# THE LANCASHIRE
# COTTON INDUSTRY

FIGURE 1. Richard Arkwright, the inventor of the water frame, which was patented in 1769. Source: E. Baines, *History of the Cotton Manufacture in Great Britain* (Fisher, Fisher & Jackson, 1835), frontispiece.

# The Lancashire Cotton Industry

## A History Since 1700

edited by

MARY B. ROSE

Lancashire County Books, 1996

*The Lancashire Cotton Industry: a History Since 1700*

edited by Mary B. Rose

First edition published 1996 by
Lancashire County Books, 143 Corporation Street, Preston

Copyright © Lancashire County Books, 1996

Text copyright © contributors, 1996

Designed and typeset in Monotype Bembo by Carnegie Publishing
Printed in the UK by The Alden Press, Oxford

ISBN 1 871236 38 X   *hardback*
ISBN 1 871236 39 8   *softback*

# Contents

# Acknowledgements

THIS PROJECT was launched in 1992 by the enthusiasm and professionalism of Zoë Lawson, then of the County Library Headquarters in Preston. I cannot thank her enough for the help and advice she gave to the planning of the book and to tracking down many of the illustrations. Anita Addiman, also of the County Library Headquarters, has also provided valuable assistance with illustrations and more generally in the production phase of the book. I should also like to thank the Pasold Research Fund for financial assistance for a planning meeting. More than anything, however, I should like to thank the contributors for their co-operation and good humour in responding to my editorial requests and meeting my deadlines. Without them there would be no book.

# Notes on contributors

**Chris Aspin** is a native of Rossendale and a retired journalist, who spent most of his professional life in Manchester writing on business, finance, music and cricket. He has been secretary of the Helmshore Local History Society since its foundation in 1953. Among his published works are *Lancashire: the First Industrial Society* and *Dizzy Heights: the Story of Lancashire's First Flying Men*. His contributions on textile history include *The Cotton Industry* and *The Woollen Industry* for Shire Publications. Mr Aspin is working on a book about the water-powered spinning mills which helped to transform the cotton trade in the north of England during the eighteenth century.

**Stanley Chapman** is Professor of Business History in the History Department of Nottingham University and Editor of *Textile History*. He is author of several books on industrial, commercial and financial history including *Cotton in the Industrial Revolution* (1972), *The Rise of Merchant Banking* (1984) and *Merchant Enterprise in Britain* (1992). he is now completing a history of the hosiery and knitwear industries since 1750.

**Marguerite Dupree** is editor of *Lancashire and Whitehall: The Diary of Sir Raymond Streat, 1931–1957*, 2 vols (1987), and articles on government–industry relations in the cotton industry in *Textile History, Business History*, and in H. Mercer, N. Rollings and J. Tomlinson (eds), *Labour Government and Private Industry: The Experience of 1945–51* (1992). She is also author of *Family Structure in the Staffordshire Potteries, 1840–1880* (1995) and articles on the social history of medicine in Britain in the nineteenth and twentieth centuries. She is a Senior Research Fellow and core staff member of the Wellcome Unit for the History of Medicine at the University of Glasgow and a Fellow of Wolfson College, Cambridge.

**Anthony Howe**, author of *The Cotton Masters, 1830–1860* (1984) is Senior Lecturer in International History at the London School of Economics. In addition to numerous entries on Lancashire cotton magnates for the *Dictionary of Business Biography*, he has published studies of London financiers, Oxford Dons and of the making of economic policy in Victorian Britain. He is currently completing a book on *Free Trade and Liberal England, 1846–1906*.

**David Jeremy** is a Reader in Business History in the Faculty of Management and Business at Manchester Metropolitan University. He has been a Visiting Research Associate in the Smithsonian Institution, Washington, DC; Curator of the Merrimack Valley Textile Museum (now the Museum of American Textile History) in Massachusetts, USA; and Research Fellow in the Business History Unit at the London School of Economics, where he edited the *Dictionary of Business Biography*, 96 vols (1984–6). He has published widely on the diffusion of textile technology, entrepreneurs and company culture and business and religion.

**Sarah Levitt** gained an MA in the History of Dress from the Courtauld Institute of Art, before embarking on a career in museums, specialising in costume and textiles. She has written and lectured extensively on the subject, concentrating on the history of clothing manufacture. Her major publications include *Fabric of Society: a Century of People and Their Clothes 1770–1870* (with Jane Toiser, 1983); *Victorians Unbuttoned: Registered Designs for Clothing, their Makers and Wearers, 1839–1900* (1986) and *Fashion in Photographs, 1880–1900* (1991). She is an Associate of the Museums Association and currently Curator of Gunnersbury Park Museum, London.

**Andrew Marrison** is a Lecturer in Economic History in the History Department, University of Manchester. In addition to his work on the cotton industry, his publications and research interests include British overseas trade in the nineteenth and twentieth centuries, tariffs and commercial policy, agricultural politics, the business community and industry–government relations.

**Mary B. Rose** is a Senior Lecturer in Business History in the Department of Economics at Lancaster University. Her main research interests lie in business and textile history, on which she has authored or edited seven books and a number of articles. Her publications include *The Gregs of Quarry Bank Mill: The Rise and Decline of a Family Firm, 1750–1914* (1986) and she is currently working on a comparative history of the British and American cotton industries. She was President of the Association of Business Historians 1993–4.

**Mary Schoeser** is a freelance design historian, who specialises in textiles and wallpaper. Trained at the University of California, California State University and the Courtauld Institute of Art, her publications include numerous articles and essays and over a dozen books and exhibition catalogues. Her most recent book is *International Textile Design* (1995). She is currently consultant curator of the Liverpool Cathedral Elizabeth Hoare Collection and of the Central/St Martin's travelling exhibition 'Bold Impressions: Block Printing, 1910–1950'. She is also a consultant archivist for Morton, Young and Borland, Ayrshire.

**John Singleton** is Senior Lecturer in Economic History at Victoria University of Wellington, New Zealand. A native of Preston, he gained his Ph.D. from Lancaster University. He has taught previously at the London School of Economics and Lancaster, York and Manchester Universities. He is the author of *Lancashire on the Scrapheap: the Cotton Industry, 1946–70* (1991) and the joint editor, with R. M. Millward, of *The Political Economy of Nationalisation in Britain, 1920–50* (1995).

**Geoff(rey) Timmins** is a Principal Lecturer in History and INSET Co-ordinator at the University of Central Lancashire. His teaching and research interests are largely in the field of local and regional history, especially of the North West. He is currently preparing a book on the history of industrialisation in Lancashire, as well as undertaking research into the development of the county's turnpike road network. He is author of *The Last Shift* (1993).

**Michael Winstanley** is a Senior Lecturer in History at Lancaster University, where he has taught modern British social history since 1978. He has contributed to G. E. Mingay (ed.), *The Victorian Countryside* (1981) and has published on rural and retail history including *The Shopkeeper's World, 1830–1914* (1983) and *A Traditional Grocer: T. D. Smith's of Lancaster, 1858–1981* (1991). His work on nineteenth-century Lancashire includes studies of the development of early policing; popular radicalism of the 1830s and 1840s; newspaper reporting; Edwin Butterworth and the researching of Edward Baines' *History of Lancashire* (1836); and a chapter on the nineteenth century in A. White (ed.), *History of Lancaster, 1193–1993* (1993). He is editor of a recent collection of work undertaken in conjunction with his students on *Working Children in Nineteenth- Century Lancashire* (1995).

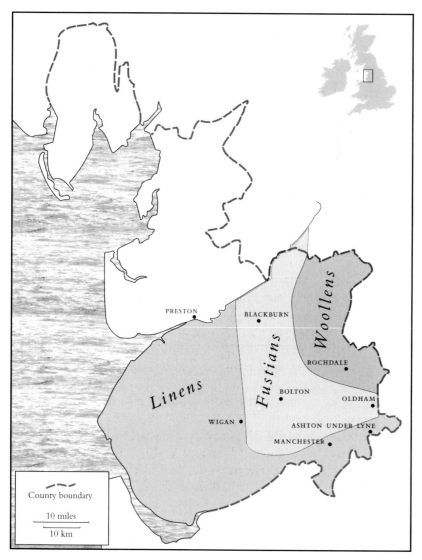

County boundary

10 miles

10 km

PRESTON

BLACKBURN

*Woollens*

ROCHDALE

*Fustians*

*Linens*

BOLTON

OLDHAM

WIGAN

ASHTON UNDER LYNE

MANCHESTER

MAP I.

CHAPTER I

# Introduction: The rise of the cotton industry in Lancashire to 1830[1]

MARY B. ROSE

B Y THE MIDDLE of the nineteenth century Manchester had been designated Cottonopolis, the cotton factory and Lancashire had become synonymous and whoever thought of cotton thought of Lancashire. The juxtaposition of factory industry and warehouses and their proximity to urban concentrations of working-class housing, in a comparatively small corner of the county, made the visual and actual impact of the industry on Lancashire, south and east of the Ribble, especially powerful. Yet, although textiles were well established in Lancashire in the seventeenth century and Manchester was an important urban textile centre, the county remained predominantly rural in this period.[2] It was during the eighteenth century and, most especially after 1780, that cotton textiles became an increasingly important dimension of the Lancashire economy.

This chapter explores Lancashire's experience of the industrial revolution, and will explain the origins and early development of the modern cotton industry. By focusing on the protracted nature and regional variations of industrial change, it will help to dispel some of the myths surrounding the transition to the factory system. It will highlight the self-reinforcing influence of locality on technological change, finance, on the structure of firms and on the labour force. In this context it will explore the impact of intraregional variations, in traditions and customs, on the distinctive characteristics of Lancashire's cotton towns. It will also demonstrate that development, in the archetypal industrial region, was gradual and that the industrial revolution was marked as much by continuity as by change. Nevertheless, it will illustrate that Lancashire's transformation was not, and could not have been, without its discontinuities, created, for example, by the shift from water to steam as a source of motive power. Many of the themes discussed in this chapter have bearing upon the subsequent development of the cotton industry and so the chapter also serves as an introduction.

1

The chapter is divided into five substantive sections. The first addresses the eighteenth-century origins of the Lancashire cotton industry, which led the county to emerge as Britain's most dominant and highly concentrated centre of cotton textile production by the middle of the nineteenth century. The second explores the expansion of demand whilst the third discusses the emergence and organisation of the factory system. The increasing concentration of the industry in the south-eastern corner of Lancashire is the focus of the fourth section. In the concluding section the themes which are to be explored later in the book will be introduced.

## The origins of the Lancashire cotton industry

The problem of why cotton, an exotic, imported fibre should lie at the heart of industrial change in a small corner of England is a complex one. A number of mutually reinforcing influences help to explain the expansion of a modern cotton industry. Growing domestic and, subsequently, overseas demand gave a general stimulus to the British cotton industry. It was, however, the industrial traditions and the attendant social structures within parts of Lancashire, combined with such natural advantages as climate, which made the county one of a few natural homes for the cotton industry in the eighteenth century.

An area's industrial traditions include a patchwork of customs, experience of work, technology, attitudes, contacts and organisation. These legacies of the past have influenced industrial development in all periods. In the case of Lancashire this meant that whilst the nineteenth-century transformation of part of the county was dramatic, 'two centuries of industrial growth lay between the introduction of cotton manufacture . . . and the first cotton factory'.[3] The establishment of a textile tradition in Lancashire by the seventeenth and early eighteenth centuries was crucial to the subsequent development of the cotton industry. Writing as early as 1835 Baines noted the important impact which the earlier pre-industrial development of Lancashire had upon its emergence as a centre of cotton manufacturing. He observed: 'the woollen and linen manufactures have existed in this county from a very early period, and both were carried on in Lancashire before the cotton manufacture, for which they prepared the way'.[4]

Such a textile tradition brought with it distinct advantages in terms of skills, commercial facilities and wealth which proved crucial to the subsequent development of the industry. It was not, however, the presence of textiles generally that was significant to the early spread of cotton manufacturing. Rather it was the early combination of linen-based cloths such as fustians, checks and smallwares with fast printing (introduced into Lancashire by 1750) that gave birth to a modern cotton industry.[5] After 1770 woollens began to give way to cottons in the Pennine valleys of Rossendale,[6] but in this period the cotton industry developed most rapidly within the Bolton, Oldham and Manchester nexus, the homes of fustians, checks and smallwares respectively and in the cotton-linen area of the south and west of the county (see Map 1). The implication here is of a particular family of textiles, for which there was a buoyant market, where cotton could be used as a complementary and ultimately a substitute fibre.

In these areas, by the early eighteenth century, there had developed an array of skills, technology and work practices, associated with extensive networks of mainly rural cottage workers,[7] which provided a valuable basis for the development of modern industry. Integral to these were a formidable array of middlemen who both co-ordinated production and were the lynchpins of the local credit and information networks which were later to play an important part in financing the cotton industry.[8] Nowhere is the development of specialist Lancashire middlemen in the seventeenth century better illustrated than in the fustian trade. At the very centre of this were the linen drapers, merchant-manufacturers, who could be described as 'buying and selling [and] putting out linen yarn [and] cotton wool to the spinning, winding, warping and weaving'.[9] Their personal and financial networks in turn linked Lancashire to London, which was then the commercial centre of the textile trade as well as of calico printing (see chapter 7 for a discussion of the development of design in calico printing). By the mid-eighteenth century, although the term linen drapers was no longer used, their successors had become the wealthy heads of the Manchester industrial and trading community as specialist commercial services began to develop.[10]

A significant proportion of the raw materials for fustian manufacture was imported and this considerably increased the complexity of the linen drapers' business. Some directly imported the raw materials they dealt in or put out for manufacture. However, it was often safer and more convenient to use the services of specialist middlemen such as yarn jobbers and raw cotton dealers in the ports. In the seventeenth century the majority of these were in London. However, the eighteenth century saw the transfer of some of this work to specialist commercial firms within Lancashire. Linen yarn from Ireland and the Continent was, for example, imported via the ports of London, Hull and Liverpool. On the other hand, raw cotton came from the Levant, the West Indies and Brazil and until 1795 London remained the most important port of entry.[11] However, Lancashire's west coast ports of Lancaster and, more especially, Liverpool were increasingly the recipients of raw cotton from the West Indies and Brazil.[12] Therefore while many of the raw cotton dealers were in London, by the mid-eighteenth century an increasing number were to be found in Liverpool with some also in Manchester, where, until the 1770s, cotton dealing was commonly combined with both yarn dealing and manufacturing[13] (see chapter 4 for an extended discussion of commercial developments within Lancashire).

London's seventeenth- and early eighteenth-century commercial importance was not confined to the import trade, for the metropolis was also the hub of both the domestic market and the export trade for textiles. The capital's specialist middlemen were therefore vital to Lancashire's linen drapers, reducing the uncertainties of dealing with distant and often rapidly changing markets. Some brought this expertise within their firms by taking a London partner. For many, however, the services of the London warehousemen, who sometimes combined selling goods with purchase of raw materials, were invaluable:[14]

> . . . so elaborate an organisation of production, involving the purchase in bulk of imported raw materials, and the lapse of an interval of several months between the time when it was distributed to the workpeople and the final sale of the finished cloth required a correspondingly elaborate financial mechanism.[15]

The importance of middlemen, within and outside Lancashire, to the linen drapers, was not confined to the purchase of raw materials or the sale of finished products. It can be shown that they played a part at every stage of the production and distribution process. Some linen drapers, it is true, operated a putting out system directly from their warehouse. But for many, as the scale of activity grew and the geographic spread of their outworkers increased, the services of middlemen, especially of the fustian masters, were crucial. Some of these were manufacturers in their own right and purchased raw materials from the linen drapers on credit, while selling the finished goods for profit. Many were, however, true middlemen, who acted as the agents of the manufacturers co-ordinating the putting-out sytem in return for commission on the delivery of finished goods.[16]

Banks did not appear in Lancashire until the 1770s and developed only slowly before the 1820s. As a result credit, prior to that date, was non-institutional, and when a formalised system did emerge, it derived much from previous personalised financial arrangements. This complex interlocking web reinforced the importance of both the linen drapers and the London middlemen and was essential to the expansion of the fustian trade.[17]

Every stage of the putting out system operated on the short term credit extended by the linen draper. The purchase of raw materials and the sale of goods was similarly underpinned by the London warehousemen. Relying for security on the standing of the London house, a linen draper received payment for goods sold in the form of a bill drawn on London. Since these bills could then be used to meet local debts, the fortunes of Lancashire and those of London became inextricably linked by a network as extensive as it would have been with a banking system. Similarly the growing commercial importance of Liverpool increased the significance of her merchants and brokers in the financial health of the fustian trade, though in the eighteenth century they remained reliant on the London houses. The sophistication and elegance of Lancashire's eighteenth-century commercial and financial network facilitated business expansion and spawned the first generation of Lancashire's bankers.[18]

The dominance of the putting out system in Lancashire's eighteenth-century textile industry made short term credit of fundamental importance. There was, however, a demand for long term loans for mining, iron founding and for building textile workshops, especially for sail cloth manufacture. Lancashire was, in the seventeenth and eighteenth centuries, predominantly rural, so that far more wealth was held in land than in trade and industry. In the absence of banks, ignorance and mutual suspicion could have restricted the long term flow of funds between landed groups and those in trade and industry. However, in both Lancashire and the West Riding of Yorkshire such difficulties were circumvented because local attorneys acted as financial intermediaries. Attorneys were involved in real estate dealings and had intimate knowledge of most aspects of their local communities. This placed them in an ideal position to co-ordinate the mortgage market. This in turn facilitated the long term flow of funds between land and industry.[19]

The growing network of Lancashire-based commercial and financial facilities meant that, by the mid-eighteenth century, the county had relatively wealthy mercantile groups in Liverpool, Manchester and in some of the outlying towns. There had also developed a reservoir of skill, especially amongst the predominantly rural outworkers in the linen/cotton regions of Lancashire. It was on the basis of these skills that Lancashire was able to satisfy demand, at home and abroad, for cheap, light textiles with a growing array of cloths. Remarkably little is known about how and among whom this reservoir of skill developed. Yet it is apparent that a sexual division of labour had developed even before the industrial revolution. In the eighteenth century, therefore, spinning and preparation, the commonest of industrial processes, were normally carried out by women and children. Commenting on the Warrington sail cloth and sacking trade in 1771 Young, for example, highlighted a significant division of tasks and observed that:

> . . . the manufactures of sail cloth and sacking are very considerable. The first is spun by women and girls who earn about 2*d*. per day. It is then bleached, which is done by men, who earn 10*s*. 0*d*. per

week; after bleaching it is wound by women, whose earnings are 2s. 6d. a week; next it is warped by men, who earn 7s. 0d. a week; and then starched . . . The last operation is weaving, in which men earn 9s., the women 5s. and boys 3s. 6d. a week. The spinners in the sacking branch earn 6s. 0d. a week and are women.[20]

The emergence of a modern cotton textile industry in parts of Lancashire was not, however, only the result of industrial traditions and the consequent networks of wealth and skill. It was also developed from pre-existing social structures and the emergence of established links and flows of information between urban and rural communities, especially between Manchester and the textile areas.[21] Given the personalised nature of early business and the intimate relationship between businessmen and the societies in which they resided, such considerations are clearly of the greatest importance.

Any survey of the historical traditions of an area would be incomplete without some consideration of the legal and institutional environment. It would be misleading to isolate the significance of the lack of legal restrictions on the development of textiles in Lancashire from other trends favouring expansion. Yet this does seem to have been a decisive factor in the county's favour. Both Lancashire and Yorkshire, where there was considerable textile expansion in the sixteenth and seventeenth centuries, were exempt from the Weavers' Acts restricting the numbers of apprentices which could be employed by a Master weaver.[22] An even greater stimulus to the development of Lancashire's fustian manufacture was the county's exemption from the Calico Acts. Originally introduced in 1721 to prohibit the importation of printed fabrics from the east, the Calico Acts were soon extended to apply to the use or wearing of all printed fabrics irrespective of where they had been dyed.[23]

The overwhelming influence of Lancashire's social and economic traditions on the eighteenth-century expansion of the cotton industry has sometimes led the significance of climate to be neglected.[24] Yet although a damp climate may not have been *the* decisive factor, it nonetheless made an important contribution to the suitability of the area for cotton textiles.[25]

## Expansion of demand and output

Fustian manufacture, organised under a predominantly rurally based putting out system, continued to dominate Lancashire's textile industries until the 1770s. The next two decades saw the replacement of linen/cotton mixes by pure cotton cloth and the gradual shift towards a modern factory system. Why this change in the organisation of production occurred when it did and why Lancashire should have been the first county in Britain to industrialise, has proved controversial and at times frustratingly inconclusive. Yet this is a healthy reflection of the complexity of the process.

Textiles are synonymous with early industrialisation. Almost everywhere, including the world's first industrial nation, some of the earliest factories have been in the cotton industry. One of the keys to the precocious mechanisation of cotton is the position of clothing as a basic necessity. In Britain until the eighteenth century, these had been made predominantly of wool and linen. However, there developed an unquenchable taste for cotton cloth which irreversibly changed the face of the British textile industry[26] (see chapter 6 for a discussion of cotton clothing). This was because it was a taste which was increasingly met, not by foreign imports, but by domestic production. As a result, during the course of the eighteenth century, raw cotton consumption in Britain grew from an annual level of a mere 1 m lbs in 1700 to 56 m lbs in 1800.[27] Table 1.1 illustrates that whilst retained imports of raw cotton grew relatively steadily until the 1770s, during the following decade there was a dramatic rise of more than 200%, with consumption virtually doubling on a decennial basis until 1840.

Table 1.1 *Raw cotton consumption, 1720–1799*★

|  | retained imports (million lbs) |
| --- | --- |
| 1720–29 | 14 |
| 1730–39 | 17 |
| 1740–49 | 21 |
| 1750–59 | 28 |
| 1760–69 | 35 |
| 1770–79 | 48 |
| 1780–89 | 155 |
| 1790–99 | 286 |
| 1800–09 | 594 |
| 1810–19 | 934 |
| 1820–29 | 1664 |
| 1830–39 | 3208 |
| 1840–49 | 4072 |

Source: B. R. Mitchell, *British Historical Statistics* (Cambridge University Press, 1988), pp. 330–3
★ Statistics for 1720–99 based upon calculations of retained imports.

It was once assumed that the industrial revolution in general, and the transformation of the cotton industry in particular, was export driven.[28] However all the evidence suggests that the initial market impulse came from the home rather than the foreign market.[29] In the 1770s, for instance, when the growth of raw cotton consumption began to accelerate, exports of cotton goods were negligible, whilst home markets swallowed around two-thirds of output.[30] The appeal of cotton cloth in England originated with the oriental imports of the East India Company in the late seventeenth and early eighteenth centuries. Despite efforts by vested interests in the woollen sector to stifle this trade between 1721 and 1774,[31] cotton cloth achieved a remarkable level of popularity very quickly. Initially a luxury good, it rapidly became accessible to a wider market through the development of the London second-hand clothing trade.[32]

FIGURE 2. Samuel Crompton. Source: G. J. French, *The Life and Times of Samuel Crompton* (Simkin, Marshall & Co., 1859), frontispiece.

It is remarkably difficult to disentangle the relationship between the expansion of demand for cotton cloth and technological and organisational change in the industry. This is because although demand can be shown to have stimulated innovation, technical change of itself created new products which, when successfully promoted, penetrated ever widening markets (see chapter 2 for a detailed discussion of technological change).

The expansion of demand for light textiles in the early eighteenth century could initially be met by traditional means. These included hand innovations such as the fly-shuttle and an extension of outwork in spinning and preparation using existing technologies, and employing growing numbers of women and children.[33] However, by the 1760s, supply bottlenecks in the hand spinning sector could only be met, first by technological and later by organisational changes. The spinning inventions, between the 1760s and 1780s, by Hargreaves, Arkwright and Crompton respectively, of the jenny, water frame and mule, helped to reduce yarn shortages. They also successively enhanced the quality and variety of the yarn produced and dramatically increased the productivity of British spinners.[34] On the other hand, a widening variety of pure cotton cloths were woven, primarily by handloom weavers rather than on powerlooms.

The British domestic market for cotton cloth was comparatively small and the Lancashire cotton industry would never subsequently have achieved the scale that it did without a rapid expansion of exports. As table 1.2 demonstrates, it was a growth which began in the 1780s, but which accelerated dramatically in the 1790s. The uncertainties of war (with France from the 1793 until 1815 and with the United States from

1812 to 1814) combined with variations in tariff policy meant, however, that although the trend was upwards, exports could be extremely volatile.[35]

Table 1.2 *Exports of cotton goods*

| Date | £ (thousands) | % total British exports |
|---|---|---|
| 1784–86 | 766 | 6.0 |
| 1794–96 | 3,392 | 15.6 |
| 1804–06 | 15,871 | 42.3 |
| 1814–16 | 18,742 | 42.1 |
| 1824–26 | 16,879 | 47.8 |
| 1834–36 | 22,398 | 48.5 |
| 1844–46 | 25,835 | 44.2 |
| 1854–56 | 34,908 | 34.1 |

Source: R. Davis, *The Industrial Revolution and British Overseas Trade* (Leicester University Press, 1979), p. 15.

The growth in exports stemmed from the increasing price competitiveness and quality of British cotton goods. It was the combination of spinning innovations, with the availability of growing numbers of specialised skilled handloom weavers, that enabled Lancashire producers to gain a foothold in the overseas markets upon which they were eventually to depend. These advantages came, in the first place, from the diffusion of power-driven carding and spinning machinery in the 1770s and 1780s. By dramatically increasing labour productivity, these innovations gave Britain an absolute cost advantage in the production of pure cotton cloth.[36] The introduction and improvement of the mule, on the other hand, meant British spinners could produce yarn which rivalled the fineness of Indian hand produced yarns.[37] Initially destined for the West Indies, British cotton cloth began to penetrate North American and European markets in the 1780s and 1790s. However, although Britain's exports of cloth continued to grow enormously during the nineteenth century, there was, from the 1790s and more especially after 1800, an expanding market for yarn. This was a reflection of the technical, qualitative and cost advantages of Britain's advanced spinning sector.[38] In addition, the ability to export so extensively was facilitated from the 1790s onwards by the development of networks of commercial agents operating abroad, reinforcing areas of influence and improving flows of market information (see chapter 4 for further discussion of commercial arrangements in this period). The widening of the export base for British cotton goods, therefore, continued throughout the nineteenth century. Before 1850 it included North and Latin America, Asia and Australia as table 1.3 illustrates.

Table 1.3 *Destination of British cotton exports by region, 1784–1856 (%)*

|  | Europe | Asia and Africa | America and Australia |
|---|---|---|---|
| 1784–86 | 40.5 | 21.4 | 38.1 |
| 1794–96 | 2.6 | 5.8 | 71.6 |
| 1804–06 | 45.5 | 4.3 | 50.2 |
| 1814–16 | 60.1 | 1.9 | 38.0 |
| 1824–26 | 51.4 | 10.1 | 38.5 |
| 1834–36 | 47.4 | 18.1 | 34.5 |
| 1844–46 | 39.2 | 36.3 | 24.5 |
| 1854–56 | 29.4 | 39.6 | 31.0 |

Source: Davis, *The Industrial Revolution*, p. 15

These, and most particularly the Indian market, were to become the foundation of the phenomenal expansion of the cotton industry in the Victorian era (see chapter 9 for a discussion of the late nineteenth-century expansion of the cotton industry).

## The emergence and organisation of the factory system

The putting out system of production was ideal where technology was rudimentary and suitable for household operation, where raw materials were not valuable, where demand was relatively stable and where there was an abundant supply of skilled and semi-skilled labour. In these circumstances a sustained increase in demand could be met by an expansion of the outwork networks.[39] The flexibility of the system, in the face of market fluctuation and uncertainty, was an additional advantage. Technological change in the Lancashire cotton industry was not immediately associated with changes in the organisation of pro-duction. It has already been shown that eighteenth-century expansion of demand was met largely by traditional means. In addition, the three spinning innovations could be hand operated and the jenny was only ever operated in hand workshops. It is therefore necessary to look beyond the technologies themselves to understand how and why change occurred. There is no single explanation of why outwork was replaced by the factory system or why, even in the Lancashire cotton industry, this was a protracted and patchy process. It is, however, important to explore the complex relationships between markets and products on the one hand, with technology, employers and the labour force on the other. Moreover, it is necessary to identify the significance of local influences in explaining the interregional variations in the pace and character of change in Lancashire in the late eighteenth and early nineteenth centuries.

A desire to exploit the workforce, or to increase efficiency by reducing the costs associated with dispersed production, are among the commonest and most plausible explanations of the transition to the factory system.[40] Yet, whilst it is hard to deny that both considerations were a dimension in the thinking of the early factory masters, historical evidence for Lancashire does not suggest that they explain either the timing or the extent of organisational change.

One of the consequences of the factory system was a greater control over employees' time and hence over their levels of effort.[41] Conversely under outwork, especially if a sector was growing and piece wage rates rising, workers had the opportunity to substitute leisure for increased income. Moreover, the absence of close monitoring gave ample opportunity for theft of raw materials. By centralising control, so the argument runs, factory owners were able to intensify the work process, reduce theft and increase their share of profits. Yet whilst there is no denying that all these consequences *flowed from* the coming of the factory system, the idea that they were the principal cause is not supported by the historical evidence for Lancashire.

There is very little evidence one way or another on the precise trends in piece rates in the eighteenth-century Lancashire. Much more research is needed to confirm or refute their role in hastening the rise of factories. On the other hand, the increasing severity of laws relating to the theft of work materials and an expansion in prosecutions, have been taken to mean that this problem was worsening in eighteenth-century Lancashire and that this did precipitate the coming of the factory system.[42] Yet the embezzlement of flax, raw cotton and yarn had a marginal, rather than a decisive, influence on employers' desire to change the organisation of production. Theft was accepted as an integral part of outwork systems by merchant manufacturers. They adjusted the wages they paid accordingly. It was predominantly during downturns, when profit margins were squeezed, that employers favoured prosecution and a rigid enforcement of legislation. In other words, the apparent increase in the problem of embezzlement in late eighteenth-century Lancashire was indicative of short term pressures facing employers, rather than of a long term trend which encouraged an abandonment of outwork.[43]

If the timing of the shift to the factory system in Lancashire cannot be explained by the quest for greater control by employers, it is not even clear that under all circumstances outwork was less efficient than factory work. In theory, centralisation of production reduced both transport costs and the reliance on middlemen, whilst limiting the stock levels necessary to maintain production flows.[44] However, in late eighteenth- and early nineteenth-century Lancashire, reliance on water power by early factories meant that such cost reductions were often fairly limited. In any event, variations in labour market conditions, the culture of the workforce, market characterisitcs and technology could all render outwork an appropriate form of organisation. Moreover the persistence of outwork outside cotton spinning and preparation, well into the nineteenth century, makes an explanation of the rise of the factory system purely on efficiency grounds untenable.

The centralisation of production in cotton spinning from the 1770s was hastened by the application of power, first horse, then water and finally, especially after 1790, steam. Prompted perhaps by favourable demand conditions which came with the Repeal of the Calico Acts in 1774,[45] this speeded up machinery and increased productivity. This was not all, however, for as it spread it simply rendered outwork in spinning impractical. During the 1770s powered cotton mills began to appear in the old fustian area and the rise of the factory system in Lancashire was underway.[46]

Technological and organisational change continued apace in spinning in the early nineteenth century. Cotton cloth, on the other hand, continued to be predominantly traditionally produced and finished, until the second quarter of the nineteenth century or beyond, in some regions of Lancashire. Indeed until the 1830s the rise of factory spinning

FIGURE 3. View of Manchester in the 1790s. Source: J. Aikin, *A Description of the Country From Thirty to Forty Miles Round Manchester* (David & Charles reprint, 1968), facing p. 212).

and preparation led to an expansion in handloom weaving. Numbers of handloom weavers reached a peak of 250,000 in 1825 with the majority residing in north-east Lancashire.[47] The persistence of hand-loom weaving can partly be explained by technological considerations. The powerloom proved unsuitable for all but the coarser cloths until the 1840s and was not successfully adapted for finer or fancy cloths before 1850.[48] Nevertheless, the flexibility of outwork, in the face of volatile fashion markets for finer cloths, combined with the long standing artisan handweaving traditions of north-east Lancashire, also explain the gradual penetration of power weaving in Lancashire.[49] In printing, too, block, as opposed to machine printing, continued in parts of Lancashire, until after 1850 (see chapter 2 for a discussion of the persistence of handloom weaving and block printing).

By the late eighteenth century most historians are agreed that factory-based spinning and preparation of cotton was becoming the norm and that, by the 1780s, an increasing proportion of new mills were in Lancashire. There remains, however, considerable doubt about the precise pace and pattern of growth, not least because there were considerable fluctuations and because bankruptcy was an ever present hazard.

## The concentration of the industry

Evidence of the early growth of the cotton industry is extremely patchy. In the 1770s, although mills were built in Lancashire, the quest for water power meant that other areas, especially the East Midlands, Yorkshire, Scotland and North Wales, saw quite considerable mill building.[50] However, it does seem as though by the late 1780s the industry was becoming more concentrated in Lancashire, with a considerable number of mills within the Oldham, Bolton, Manchester triangle. By 1787, of 145 Arkwright-type mills, 43 have been identified as in operation in Lancashire.[51] By 1791 there were 18 mills in Oldham alone, though competition for water power meant that many were horse-powered. Thereafter millbuilding expanded dramatically. By 1811 Crompton's census of spindlage pointed to upwards of 650 cotton mills operating within 60 miles of Bolton.[52] However, he was trying to gain recognition and financial compensation for the impact of the mule on the cotton industry. As a result, he underestimated the numbers of water frames and jennies and hence the overall scale of the cotton industry. In addition, he may have exaggerated the concentration within Lancashire at this time.

The nineteenth-century development of the cotton industry witnessed a growing localisation in Lancashire. By 1841, 70 per cent of those employed nationally in an estimated 1,105 cotton firms resided in the county. These figures, collected by Factory Inspector Leonard Horner, should not be confused with the number of mills, since some mills were in multiple occupancy and some firms owned more than one mill. However, they confirm the continued growth of the factory-based cotton industry in Lancashire in the nineteenth century.[53] In 1840 some 127 calico printing works, the majority either within north-east Lancashire or close to Manchester, were also active.[54]

As the cotton industry expanded so its impact upon employment grew. Therefore, although no more than 5.95 per cent of the UK labour force was ever employed in the cotton industry at any time in the nineteenth century, its impact upon employment patterns in Lancashire was profound. The marked labour intensity of the cotton industry, at the beginning of the nineteenth century and the relatively narrow industrial base of Lancashire, meant that in 1811 over one third of the county's population was employed in cotton.[55] A widening industrial base meant that the relative importance of cotton as an employer in Lancashire declined as the nineteenth century progressed. However, the absolute numbers continued to grow so that, as table 1.4 shows, by 1861 some 446,000 people were employed in the Lancashire cotton industry.

Table 1.4 *Employment in the Lancashire cotton industry, 1801–1861*

| Date | Number of workers | Equivalent of % of Lancashire population |
|---|---|---|
| 1801 | 242,000 | 35.96 |
| 1811 | 306,000 | 36.96 |
| 1821 | 369,000 | 35.04 |
| 1831 | 427,000 | 31.94 |
| 1841 | 374,000 | 22.44 |
| 1851 | 379,000 | 18.66 |
| 1861 | 446,000 | 18.36 |

Source: D. A. Farnie, *The English Cotton Industry and the World Market, 1815–96* (Oxford University Press, 1979) p. 24

During the nineteenth century the modern cotton industry became concentrated 'over an extensive area of south-east and central Lanca-shire, from Preston and Wigan in the west to the Pennines in the east, spilling over into north-west Derbyshire around Glossop, and north-east Cheshire around Stockport'.[56] Precisely why this should have happened is a complex issue and has invited extensive discussion.

The emergence of modern industrial regions in Europe has been ex-plained in terms of the early development of pockets of rural handicraft producers, supplying overseas markets. This 'proto-industrialisation' was in turn the inevitable response to the infertility of small landholdings in upland regions which made family income supplements from industry vital for survival. These rural proto-industrialists were linked to adjacent areas by a web of mercantile credit. It has been argued that the wealth and skills created by the process, combined with the acceleration of population growth, which proto-industrialisation encouraged, formed the basis of the future industrialisation of individual regions.[57]

Superficially the development of the cotton industry in Lancashire, south of the Ribble, followed this pattern. There was an almost perfect geographic coincidence of eighteenth-century fustian manufacture with the location of the modern cotton industry. Fustians were often produced in upland areas where poor agricultural land made supplementary employment in outwork inevitable. Equally it has already been shown that there had developed, in seventeenth- and early eighteenth-century Lancashire, a complex network of middlemen and commercial credit which connected rural producers to their markets. In addition, the evolution of rural pockets of skill were of critical importance to the subsequent development of the cotton region in Lancashire.

It is tempting to assume that the transition from proto-industry to a modern factory system was, therefore, a natural progression as the cotton industry expanded. Equally, it could be supposed that the emergence of rural manufacturing in impoverished upland areas was an automatic precursor of industrial change. However, the wide variations in experience within Lancashire suggest that the process of industrialisation was infinitely more complex.[58] One of Lancashire's most important specialisms in the seventeenth and early eighteenth centuries was, for example, smallwares produced, not in rural areas, but in Manchester.[59] Equally, the existence of proto-industry was by no means an automatic passport to industrialisation. This is not, of course, to deny that the shape and pace of the development of Lancashire's factory based cotton industry *was* critically influenced by past traditions. Rather, it is to emphasise that, even within a single county, regional differences in economic, social and cultural characteristics may lead down different paths towards industrialisation.[60]

During the late eighteenth century, although the exact numbers or location of the all early mills are not known, the influence of the established fustian regions on the development of the factory system was considerable. Between 1776 and 1778, for example, six small mills were erected in Oldham where three were worked by water and three by horses. In the surrounding townships of Chadderton, Royton and Crompton there was also a handful of water and horse powered mills. By 1788 there were around 25 in the parish of Oldham, whilst three years later 18 were recorded in Oldham alone. Some water mills were built in other towns including Rochdale, Blackburn and Burnley in the early 1780s. However, relatively limited water supplies in Oldham itself encouraged the persistence of horse power, alongside water, quite late in the eighteenth century. Large numbers of early mills were also sited on the banks of the Irwell, Irk, Tame, Roch, Calder and Darwen and their tributaries. These sites, although isolated below the Pennine and Rossendale Moors, were within easy reach of established textile areas.[61]

During the 1780s overcrowding on water sites sent industrialists to the periphery of the county, well away from concentrations of skilled labour and from established networks of connections. There were, as a result, several early mills in north Lancashire. At Caton, near Lancaster, for example, there were five mills in the late eighteenth century. Three were on Artle Beck and two, including Low Mill founded in 1784 by Thomas Hodgson a Liverpool merchant, on another small tributary of the Lune.[62] Similarly, in about 1782, Birch Robinson and Walmsley built a cotton mill at Backbarrow, in Furness, not far from the borders with Westmorland.[63]

Water power led to the dispersal of the cotton industry in Lancashire. The spread of steam power was, however, eventually to help reverse this trend, though it was initially a slow process. The first recorded use of a steam engine to drive spinning machinery was in 1789 at Peter Drinkwater's mill in Piccadilly, Manchester.[64] Thereafter, despite a steady spread of steam power, water continued to be important until at least the 1820s. As late as 1838 21.7 per cent of motive power in the cotton industry was from water.[65] The technical limitations and unreliability of early steam engines, combined with the continued improvement of water technology, meant that steam power brought

FIGURE 4. Low Caton Mill, near Lancaster. The original water-powered mill was built by Thomas Hodgson in 1784, passed to Samuel Greg in 1817, and was largely destroyed by fire in 1837 and rebuilt. (Photograph courtesy of Robert Alston.)

few cost advantages before the 1830s. Even then, on exceptional water sites, new investment in water power continued to be cost effective. On a few of these, such as Low Mill Caton, water turbines replaced wheels after 1860.[66] More generally, however, the sojourn of the cotton industry north of the Ribble was relatively shortlived and largely vanished after the Cotton Famine. Increasingly, after 1830, as table 1.5 shows, therefore, the Lancashire cotton industry was concentrated within established cotton areas within easy reach of the coalfield in the south of the county.[67]

Table 1.5  *Distribution of cotton factories within the main Lancashire parishes 1838*

| Town | Number of factories |
| --- | --- |
| Manchester | 182 |
| Oldham | 213 |
| Bury | 114 |
| Ashton | 82 |
| Rochdale | 117 |
| Blackburn | 44 |
| Whalley | 113 |
| Bolton | 69 |
| Preston | 35 |
| Wigan | 37 |

Source: H. D. Fong, *Triumph of the Factory System* (Tientsin, China: Chihli Press, 1932), p. 29

It is true that the pursuit of water power widened the boundaries of the cotton industry beyond the confines of the traditonal textile areas in Lancashire. However, it is misleading to assume that the relative cost of power was the only, or even the most important reason, why cotton manufacturing became so concentrated in south-east Lancashire. Despite the relatively short extension of cotton manufacturing to Lancashire's periphery, industrial and commercial growth of the 'core' areas served to reinforce pre-industrial advantages. The industrial revolution encouraged further development of industrial skills and wealth in such towns as Oldham, Bolton, Manchester, Preston and Rochdale. In addition, the growing specialisation of commercial and financial institutions in Liverpool and Manchester, combined with infrastructure development, increased the locational advantages of the south-eastern corner of Lancashire (see chapter 4 for a further discussion of the development of business communities). These not only brought significant cost advantages, but also improved flows of information, which were vital in the intensely competitive world of the nineteenth-century

FIGURE 5. Raw cotton bales, Prince's Dock, Liverpool, *c.* 1833. Source: S. Austin *et al.*, *Lancashire Illustrated* (Fisher, Fisher & Jackson, 1833), facing p. 62.

cotton industry.[68] In addition, from the 1820s and especially the 1830s, industrial concentration also spawned important ancillary industries such as textile machine making. Machine makers served Lancashire's requirements whilst some, such as the engineering giant, Platt Brothers of Oldham, were instrumental in the international diffusion of textile technology in the late nineteenth century[69] (see chapter 8 for a discussion of technological diffusion).

The concentration of the Lancashire cotton industry was, therefore, a cumulative process where pre-industrial influences were reinforced by the industrial revolution. Yet despite the remarkable geographical concentration of the cotton industry, experience of the industrial revolution varied considerably in Lancashire. It was not simply the case that large tracts of the county were untouched, or only fleetingly touched, by the cotton industry. Even where cotton predominated there emerged sharp contrasts in the sources of enterprise, the organisation of firms, in the division of labour, in labour relations, in technological traditions and in products and markets served. These differences highlight the extent to which business development in eighteenth-century Lancashire was inseparable from the evolution of distinctive local communities.

In the early eighteenth century it is not surprising that businessmen preferred, where possible, to conduct their business dealings on a largely local basis or through a trusted friend or relation. It was a time when bankruptcy rates were relatively high, communications poor and markets relatively limited. Yet the economic, social and demographic changes of the industrial revolution increased rather than reduced the role of the local business community.

FIGURE 6. Cotton factories, Union Street, Manchester, *c.* 1833.
Source: S. Austin *et al.*, *Lancashire Illustrated* (Fisher, Fisher & Jackson, 1833), facing p. 41.

Between 1788 and 1800 the level of investment in buildings and machinery in the cotton industry rose from £1.86m to £4.82m and by 1830 had reached £14.99m.[70] In the 1780s a high proportion of this investment went into the factory-based spinning sector of the industry, with almost 25 per cent of investment in Arkwright type-mills, £55,000 in mule spinning mills and £141,000 in jennies. In Lancashire in 1787, the vast majority of the owners of early mills of whatever type came from a textile background. State of the art mills of the Arkwright-type held around 1,000 waterframe spindles and cost around £3,000 to build.[71] These and the early mule mills were inevitably beyond the reach of men of small means without a wealthy partner. Amongst the early factory masters were several of the future giants of the industry. Horrocks of Preston and Ashworth of Turton near Bolton had been fustian manufacturers, whilst Samuel Greg of Quarry Bank Mill, Styal was heir to the Hyde's merchant-manufacturing partnership. Peel on the other hand had been a calico printer and manufacturer.[72] This suggests that the dynastic tendencies, which have been identified in Lancashire by the 1830's, could be traced back to the eighteenth century.[73] If the financial outlay on these purpose-built, best practice, factories required substantial resources they were by no means the norm in the late eighteenth century. Small jenny and handweaving workshops cost a few hundred pounds to build and equip. Similarly a converted cornmill, filled with second-hand machinery was also relatively inexpensive.[74] When larger, steam powered mills developed from the 1790s, in Manchester and elsewhere, the opportunity to rent space and power left opportunities for 'men of modest means'. Consequently, behind the

vanguard of the industrial revolution, there emerged a myriad of very small, usually shortlived firms. These firms were heavily reliant on trade credit from their locality and from Liverpool and Manchester, to meet their raw material and other short term requirements. However, they lacked the financial resources and the goodwill that comes from long establishment and so they were increasingly vulnerable to failure.[75] The susceptibility of mainly smaller, new firms to collapse during the industrial revolution is clear with 15 per cent of Britian's textile bankruptcies between 1781 and 1800 falling in Lancashire. Although some of the most spectacular failures, such as that in 1788 of Livesey, Hargreaves & Co., calico printers, millowners and bankers, were large established firms, the majority were recently formed.[76]

FIGURE 7. The large cotton mill of Swainson, Birley & Co. of Preston, *c.* 1830. Source: E. Baines, *A History of the Cotton Manufacture in Great Britain* (Fisher, Fisher & Jackson, 1835), facing p. 185.

In such an uncertain environment it was inevitable that, in order to reduce the likelihood of failure, entrepreneurs would conduct as much of their financial arrangements as locally as possible. In addition, the liability for debts of all participants in the myriad of firms was unlimited. It was normal therefore to turn to one's family and local community for associates and financial assistance.[77] It was a trend which was reinforced during the industrial revolution and localised financial networks remained important well into the nineteenth century. In the second quarter of the nineteenth century, for example, banks became growing sources of overdrafts and mortgage finance for the increasingly capital-hungry cotton industry. Analysis of the Security Books of the Preston Bank, for example, reveals a heavily localised pattern of lending. Decisions to lend were based as much on the local standing and non-business assets of the partners, as the resources of the firm.[78]

The role of community in the industrial revolution was not confined to financial arrangements because local pockets of pre-industrial expertise were vital to the location of early factories. This is not to imply that all or even the majority of jobs in the early factory system were skilled, many were not. Nevertheless familiarity with such processes as carding and spinning was important. This meant that the division of labour in spinning, identified in the early eighteenth century, was often replicated during the industrial revolution. In spinning, for example, especially water frame spinning, and carding there was a predominance of female labour, with children employed as helpers and in numerous unskilled tasks[79] (see chapter 5 for a discussion of changes in the sexual division of labour in mule spinning). Significant colonies of handloom weavers also meant that prior to the 1820s and beyond in some parts of Lancashire the demand for a wide variety of cloth could be met without either mechanisation or centralisation of production.

The transfer of skills from cottages to factories was not always a simple process. In the first place prejudice against factory work and fear of loss of status and income, by cottage workers, significantly complicated the process and had a lasting influence on the organisation of work within mills. Early use of water power, whilst initially within the traditional textile areas, took factory masters to such places as Backbarrow and Caton, where indigenous population was scarce. Early rural factory masters did not, however, face an absolute shortage of labour. Welcomed as potential employers of the poor, they were able to turn to the parish authorities. Both child and adult labour came from this source often from the locality of the mill. Since spinning was often a spare time occupation for those in receipt of poor relief, many would have already been familiar with the hand process.[80] Larger employers whether outside or within the traditional textile areas of Lancashire looked further afield, bringing batches of children from large towns, such as London, to expand their workforces. By no means an innovation of the industrial revolution, the use of pauper children in industry was a time honoured way of reducing parish costs on the one hand and providing employers with labour on the other. The practice gathered momentum in the 1780s reaching a peak in the early 1800s and it has been suggested that about one third of the cotton factory labour force in the industrial revolution came from this source. In the traditional textile areas, such as Oldham, parish apprenticeship was fairly uncommon and probably unnecessary. However, for some larger employers predominantly, but not exclusively, in rural areas, parish apprentices made up the bulk of their workforce in the late eighteenth century. Of the 310 workers employed by Birch Robinson and Co. of Backbarrow in 1797, for example, 210 were parish apprentices.[81]

The poor conditions in many early mills meant that the wholesale and unregulated apprenticeship of poor children to the cotton industry was relatively shortlived. Even before 1802 and the somewhat ineffective government restrictions on the hours parish children could work,[82] rumours of maltreatment in cotton mills caused disquiet in some parishes. Somewhat tellingly some of the earliest concern was shown in Lancashire itself. In 1784, Dr Thomas Percival and several other Manchester physicians were appointed by the Lancashire magistrates to investigate an outbreak of fever at one of the Peel family's mills at

FIGURE 8. 'Love Conquered Fear'. Cartoon of child labour in mule spinning. Illustration from F. Trollope, *The Life and Adventures of Michael Armstrong, the Factory Boy* (Henry Colburn, 1840), facing p. 82.

Ratcliffe near Bury. The report was sufficiently damning for Lancashire's magistrates to resolve

> that it is the opinion of this court that it is highly expedient for the magistrates of this county to refuse their allowance to all indentures of parish apprentices who shall be bound to owners of cotton mills or other manufactories in which children are obliged to work at night or for more than ten hours a day.[83]

It is not clear how rigidly this resolution was implemented, however. Manchester magistrates retained a deep antipathy to parish apprenticeship in cotton mills, one observing in 1816 that:

> it is not customary with the magistrates of that district to bind children to cotton mills or to any other business in which children or other are employed in large bodies, it being their conception that the principle of parochial apprenticeship is best provided for by an immediate or domestic connection between master and apprentice and consequently children are hardly ever bound apprentice except to weavers or other persons with whom they form part of their family . . . the children being employed in cotton factories being either in a state of free labour or apprentices bound from distant parishes.[84]

Such disquiet eventually reached more distant parishes such as some of those in London. For example, a series of visits by the Officers of St Clement Dane's to Birch Robinson and Co.'s Backbarrow Mill between 1797 and 1801 pointed to a deterioration of conditions for apprentices there. Whilst this did not lead St Clement Danes to stop sending children to the mill it led them to regularise their inspection procedures.[85]

The availability of parish children reduced the incentives for rural mill owners to build their own communities. This is not to say that factory owners did not offer housing to induce migration. But where a high proportion of their requirements for child labour could be met through parish apprenticeship, this reduced the level of cottage building. This was because it was less necessary to accommodate whole families, whilst parish children could be housed in a single apprentice house. It was only when parish apprenticeship ceased to be an accessible, renewable source of labour that many rural millowners really began community building in earnest. A few, such as the Ashworths of Turton and New Eagley near Bolton, provided schools, shops, chapels and recreational facilities in the 1820s and 1830s. In so doing they created a community-based labour market which they controlled. They tried to improve work efficiency by reducing labour turnover, increase loyalty by offering decent working conditions and regular employment and reduce labour unrest through community control.[86] Yet such paternalism, where employers attempted to a create a community and bind the workforce to the objectives of the factory, was costly and remained the preserve of relatively few, much quoted, large firms.

This type of community building remained exceptional, especially as water gave way to steam. Within the traditional textile areas the expansion of the cotton towns meant that from the 1820s, if not before, the cotton industry became increasingly urban based. With the exception of Manchester, few of the cotton towns relied heavily on Irish migrants. Instead, all categories of labour were increasingly drawn from the locality of the mill from within the existing community of textile workers, or through short-distance migration of young adults as out-work and rural industry declined. Family and community remained closely linked, whilst the organisation of work in many factories ensured these ties extended to the shopfloor. Factory mule spinners, for example, controlled virtually all aspects of their work from maintenance of their machinery to the choice of helpers. Out of piece-rate wages they recruited, trained and remunerated their piecers, who in turn could look forward to the prospect of rising to become spinners. It was a hierarchical system, which had evolved out of pre-industrial practice and helped to overcome early prejudice against factory work, when power was first applied to the mule from the 1790s.[87] It proved to be an effective method of labour management during the industrial revolution since

> the spinners had an economic interest in seeking out the most dependable assistants, while at the same time their location in the families or communities. . . gave them advantage in assessing the likely qualities of recruits.[88]

The importance of community to the rise of the factory system in Lancashire had moulded the industry before 1830 and had lasting consequences for its subsequent development and performance. There were considerable variations in the pre-industrial traditions and in the social and economic construction of the evolving towns. This meant that even within the small geographic area of Lancashire affected by the cotton industry the experience of the industrial revolution was not uniform. Variations have been detected from an early date in, for example, the origins of enterprise, technology, product, the size of firms and the economic profile of towns.

Some of the most profound contrasts have been detected if the two spinning towns of Oldham and Bolton are compared in 1811. In Oldham the majority of firms were small, and spun mainly coarse counts. The majority of cotton manufacturers had originally either been small landholders, had coalmining links or had been involved in hatting,

Oldham's previous specialism. Bolton mills were, in general, larger than those in Oldham and were generally established by those who had amassed previous experience and wealth in textiles. They produced fine yarns, a reflection of a pre-industrial concentration on muslin manufacture and the local invention of the mule by Samuel Crompton.[89] Inevitably variations in the economic characterisitics of the towns were a reflection of social differences. Moreover the reinforcement of these trends during the industrial revolution meant that by the 1830s the culture of the two towns, in terms of politics and labour relations as well product and technology, had diverged (see chapter 5 for a discussion of the factory workforce).

Differences in experience are, therefore, especially striking between Bolton and Oldham, but they were to be found throughout the cotton area during and after the industrial revolution. The persistence of handloom weaving especially in the finer branches and in the rural parts of north-east Lancashire, has been linked to the long-standing tradition of craft organised hand work. In these areas, therefore it was not until the 1880s that handloom weaving was finally extinct.[90] Similarly the survival of tiny small scale jenny workshops in Wigan, until at least the 1820s, is inexplicable without reference to the characterisitics of the local economy and to the technological traditions which had developed there. The jenny has been portrayed as the least enduring of the key cotton spinning inventions. Never a powered machine, it was overhauled in terms of both quality and efficiency, first by the water frame and then the mule by the early nineteenth century. By 1811 Crompton's evidence suggests that only 3.1 per cent of the 5,066,396 spindles in use in the cotton industry were jennies in small hand workshops operated by marginal producers.[91]

What is striking, however, is that nearly 80 per cent of the surviving jennies in 1811 were in just two centres – Stockport in Cheshire and in Wigan, with a further 8 per cent in Manchester.[92] In Wigan there were 40,386 jenny spindles in use often in small workshops. Of the 28 mills recorded by Crompton in Wigan 16 used jennies exclusively. These were tiny hand workshops, employing on average around 13 spinners typically on 126 spindle jennies.[93]

The concentration of jenny workshops has not gone without comment,[94] but more research is needed to explain the phenomenon fully. It is unlikely, however, that the Wigan jenny cluster could be explained without reference to the local economy, its traditions and resources. Local labour market conditions meant that there were better employment opportunities for men in mining than in cotton. In addition an early technological and machine making tradition centred on the jenny, poor water power and demand from the local sail cloth and sacking industries all seem likely to have contributed to the persistence of jennies and inhibited the spread of first water frames and then mules.

It would seem that although there was some convergence, within the cotton areas of Lancashire before 1830, the experience of the industrial revolution in the Lancashire cotton industry reinforced many pre-industrial differences. By 1841 the majority of firms in Lancashire remained small and single process, using limited amounts of power and employing a small number of workers. Even in Manchester where there were a number of large firms like McConnel and Kennedy, the typical firm was at best medium sized and employed between 150 and 500 operatives.[95] Yet what is even more striking, than the relatively modest size of firms generally, is the considerable variation in scale between the main cotton parishes as table 1.6 demonstrates.

Table 1.6 *Average employees per factory
in the principal cotton parishes in Lancashire, 1838*

| Town | Employees per mill |
| --- | --- |
| Manchester | 216.3 |
| Oldham | 78.1 |
| Bury | 119.8 |
| Ashton | 148.1 |
| Rochdale | 89.9 |
| Blackburn | 237.7 |
| Whalley | 88.1 |
| Bolton | 143.7 |
| Preston | 204.6 |
| Wigan | 165.9 |

Source: H. D. Fong, *Triumph of the Factory System*, p. 29

## Conclusions

The output of the cotton industry grew at an annual rate of 12.76 per cent *per annum* in the 1780s, and by 1801 accounted for 17 per cent of British industrial output and 13.5 per cent of industrial value added.[96] As a result cotton and Lancashire have often been placed at the heart of the British industrial revolution. The cotton industry has variously been described as 'the original leading sector in the first take-off'[97] as 'the pacemaker of industrial change'[98] whilst the cotton mill has been seen as 'the symbol of Britain's industrial greatness'.[99] Yet if the growth of the cotton industry was impressive in the industrial revolution, its impact on the British economy was, in reality, relatively limited. By

1811 'its contribution to British national income was only between 4 per cent and 5 per cent; [and] it offered employment opportunities on a smaller scale than the armed forces'.[100]

It is only when viewed at the level of the region that cotton can be seen as an engine of growth in any meaningful sense. Thus

[if] cotton was the motor . . . in the first instance it was Lancashire, rather than England that was the vehicle driven by it.[101]

Lancashire and its environs have, therefore, been described as the 'classic industrial region', with cotton the major industry. This predominance, in turn, stimulated the Lancashire economy. The cotton industry, therefore encouraged the development of commerce, finance, transport, mineral extraction and ancillary industries, especially after 1830. This meant that the cotton industry fulfilled the role of leading sector in the region. In addition the substantial cost and information advantages of location within reach of both services and raw materials, after 1830, reinforced trends which had begun during the industrial revolution.

Yet, if in the nineteenth century the British cotton industry was increasingly concentrated in a single county, the popular image of its overwhelming dominance should not be exaggerated. Nor should the early impact of the factory, during Lancashire's industrial revolution, be taken for granted. Lancashire certainly became the single most important centre of the British cotton industry by 1830. However, throughout the nineteenth century, the majority of Lancashire's population was employed in other sectors, with vast tracts of the county virtually untouched by cotton. During the industrial revolution the quest for water power sent industrialists to the very margins of the county. However the lasting and cumulative impact of the cotton industry was increasingly restricted, as the nineteenth century progressed, to its south-easternmost corner. Even amongst the cotton towns there were, by 1830, considerable variations in their employment profiles.

Before the middle of the nineteenth century, factories did not dominate Lancashire industry. Between 1780 and 1830, there developed in the county a 'small island of modern industry' amidst a 'veritable sea' of pre-industrial sectors and a worker was as likely to be employed in a cottage or small workshop as in a factory.[102] Even in the cotton industry the factory system was initially confined primarily to carding and spinning. In weaving and calico printing the process of mechanisation and centralisation of production was patchy and protracted.

Lancashire's long tradition in textiles and the variations in the economic, technological, social and cultural characteristics of the cotton towns, which were reinforced by the industrial revolution had important consequences for the subsequent development of the industry. In the first place, the development, by the 1840s, of established commercial networks and ancillary industries removed the incentive to integrate production and commerce in a single firm. In addition the sustained expansion of diverse export markets in the second half of the nineteenth century served to reinforce patterns of spatial specialisation already evident during the industrial revolution. Conversely it was the very diversity of experience within Lancashire during the industrial revolution which meant that firms were able to specialise by process and by market (see chapter 9 for a discussion of the late nineteenth-century development of the cotton industry).

By the interwar period and beyond, however, the collapse of many of those markets caused serious problems of readjustment. In this environment, the vertical and spatial specialisation of the industry made it difficult to develop an industry-wide response to problems (see chapter 10 for a discussion of the experience of Lancashire from 1914–39). The shrinkage of the Lancashire cotton industry, however, began in the interwar period. It has variously been blamed on a combination of technological and organisational interia which meant that her firms were increasingly unable to compete with new industrialisers such as the Japanese (see chapter 8 for a discussion of the international diffusion of cotton textile technology). However, it is doubtful whether the late nineteenth-century level of output was sustainable in the long term or whether the profound concentration of a corner of Lancashire on cotton textiles was desirable in the changing world after 1945 (see chapter 11 for a discussion of the decline of the Lancashire cotton industry since 1939). Yet a more satisfactory movement up market, in line with developments elsewhere in the Western world might have prevented the annihilation of cotton textiles in Lancashire. The decline of cotton in Lancashire has, from the 1930s onwards, drastically altered the visual appearance of the cotton towns with the factory chimney virtually vanishing. However the legacy of cotton remains. Throughout the old cotton area of Lancashire it lives on in street names, buildings and in the proliferation of industrial museums (see chapter 12 for a discussion of the remains of the industrial revolution).

CHAPTER 2

# Technological Change

GEOFFREY TIMMINS

HISTORIANS see the relationship between technological innovation and the success of the cotton industry as being of fundamental importance. Indeed, S. D. Chapman has remarked that this aspect of its history has received more attention than any other. He notes particularly the interest in that famous trio of multi-thread spinning machines, Hargreaves' jenny, Arkwright's water-frame and Crompton's mule, along with the associated machinery used for carding and pre-paring rovings.[1] His comment was made more than 20 years ago, but, judging by the steady flow of contributions that have since appeared, its force remains undiminished.

In addressing the theme, two closely-related issues have been em-phasised. One examines the type of technological advances that took place and the impact they had on the growth of the industry. Essentially, it considers the degree to which more technically-advanced machines both increased the productivity (output per person) of those employed in cotton production and influenced the move from domestic to factory work. The other deals with the pace at which improved technology was introduced in the industry and the degree to which it was adopted. Of concern here has been the replacement of hand technology by powered machinery, especially in weaving, as well as investment in im-proved types of powered machines to replace those already in use.

In this chapter, both these matters are considered. Each of the three main branches of the industry – spinning, weaving and finishing – are covered, emphasising developments from the late eighteenth century to the mid-nineteenth. In part, this period is chosen because of the importance that technological change assumed in the industry as powered machinery became widely adopted. It is also because discussion on subsequent technological development, associated particularly with the invention of ring spinning and the automatic loom, becomes subsumed into a broader debate about the alleged failure of British entrepreneurs during the late nineteenth century and the impact this had on Britain's relative economic decline. Such matters require detailed consideration in their own right and are accordingly left to chapter 9.

## Technological change and its impact

### 1. *Traditional hand techniques*

References to cotton production in Lancashire go back to the early 1600s. They are concerned with the weaving of fustians, cloths comprising a linen warp and a cotton weft. These were one of several

FIGURE 9. Hand cards and Jersey spinning wheels.

In the left foreground is a pair of hand cards, essentially wooden blocks fitted with handles and covered with short metal spikes. The spikes were angled and set in leather. The fibres were worked between the spikes and, by reversing the cards, scraped off in rolls (cardings) about 12 inches long and ¾ inch thick.

The spinner on the right has several cardings in her lap. She is producing rovings, lightly twisted threads. The carding has been attached to the roving which has already been spun and wound onto the spindle. As she turns the wheel, the spindle revolves, twisting the carding fibres together. At the same time, the spinner draws out the carding, holding it at about 45° to the point of the spindle. Spinning completed, she winds the new length of roving onto the spindle, holding the roving roughly parallel to the wheel.

The other spinner is twisting and drawing out (drafting) the rovings to produce thread (there is a roving on her lap). She works in a similar way to her companion, but holds the roving at a shallower angle. After drafting, she turns the spindle a few times in reverse. This is known as 'backing off' and is done to remove the few coils of yarn that have formed near the top of the spindle. She then winds on, turning the wheel in the original direction, and forms a cop on the spindle.

Source: R. Guest, *A Compendious History of the Cotton Manufacture* (Joseph Pratt, 1823), plate 3.

'new draperies' introduced into England by Flemish refugees during the latter half of the sixteenth century. In Lancashire, early centres of fustian production were at Bolton and Blackburn, but the industry eventually expanded throughout most of the county's textile zone.

During this early phase of industrialisation, often referred to as the proto-industrial era, textile production largely took place in rural cottages. Merchants in Manchester and other main towns gave out materials on credit to independent 'putters out' or 'manufacturers'. In turn, they supplied the domestic spinners and weavers, paying them a piece rate and returning their products to the merchant for finishing and marketing.[2]

The raw cotton received by domestic producers might first require beating to remove impurities, including cotton seeds, and to open out the fibres. Next it was carded. The aim was to disentangle the fibres and produce a roll (or carding) of fairly even density. This was achieved with hand cards (figure 9).

The cardings were then spun, which involved drawing out the fibres (drafting), whilst, at the same time, twisting them together. It also entailed 'winding on' the spun thread. This was done either onto a bobbin held by the spindle, or onto the spindle directly to form a cop – a cylinder of yarn with conical ends, which fitted into the weaver's shuttle. Two types of hand wheel were used, each with a single spindle. One was the Jersey or muckle wheel. With this, the operative first spun rovings and then thread, building up a cop (figure 9). The other was the Saxony wheel, which was operated by a crank and foot treadle (figure 10). This left the spinner's hands free for drafting, a crucial matter in flax spinning. The spun thread was wound onto a bobbin.[3]

Domestic carding and spinning would normally have been undertaken by women and children. Weaving was left to men and the type of handloom they used can be seen in figure 11. Men would also have been responsible for warping. This process created parallel warp threads of a given length and was achieved by means of a series of wooden pegs set into a wall (figure 12).[4]

In finishing fustians, the most important process was bleaching. Traditionally, this was accomplished by steeping the cloth in an alkaline solution made from plant ashes and then spreading it out in a bleaching field (or croft) for some weeks. The process was repeated several times. Next, the cloth was soaked in buttermilk (souring) before being returned to the croft. Again the process was repeated several times. Not surprisingly, up to eight months could elapse before the cloth was bleached.[5]

Each of these processes was extremely labour-intensive and time-consuming. That they did not require highly-skilled, expensive labour, however, meant that the incentive to innovate was not especially strong.

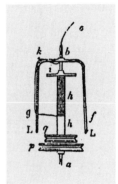

FIGURE 10. The Saxony Wheel.

The illustrations show a spinner using the wheel, along with the spindle, flyer and bobbin mechanism. The latter was mounted horizontally on two uprights at one end of the wheel. The thread was spun from fibres held by the spinner and was fed through a short, hollow section (*b*) at the top of the spindle. After re-emerging, it passed around hooks at *k* and *g* on one of the flyer's arms, before being wound onto the wooden bobbin (*h*) placed on the spindle.

At the other end of the spindle were two grooved discs or 'whorls' (*p* and *q*). Whorl *p* was attached to the spindle and flyer and whorl *q* to the bobbin. Both were connected by endless cords to the wheel. Because the bobbin whorl had the smaller diameter, it revolved faster than the spindle and flyer whorl. As a result the spun thread could be wound onto the bobbin. The point at which this took place could be varied by moving the thread to another hook on the arm of the flyer, several being provided.

The spinner drafted the fibres, which were combed rather than carded, as they were spun and wound, replacing the bobbin when it was full. The process was thus continuous, whilst that using the Jersey wheel was intermittent. The fibres were held on an upright stick, the distaff, attached to the frame of the wheel.

Source: A. Ure, *The Cotton Manufacture of Great Britain* (H. G. Bohn, 1861), vol. 1, pp. 234–5.

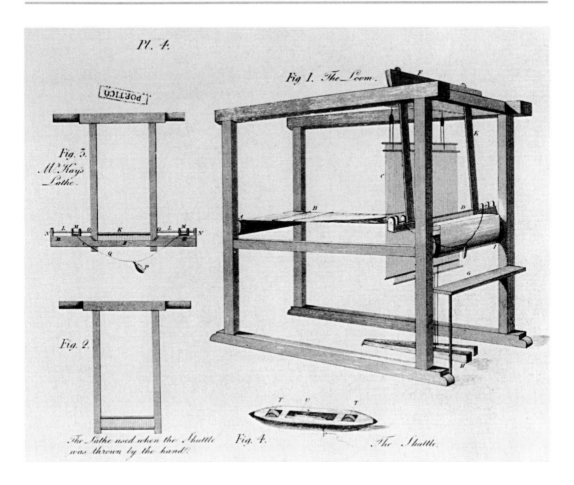

FIGURE 11. Handloom and Kay's fly shuttle.

In the loom illustration, the warp is wound from the warp beam (A), half the threads passing through loops in one heald (C) and half through loops in the other. The warp also passes through the reed (D), which is fixed to the lower part of the lathe (E).

The weaver, sitting on the seat (G), used his foot to press down one of the treadles (H). This raised one of the healds, creating a passage (or shed) in the warps through which the shuttle could pass. This was originally done by hand, but in this loom, a fly shuttle was used. The weaver held the picking stick (P) in his right hand, jerking it sharply to propel the shuttle across the lathe and through the shed. As the weaver pulled the lathe towards him with his left hand, the reed drove the weft thread left by the shuttle against the finished cloth. The woven cloth was wound onto the cloth beam (I).

Periodically, the weaver dressed the unwoven warp threads by brushing them with size, often a mixture of flour and water. This strengthened the warps so that they could resist the friction from the shuttle and reed.

In the illustration of a lathe fitted with a fly shuttle mechanism, the moveable slides (MM) are fixed on iron rods (LL). The slides are fastened by a cord (Q) to the picking stick or peg (P).

The other illustrations show the type of lathe used when the shuttle was thrown by hand and the underside of a fly shuttle.

Source: R. Guest, *A Compendious History of the Cotton Manufacture* (Joseph Pratt, 1823), plate 4.

FIGURE 12. Peg warping. A thread was attached to the outer peg and then under and over the other pegs alternately. Having passed round the peg at the other end, the thread was returned to the start, again passing under and over the pegs. The process was repeated until the required number of warp threads was obtained. Before removing the warps, cords or rods were inserted in place of the pegs. These kept each thread separate. The crossing of the threads is called the lease. Source: R. Marsden, *Cotton Weaving: Its Development, Principles, and Practice* (Bell, 1895), p. 251.

Indeed, it was not until the middle decades of the eighteenth century, when the long-term demand for fustians began to show a marked and sustained rate of increase, that the need for improved technology became of more pressing concern.

### 2. *Developments before the Industrial Revolution*

The major technological advances achieved in multi-thread cotton spinning during the late eighteenth century had long been anticipated. As early as 1678, Richard Haines of Sullington in Sussex and Richard Dereham of London obtained a patent for a machine that would spin from six to a hundred threads at once. Compared with the single-thread spinning wheels then in general use, this new invention promised a notable rise in spinners' productivity. However, as with other early hand-powered spinning machines, there is no indication that it proved commercially viable.[6]

Nor was any high degree of success achieved with the earliest power-driven spinning machine. Intended for the woollen trade, but probably used only with cotton, it was patented in 1738 by Lewis Paul. Working in association with John Wyatt, he developed a means of drafting slivers (carded, unspun threads) by passing them between pairs of rollers, each pair turning faster than the one before. Revolving spindles provided the twist (figure 13). The machines were installed in premises at London, Birmingham, Northampton and Leominster, but technical shortcomings made them costly to operate and prevented

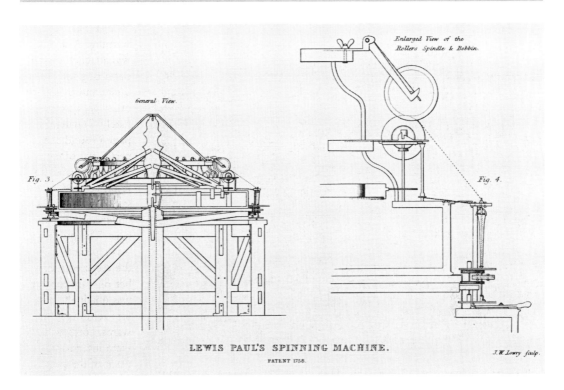

*General View.*

*Enlarged View of the Rollers Spindle & Bobbin.*

*Fig. 3.*

*Fig. 4.*

LEWIS PAUL'S SPINNING MACHINE.

PATENT 1758.

*J. W. Lowry sculp.*

FIGURE 13. Lewis Paul's spinning machine. The illustration is from a second patent taken out by Paul in 1758. It shows a variant of the mechanism described in the earlier patent. Only one pair of rollers was used, the sliver being both drafted and twisted by the spindle, which rotated faster than the rollers. Source: E. Baines, *History of the Cotton Manufacture in Great Britain* (Fisher, Fisher & Jackson, 1835), facing p. 139.

their widespread adoption.[7] There is no evidence to show they were used in Lancashire.

Lewis Paul also took out a patent for hand-powered carding machinery. Granted in 1748, it comprised two different machines, one having the cards laid flat and the other with the cards placed around a horizontal cylinder (figure 14). Edward Baines saw the latter as the more important, since it closely resembled the type of carding engine that eventually came into general use.[8]

The evolution of these new techniques was encouraged by a growing demand for cotton goods, both at home and abroad, as well as by annual yarn shortages that arose when wool, linen and cotton spinners undertook harvest work.[9] But the more immediate stimulus to the introduction of roller spinning was the scarcity of imported cotton yarn during the mid-1740s. Furthermore, this may have prompted Paul and Wyatt to concentrate on spinning cotton rather than other types of fibre.[10]

In developing these improved machines, inventors were aware that operatives of traditional spinning wheels might face reduced employment opportunities. Since this could have prevented their patents being granted, defensive argument was required. Thus, Paul and Wyatt took the line that displaced labour could be readily absorbed into other jobs, with young women, who would be most affected, turning to agricultural work. This would have the further advantage of meeting the 'just complaints' of farmers about labour shortages, especially during the summer, whilst the livelihood and even the morals of the women would be protected. To strengthen their case, they suggested that roller spinning machines would employ paupers, including children and those who were infirm. Their arguments satisfied the attorney general, who reported favourably on the application. However, whether farming could in reality have provided enough jobs for displaced spinners is questionable, as is the notion that roller spinning would have given employment to infirm paupers. And young women would not willingly have turned from spinning, since, as Paul and Wyatt recognised, they preferred such work 'for the sake of their liberty'.[11] In their view, seemingly, greater freedom for females inevitably led to moral decline.

Meanwhile, technical innovation was occurring in textile weaving. Around the 1660s, the Dutch or engine loom, which could weave simultaneously a dozen or more smallware items (ribbons, tapes, garters and the like), spread from London to Manchester. It soon gave rise to

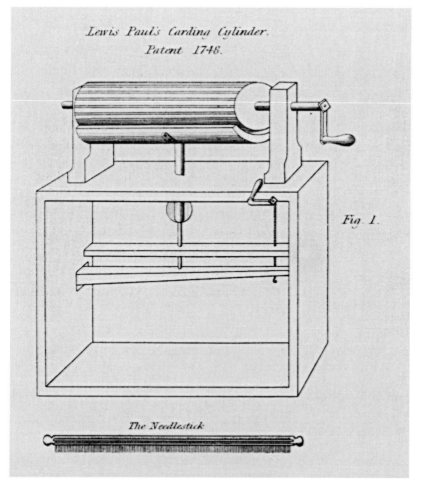

FIGURE 14. Lewis Paul's carding cylinder. Both the cylinder and the curved frame beneath it were fitted with cards. They worked against each other when the handle was turned, thereby carding the fibres. The frame could be lowered and rotated, so that the carded fibre could be stripped off by hand using the needlestick, in effect a long metal comb.
Source: E. Baines, *History of the Cotton Manufacture in Great Britain* (Fisher, Fisher & Jackson, 1835), facing p. 152.

a prosperous industry and by the mid-eighteenth century, at least 1,500 Dutch looms were at work in Manchester parish. About this time, the industry received a further boost with the invention of the swivel loom, an improved version of the Dutch loom, which enabled finer fabrics to be woven.[12]

Of more general significance to the weaving trade, though, was the fly-shuttle, patented in 1733 by John Kay of Bury. This was wheeled and the weaver propelled it between the warps by pulling a cord attached to moveable slides placed at each side of the lathe. These struck the end of the shuttle, sending it to and fro (figure 11). In weaving wider cloths, the fly-shuttle dispensed with the need to have

FIGURE 15. An improved jenny.
The rovings are held in bobbins on the sloping frame. At the outset, the drawbar, held in the spinner's left hand, is at the other end of the machine. Lengths of roving, which are attached to the spun thread on the spindles, are released from the bobbins and clamped in the drawbar. As the wheel is turned, the spindles rotate, imparting twist. At the same time, drafting is achieved as the spinner walks backwards pulling steadily on the drawbar.

The spun thread is wound onto the spindles as the spinner returns the drawbar. This is done by means of a thin wire, called a faller, situated above the spindles. By operating a lever with her left hand, the spinner enables the faller to drop down onto the spun threads to form a cop.

Source: C. Aspin and S. D. Chapman, *James Hargreaves and the Spinning Jenny* (Helmshore Local History Society, 1964), facing p. 52.

COTTON MANUFACTURE.

*WATER SPINNING FRAME.*

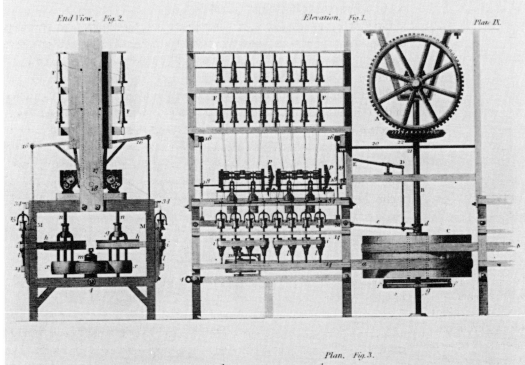

End View. *Fig.2.*                    Elevation. *Fig.1.*                    Plate IX.

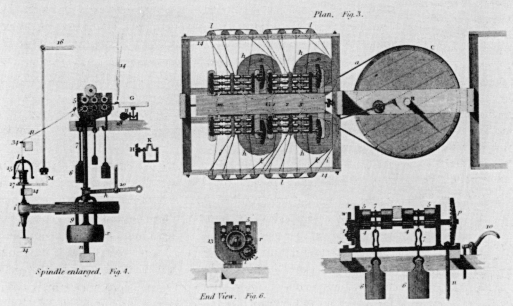

Plan. *Fig.3.*

Spindle enlarged. *Fig.4.*

End View. *Fig.6.*

Elevation of Rollers. *Fig.5.*

W.Lowry sculp.t

a person at each side of the loom. Its other main advantages were the higher speeds at which it could be operated and the evenness with which it laid the weft. The indications are that the fly-shuttle did not make rapid progress until the 1750s, when it became widely used in weaving fustians on narrow looms.[13]

One other noteworthy development that took place in weaving during this period was the drop-box. Introduced by John Kay's son Robert in 1760, it enabled the quick interchange of shuttles containing different colours of thread.[14]

For the most part, technological change in the cotton-using branches of the textile trade prior to the later decades of the eighteenth century was directed at hand-powered machinery. Accordingly, the degree to which operatives' productivity was raised and hence labour costs per unit of output reduced, remained limited, though by no means insignificant. Not until the adoption of powered machinery could the impact of technological change on cotton production be more fully demonstrated.

### 3. Developments during the Industrial Revolution

#### (i) Spinning

FIGURE 16. Arkwright's water frame. The rovings were led from the bobbins (F) through three pairs of rollers (4 and 5), each pair revolving faster than the one before, to allow drafting. The revolving spindles (15) provided the twist and the flyers wound the spun thread onto bobbins. The fluted rollers (4) and the weights attached to them (6) can be seen. Source: *Rees's Manufacturing Industry (1819–20) vol. 2,* 'Cotton Manufacture', plate 9 (David & Charles reprint, 1972).

A doubling of raw cotton imports into Britain during the middle decades of the eighteenth century reflects a steadily-rising demand for fustians and cotton-linens.[15] Whilst this had a marked, if unspectacular, effect on the growth of these trades, it also brought the threat of labour shortages. This was particularly so in spinning, because yarn production remained largely dependent on hand spinners using traditional, single-spindle wheels, whilst weavers' output was greatly enhanced by the widespread adoption of the fly-shuttle. A technological inbalance was thus created in the industry, with the result that, all too often, weavers were unable to obtain the amounts of yarn they needed. And the problem was exacerbated by the difficulty of increasing the supply of labour without employing, as spinners, men who would have demanded higher wages than women.[16]

Concern over the impact labour shortages might have on production costs and product prices, coupled with limited progress made in textile technology during the 1740s and 1750s, prompted the Royal Society of Arts to offer premiums for the invention of a loom which would double a weaver's output and a spinning machine which would spin six threads at once. Several machines were created, but none proved adequate. With trial and amendment, success might have been attained, but perfecting new machinery could prove extremely costly for inventors and sponsors alike. To serve as a reminder, John Wyatt's spell in a debtor's prison need only be recalled, as well as the limited achievements he and his associates made in the cotton spinning business.[17]

Nevertheless, with the prospect of high rewards from the successful development of improved textile machinery, inventors persisted and during the 1760s, two major breakthroughs were achieved, both in spinning. The first was James Hargreaves' jenny. This incorporated a carriage to draw out the threads as revolving spindles twisted them together (figure 15). Hargreaves, a hand weaver from Stanhill, near Blackburn, developed his machine around 1764, taking out a patent in 1770. At first, the jenny could spin no more than 16 threads simultaneously. That it remained a hand-driven machine limited its capacity, though improved jennies were eventually constructed with

FIGURE 17. Three views of a carding machine.
The raw cotton was fed through rollers (B) onto the carding (great) cylinder, around which was a convex cover (D) made from strips of cards (or flats). The carded cotton was removed from the great cylinder by the doffing cylinder (E) and from the latter by the crank and comb mechanism (F). It then passed into a funnel (G) and through rollers (HH), emerging as a sliver (I). This was fed into a can (K).
Source: R. Guest, *A Compendious History of the Cotton Manufacture* (Joseph Pratt, 1823), plate 10.

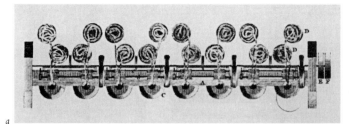

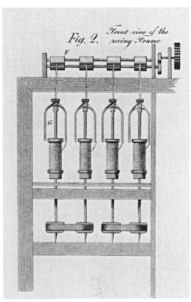

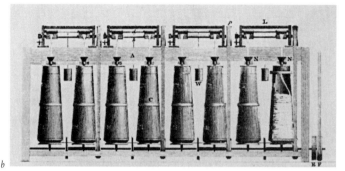

FIGURE 18. Roving frames.

As the plan drawing (*a*) shows, each pair of slivers were drawn from the cans, and drafted between a pair of rollers, so they became longer and thinner. Twisting occurred as the slivers were fed from the rollers into revolving cans. The cans had doors in the side by which the rovings were removed to be wound by hand onto bobbins.

Around 1815, the fly frame (*c*) was introduced. As the front elevation drawing reveals, this used flys or flyers and spindles to provide the twist instead of the revolving can. One leg of the flyer was hollow, so the sliver could be fed through it and then conveyed to the bobbin. Using the fly frame saved having to wind rovings onto bobbins by hand.

Sources: R. Guest, *A Compendious History of the Cotton Manufacture* (1823), plate II and *Rees's Manufacturing Industry (1819–20), vol. 2*, 'Cotton Manufacture', plate 5 (David & Charles reprint, 1972).

as many as 130 spindles. The thread produced by the jenny was relatively coarse and weak, but was eminently suitable for use as weft.[18]

The second breakthrough was made in 1769 with the patenting of the water-frame, a more advanced roller-spinning machine. The patentee was Richard Arkwright, but the machine may have been devised by Thomas Highs of Leigh. Part of its success lay in grouping the rollers in sets of three rather than two and in spacing sets of rollers to take account of the length (or staple) of the fibre. The rollers were also made to grip the fibres firmly without damaging them. This was partly achieved by covering the top sets with leather and making the bottom sets from fluted cylinders of wood held on a metal core. In addition, metal weights were suspended from the top sets of rollers. As with earlier roller-spinning machines, flyers provided the twist and wound the spun thread onto bobbins (figure 16). The water-frame used mechanical power and produced a strong, coarse thread suitable

for warps. It thus complemented jenny-spun yarn and facilitated the production of all-cotton cloth.[19] Under an Act passed in 1721, however, making such cloth was illegal and to protect their interests, Arkwright and his partners successfully petitioned Parliament to secure its repeal in 1774.[20]

Arkwright contributed further to the cotton industry's technological progress when, in 1775, he patented improved preparatory equipment. It included a cylinder carding engine, incorporating a crank and comb mechanism. The comb moved up and down, removing the carded fibres from the doffing cylinder in a 'continuous filmy fleece'. This was next passed through rollers and a funnel to reduce it to a sliver, which then fell in coils into a cylindrical can (figure 17). In a further process, known as drawing, several slivers were taken from their cans, joined together and drafted between pairs of rollers. More uniform slivers were obtained. They were then drafted in a roving frame and fed into conical (or lantern) cans. These revolved, twisting the slivers into rovings (figure 18). Arkwright may not have invented these machines, as those opposing his patent rights, and later critics, have claimed, but he did combine them together effectively with the water-frame, so that, for the first time, cotton yarn production became a continuous process largely using powered machinery[21] (figure 19).

Neither the jenny nor the water-frame were introduced without opposition. During the late 1760s, Hargreaves' early machines were

FIGURE 19. Carding, drawing and roving at Swainson and Birley's mill, Preston, 1836. Carding machines can be seen on the left and a fly frame on the right.
Source: E. Baines, *History of the Cotton Manufacture in Great Britain* (Fisher, Fisher & Jackson, 1835), p. 182.

destroyed and this probably influenced his departure to Nottingham. However, that he would have gone anyway remains a possibility, being attracted, as was Arkwright, by economic opportunity in the local hosiery industry.[22] More serious and general opposition to the new technology occurred in 1779 as trade depression became severe. Machine breaking again took place, rioters seeking to maintain employment levels, as well as traditional types of employment, by destroying machines they thought more suitable for use in factories than in domestic premises. These included jennies with more than 24 spindles.[23]

But such actions did not prevent the growing use of improved machinery. Nor did the patents by which they were supposedly protected. Thus, in the case of the jenny, patent rights were difficult to enforce because the machine was widely dispersed amongst domestic producers.[24] As to the water-frame, Arkwright probably tried to restrict the number of firms using his system under licence. Yet, as was often the case, he could not stop infringements or competitive patents, both of which were doubtless encouraged by the high royalties he demanded.[25]

The jenny and water-frame were soon outpaced by Samuel Crompton's mule, however. Introduced in 1779, the mule borrowed rollers and a drafting frame from earlier machines and spun a fine, strong thread, suitable for such high-value cloths as muslins. For some time, the mule carriage was hand-driven, requiring great skill from spinners and limiting the number of spindles they could turn to around 144. In 1790, though, William Kelly of New Lanark utilised water power to push the carriage outwards and, before long, steam power was being used for the same purpose. This increased the number of spindles per frame and the speed at which they rotated. Moreover, it enabled one spinner to operate two frames placed parallel to one another and hence twice as many spindles (figure 20). The mule was further improved when power was also applied to the return (putting up) action of the carriage, albeit partially. This was achieved by the early 1830s, allowing one spinner to drive upwards of 1,200 spindles. But by then, Richard Roberts had developed a virtually automatic (self-actor) mule, for which he took out patents in 1825 and 1830. In a given time, this could spin up to a quarter more yarn of the same quality than the power-assisted mule and with far less effort from the spinner. It was also said to wind yarn more evenly and firmly onto cops, thereby reducing yarn breakages in weaving.[26]

Other advances in spinning and preparatory technology during this period may be briefly noted. One was the throstle, a faster, more flexible version of the water-frame. Dating from about 1815, it met a rising demand from power weavers for a coarse, strong yarn, which was cheaper to spin than on the mule. Around the same time, rovings began to be made on fly frames. Instead of rotating cans, these used

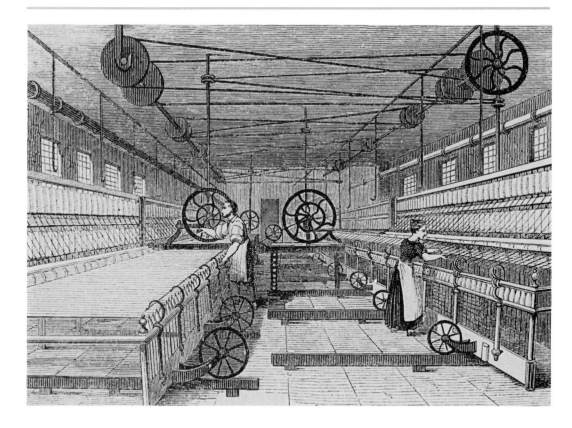

FIGURE 20. A mule spinning room.

Unlike the jenny, the spindles on the mule were placed on the carriage. The spinner is operating a pair of hand-assisted mules. He is helped by a female piecer, who joined any broken threads. The frame on the left has been drawn out using steam power, demonstrating the improvement arising with the application of power. The other has been backed off and returned (put up) by the spinner, who has also wound the spun thread onto the spindles. He is now putting up the other frame.

Putting up required considerable skill. This was because the spinner had to wind the spun thread onto the cops at an even rate, using a faller wire similar to that found on the jenny. The speed at which the carriage was returned had to be kept in the correct relationship to the speed at which he turned the spindles (using the wheel to his right) for this to happen.

Source: *An Illustrated Itinerary of the County of Lancashire* (How and Parsons, 1842), p. 20.

spindles and flyers for twisting. Meanwhile, willows and scutchers, which broke up raw cotton and removed impurities, also appeared, along with lapping machines, which wound raw cotton evenly onto rollers for the carding engine [27] (figure 21).

That, except for the jenny, the new spinning machines adopted in the cotton industry during the late eighteenth and early nineteenth centuries used mechanical power, had a remarkable impact on spinners' productivity. This can be seen from Catling's calculations of the number of operative hours that each machine took to process 100lbs of cotton. For single-spindle hand spinning the time might exceed 50,000 hours.

FIGURE 21. Willowing and scutching.
The illustration is of a willowing machine. It contained a large drum filled with iron spikes, which loosened and separated the fibres, and a powerful fan which blew away dust and other impurities through a large pipe. The scutcher, invented in 1797, removed further impurities from the willowed cotton by beating it with rapidly revolving metallic blades.
  Source: J. R. Barfoot, *The Progress of Cotton* (Helmshore Local History Society 1973 reprint of *c.* 1840 edition), facing p. 2.

Paul and Wyatt's machine reduced this to perhaps 600 hours,[28] but by the 1790s, the water-frame and mule needed only around 300 hours. By the mid-1820s, a 600-spindle power-assisted mule might take as little as 135 hours.[29]

(ii) *Weaving*

During the late eighteenth and early nineteenth centuries, much effort went into mechanising the cotton weaving processes. In the mid-1770s, Robert and Thomas Barber patented a powerloom that appeared technically sound, but nothing came of it. Nor was any marked success achieved by the better-known powerloom invented a decade later by Edmund Cartwright. He established a 20-loom factory at Doncaster in

1787, but went out of business within a few years. Moreover, the twenty-four Cartwright looms installed at Grimshaw's Manchester factory in 1790 were destroyed by fire two years later. Reasons suggested for Cartwright's failure include the crude construction of his looms, along with the lack of machinery in his mills for dressing the warps (applying a starch paste to strengthen them) and winding the warp onto a beam ready for the loom.[30]

The earliest powerloom to have any marked degree of commercial success was patented in 1802. Devised by William Horrocks, a Stockport cotton manufacturer, it featured a more effective means of 'taking up', the process of winding the woven cloth onto a beam at the back of the loom. It was further improved by several patents, including that of Sharp and Roberts in 1822, which, besides modifying further the taking up device, introduced a better way of applying power to the healds (figure 22).[31] As in the spinning branch of the cotton industry, early mechanisation in weaving was perceived as a threat to jobs and led to periodic outbreaks of machine-breaking. The most serious occurred during April, 1826, as trade took a sharp downturn. This brought large-scale unemployment and short-time working, as well as marked reductions in weavers' piece rates. In several days of rioting, more than 1,000 powerlooms in twenty-one East Lancashire mills were destroyed. For the part they played in the riots, forty-three individuals were transported or imprisoned. Because local communities were held partly responsible, they were required to pay a special rate levy to meet the cost of loom replacement.[32]

Whether, by the time of the riots, the technical capability of the powerloom had reached the stage where it posed a severe threat to hand weavers is doubtful. This is so despite the improvement in labour productivity it was said to have achieved. Writing in the early 1820s, Richard Guest, one of the cotton industry's first historians, maintained that a boy or girl aged fourteen or fifteen could manage two power-looms and could produce three and a half times as much as the best handloom weaver. He thought, too, that the powerloom wove cloth of a higher quality than the handloom, because the hand weaver could not draw back the lathe with constant force, so that his cloth varied in thickness. In contrast, the powerloom lathe gave a steady, constant blow, achieving a much more regular weave.[33]

A decade later, an unnamed manufacturer was making even more striking comparisons between the performance of handlooms and powerlooms. Taking cloth of a given size and quality, he maintained that a 'very good handloom weaver, 25 or 30 years of age' could produce two pieces per week, whereas a steamloom weaver of about the same age, assisted by a girl around 12 years old, could weave eighteen or twenty pieces.[34]

Such figures doubtless highlight the capabilities of the most efficient looms rather than those in general use. Accordingly, they probably exaggerate the degree of productivity improvement that most power-looms could attain. Indeed, in weaving fine and fancy wares, powerlooms may still have been uneconomic.[35] Of particular concern here is the number of looms that a weaver could actually manage. According to Richard Marsden, two was the maximum for the most skilful weavers prior to the early 1840s, whilst many weavers could only operate one. This was because the powerloom still required 'the closest and most unremitting attention' of the weaver to ensure that the loom was stopped when the weft thread broke or when the shuttle pirn became empty.[36] That weavers in Grimshaw's shed at Barrowford mostly worked two looms during the mid-1830s indicates that Marsden may have understated the labour savings that powerlooms could attain.[37] Yet his cautionary tone is by no means misplaced and it was not until 1841, when William Kenworthy and James Bullough of Blackburn patented

FIGURE 22. Powerloom weaving at Swainson and Birley's mill, Preston, *c*. 1835.
These looms are probably of the type supplied by Sharp and Roberts. Each loom appears to have two healds, indicating that plain weaving was being undertaken. The cloth being woven is likely to have been coarse calico, perhaps a yard and a half wide (six quarters or 6–4 cloth). Each weaver seems to have been operating two looms.
  Source: E. Baines, *History of the Cotton Manufacture in Great Britain* (Fisher, Fisher & Jackson, 1835), facing p. 239.

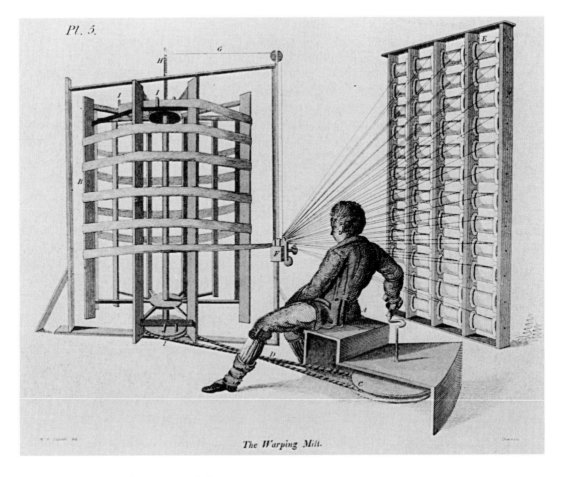

*Pl. 5.*

*The Warping Mill.*

FIGURE 23. Improved warping techniques.
The warping mill was introduced in 1760. It comprised a bobbin creel and a large vertical reel
mounted in a frame. The reel was turned by a pulley. The warps were gathered together at the
slide (*F*) and then fixed to pegs in the upper part of the creel (*I*). The slide was attached by a cord
and pulley to the top of the reel axle (*H*). As the warper turned the handle, the warps were wound
onto the reel and kept in place by the descending slide.
     Source: R. Guest, *A Compendious History of the Cotton Manufacture* (Joseph Pratt, 1823), plate 5.

their weft stop motion, that the technical problems he highlights were
largely overcome. The same patent specified a roller temple, an improved
means of keeping woven cloth at its proper width, whilst, in the
following year, James Bullough patented a loose reed, which allowed
the lathe to back away when it encountered a shuttle trapped in the
warps.[38] Collectively, these developments made the powerloom a far
more efficient, though by no means a perfect, machine.
     The improvement of the powerloom was also assisted by advances
in warp preparation, with two further inventions of William Kenworthy,
namely the warping frame (1843) and tape-sizing (1839), being especially

FIGURE 24. Warp beaming.
In 1803 Thomas Johnson of Stockport developed the beaming machine, which provided an alternative means of warping. Essentially, the warp threads were led from bobbins on a creel, through comb-like guide wires and then between two beams. The upper beam took the threads and the lower one provided the drive.

A major improvement was made to the process by William Kenworthy of Blackburn in 1843. He passed each thread through a hole at the top of one of a row of short, upright rods placed in front of the beams. The rods were supported by the threads, so the threads were held slightly in tension. When a thread broke, causing a peg to fall, the beam was reversed. This allowed several yards of warp to be rewound, facilitating the piecing of the broken ends. Later improvements stopped the beam immediately a thread broke, so there was no need to reverse the cylinder.

Source: J. R. Barfoot, *The Progress of Cotton* (Helmshore Local History Society, 1973 reprint of *c.* 1840 edition), facing p. 8.

notable. Both required mechanical power. The former involved taking warp threads from bobbins attached to a frame and winding them onto a warp beam (figure 23). The latter enabled parallel strips of a warp to be completely immersed in size and then dried by passing over steam-heated cylinders.[39]

Although efforts to improve weaving technology centred on the powerloom, attempts were also made to create more efficient hand-looms. The most successful was probably the dandy loom, developed by Thomas Johnson and William Radcliffe of Stockport and patented by the latter in 1802. Radcliffe's aim was to curb yarn exports in an attempt, however misplaced, to protect British weavers from overseas competitors. The new loom contained a mechanism linking the lathe to the taking-up beam, so that the cloth could be wound continuously as it was woven. According to Radcliffe, William Horrocks pirated this mechanism and used it in his powerloom. Radcliffe also invented a machine for dressing the warps with size before they were placed in the loom. In line with the needs of hand weavers, it coated rather than saturated the yarn.[40] Freed from the need to take up the cloth and dress the warps, dandy loom weavers could work a good deal faster than other hand weavers, perhaps producing fifty per cent more cloth.[41]

### (iii) *Finishing*

In common with spinning and weaving, the finishing branches of the cotton industry saw major technological advance during the Industrial Revolution. Additionally, the bleaching section especially benefited from developments in the chemical industry which had a dramatic impact on the time the process took.

As has already been noted, the traditional method of open-air bleaching required several months to accomplish. By the mid-eighteenth century, however, sulphuric acid was replacing buttermilk in souring, allowing the work to be completed in only half the time. But it was

FIGURE 25. Finishing works machinery. This illustration shows three dash wheels. These were large hollow wheels, divided into four compartments, into which bundles of cloth and water were placed. Impurities were washed out of the cloth as the rapidly revolving wheels threw it backwards and forwards. From 1828 dash wheels were gradually replaced by washing machines. For details of these and other machines see G. Turnbull, *A History of Calico Printing in Great Britain* (Sherratt & Son, 1951), pp. 35–43. Source: *An Illustrated Itinerary of the County of Lancaster* (How & Parsons, 1842), p. 51.

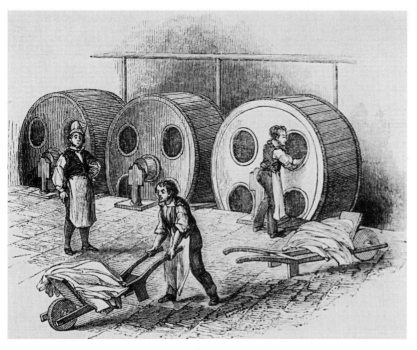

FIGURE 26. Block printing. The illustration shows a block printer and his child assistant or tierer. The printer's block has a pattern cut in relief. After the printer applies it to the cloth, he strikes it with an iron mallet. The block has metal pins at each corner so that he can position it correctly. The tierer brushes the printing colour evenly over the surface of a wooden sieve and, before each print is made, the printer places the block on the sieve in order to 'serve it' with colour. Source: BPP, *Children's Employment Commission: Second Report, Part 1* (1842), p. B8.

at the end of the century that a far more spectacular breakthrough occurred. This was the introduction of bleaching powder, which reduced the time taken for the process to little more than a day.[42]

Meanwhile, mechanisation was also occurring in bleach works as water or steam power was applied to various types of machine. These included dash wheels, which washed the cloth between the various chemical processes; drying machines, in which the cloth passed over heated copper cylinders; and calenders, the wooden and iron rollers of which gave a glossy surface to the cloth (figure 25).[43] Dyehouses, too, employed mechanical power. These were commonly found within bleach works, the imported dyewoods they used having to be ground before being mixed.[44]

In the printing branch of the trade, which may not have begun in Lancashire until the early 1750s, hand processes initially held sway. Both wooden blocks, with patterns cut in relief, and copper plates, with engraved patterns, were used (figure 26). During the mid-1780s, however, printing by means of engraved copper rollers was invented. Credited to Joseph Bell, the process was first used successfully by Livesey, Hargreaves & Co. at Walton-le-Dale, near Preston. Since the rollers were mechanically powered, the speed of printing increased dramatically. Indeed, by the mid-1830s, Edward Baines claimed that a cylinder printing machine operated by a man and a boy could produce as much as one hundred block printers, each with a boy assistant (figure 27).

FIGURE 27. Machine printing.
The engraved printing cylinder was placed horizontally with another cylinder above it. The bottom of the lower cylinder took up the printing colour from a trough, the excess being scraped off by a closely fitting steel blade known as a doctor. The cloth to be printed passed between the cylinders and then over several steam-heated drying boxes. More than one printing cylinder could be used, each providing part of the pattern. The colour was fixed by exposing the cloth to steam.
Source: *An Illustrated Itinerary of the County of Lancaster* (How & Parsons, 1842), p. 62.

Whilst roller printing is perhaps the best known amongst the technical advances made in the cotton printing trade during the late eighteenth and early nineteenth centuries, others also occurred that were of considerable importance. They include the use of small steel cylinders to create the printing pattern on copper rollers. This technique was devised by Joseph Lockett of Manchester around 1808. It meant that the copper roller no longer had to be engraved entirely by hand. Instead, the steel cylinder, on which the pattern was created in relief, was pressed against the copper cylinder, transferring the pattern a length at a time. With a complex pattern, the time taken to complete the copper roll was reduced from several months to a few days.[45]

## The emergence of factory production

The impact of improved technology, both in the cotton industry and more generally, forms a key element in discussions on why the factory system developed, often replacing domestic industry. The traditional view is that centralised production in factories or workshops resulted largely from the development of powered machinery which, because of the relatively high costs involved, could not be used economically in domestic premises.

Other explanations for the rise of centralised production have also been given, however. They focus on the savings that could be obtained by transferring work from domestic premises to factories. Included amongst them are reduced transport charges, lower losses through embezzlement and the need to keep smaller stocks of raw materials. Additionally, it is argued, factory work allowed closer supervision of employees, thereby improving work rate and easing the problems of quality control.[46]

In assessing which line of explanation most applies to the cotton textile industry, it must be noted that centralised production occurred in the spinning, weaving and warping branches, as well as in finishing, without the use of powered machines. This has received most comment in relation to weaving. Thus, in the mid-eighteenth century, the Manchester smallware weavers frequently worked as journeymen for 'men of moderate capital who could bring a number of Dutch looms together in a small workshop . . .'[47] Around the same time, rather larger concentrations of sailcloth weavers and ancillary workers were to be found at Warrington, one manufactory containing no fewer than forty looms, as well as preparatory and finishing equipment.[48] By the early nineteenth century, moreover, handloom weaving sheds were found in various parts of the cotton districts, the largest employing as many as 150 or 200 people, though this was exceptional.[49] Not all were operated by private concerns, workhouse and penal institutions often establishing them to give gainful employment to inmates, sometimes with telling effect. In 1821, for example, hand weaving prisoners at the Preston House of Correction made a profit of almost £1,400 for the town's ratepayers.[50]

The existence of these hand-powered workshops or factories demonstrates that centralised production in the cotton trade did not necessarily await the appearance of powered machinery. In fact, the more crucial consideration was the amount of fixed capital expenditure incurred, irrespective of whether or not powered machinery was involved. Beyond a certain level, this became too high for domestic producers and could only be met by those with long-term capital to invest. In weaving, for example, much of the hand-powered equipment found in centralised production was relatively expensive, including the smallware weavers' Dutch loom, Radcliffe's dandy loom and dressing machine, which were worked in combination to weave calico, the broad looms required for making sailcloth, and the warping mill, which began to replace peg-warping from the mid-eighteenth century (figure 23).[51] That much of this machinery was cumbersome added further to the difficulties of using it in a domestic setting. At issue in the finishing branch of the industry was the cost of hand printers' blocks and stone printing tables, along with provision of sufficient indoor space to dry printed cloth. And printing was often associated with bleaching, a process which incurred its own substantial fixed costs, not least from the construction of reservoirs for water storage.

Such considerations are not intended to deny that the introduction of powered machinery in the cotton trades strongly influenced the move towards centralised production. Clearly, it added appreciably to fixed capital costs, not only in terms of equipment, but also in the provision of mechanical power, especially if a steam engine was installed. Moreover, as in the silk industry, the tendency was for efficient powered machines to appear before factories became usual, rather than the other way round.[52] This strongly suggests that most cotton producers did not believe they could make any worthwhile savings by establishing hand-powered factories, especially when set against the risks involved in extending fixed capital expenditure. However, to take advantage of powered machinery once it had become an economic proposition, they had to enter factory production.

## Pace of technological change

### 1. The supersession of hand techniques

Not unexpectedly, discussions on the survival of hand technology in nineteenth-century Britain make little reference to cotton spinning. After all, it was this trade that, in Samuel's words, saw 'the most complete triumph of the machine'.[53] Its transition to a technology dependent on the application of mechanical power was already well advanced by the early nineteenth century, bringing massive increases in output and productivity and ensuring that it had become largely a factory-based activity.

This is not to say, however, that cotton spinners had abandoned hand techniques. In part, this is because the jenny, a hand-powered machine, continued to be used in the trade during the early decades of the nineteenth century, if not beyond. Moreover, not only was the appearance of the self-actor mule delayed until the 1820s, it was by no means universally accepted as a replacement for power-assisted mules or hand mules, as they became called.

With regard to the continuance of jenny spinning, Crompton's survey of 1811 noted nearly 156,000 jenny spindles were still at work. It is true that this was only half the number of water-frame spindles and a tiny fraction of the 4.6 million mule spindles, the bulk of them power-assisted, which were also recorded. That the survey was compiled by the inventor of the mule inevitably raises concerns about its accuracy. Yet, whilst the total spindle count for each of the three machines is incomplete, the mule had without doubt risen to a dominant position.[54] And that it had done so quickly was partly the result of applying steam power to the outward movement of the frame, a practice which had become common by the late 1790s, and to Crompton's failure in securing a patent.[55]

Crompton's survey was made almost half a century after the jenny was invented. Whether it records the peak number of jenny spindles is uncertain, though M. M. Edwards believes that jenny spinning reached its height as early as the 1780s,[56] presumably on the grounds that, from the outset, the mule competed effectively in spinning weft. Yet this is by no means certain, since, compared with the jenny, the mule was an expensive machine for spinning coarser threads. Accordingly, jenny numbers would have continued to rise even after the mule was adopted. As late as the second decade of the nineteenth century, the machine was still favoured by those with limited capital as a means of entering the cotton trade.[57] How long jennies remained at work is uncertain, though in 1833, one commentator observed that jenny spinning at Stockport, by far the most important centre of the trade during the early nineteenth century, was 'decayed'.[58] And two years later, Edward Baines could imply that the jenny had been going out of use for some time.[59]

As to the replacement of hand (power-assisted) mules by self-actors, a gradual change took place. It is true that appreciable numbers of self-actors were installed during the major trade upturns of the mid-1830s and mid-1840s,[60] but they had by no means displaced hand mules at mid-century. In fact, not all firms found that the early self-actors met their needs. Thus, the Ashworths, leading cotton spinners of Egerton, near Bolton, made several attempts to introduce them at their New Eagley Mill. They did not succeed until the late 1860s, however. A decade later, the firm had installed nine self-actor mules, but they continued to operate twenty, 810-spindle hand mules. At the same time, more hand than self-actor mules were at work in the Bolton district (1,231 compared with 1,191), though numbers declined thereafter, 516 surviving in 1882.[61] Long after their introduction, therefore, self-acting mules were only partly meeting the needs of cotton spinning firms and their requirement for a technology that relied partly on hand labour remained strong.

It should also be noted that, despite its name, the self-actor mule was not completely automatic. It still required piecers to join broken threads, whilst the quadrant mechanism, which controlled the speed at which putting-up took place, had to be adjusted by hand. Spinning yarn of an 80s count (a relatively fine yarn), about 90 such adjustments were needed during a twenty-hour spinning cycle. They all took place within four hours of the start, when the bottom part of the cop was formed.[62]

Whilst it is easy to exaggerate the speed at which hand technology was superseded in cotton spinning, there is no doubt that it took place at a far faster rate than in cotton weaving. According to estimates made by Edward Baines, only 2,400 cotton powerlooms had been installed in British factories by 1813, a decade after the improvements made by William Horrocks.[63] Thereafter, numbers grew more rapidly, reaching 108,109 by the mid-1830s, of which 61,176 (57 per cent) were in Lancashire. At the same date, however, the country's cotton hand weavers numbered at least 200,000, of whom around 165,000 (perhaps 80 per cent) were in Lancashire. The productivity of the power weavers would have been appreciably higher than that of the hand weavers, so that, in terms of output, the impact of the powerloom was stronger than these figures imply. Yet, because the hand weavers were the more numerous group and because they tended to produce higher-quality cloths, the total value they added may still have exceeded that of the power weavers.[64]

By 1850, though, the balance had swung decisively in favour of the powerloom. At that time, almost 250,000 cotton powerlooms were to be found in Britain, of which nearly 177,000 (70 per cent) were in Lancashire. Within a fifteen-year period, therefore, the country's stock of cotton powerlooms had increased by 140,000, substantially more than in the previous half century. Little of this new investment was undertaken in the mainly depressed years of the late 1830s and early 1840s. However, there is ample evidence from factory inspectors' returns to show that it occurred on a very substantial scale as the trade cycle reached a major peak during the mid-1840s.[65] And, as an additional incentive to invest, manufacturers could take full advantage of the key improvements that, just a few years earlier, had been made to the powerloom by Kenworthy and Bullough.

This rapid expansion in cotton powerloom capacity had a marked impact on the size of the hand weaving labour force. During the 1840s, as many as 100,000 hand weaving jobs were lost in Lancashire, leaving perhaps 55,000 hand weavers still at work. Of these, about two-thirds produced cotton cloth or cotton-mixture cloth. The remainder chiefly worked with silk.[66]

Whilst the decline in the use of hand looms during the 1840s was dramatic, its impact must not be exaggerated. In the first place, redundant hand weavers often found other occupations, even if it proved difficult for the older ones amongst them to obtain factory jobs. Secondly, in rural districts especially, the dependency on hand weaving could still remain strong, with hand weavers constituting the largest occupational group. Thirdly, hand weaving proved a resilient trade in Lancashire beyond mid-century, with a labour force of around 30,000 in the early 1860s, half weaving cottons, and of some 10,000 a decade later. Even at the time of the 1881 census, they were still being recorded, though their numbers cannot have been large.[67] Plainly, the demise of hand technology in Lancashire's weaving trades was a protracted affair and handlooms continued to make a significant contribution to output well into the mid-Victorian era.

Turning lastly to the finishing trades, there is again evidence that hand technology long remained in use. This is despite a move towards powered machinery that was probably well advanced by the early nineteenth century. The main exception was in printing. As late as 1842, 8,324 block printing tables were counted in Lancashire, Cheshire and Derbyshire, to operate most of which required a printer and his child assistant (or tierer).[68] Four years later, John Graham noted that English print works normally contained printing tables as well as printing machines. For example, at Fort Brothers' Oakenshaw Works, near Blackburn, no fewer than 229 tables and 243 block printers were employed, along with 8 printing machines. Not all the industry's print tables were in use, though, and permanent excess capacity may have been developing. Thus, the Oakenshaw block printers were 'very short of work', whilst London Vale Printworks, Prestwich was 'busy with Machines, but very slack with Blocks'.[69]

Given the massive productivity difference between block printers and machine printers, the latter may soon have produced the bulk of the industry's output. Indeed, by the mid-1830s, Baines thought that the proportion was as high as 75 per cent.[70] Probably, though, block printers were making higher-grade wares, so their overall contribution to the value of output remained substantial. How long block printing survived on any appreciable scale has yet to be determined. Some firms certainly continued to use block printing throughout the mid-Victorian years and probably beyond. This is evident from census returns, those for Oswaldtwistle and Church recording 54 block printers in 1871.[71] However, a rather greater number would have been expected had the local printworks at Foxhill Bank maintained anything like the 239 it employed at mid-century; the trade was plainly much diminished.

### 2. Reasons for the continuing use of hand techniques

In discussing why entrepreneurs in the cotton trade continued with hand technology once powered machines became available, several issues arise. Firstly, powered machinery did not always prove to be efficient, despite the claims made for it. Secondly, even when its efficiency could be demonstrated, entrepreneurs might still be unwilling, or even unable, to incur the costs of installing and running it. Thirdly, relying solely on powered machinery could make it difficult for entrepreneurs to respond as effectively as they might wish to their customers' requirements.

With regard to the first of these matters, there is evidence from all three branches of the cotton industry that powered machinery was only very gradually adapted to certain processes. This was especially so in producing finer goods. The problem was that the action of powered machinery could prove too harsh for fine yarns, leading to frequent breakages and hence production stoppages. It was largely for this reason that the hand mule was long preferred in spinning muslin yarn and the handloom in muslin weaving. In muslin spinning, two difficulties arose. One concerned the varying rate at which the carriage of the self-actor mule terminated its inward run. Sometimes it barely touched the back stops; at other times, it struck them with enough force to vibrate the carriage and rollers, causing numerous thread breakages. With the hand mule, however, the spinner could bring home the carriage 'so gently as to avoid the final concussion', thereby minimising breakages. The other difficulty was that the faller wire on the mule, which wound the spun thread into cops, could be operated more sensitively on the hand mule than on the self-actor, again reducing breakages.[72] Even the skill of the mule spinner, though, could not make up for a dry atmosphere, which particularly impaired the spinning of finer threads, sometimes to the point where piecers were unable to cope.[73] Nor could it compensate for uneven rovings, which led to frequent yarn breakages.[74]

To illustrate the type of problem that arose in using powerlooms to weave muslin, the patent granted in 1855 to Valentine, Foster and Haworth may be taken. The patentees noted that fine or weak yarn was liable to break when, with the shed open, a weft thread was driven up by the reed against the finished cloth. The problem was that the tension of the warps varied as the healds were raised and lowered. To overcome this, the patentees incorporated a device which took up the slack when the shed closed and let it out again when the shed opened.[75]

Such an example serves as a reminder that useful alterations could still be made to the powerloom despite the important advances made by Kenworthy and Bullough during the early 1840s. In fact, this patent was one amongst hundreds relating to the powerloom that were granted during the mid-Victorian years. Many, perhaps most, were not especially significant, since they specified alternative arrangements to those already in use. Yet such a high level of activity amongst patentees suggests that the scope for further advance was by no means minimal. Nor was opportunity lacking to exploit earlier innovation, not least the dobby. This device enabled fancy goods to be woven on the powerloom and though invented in the 1820s, it does not seem to have been widely used before the late 1850s.[76]

As to the finishing trades, it is less evident that powered machinery was found lacking, except with regard to cylinder printing. Writing in the mid-1830s, Edward Baines remarked that block prints still had to be used in finishing patterns on fine goods after most of the design had been printed by cylinders. This was because parts of the pattern could not be made 'so exactly to fall into and fit with the other parts, by the cylinder as by the block'.[77] Further, the cylinder could not apply as many colours as the block, nor achieve the same 'purity, richness and transparent quality' in terms of colour.[78] And block-printing long continued to have a use in making trial design patterns.[79]

Turning to the question of the costs arising in moving from hand to mechanised techniques, discussion has centred on weaving, in which trade a substantial body of domestic hand workers long remained available. This was partly a result of the difficulty they could have in finding other jobs. But it also reflects a desire amongst many of them to preserve a traditional way of life, which, though it could not have provided a generous income, nonetheless gave a high degree of freedom from work supervision and allowed the continuance of family working groups.[80]

By switching to powerloom weaving rather than continuing to draw on this workforce, manufacturers faced appreciable increases in both wage and fixed capital costs. With regard to the former, power weavers normally earned a good deal more than hand weavers, though fewer of them might be required. Moreover, as H. J. Habakkuk has suggested, falling piece rates for hand weaving during the early decades of the nineteenth century would have encouraged hand weavers to increase their productivity. Accordingly, the price of cloth and the profits arising from its production, remained relatively low, reducing the incentive and ability of handloom manufacturers to invest in powerlooms.[81] Wage figures for the Manchester area during the early 1830s suggest that earnings differences between hand and power weavers were more marked for men than for women, but that they commonly amounted to at least fifty per cent.[82] As to higher fixed capital costs, the impact was appreciable, even though it might be lessened by renting rather than purchasing. Moreover, the working equipment that weavers required, including looms, shuttles and healds, had to be provided, whereas, under the domestic system, this was generally left to the weavers themselves.[83]

The additional profit that might be anticipated by using powerlooms, along with savings that would arise through centralised production and fewer workers, might often have provided more than adequate compensation for higher fixed capital and wage rate costs that transferring to powerloom weaving entailed. Yet this was by no means assured and the would-be powerloom manufacturer had to bear in mind that, during trade recessions, the cost of fixed capital would have to be maintained, even though it might be appreciably under-employed. Accordingly, a move into powerloom weaving could add considerably to the level of business risk he incurred.

In the spinning branch of the industry, additional fixed capital costs were incurred by switching from hand-assisted to self-actor mules. In making the change, however, entrepreneurs might hope to save on labour costs by replacing skilled, male labour with unskilled women and boys. In the event, though, relatively well-paid males remained predominant. Amongst the explanations offered have been the ability of male mule spinners to exclude women from entering the trade and the desire amongst employers to retain the supervisory role that male spinners exercised over piecers. But it has also been suggested that women were largely ousted from the trade as longer hand mules became widely used in the 1830s and 1840s. These were supposedly too heavy for women to operate. The resultant loss of female labour enabled male exclusionary policies to be effectively applied, including the refusal to train girls as self-actor spinners.[84] The difficulty with this theory, however, is that longer mules were being adopted because power was being applied to the putting-up action of the carriage. Accordingly, it is not clear that women lacked the strength to operate longer mules, even if the longest ones did prove too heavy.

The cost of installing longer hand mules could be minimised by joining together machines that were already in use, a process known as 'double decking'. This, in addition to the productivity improvements that longer mules brought, strengthened the incentive to remain with hand-assisted technology. The rates paid to spinners may not have fallen, but smaller labour requirements could bring useful reductions in firms' overall wage costs or enable them to expand output appreciably without adding to them.

It remains to consider how far cotton firms were likely to have persisted with hand technology in order to meet abnormal or specialist demands for their products. The essential point here is that where market opportunities were limited, to install powered equipment, or to invest in it further, would be risky and not necessarily cost effective. This was the more so whilst the technical shortcomings of powered machinery remained unresolved.

Abnormal demand for cotton products occurred periodically as the trade cycle reached major peaks of activity. During the mid-1830s upturn, for example, a serious shortage of cotton weaving capacity arose. This was partly met by investment in powerlooms, but also by extending employment opportunities for hand weavers and by offering them much higher piece rates. Thus, in July, 1836, the *Preston Chronicle* reported that whereas hand weavers were being paid 4s. per piece in the previous month, they were now receiving 5s.[85] Perhaps this temporary increase in demand could have been more fully met by additional investment in powerlooms, but, for many manufacturers, a greater use of handlooms represented a cheaper and more profitable alternative.

Cotton producers also had to consider the problem of meeting specialist demand for their wares, a reflection of their link with the fashion trade. This brought frequent changes in consumer preferences, mainly for higher grade cloths of fine quality and fancy design. As a result, short production runs became inevitable. To meet them by the use of machinery might well have been possible and certainly became more so as the technical capability of machines improved. Yet, as Turnbull remarks with regard to printing complex coloured designs on cloth, the level of demand was insufficient 'at the price necessary to run a machine at a profit'.[86] And William Hickson, writing in the 1840s, argued that handlooms would always be needed because the demand for some fabrics was so limited and uncertain that it would never pay to 'erect complicated and costly machinery'.[87]

There was good reason, therefore, for Lancashire's cotton entrepreneurs to remain at least partially committed to hand technology once powered machinery became available. For many of them, the costs of transfer and the risks arising might well be considered unacceptably high. And this was so despite the higher returns they might realise from using improved machines. Evidently, such men were content to earn acceptable returns on their investment rather than seek to maximise them.

## Conclusion

Without doubt, the technological change that took place in the Lancashire cotton industry during the late eighteenth and early nineteenth centuries was of fundamental importance. For the first time, powered machinery was introduced on a substantial scale, increasingly replacing the traditional handicraft techniques that had long prevailed. Not only did it enable output and productivity in the industry to increase dramatically, but it also gave a powerful stimulus to the development of factory production.

Yet its significance should not be exaggerated. In the first place, notable advances in textile technology took place before the late eighteenth century. These mainly related to hand techniques, but included the introduction of roller spinning, which was at first operated with animal and water power and was to become a vital component in the water-frame and mule, as well as in the fly frame. In other words, the success of spinning machinery developed during the late eighteenth century owed much to a technique that an earlier generation pioneered.

It must also be stressed that powered machinery was adopted at a varying pace within the industry. In general, quicker progress was made in spinning and finishing than in weaving, the technical problems in developing an efficient powerloom proving especially intractable. But even in spinning, the hand-driven jenny continued to produce cotton until the 1830s at least, whilst hand-assisted mules were still widely used at mid-century. This did not prevent a fairly rapid switch from domestic to factory spinning, however, since both the hand-assisted mule and the water-frame required mechanical power.

The adoption of powered machinery in the Lancashire cotton industry was thus a protracted affair and, as in other industries, mechanised and handicraft techniques long co-existed. Only gradually, often on a piece-meal basis, were the limitations of this machinery overcome, especially with regard to the production of fine and fancy wares. Yet, even when the technical proficiency of new machinery could be demonstrated, its adoption was not necessarily widespread, at least in the short term. For many entrepreneurs, the continued use of hand technology, either wholly or in part, might still appear advantageous, especially if they sought to maintain profitability through minimising costs rather than through maximising revenue.

# CHAPTER 3

# The Commercial Sector

STANLEY CHAPMAN

The eighteenth-century Lancashire cotton industry still found its main source of supply and its principal market in London; like so many other English manufacturing regions, it grew to strength as a satellite of London. London had much the biggest port and the greatest concentration of population and wealth in England, and it led the country in fashion and conspicuous consumption. Consequently provincial merchant enterprise was the last, slowest and least distinctive of the numerous specialisms of the cotton industry to emerge, and the handful of Manchester entrepreneurs who won fortunes in trade and finance, as distinct from production, before the middle of the eighteenth century, did so by migration to London.

## A gallery of merchant pioneers

When the earliest Manchester trade directories were published – Raffald's in 1772–3 and Bailey's in 1784 – the small group of 30 or so traders describing themselves as merchants were nearly all suppliers of the raw materials, cotton and linen yarns, to the entrepreneurs who organised production in the circle of villages and small towns round Manchester. The cotton was imported from India by the East India Company and from Turkey by Levant merchants while linen yarns largely came from Ireland, Hamburg and the Baltic ports. A more numerous category of traders – already 57 at the time of the first directory – described themselves as 'warehousemen'. They had assumed the function of collecting the production of the country manufacturers (or at any rate the smaller ones) for sale to textile merchants in London who were sufficiently specialised to be designated Manchester warehousemen in the London trade directories; 24 of them are listed in 1776.[1] The country manufacturers had their town bases in one of the numerous small inns that crowded the narrow streets round Manchester's old church. The most popular was the New Boar's Head in Hyde's Cross where, by the early 1790s, over fifty country producers reserved lodgings and kept small stocks; other popular venues were the George and Dragon in Withy Grove (16) and the Lower Ship just across the river in Salford (15), while the Griffin in Long Millgate and the Higher Swan in Market Street Lane had 13 industrial tenants each.[2]

The limitation of the directories is that they fail to give any indication that these country manufacturers were gradually assuming mercantile functions, as well as being the leaders in the increasing variety and quantity of textile fabrics made in Lancashire. They sold direct to an ever-growing list of provincial markets, fairs and retailers, established their own connections with London warehousemen and, before the American War of Independence, were selling direct to merchants in Philaelphia and New York. The domestic market was already served by 'Manchester men' in the seventeenth century, travelling countless miles with droves of packhorses and offering substantial credit to retailers in country towns.

FIGURE 28. Bulls Head Yard, Market Street Lane, Manchester, one of the numerous inn yards where country manufacturers stayed while visiting the market to sell their fustians and other cloths. From the end of the eighteenth century inn yards were superseded by warehouses (J. Loudon, *Manchester Memoirs* (1916), p. 45).

By the middle of the eighteenth century these pioneers were largely superseded by 'riders out' (or commercial travellers) dispatched by Manchester manufacturers on regular rounds carrying patterns of their wares, and followed at short intervals by the carriers' carts. The most successful of this rising class of itinerant tradesmen was probably Joseph Hague, who began life as a hawker, first with a basket, then with an ass. He settled in London in 1716 and acquired an 'immense fortune' as a dealer in Lancashire goods and an importer of yarn. There is evidence that other fortunes were made, though actual details are sparse.[3]

The variety of mercantile enterprise in the later eighteenth century is best conveyed by the stories of some of the best-known figures in the Manchester trade. Thomas Touchet moved to Manchester shortly after his marriage to begin business as a manufacturer and trader of linen and cotton goods. By 1714 he was exporting ticks and fustians to the West Indies. His eldest son Samuel went to London as the representative of the family firm where he developed rapidly into a merchant with extensive overseas interests, importing raw cotton from the Levant and West Indies and linen from the Continent. Titus Hibbert spent his career as a yarn merchant in Manchester, importing linen yarn from Ireland (via the Chester fair, Dublin and Drogheda), from Hamburg, Bremen, Danzig and other parts of Germany. Much of the expertise of the yarn merchant was in recognising

FIGURE 29. Cromford Court, Manchester, showing some of the earliest warehouses built in the town, in the 1780s. Sir Richard Arkwright's earliest factories were at Cromford (J. Loudon, *Manchester Memoirs* (1916), p. 130).

the varying qualities of different sources for traditional and new Lancashire fabrics.[4]

In the course of the eighteenth century Liverpool moved up the league table of English ports from fifth to third place (after London and Newcastle) but for much of the century was a small isolated harbour with one dock. As late as 1788 shipping in the Mersey was less than a quarter that in the Thames. Consequently Liverpool's eighteenth-century leadership consisted of a handful of merchants who lifted themselves from obscurity over two or three generations. The best-documented family is the Rathbones, the most able and powerful representative of which was William Rathbone IV. As a young man he re-established the American trade after the War of Independence and in 1784 sold the first American cotton grown in the US ever imported into Britain, thus laying the foundations of the nineteenth-century prosperity of the port. By the end of the eighteenth century Rathbone had forged strong links with fellow Quaker merchants in America and other Quaker families prominent in manufacturing round Britain, notably with the Darbys and Reynolds of Coalbrookdale (ironmasters), Lloyds of Birmingham (ironmasters), Wakefields of Kendal (textile manufacturers) and Foster of Bromley Hall (East London), the famous textile printer. Wedgwood, the celebrated potter, was a close friend.[5]

The import of linen yarns and the export of fustians were trading specialisms that evolved over several generations, but the explosion in the demand for cotton from the 1780s found Liverpool's merchants unable to cope. A new order of traders called cotton brokers appeared, nearly all of them migrants from Manchester and the surrounding manufacturing districts, and from London. The doyen of the first generation of this order was Nicholas Waterhouse who served an apprenticeship to a fustian manufacturer in Bolton and started business in Liverpool in 1782. Waterhouse sold by sample and charged both the buyer and the seller 10s. (£0.50) per £100, or one per cent in all, a modest charge that became general as imports multiplied rapidly and Liverpool overtook London as the premier port of entry. No doubt Waterhouse, a Quaker, was one of the brokers who created the business ethics of the system, 'the strict probity and honour' that sustained the smooth running of the cotton market. A protracted Exchequer Court case of 1794 shows that this could not be taken for granted in the early years of the system.[6]

Thomas Smith was a Manchester fustian and smallwares manufacturer who, according to his own account, was 'bred a weaver'. By 1785, when he gave evidence for the Lancashire trade to a House of Lords inquiry, he had customers in London, Ireland and America. His route to success is amply indicated in an autobiographical aside in his evidence,

FIGURE 30. The Customs House and the Old Dock, Liverpool. Source: *Bygone Liverpool* (Henry Young & Sons, 1913), plate 4.

'I have always found from experience that it is absolutely necessary for the proprietor of every manufactory to be a judge of every minutiae of the trade he is engaged in and if that trade must flourish he must not only be a competent judge of every minutiae but that judgement must likewise be enforced with the strictest attention and assiduity'. Merchants had to pay strict attention not only to the quality and ever-changing market for their products but, even more importantly, to the creditworthiness of their customers. The American and Irish markets customarily demanded twelve months' credit, but it frequently happened that it was fifteen, eighteen or even twenty-four months before they received payment, Smith complained. The other rule for success in most lines was to focus on the popular end of the market. As Smith put it, 'the lower and middling kind of articles are undoubtedly the most valuable to every person concerned in the fustian manufacture . . . having always a ready sale for them'. Smith's evidence harmonised with that of Thomas Walker, another Manchester fustian manufacturer, whose firm was described as the first in the trade in 1785.[7] However it is clear that the problems of recovering debt did little to restrain many Manchester merchants. One American importer snorted in 1789 that 'credit is as *cheap* this year as it was in 1784 – The Manchester folks have made all the retail shopkeepers and merchant apprentices importers!' From the middle of the century to 1790, the constant cry in Philadelphia, with few intermissions, was that the city was glutted with textile imports and that cloth was cheaper in the city than in Manchester.[8]

Smith and Walker had the advantage of being at the centre of the system in Manchester. Pennine manufacturers often found business a greater struggle, particularly if they tried to become export merchants. James Longsden was a farmer and fustian manufacturer at Little Long-stone, near Bakewell, 35 miles south-east of Manchester. In the early 1780s he was in partnership with Andrew Morewood who had moved to Salford and his brother-in-law John Morewood who had gone out to St Petersburg in a venture designed to generate 'ready money or barter for saleable Russian produce.' The partners also had a warehouse at Cromford, close to Arkwright's cotton mills. Correspondence between Russia and Little Longstone graphically sets out the problems of the small merchant enterprise at the period. John wrote from St Petersburg in 1785 that 'if it was not for our circumscribed capital he should be filled with very gay hopes, but with it he sees it as utterly impossible to make any figure in trade, for when business promises well we have it not in our power to take advantage of it by materially increasing our manufactory, and when it wears an unfavourable aspect we are not in a situation to keep up [i.e. hold back] our goods but are under the necessity of selling them to keep the little machine [i.e. the cotton enterprise] in constant motion.' It was under-capitalised enterprises of this kind that were in turn squeezed out of the trade in the difficult trading conditions of the French Wars and post-war slump.[9]

The prospects of those who entered the industry with some capital were more rosy. Thomas Potter and his brother Richard inherited £12,000 when their father, a Tadcaster draper, died in 1802. They reckoned this was 'a capital possessed by few beginners' and made all the more valuable by a London bank account carefully prepared for them by father in preparation for the launch of the Manchester warehouse business. At this period of the war manufacturers were glutted with goods so that warehousemen with ready cash could buy at less than cost price and were able to undersell the manufacturers among their country customers and drive them out of merchanting. It was in this setting that the brothers could write 'nothing but sottish indolence, indiscretion, or want of judgement can render abortive the starting in trade on such a capital as we have.' In fact the brothers were able, in the next thirty years, to win a large fortune, which they used to advance their radical political ideology. Thomas was knighted as the first mayor of Manchester, while Richard became MP for Wigan in 1832.[10]

Meanwhile, in the City of London, James Morrison was discovering the cheap warehousing system, leading the market in low-quality high-turnover textiles and haberdashery by buying up bankrupt stock and squeezing numerous small producers. He attracted high-spending country drapers to his Fore Street warehouse by sending out hundreds of trade circulars advertising the latest scoop purchases. A friend of later years wrote that 'Morrison told me that he owed all his prosperity to the discovery that the great art of mercantile traffic was to find [low-cost] sellers rather than buyers; that if you bought cheap and satisfied yourself with a fair profit, buyers – the best sort of buyers, those that have money to buy – would come of themselves.' Consequently he employed travellers in the northern manufacturing districts to buy, but saved himself the considerable expense of men paid to sell. Morrison, Dillon & Co. maintained their leadership of the City until the 1860s and were one of the major forces that kept London ahead of Manchester in the home trade through the nineteenth century.[11]

## Cotton manufacturers as merchants, 1780–1815

The chequered experience of these pioneers did not discourage hundreds of other men who crowded into the cotton trade in the late eighteenth and early nineteenth centuries. It was a time for winning fortunes, of energetic extension of functions on every side, with fustian manufacturers simultaneously opening cotton mills *and* launching themselves into mercantile enterprises. A few of the bolder spirits – Peel in calico printing, Horrocks in woven cottons, and Philips in smallwares – opened warehouses in the City of London, while Peels took the initiative in creating a whole new warehouse district in Manchester. The Manchester section of the *Universal British Directory* (1794) listed sixty firms that combined manufacturing and mercantile functions. An American visitor to the town in 1799 (Joshua Gilpin) wrote in his journal that 'in general most of the Manufacturers of Manchester have cotton mills; many of these are in the town and many on streams and places at a distance'.[12]

A few of the biggest merchant-manufacturers evidently sold in several overseas markets; Lingards of Manchester, for instance, sold their fustians and cottons direct to agents in Russia, Italy, the United States and Prussia, while Peels had an extensive sale in North America and continental Europe, employing both resident agents and travellers working on commission. Some firms in a more modest way of business evidently specialised, or rather pursued a limited connection abroad. Thus Samuel Greg found the main outlet for his fustians in his agent in Philadelphia and Robinsons & Heywood appear in the 1794 directory as 'Merchants and Manufacturers of African Goods'. Other merchant-manufacturers from Manchester and Leeds attempted to find their own customers at the continental fairs. William Radcliffe of Mellor (Stockport), who began his working life as a handloom weaver and was

FIGURE 31. Calico printer's pattern (or sample) book used by Peels at the end of the eighteenth century. The firm's outriders (travellers) used them to sell cotton prints to retail drapers around the country. (Photograph courtesy of Bury Public Library)

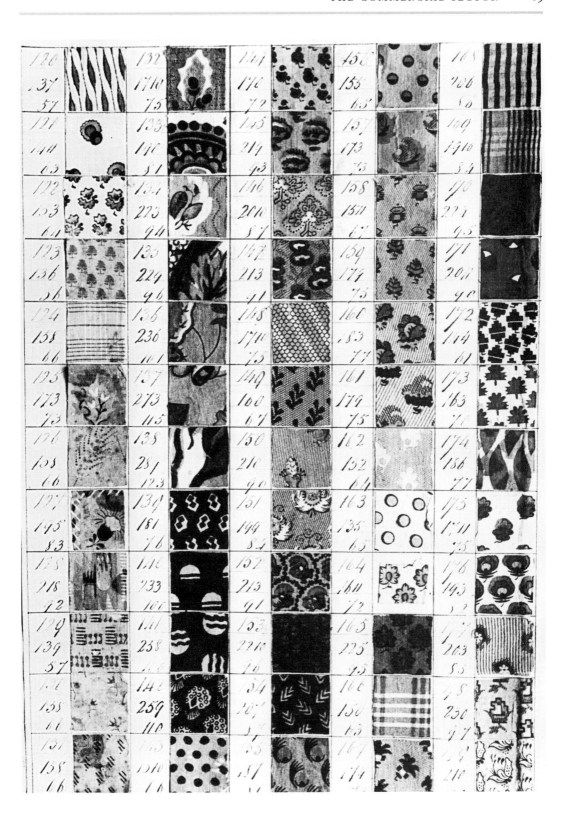

employing a thousand country weavers before the end of the century, sold first to visitors from Berlin and Copenhagen, then at the Frankfurt and Leipzig Fairs. Meanwhile his neighbour Samuel Oldknow, the pioneer of the muslin manufacture, took leave of his dependence on his London wholesaler to sell at the great European fairs.

In the 1780s and 1790s the northern industrial regions also set the pace in the provinces by sending partners to reside in foreign commercial cities. Occasionally agents abroad were invited to become a member of the family partnership, but it appears to have been more usual to follow the London practice of sending a junior partner to prove himself abroad, as when Longsdons & Morewood sent John Morewood to St Petersburg in 1784, or Wardle & Tillards, Manchester cotton manufacturers and Liverpool merchants, sent William Tillard to take charge of its trade in Jamaica. The premier Liverpool merchant houses sent junior partners to North America for two or three years at a time, while leading New York, Philadelphia and Baltimore merchants sent their sons to Britain for training. Young migrants in both directions sometimes settled and in a few notable cases became the leading houses in their adopted towns.

The counterpart of this well-known migration of enterprise to and from the New World was the settlement of increasing numbers of European – mostly German – merchants in industrial towns. Before the end of the eighteenth century at least fifteen foreign merchants and manufacturers had settled in Manchester. However, their numbers were not sufficiently large to make a major impact on the rapidly-rising

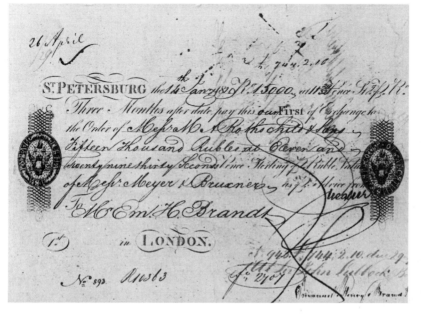

FIGURE 32. An early bill of exchange. Most domestic and export business in the eighteenth and nineteenth centuries was done with these dated IOUs. This example emanated from Rothschilds, the famous London banking house that began in Manchester in 1798, exporting cotton prints and fabrics in the family business in Frankfurt. (Author)

provincial trade before 1815, so that a full analysis of their significance will be consider later in this chapter.

The emergence of this new breed of merchant-manufacturers in the provincial industrial regions was facilitated by the increase in size, wealth and expertise of the merchants of Liverpool. Already in the 1790s there was specialisation by export destination and by commodities. The American Joshua Gilpin listed ten 'American' merchant houses, eleven West Indian merchants, a dozen corn merchants and a number of 'American' shippers. Liverpool shippers provided a service for manufacturers with customers abroad, while the merchants assumed the role of their London antecedents by purchasing on their own account from inland manufacturers or from various trade warehouses that stocked goods for export. Thus Sparling & Bolden, who exported woollen goods, printed cottons, carpets, hosiery, linens and a variety of other manufactured goods to Virginia, drew their supplies from a circle of firms in Manchester, Halifax, Colne, Rochdale, Leeds, Wakefield,

FIGURE 33. Liverpool merchants meeting on the Exchange flags in 1847. Source: *Bygone Liverpool* (Henry Young & Sons, 1913), plate 34.

Kendal, Keswick and Mansfield. They followed the trade practise of paying in bills on London at two or three months' date. London merchant houses, acting generally as bankers, accepted bills for consignments to America and other markets from all parts of the world and paid the drafts of foreign merchants to the order of British manufacturers. Bills on London houses also financed the purchase of cotton and other Liverpool imports, so the port was financially dependent on its southern rival to a large extent.

While the extension of the role of the country manufacturers to overseas marketing, and of merchants into manufacturing, was evidently familiar in all major manufacturing regions of Britain in the last two decades of the eighteenth century, no contemporary seems to have provided a precise explanation of it, but the reasons are sufficiently clear. For more than a century, dynasties of provincial manufacturers had been growing in experience, capital and connections, gradually freeing themselves from dependence on London merchants and factors by opening their own offices in the capital and selling direct to domestic customers and overseas importers. The great spurt in British manufacturing that took place after about 1770 found the existing marketing structure inadequate to meet the aspirations of the most ambitious northern industrialists. Moreover, much greater fixed capital formation (factories, warehouses, etc.) compelled them to try to maintain their investment more fully employed all the year round, rather than following the seasonal cycles, as the organisers of domestic industry had done. The vanguard of entrepreneurs in this energetic period, following the example of Arkwright, Oldknow, Peel, Greg and other celebrated leaders of industry, built up complex integrated concerns, not only in manufacturing and marketing but also, characteristically, in importing supplies, factory building, transport, banking, machine building and estate development. This forward and backward integration, that is to say, was characteristic of the dramatic period of growth on the 'new frontier' regions of Britain. We shall see that as the ancillary transport, financial and marketing services reasserted the economies of specialisation, so the empires built by the Industrial Revolution pioneers were dismantled.[13]

### The rise of commission agents
### and merchant banks *c.* 1800–1836

A combination of circumstances in the closing years of the French Wars led to the bankruptcy, enervation or retirement of many of the old merchants of London, Liverpool and Bristol, and the simultaneous withdrawal of a large number of northern manufacturers who had ventured into overseas marketing. In their place emerged a new generation

FIGURE 34. The first Sir Robert Peel (1750–1830), the most successful of the first generation of Lancashire cotton manufacturers that extended into merchanting. His firm was exporting prints to America before the War of Independence. (Photograph kindly loaned by the Earl Peel.)

of specialists, commission agents resident in foreign commercial centres (but usually having a partner or agent in Britain) and acceptance houses, that is wealthy merchants who had graduated to pure finance and provided the credits for manufacturers to send their goods to agents abroad. During the course of the nineteenth century, the latter came to be known as merchant banks and were increasingly concentrated in the City of London. The commission agents were characteristically young men of modest capital who went to seek their fortunes abroad. At the end of the French Wars most of those selling British goods appear to have been British born, but during the next twenty years, and particularly after 1825, the European and North American markets were increasingly served by the junior partners of the United States,

German, Greek and other foreign merchant houses who came to British industrial towns to buy their own goods. British commission agents moved out into the less developed and more geographically remote markets, particularly Latin America and the Orient, no doubt hoping for less competition and more profit.

The losses of the Napoleonic War are not precisely documented, but it is clear that the continental blockade caused merchants to turn to Latin America and there were severe losses in Buenos Aires in 1806 and Rio in 1808–9. The American War of 1812–14 caused extensive losses in Glasgow and Liverpool, and the post-war flooding of the European market led to further losses in 1815–16 and 1819. After 1814, United States' tariff policy was designed to exclude British goods – and more particularly coarser fabrics – from the American market. A French authority maintains that 90 per cent of London's continental houses were eliminated after the war, while in Manchester four out of five manufacturers (many no doubt with marketing interests) disappeared during the twenty years or so of war. A few of the names that left the pages of the directories in these years included those who, like the Peels and Arkwrights, withdrew to landed estates.

The early retirement of merchants and merchant-manufacturers was also accelerated by changes in trading habits. We have already noticed evidence to suggest that the tempo of trade was quickening in the second half of the eighteenth century. During the Napoleonic War, sudden scarcities and gluts encouraged stock-piling and speculation, practices that regularly led the less cautious to bankruptcy and the more prudent to withdraw in despair. In the post-war years, increased competition among exporters slimmed profit margins, but growing trade rapidly increased the turnover of the more capable entrepreneurs, further increasing the lead of the pacemakers over the 'old guard' and the struggling newcomers. This situation was responsible for the precipitate post-war decline of such old centres of trade as Norwich and Exeter, for a time centres of the new cotton industry. Many established merchants preferred to retire to their country estates than to change their way of life.

Increasing post-war competition was the consequence not only of a new generation of fortune hunters, but also of the introduction of new types of trading organisations. London had harboured a colony of foreign merchants from the middle ages, but the settlement of foreign commission agents in northern industrial centres was a consequence of the French wars. N. M. Rothschild and his countrymen brought a tradition of cash buying when the market was low, small profit margins, volume trade, and rapid turnover of stock that set a cracking pace in Manchester and, by degrees, brought most of the continental trade into their warehouses. Backed by Frankfurt and Hamburg capital, their resources were often superior to those of local merchants served by Manchester's under-developed banking system. In much the same way, young Alexander Henry from Philadelphia, enjoying connections with 'first class' American houses, was able to take a lion's share of the North American exports of cotton goods. Rothschild came in 1799 and A. & S. Henry in 1804, and the developments they initiated were well under way when peace was finally attained.

British and foreign commission agents were also encouraged by the emergence of the wealthy acceptance houses specialising in the finance of particular branches of trade. The leading firms were Barings, Brown, Shipley & Co. and (until 1836) the 'three Ws' (Wiggins, Wilsons, and Wildes), all specialising in trans-Atlantic finance, and various firms of European origin, notably Rothschilds, Huths, and Lizardis. The distinguishing feature of the accepting houses was a large capital linked with intimate knowledge of some foreign markets, acquired by one or more of the partners having spent part of his (or their) careers abroad. A number of the best-known accepting houses were founded on fortunes made in the textile trade, including Browns in the Philadelphia linen trade, Rothschild and Wiggin in Manchester, Wilson in Liverpool and Morrison in London wholesaling. Most based themselves in London but had offices or partners in Liverpool; Browns was the only firm that retained its headquarters in the northern centre of trade. The acceptance houses were prepared to advance up to two-thirds of the invoice to recognised clients for limited periods, three to four months for sales in north America and up to twelve months for Oriental markets.

In the boom trading conditions of the middle 1830s, accepting houses competed with each other for business. 'I learn that one of the partners in Overend's house is now in Birmingham offering round at the houses of foreign merchants [with] money at 3½ per cent on first rate acceptances', the Bank of England Agent there reported to his directors. At the same time, Rothschilds of London was trying to secure a bigger share of the French trade with British India by charging one per cent less than other houses, while Lizardis was investing heavily in its newly-opened New Orleans office. The collapse of the 'three Ws' in 1836 checked rather than reversed the rise of the surviving acceptance houses. And one of the casualties, George Wildes & Co., took on a new lease of life as Wildes Pickersgill & Co. of Liverpool with the financial support of Fielden Brothers, the Todmorden family of cotton spinners and weavers. This is a complex story to which we shall return.[14]

It was in this period that Manchester emerged as 'cottonopolis', the world centre for the sale cotton piece goods. At the end of the French wars about a quarter of all British cotton spinning was done in Manchester, but the investment in warehouses (as measured by rateable values) was already *six times* that in mills in the town. Between 1807 and 1825 the number of warehouse units increased more than 50 per cent to over 1,800.[15] However, it should be added that most of these 'units' were still very small, typically a room or two in a converted house and employing, in addition to the merchant, only a book-keeper, a salesman, a packer and perhaps one or two travellers. Very little stock was kept; the orders were taken from sample books and the goods obtained afterwards from the respective manufacturers of them. The best-known of the new generation of merchant entrepreneurs was Richard Cobden, who was trained as a clerk in his uncle's London warehouse and recognised the potential of the northern cotton trade as a commercial traveller in Lancashire. He and two young partners started business in Manchester in 1828 with only £1,000 capital between them which they employed building a connection in printed cottons from the Sabden (Accrington) works. In eight years of booming trade the partnership accumulated a capital of £80,000, though in the trough of the early 1840s Cobden was only rescued from financial embarrassment by his political friends.[16]

FIGURE 35. John Fielden of Todmorden (1784–1849), who with his three brothers won the largest fortune in the Lancashire cotton industry and trade before the crisis of the American Civil War. From 1824 Fielden Bros shifted their capital from manufacturing goods towards the export trade to North and South America. (Photograph courtesy of Manchester Public Libraries)

## Problems of manufacturers that exported, 1815–1850

The mechanisation of cotton spinning and the marketing energy of Lancashire entrepreneurs were so successful that by the end of the Napoleonic War cotton goods represented 42 per cent of all British exports. The success was won despite the most difficult exporting conditions, with war on the continent and for a period (1812–14) with America, the Napoleonic blockade, financial crises and high taxation. After a long period of almost uninterrupted warfare (1793–1815), the trade looked forward to an era of peaceful commerce, but the post-war years brought their own problems. Overseas markets quickly became glutted, prices tumbled, competition increased sharply and profit margins tightened until many claimed that there was no profit left in the business. The successful business was now the one that could achieve high turnover to compensate for low margins, and overseas markets were often targeted as part of this strategy.[17]

The problems of overseas markets were, as always, ignorance or uncertainty about fluctuating demand there and slow financial returns.

FIGURE 36. Jones & Co.'s Bank in King Street, Manchester, which was founded c. 1772, the second in the rapidly growing town. The building still stands, a handsome monument to the commercial prosperity of Manchester in the later eighteenth century. (Photograph courtesy of Manchester Public Libraries)

It was possible to smooth the path of export sales by good agents or partners in commercial cities overseas, ideally a member of one's own family or religious group (church, chapel, or synagogue), or former apprentice, so that he could be relied on to carry out the firm's policy without continuous instruction by the agonisingly slow and irregular mail service. A lot of firms achieved this type of relationship so that the outstanding problem was one of financial support, more particularly during the recurrent periods of trade crisis. Banks were late and slow in developing in Lancashire and the private family banks of the late eighteenth and early nineteenth centuries had very small capitals. New legislation allowed the establishment of joint stock banks, which began to multiply in the 1830s, but they were characteristically inexperienced and too often committed themselves to one major client who was a major shareholder and director. All in all, it has been estimated that inadequate finance imposed more restraints on the growth of Lancashire firms than any other single cause and the problem of financing smaller firms continued well into the nineteenth and twentieth century. The export of cotton goods nearly doubled, by value, between 1815 and 1855, but this growth covered a multitude of losses and several spectacular bankruptcies. The nature of the problems faced by particular firms is best appreciated by a couple of case studies.

Robert Gardner was probably the most successful of Manchester's self-made men of the postwar generation. Entering business about 1810, he bought a large spinning mill in 1824 and by 1835 had 4,500 handloom weavers on his pay-roll, mostly in the Preston area; but his main investment was in selling overseas. When he was forced into bankruptcy in the crisis of 1847, it was revealed that his debts, mostly for bills payable, were only a little over £100,000, while his assets were valued at nearly £350,000, almost £200,000 of which were in goods shipped to Brazil, the USA and other parts of the world. Freehold property – warehouses, spinning and weaving mills – were worth £92,000. Gardner's evidence to parliamentary inquiries shows a man with a liberal mind and a sound grasp of the problems of the cotton trade and industry. But the Bank of England Manchester bank manager took of poor view of him; he had 'risen from nothing' and was 'a wild speculative man, dogmatical in all his opinions and views, and not easily guided . . . he is always borrowing money and he conceives the only use of a Banker is to lend money'. Such views no doubt contributed to Gardner's fall.

Even firms with partners who were bankers were not impregnable. Butterworth & Brooks were one of half a dozen big calico printers with such advantageous connections; the works at Sunny Side, near Burnley, were founded about 1798 by Henry Butterworth, who took John Brooks of the Blackburn bankers Cunliffe, Brooks & Co. as a partner. In 1834, Brooks had a personal fortune of over £300,000, including £214,000 invested in the print works. He embarked on a programme of exporting to various countries, particularly Latin America, India and China, selling through leading commission houses. In 1836 it was reported that he was 'short of cash to carry on his current operations while the market is unfavourable for selling' and that he had £50,000 worth of unsold stock in South America. The next year, Cunliffe, Brooks & Co. attempted to restrain Brook's operations by withholding facilities and in May he had debts on his books of £259,000, all due from export houses and agents abroad. By 1846 Brooks had had enough and determined to retire from business 'while he has yet a considerable surplus' – in fact £150,000 to £200,000, little more than half his capital of ten years earlier.[18]

The biggest change in the export market for cottons in the first half of the nineteenth century was the shift in destinations from Europe and America to India and the Far East. The achievement was a remarkable one as for two centuries the flow to textiles had been from India to Europe and most of the quality goods were originally imitations of oriental techniques and designs. Exports of cottons to Asia and Africa rose from under two per cent of the total at the end of the French wars (1815) to nearly 40 per cent in the mid-1850s.[19] The Indian and Chinese markets were already dominated, so far as British trade was concerned, by the so called 'agency houses', the British merchant houses that kept permanent staffs in Calcutta, Bombay, Madras, Shanghai and other centres, and entrenched themselves there by extensive investments in godowns (warehouses), docks, harbours and other transport facilities, and providing banking and insurance services. A handful of Liverpool merchant houses – notably Gladstones and Brocklehursts – forced their way into this fast-growing market, but Lancashire manufacturers lacked the resources needed to challenge the established firms and consequently had to become their clients. This development reinforced the trend towards division of the trade into distinct sectors, manufacturers, commission agents, or merchants, and merchant bankers, as already described.[20]

The difficulties encountered by agents selling in the more distant foreign markets are well illustrated in the letter books of Hodgson & Robinson, Buenos Aires commission agents importing 'Manchester goods' and sending hides, tallow, bullion and other South American products to Liverpool. Hodgson canvassed for commissions by assuring manufacturers that in general they could expect returns within a year, but in practice trade proved to be much slower as the Spanish-American dealers were reluctant to meet their debts. Moreover, the market suffered from recurrent gluts and shortages because communications with Britain were irregular so that the foreign agents' connections at home all received information about profitable lines at the same time. These difficulties were exacerbated by spasms of civil war and subsequent falling exchange rates that could drastically reduce the value of remittances or compel British manufacturers to accept payment in kind. Local fashions could be as erratic as politics, and indeed at times the two were not unconnected. Hodgson wrote to a manufacturer in 1840 that 'there are some pieces [of printed cottons] which have the colours of Light Blue & Green very prominent & which would be unsaleable under the present regime here'. Hodgson & Robinson's best connection was Fielden Brothers of Todmorden, whose £500,000 capital made them one of Lancashire's biggest manufacturers. Yet even Fieldens, with their vast resources, ran into liquidity problems in the trade depression of 1837–42 and had to be baled out by the Bank of England.[21]

## Foreign merchants in Manchester

In the first half of the nineteenth century Manchester was the principal attraction for numbers of continental merchants that settled in Britain, drawn by the rapidly expanding textile trade. The actual numbers at a few key dates are set out in table 3.1. Smaller numbers settled in London, Bradford, Nottingham, Belfast and other textile centres. They not only brought first-hand knowledge of the markets of their home countries, but also extensive mercantile connections across the Continent and the Ottoman Empire, and in some instances valuable links with City of London merchant banks, several of whom were also of foreign origin.

Table 3.1 *Numbers of foreign merchants in Manchester, 1800–70*

| Date | Germans | Greeks | Others | Total |
|------|---------|--------|--------|-------|
| 1800 | 9 | 0 | 3 | 12 |
| 1810 | 19 | 0 | 5 | 24 |
| 1820 | 28 | 0 | 7 | 35 |
| 1830 | 61 | 0 | 13 | 74 |
| 1840 | 84 | 9 | 17 | 110 |
| 1850 | 97 | 55 | 31 | 183 |
| 1860 | 114 | 87 | 41 | 242 |
| 1870 | 143 | 167 | 80 | 390 |

Source: John Scholes, *Foreign Merchants in Manchester 1784–1870*, ms, Manchester Public Library. Americans were not included in this compilation as their numbers were very small.

The principal immigrants were Germans (about half of them German Jews), Americans (often of Irish Presbyterian extraction) and, later in the century, 'Greeks' from the Ottoman Empire. (The so-called 'Greeks' included Turks, Armenians, Arabs and several other ethnic groups from Asia Minor.) Though they were all drawn to Britain by the unprecedented trading and manufacturing opportunities that were opening up, the religious toleration extended to German Jews and Ottoman Christians was also a factor in their migration. The Napoleonic occupation of Frankfurt and Hamburg, and the post-war anti-semitic reaction, also encouraged emigration from Germany.[22]

There can be no question that Germans and German Jews made a major contribution to creating, financing and sustaining the British export trade in cottons in the first half of the nineteenth century, but it is difficult to quantify this. The only early attempt is an estimate made in Manchester in 1839 of the British contribution to the capital needed to finance its overseas trade. In general, as might be expected, this amounted to 80, 90 or 100 per cent according to the sector, but in the trade with continental Europe it was reckoned to be no more than 33 per cent. The remainder of the capital – 66 per cent – was presumably provided by the German merchants and their connections. At this time nearly half the goods being exported from Britain still went to the Continent, so it is not too much to suggest that this foreign enterprise was crucial to British commercial success in the period.[23] A much later (1886) estimate by Sir J. C. Lee of Tootal, Broadhurst, Lee & Co., one of the biggest Lancashire manufacturers at the period, was that three-quarters or seven-eighths of the export business of Manchester had been conducted by these houses, but that was apparently an impression rather than a calculation. Later in this chapter we shall see just how difficult it proved for Lancashire producers to learn the business of exporting, even in the twentieth century.[24]

The foreign shipping houses varied enormously in size and importance and it is impossible to do justice to their rich variety of backgrounds in this chapter. The early giants of the business, Schunk, Souchay & Co. (from Frankfurt) and Ralli Brothers (from Constantinople) were in the same league as merchant princes of British origin, but there were many 'middling' firms and a long tail of small ones, especially in the Greek community. The most successful of the early arrivals, N. M. Rothschild, migrated from Manchester to London in 1805 and in the early post-war year emerged as the premier merchant bank for continental trade while Brown, Shipley & Co. of Liverpool (originally a branch of Brown Brothers of Baltimore) competed with Baring Brothers of London to be the number one accepting house serving the Anglo-American trade. Towards the middle of the nineteenth century the more representative ('middling') foreign houses had capitals of £100,000 – £200,000, which means that they were in a superior league of wealth to the representative Lancashire manufacturer. As late as 1877, the average capital of all cotton mill firms was said to be less than £40,000.

Actually, most of the large and middling firms were not simply Manchester enterprises, and are more properly called 'international houses'. That is, they operated in several trading cities through linking partnerships, their home towns (Frankfurt, Hamburg, Baltimore etc), Manchester, Bradford, and often London as well. The biggest of them, Ralli Brothers, had family partnerships linking fifteen trading centres at mid-century, from Karachi in the east to New Orleans in the west. As Germany industrialised and the profitability of exporting to the Continent declined, the international houses established new partnerships in more distant markets, such as Reiss Brothers in Shanghai and Hong Kong and Salis Schwabe in Singapore, Manila and other centres in the Far East.[25]

In this way, German, Greek and other foreign-born merchants continued to play a large role in the cotton trade down to the First World War and, if they appeared less prominent after 1914, it was often because they Anglicised their surnames. (The Hertz family, for instance, changed its name to Hurst and as such were still leading shippers in the 1920s.) Edgar Jaffe, whose family fortune was made in Manchester, sketched the historical development of the German merchant houses in 1900 and emphasised that 'in spite of their German origin and even though some of the owners were still born in Germany, they mostly do not consider themselves German'. Most of them, he might truthfully have added, were happy to think of themselves as Mancunian.[26]

## Merchants dominate the industry

Towards the middle of the nineteenth century a system of specialisation emerged in the cotton trade (as distinct to the cotton industry) based on the 'home trade houses' (warehouses serving the domestic market) and 'shipping houses' (export houses specialising in different overseas markets). Many of the latter group were, as we have seen, of foreign origin and were consequently often loosely called 'foreign houses'. Despite the problems indicated earlier in this chapter, a handful of manufacturers continued to act as merchants for their own production and to maintain their own warehouses in Manchester. Horrockses, Fieldens, and Thompson & Chippendall, the quality textile printers, were the best-known examples of this practice at mid-century. The elements of the system, with a few well-known examples, are set out in table 3.2:

Table 3.2 *Main categories of Manchester merchants c. 1860–1940*

| Main category | 'Generalists' (big firms) | Specialists (small firms) | Manufacturers (big firms) |
|---|---|---|---|
| Home trade houses (warehouses) | John Rylands S. & J. Watts | e.g. Richard Cobden | e.g. Horrockses Fielden Bros. Thompson & Chippendall Tootalls |
| Shipping houses (exporters) | e.g. A. & S. Henry De Jersey & Co. Ralli Bros. | e.g. John Owens | |

The export business was divided among several hundred small family enterprises, characteristically supplying a handful of correspondents in a single overseas market. There were however a small number of houses which, because of their early start or exceptionally good connections in overseas markets, grew to much larger size; such were for instance A. & S. Henry in the American trade, Ralli Brothers in the trade to India, and De Jersey in the Russian trade. The home trade houses were also a numerous order with big differences between a few leaders and many small specialists, but it was the continuing hegemony of the City of London textile houses that placed the main constraints on this group. Despite the location advantages and the enterprise of Manchester, the

FIGURE 37. John Rylands, the most successful Manchester merchant manufacturer between the American Civil War and the end of the century. Most of his business was with drapers in the home market, but from the 1880s his firm extended into the Empire market, as numerous other 'home trade' houses did.
Source: W. A. Shaw, *Manchester Old and New* (Cassells & Co,. n.d.), vol. 2, p. 36.

home trade warehouses never quite managed to catch up with the old-established metropolitan centre of the textile trade. According to Reuben Spencer of John Rylands & Co., writing in 1889, Manchester home trade houses failed to respond to changing opportunities such as diversification into ready-made clothing, carpets and the colonial trade, 'most of the large wholesale houses in the city jogging along on the old lines'. In 1914 an authoritative text written for the trade, Murphy's *Modern Drapery*, affirmed that 'drapery commerce tends more and more to concentrate in London and most of the important manufacturing firms have either offices or agents in the metropolis.' Manchester's biggest home trade house, Rylands, responded to the challenge by opening a London warehouse in 1849 and extending operations there until, early this century, it became the biggest textile operation in the metropolis.[27]

Though Rylands was customarily referred to as a home trade house, and indeed had most of its business in this sector, it was very much bigger and more active in other areas than any other Lancashire firm. It was the colossus of the trade *and* industry with seventeen cotton spinning and weaving mills at Manchester, Wigan and other centres, a bleach works at Liverpool and five clothing factories in various parts of the country, a unique venture in vertical integration. In the 1870s Rylands responded to problems in the domestic market by launching into exports, particularly in the imperial market. The firm's payroll reached 12,000 in the 1880s while the capital topped £4 million in the 1890s. As a point of comparison, the average capital of public companies in the industry was calculated at just under £76,000 in 1890 and fell continuously to the First World War (table 3.3). Other firms such as S. & J. Watts tried to follow Rylands but none came anywhere near them.[28]

The merchants became the linchpins of the system for several reasons. The shipping houses were more than mere distributors; their function was better expressed by the American term 'convertor'. In addition to finding customers and making arrangements for credit, transport and payment, they usually bought the cloth in its unfinished or 'grey' state and had it finished according to their own very precise specifications, so that the bleachers, dyers and calico printers worked for them. As a rule shippers confined themselves to a single market (e.g. India, Latin America, continental Europe) or a group of related markets, and so became experts on specific foreign market cultures, laws, customs and distribution networks. Trade marks, which came to play an important part in the trade, were nearly always the property of the merchant, not of the manufacturer. The manufacturing side consisted of a large number of small (or small-to-middling) family firms with limited capital making similar goods in conditions approaching the economist's definition of perfect competition, so that each firm made an imperceptible contribution to total output and merchants could pick and choose their suppliers at will. Competition among spinners and weavers guaranteed cheapness, while the merchants' insistence on perfection and exact adaption to particular consumers' wants was a guarantee of quality.[29]

The home trade houses sometimes boasted of the invaluable service they provided for the manufacturers, channelling the products of hundreds of mills to 50,000 or more drapers at home and many more customers with the most heterogeneous demands in overseas markets. They devoted a quarter or more of their capital to financing retail trade by providing credit facilities and 45 per cent (or so) to supporting

FIGURE 38. The Manchester Royal Exchange building, where manufacturers and merchants met every Tuesday to transact business. Source: W. A. Shaw, *Manchester Old and New* (Cassells & Co., n.d.), vol. 2 facing p. 33.

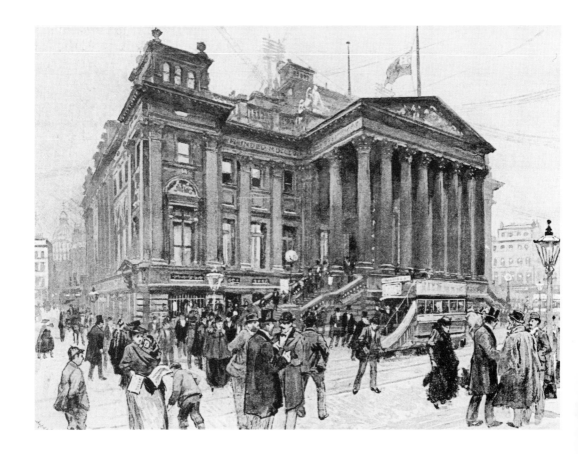

manufacturers by holding stocks which (they claimed) they customarily paid for within seven days of delivery. But the manufacturers did not always see the system in such a favourable light. Dependent producers spoke bitterly of the 'merchant's yoke' and being 'downtrodden', while the connection between the two parties was compared to the tied house system established by the brewers in the period. Heylin maintained that 'it has not been uncommon for spinners to find that cloth agents or merchants, in addition to holding unsold stock of manufacturers, have had a lien on the manufacturer's business and practically controlled it.' Meanwhile some merchants invested large capitals in cotton mills in India, Russia and other cheap labour areas to undercut the home producers in popular lines, increasing the sense of betrayal.[30]

Apart from John Rylands & Co. the earliest and most successful firms to make direct connections with retail trade were Horrockses of Preston and Tootal Broadhurst Lee & Co. of Bolton and Manchester. In the 1870s Frank Hollins, heir to a small family firm in Stockport, initiated the practice of direct trading with retailers to save his struggling mill. In 1885 he boldly acquired control of Horrockses in a reverse takeover and in the next few years successfully applied his system to the vaster custom of Horrockses. In 1887 Hollins succeeded in merging Horrockses with Crewdson, Cross & Co. of Bolton to produce one of the most profitable enterprises in the cotton industry, but there were few who thought of responding to this path-breaking challenge. Forward integration continued to be regarded, as Heylin wrote in 1913, as 'the outcome of being driven to desperation'.[31]

Tootals were driven to desperation by the situation that developed in their US market in the 1880s. It was reported to the directors that the New York importers were apparently abandoning the trade in plain and white goods so that sales had fallen by half in five years (1882–7), while their direct sales to major retailers had quadrupled in the period. The only realistic solution was to open a New York office to sell direct to retailers and to the ready-made clothing manufacturers in that city and Philadelphia. The export manager clinched the argument by declaring that 'our present trade with the importers and jobbers has now fallen to such a figure . . . that we run little risk of losing anything by the proposed change.' This resolution shortly encouraged Tootals to open up direct trade with various parts of India and agents in most European countries, Australia, Persia, the West Indies and other principal markets, so by-passing the Manchester shippers.[32] Tootals' marketing strategy was evidently a major factor in the continuing success of the business, but it found scarcely any imitators so that half a century later (in 1931 to be precise) the firm was reported as unique in the Manchester trade in going direct to retailers. This was not strictly true as Horrockses and Rylands also had a vertical structure but the absence of further names is a telling comment on the paucity of enterprise among Lancashire manufacturers.[33]

Table 3.3 *The major vertically integrated firms in the Lancashire cotton industry, c. 1890*

|  | capital | payroll |
|---|---|---|
| John Rylands & Co. | £3.0 million | 12,000 |
| Horrocks, Crewdson & Co. | £0.8 million | 6,000 |
| Tootal, Broadhurst, Lee | £1.1 million | 5,000 |
| Average size of public companies in the cotton industry | | |
| Date | Capital | |
| 1890 | £76,000 | |
| 1911–13 | £63,000 | |

Source: *Dictionary of Business Biography* articles on John Rylands, Sir Frank Hollins and Sir E. T. Broadhurst.

Sir Sidney Chapman wrote in his *Lancashire Cotton Industry* in 1904 that the 'cloth market is somewhat the same as it was at the end of the eighteenth century.' He went on to record that because of the increased scale of production and growing specialisation of the products, greater efforts were being made by the manufacturers to reach the buyers, but he offered no evidence of achievement beyond the 'enormous increase of manufacturers catalogues of late years.' H. B. Heylin's *Buyers and Sellers in the Cotton Trade* (1913) noted that 'some large spinning and weaving concerns now do a direct shipping business with the continent, India and the British Colonies', but he explained this by reference to mercantile exploitation rather than producers' strategy and offered no examples so the reader may well surmise that he had little more in mind than the names already mentioned. In other words, almost the whole of the trade and industry was locked into the traditional horizontal structure until well into the twentieth century.[34]

## Merchants' problems

In the last two or three decades of the nineteenth century, both home trade and export merchants were beset by new problems. The basic cause was dramatically improved communications. The spread of the telegraph network brought the producer, merchant and retailer much closer and made increasing numbers in the chain of intermediaries that linked them redundant. Competition in domestic and overseas markets sharpened and margins became tighter. Parallel changes took place on the cotton supply side. The movement of raw cotton from America to Europe involved a long chain of traders including merchants or agents in the southern ports of the USA (Charleston, Savannah, New Orleans etc.), shippers, merchants at the British ports, cotton brokers in Liverpool and cotton dealers in Manchester, Blackburn and other centres, and buying brokers who represented several hundred spinning mills. New York forced the pace of change after 1870 when the cotton market there was organised exclusively for futures trading (i.e. contracts were agreed for delivery of standard quantities and qualities of baled cotton at dates up to a year ahead) as distinct from the traditional commodity (or 'spot') trading. The American pacemakers undermined the Liverpool system by bypassing the traditional buying agencies in the plantation states and the selling agencies in Europe. Cotton broking changed from being a regular and low-risk business to a speculative one, and half the old broking houses disappeared between 1885 and 1905, while several American merchants opened selling offices in Liverpool and Bremen. However after the initial onslaught, Liverpool mounted a strong resistance, some merchants opening buying offices in the American south, Calcutta and Alexandria.[35]

The most successful was Smith, Edwards & Co., whose principal partner, Samuel Smith MP, conveyed some of the trauma of change in an autobiography called *My Life-Work* (1902). Starting business as a broker in 1860, Smith crossed the conventional cotton trade boundaries to become a partner in James Finlay & Co., the Glasgow-based agency house with a strong piece goods trade to India, and owner of two large mills at Staleybridge. By the turn of the century his business was much the biggest in cotton in Liverpool with a capital of £500,000, and exceeded by only one American house in the trade. Smith's management style is conveyed by a few sentences in his autobiography: 'the head of a great firm dealing with foreign countries needs to be a statesman, an economist and a financier, as well as a merchant. He must have the power of taking a bird's eye view of the whole situation; like the general of an army, and like all great commanders, he must be able to discern talent, and to promote it to a high position. A first-class merchant does not burden his mind with a multitude of details, and is always seemingly at leisure, while intent on great issues.' Smith was one of the few that brought strategic planning to a large organisation, something that was increasingly needed in the cotton trade but too often in short supply.[36]

Intense competition induced Manchester merchant houses to offer longer credits and put more and more travellers on the road. This 'reckless' policy brought many new and old firms to grief in both Manchester and London in this decade while some of the most eminent City houses (notably Morrisons) struggled for survival. Several second and third generation leaders found it necessary to incorporate their family businesses, but limited liability was still widely distrusted and dynasties were thought inherently superior to meritocracy in retaining the loyalty of customers, suppliers and workpeople. Indeed one of the two most successful Manchester textile houses, S. & J. Watts, remained a family enterprise until after the First World War.

These problems were exacerbated as manufacturers and major retailers began to forge direct links. There had always been connections at the fashion end of the market, but they multiplied in the 1870s and 1880s. In the late 1880s the shareholders of Morrisons (now the Fore Street Warehouse Co. Ltd) were told 'things are much changed now, those great retail houses go to the manufacturers and are larger purchasers than ever wholesale houses can be of certain specialities.' Towards the end of the century the traditional piece goods trade with the drapers declined in favour of the ready made garment trade, where the great retailers had the advantage of the wholesalers. By the mid-1890s the leading London stores were already rivalling most of the wholesalers in capital assets. The accounts of the public companies show that they were already tightening credit in the 1880s. The clearest comments on this process come from Reuben Spencer of Rylands, writing in 1889. At that time some 40,000 commercial travellers were competing for the business of some 50,000 drapers, who were frequently tempted to overstrain their credit. He urged that a retailer should never allow his liabilities to trade creditors to exceed 2 to 2.5 times his capital, and that he should do a cash business. Spencer's work seems to have been very popular.

The Wholesale Textile Association was formed in London in 1912 to resist the encroachments of the manufacturers and major retail houses. It was always a very secretive organisation and not much is known about its activities. Its main offensive activity consisted, it seems, in blacklisting manufacturers who contracted directly with retailers. Its leading light for many years was the head of I. & R. Morley of London and Nottingham, Lord Hollenden. The pressure of the WTA is evident in the advertisements of branded goods manufacturers, in which they insisted that they sold only through the wholesalers; in reality many of them were simultaneously involved in subterfuges to sell direct to the chain stores. As late as 1953, the WTA were advertising in the *Drapers Record* that 'the Wholesaler ensures that only the cream of the world's production is presented to the retail trade. He enables the Shopkeeper to examine the products of hundreds of manufacturers under one roof . . .' By such pressures, the old merchant houses were able to resist the tide of change for a couple of generations. It was not until the period of mergers and takeovers of the 1960s that the last of the old firms were incorporated into vertical combines.[37]

## The inter-war years

In the economy as in politics, the 1920s was a decade in which nearly everyone thought or pretended that nothing that mattered had been changed by the First World War and that trade would soon be restored to its pre-war level. The contraction of the cotton industry soon forced many manufacturers into mergers and closures but on the marketing side the old structure changed surprisingly little. Exports, though declining steeply, especially after 1929, continued to be handled by a large number of firms, even more than those engaged in manufacturing. A lot of firms closed and others were forced to curtail the scale of their operations, but even after two decades of discouragement, there were still more than 1,200 merchant convertors (i.e. firms that 'converted' grey cloth into particular finishes, shades or designs to suit the needs of specific markets) (table 3.4).

Table 3.4  *Number of firms in different branches of the cotton industry and trade, c.1930*

| | | |
|---|---|---|
| MERCHANTING: | | |
| Home trade | | 150 |
| Shipping merchants | | 1,200+ |
| MANUFACTURING: | | |
| Spinners, weavers and integrated firms | | 1,193 |
| FINISHING: | | |
| Bleachers | 190 | |
| Calico Printers | 145 | 595 |
| Dyers | 260 | |
| Total | | 3,138 |

Source: Henry Clay *Report on the Position of the English Cotton Industry* (privately printed, October 1931). There were more home trade houses in London not included in this count.

Actually, there were so many export houses that nobody ever made a final count of them. The clearest report, that by the economist Henry Clay in 1931, maintained that 'their number cannot be less than a thousand' but he later quoted 'a prominent Manchester shipper' that there were 742 shippers in that year. However Clay's own estimate was evidently nearer the mark because a calculation made from official returns during the Second World War produced a figure of 1,210 in 1940. The total could not have been less than that a decade earlier and so is used in table 3.4. Membership of Manchester Royal Exchange, the market for exports, peaked at 11,539 in 1920 then tumbled year by year to just over 5,000 in 1939.[38]

Manchester continued to have a large number of shipping houses because anyone with a little experience of the export trade and some appreciation of the fabric specifications of particular markets who could get a few orders to start with could set up in competition with the oldest-established merchanting houses. Most export houses rented premises (often a room or two) and had their packing done by specialised packing firms, so that it was not necessary to have a permanent office or a warehouse to commence business. The banks were willing to open new accounts and sometimes manufacturers might help with credit. New firms were constantly being formed in the 1920s as managers and travellers in established houses launched out on their own, partnerships split up, and overseas traders (particularly from the Middle East) continued to be attracted by Manchester's historical reputation. It was only after the economic catastrophe of 1929–31 that this century-old system began to expire.[39]

There had always been a high turnover of firms, as would be expected in a trade where entry was so easy. But there were also family firms that lasted two or three generations and came to control a large proportion of the trade in their chosen export sector. Table 3.5 shows that about 50 of the 1,200 or so firms (4 per cent of them) controlled half the export trade. Among the family dynasties that continued to lead in their respective sector in the early 1920s were A. & S. Henry in the American trade, Reiss Brothers in China, De Jersey in Russia, and S. L. Behrens on the continent. Some of the old-established home trade houses like Rylands and S. & J. Watts continued to export to the continent, the Dominions, and the USA. The losses consequent on the Bolshevik Revolution brought down De Jersey, and Reiss Brothers made an early capitulation to the Japanese, but for most merchant houses the 1920s and 1930s were a long period of attrition rather than early surrender.[40] Data on the home trade houses is even more difficult to find but a similar concentration is apparent: in 1942 75 per cent of all the wholesale trade was done by firms with a turnover of £100,000+.

Table 3.5 *The size of merchant convertors in 1940*

| Quantity converted | Number of convertors | Share of total exports |
|---|---|---|
| 5m + yards | 49 | 50.0% |
| 0.5m − 4.99m yards | 257 | 40.0% |
| 0.05 − 0.049m yards | 468 | 9.5% |
| 5,000 − 49,000 yards | 306 | 0.5% |
| less than 5,000 yards | 130 | 0.03% |

Source: H. Kenyon, 'The Shape and Size of the Export Merchanting Section of the Cotton Industry', *Trans Manchester Statistical Society* (1944).

The difficult trading conditions persuaded numbers of spinning, weaving and 'combined' firms to set up their own merchanting operations. Clay identified eight public companies and eighteen private companies in this category; the former included Amalgamated Cotton Mills Trust Ltd, a conglomerate of fifteen firms formed round Horrockses, and Joshua Hoyle & Sons, that absorbed seven other firms. The published results of these firms were much better than the industry generally, but this may have been because they were simply better-managed firms; certainly Horrockses had had a lot of experience of merchanting.[41]

In fact the only in-depth study of a group of manufacturers that tried to extend into merchanting proved to be a dismal failure. The Calico Printers Association was formed at the turn of the century as an amalgamation of forty-six printing firms and thirteen merchant convertors. Calico printing had seen a succession of firms at the top end of the market marketing their own goods, for instance Peels in the last quarter of the eighteen century, Thompson & Chippendall in the first half of the nineteenth century, and Frederick Steiner of Accrington in the second half. Some firms in the more popular sector like Butterworth, Brooks & Co. and Schwabe had, as we have seen, a more patchy record. In 1900 the CPA had 70 per cent of British capacity including quality and middle range printing, so should have made a major impact. But the shippers were hostile to the CPA from the outset so that in the early 1920s the CPA's overseas distribution network was still centred round a mass of agents who were linked to Manchester by independent merchant houses. Lennox Lee, the Association's chairman for nearly 40 years (1908–1947), recognised the problems of relations with the merchants and pushed the focus of the organisation from production towards marketing, but never tamed the power of the merchants. An inflexible policy of fixed prices allowed the Japanese to encroach on the most important export market, that of India and the Far East, where the powerful agency houses maintained their traditional independence. Ralli Brothers, the most successful agency house, discussed the possibility of establishing a direct trade organisation with the CPA in India in 1933 but pulled out when the CPA would not allow them to be sole distributor; by the late 1930s Rallis were distributing a lot of Japanese output. CPA policy in the home market showed similar lack of ability to recognise their own best interests; in particular the directors were wary of selling direct to major retail chains and rejected a deal with Marks & Spencers in 1937. In a nutshell, the conglomorate failed to make the strategic breakthrough that was so necessary to lift its flagging sales. The CPA remained a prisoner of the nineteenth-century system and so, it seems, did most of the rest of the Lancashire cotton trade and industry.[42]

## Conclusion

Henry Clay, the most perceptive of the commentators on the inter-war problems of the cotton industry shrewdly observed that 'it is hardly a paradox to say that the cotton industry, in the sense of the manufacturing industry, has never had a marketing organisation of its own'.[43] He meant that the historical evolution of the industry determined that the merchants represented the consumer, not the spinners, weavers or finishers; they came to Manchester form Scotland, Germany, the US, Asia Minor, India and other distant parts because Manchester was the best place to buy yarns and cotton piece goods of every description, and they effectively separated the producer from his ultimate market. These merchants were consequently entrepreneurs with no permanent commitment to Manchester, British produce, or the maintenance of Lancashire as an industrial region, and when the balance of advantage shifted to other production locations, there was no hesitation in switching their orders.

The producers were not blind to the situation and the bolder spirits of successive generations tried to add the profits of the merchant to those of the manufacturer. With very few exceptions they failed. The main reasons are fairly clear: that for centuries Manchester was satellite to London and so its experience and originality was in production rather than international trade; and when unprecedented opportunities suddenly appeared at the end of the eighteenth century, the indigenous trading community lacked adequate capital and an effective banking system. The American war and the French wars destroyed or enervated most of the pioneer family enterprises. As a result, manufacturers were typically small and specialised, and produc- tion- rather than market-orientated. After the first Industrial Revol- ution generation (1780–1815), scarcely any producers could even contemplate a marketing role. For the remaining generations, the merchants were a separate business class.

Chapter 10 of this book shows how integration of firms was forced on sections of the cotton industry by the financial pressures of the inter-war years, while chapter 11 describes how this became government policy after the Second World War. Nevertheless, the integration of merchant convertors with other sections of the industry ran contrary to long-established practice and the conventional wisdom of the trade, and developed only slowly. The Cotton Board calculated that by 1939 firms engaged in converting controlled as much as 44 per cent of the looms in the industry, and by 1956 this figure had risen to 63 per cent of a smaller industry.[44] This sounded impressive progress to politicians and industrial spokesmen who saw integration as the best strategy for the salvation of the Lancashire industry, but it did little to arrest continuing decline. For generations merchant enterprise had evolved separately from industrial enterprise while the most able entrepreneurs had been unable to integrate the two activities, so it was hardly to be expected that shot-gun marriages, even in the dire situation of the industry in the 1950s and 1960s, would reverse the rapidly declining fortunes of the industry.

# CHAPTER 4

# The Business Community

ANTHONY HOWE

THE Lancashire cotton industry spawned a brand of businessmen who uniquely in Britain's industrial revolution acquired a well-defined collective identity – the millocracy, cottonocracy, steam lords, Manchester School.[1] As such, they seemed not only to control an industry and a county but at times to lay a strong claim to direct the affairs of the nation. Much more so than, say, Sheffield steel masters, Sunderland shipowners, or Staffordshire potters, the cotton masters were the archetypal 'new men' of the Industrial Revolution, the bearers of a pride of order, based on the factory system, and ready to challenge the cultural values and distribution of power in aristocratic and rural Britain. Even more than this, the cotton masters were a cosmopolitan breed, in part reflecting the presence in their midst of migrants from abroad, but much more so because they were intimately tied into an international division of labour, technology and markets, which carried to the world the message of free trade, peace and goodwill. 'Manchester man' was also 'International man'.

Despite this readiness of contemporaries to identify 'a cottonocracy', in fact the business community engaged in the cotton industry em-braced a wide variety of different characteristics and lacked much of the homogeniety which held together narrower, more cohesive groups, whether the territorial aristocracy or even London's 'moneyocracy'.[2] Moreover, to a large extent, those engaged in cotton self-consciously repudiated collective action, upholding an ethic of individual endeav-our, 'self-help', connected with their peers merely by the toils of competitive markets, and the accident of geographical proximity: or as one contemporary put it, 'a dominance of mere individualism, each stretching as high and as wide as possible, without regard to his neighbours'.[3] Yet in attempting to understand this business community, we may do so by examining the characteristics which defined those engaged in it, by analysing the forms of collective action into which they were necessarily drawn and by identifying values and beliefs which they shared in common.

## Unity and diversity within the business community

The nature of the business community is most readily revealed if we briefly consider its composition, defined by function, numbers and scale of operations. Very broadly, it may be divided into four sections. Firstly, the typical cotton lords of Victorian Lancashire were the owners of sizeable family firms, whether engaged in spinning, weaving, bleaching or calico-printing, employing several hundred workmen and by the 1850s accounting for the bulk of the employment in the cotton trade.[4] This group had only decisively emerged in the previous decades, finally separating itself from the earlier 'warehouse' and 'factory' form of enterprise in the decade after 1815.[5] But in this category we find the most familiar names of the early Victorian cotton industry, Ashworths, M'Connel & Kennedy, Gregs, Brights, Horrockses, and Fieldens.[6]

Secondly, there were a vast array of small manufacturers, sometimes employing only a handful of men, hiring room and power in multi-occupied mills, living a hand-to-mouth existence and often engaging in cut-throat competition. In this category were several hundred firms in Lancashire by 1850.[7] Taking these two groups together by 1861 1,979 firms were enumerated by the Factory Inspectors, while Worrall's first textile directory in 1882 listed some 1,948. Given the complexities and obscurities of definition ('firm', 'mill', and 'factory' were by no means uniform), this suggests some stability in total numbers but there

FIGURE 39. Lark Hill, the residence of Samuel Horrocks. The Horrocks family dominated business and politics in early nineteenth-century Preston. The death of Samuel Horrocks brought their presence but not the business name to an end. (Illustration courtesy of Lancashire County Library, Preston Local Studies Collection)

were to be important changes in the structure of the industry after mid-century. In particular, the rise of the 'Oldham Limiteds' in the 1870s offered an alternative form of business organisation, diffusing ownership amidst considerable numbers of small shareholders, and concentrating control in the hands of company promoters, directors and mill brokers.[8] This in turn contributed to the increasingly marked geographical specialisation in the industry, with its weaving sector concentrated in north and north-east Lancashire and the spinning sector centred in south-east Lancashire.[9] This did not change the nature of the business community but served to emphasise its efficiency, with high levels of specialisation by product, market and location.

Table 4.1 *Distribution of cotton firms by numbers (1841)*
*and capital (1877)*

| Employees | 1841 | Capital invested(£) | 1877 |
|---|---|---|---|
| 1–50 | 357 | under 10,000 | 667 |
| 51–100 | 207 | 10–19,000 | 258 |
| 101–150 | 150 | 20–29,000 | 155 |
| 151–200 | 102 | 30–49,000 | 106 |
| 201–250 | 62 | 50–74,000 | 101 |
| 251–500 | 147 | 75–99,000 | 72 |
| Over 500 | 80 | 100,000+ | 94 |
| Total | 1,105 | | 1,453 |

Sources: Howe, *Cotton Masters*, p. 5; Farnie, thesis, appendix 15.

Specialisation of function, as Professor Chapman has shown above, had also lent clear definition to the third group within the business community, its merchants, serving both to supply manufacturers with raw materials and to dispose of their produce in the home and world markets.[10] In some cases, manufacturers combined both roles but by the 1830s this had become much more rare. Merchanting was to a large extent focussed on Manchester itself rather than its satellite towns, with the warehouses of its merchant princes dominating the appearance of central Manchester. Yet not all merchants were princes, and equally central to the cotton industry were a host of yarn agents, brokers, commission agents, warehousemen, shipping agents and others, comprising a huge range of middlemen within the commercial sector.[11] For the most part, merchants and their auxiliaries worked harmoniously with the spinners, manufacturers and finishers, forming a network of economic interdependence which carried over into social and political spheres. Thus by the 1830s, families such as the Potters played a pre-eminent role in public and commercial life, 'the energetic pioneers of Manchester's radical politics . . . the founders of the civic life of the town', as one of their descendants, Beatrice Webb, recalled.[12] As we will see below, institutions such as the Manchester Chamber of Commerce underpinned this commercial harmony and it was only in the twentieth century that growing conflict between merchants and manufacturers both reflected and intensified the challenges facing the cotton industry.[13]

Finally, a vast number of professions and ancillary trades ranging from bankers, accountants, architects and lawyers to bobbin-makers, machine makers, engineers, dyers and chemical manufacturers, were all directly or indirectly dependent upon the cotton industry.[14] This fourth group within the business community was virtually limitless. Its size and importance had led by the 1880s to the creation of directories to guide middlemen to their mill-owning customers.[15] To some extent cotton fortunes themselves had been invested in subsidiary services and industries, including banking, transport and insurance, contributing to an increasingly well-defined network of interdependence between the four leading groups within the business community.[16] Yet, despite this degree of co-operation, within and between the members of each group was also a highly competitive market, for cotton remained an industry with a 'lottery' attraction, drawing in many at the lower echelons where entry remained cheap and easy, yet in which 'winners' were relatively few.

## The pursuit of success

Within the manufacturing sector, those drawn into the cotton industry were primarily local men. Over eighty per cent of mid-century masters were born in Lancashire, familiar with the perils and rewards on offer, although cotton continued to draw in outsiders, for example, some foreign merchants, or occasional fortune-seekers from southern England.[17] But by and large, Lancashire's important ethnic minorities, Germans, Italians and Jews, only rarely became millowners, rather than merchants and agents, allowing the perpetuation of a spurious racial interpretation of Lancashire's industrial prowess as the result of the qualities of her Frisian population, untouched by the Norman Conquest.[18]

The conditions, besides race, which favoured business success in the cotton industry have naturally given rise to much discussion, with no myths more hoary than those of the 'self-made man' and of 'clogs to clogs in three generations'.[19] Neither of these myths is without foundation, for given the relative ease of entry into textiles, say compared with brewing, mining, or banking, the talented artisan continued into the late nineteenth century to make his way to the top in the cotton industry. For example, John Mayall of Mossley, the largest cotton spinner in the world in the 1870s, had begun his career as an operative spinner.[20] Similarly, among the first generation of British industrialists studied by Crouzet many were of relatively 'humble' origins, reflecting the real possibilities of fortune-making in a new industry at the time of its most rapid expansion.[21] Yet much more representative by the mid-nineteenth century was the dominance of second generation, 'hereditary' entrepreneurs, the beneficiaries of the growth and success of their fathers and a group who would by and large leave sizeable fortunes rather than the prospect of a return to clogs to their progeny.[22]

The phenomenon of third-generation entrepreneurship (and even more so that of downward social mobility) has been little studied but recent evidence drawn from a sample of over 400 Manchester businessmen in the later nineteenth century reveals 17 per cent to have been drawn from the third generation, while many younger sons had set up new businesses.[23] Despite therefore some influential but flawed early twentieth-century evidence which suggested the continued possibility of manual workers rising into ownership, this was uncommon.[24] Earlier, in the co-operative wave of the mid-nineteenth century some idealistic employers had been ready to transfer mills to their workers, but far more representative were strategies designed to retain firms in family control.[25] It was rare for a firm to pass beyond family control save from biological or business failure. Yet the former included such leading firms as Horrockses and Rylands. For the death of Samuel Horrocks in 1846 severed the 'last link of the chain which has so long and so honourably connected his family with the commercial prosperity of Preston' while the latter, after the death of Rylands' heir, passed to the control of its managers.[26] But much more typical 'exits' from cotton were the result of bankruptcy, the harsh discipline of the market, which remained an ever present fear for the large and small alike. The trade cycle depressions and commercial crises of 1837–42, 1847, and 1857 cut a swathe through the trade directories, while later years saw a fluctuating but usually sizeable culling of the improvident, the immoral and the unlucky.[27]

For the survivors, the rewards were considerable. For while the cotton industry produced fewer millionaires than either land or the City of London, it produced fortunes in depth of numbers. Thus, a sample of 330 probate valuations of textile fortunes between the 1830s and 1900s reveals an average value of £126,000, although only a handful of cotton men entered the ranks of Victorian millionaires, headed by Rylands, four Fieldens, and the less well-known Salford master E. R. Langworthy.[28] Moderate wealth may in some senses have benefited the industry, for it probably encouraged the retention of capital in family firms – although this in turn may have had the drawback that firms became quasi-trusts for families, designed to provide a livelihood for numerous sons and daughters, arguably at the expense of capital investment, and the inflow of non-family talent.

Wealth also, of course, offered an escape-route from business, the prospect of an elite education, as a stepping-stone to the 'upper Ten Thousand' or the ability to purchase a landed estate. Both routes proffered those aristocratic social values which were supposedly to sap Britain's industrial spirit.[29] Yet it is doubtful if either was followed to an extent which threatened entrepreneurial success. Firstly, even second-generation industrialists had gained considerable experience of public schools without an overly-deleterious impact on firms, and this pattern does not seem to have changed much in the later nineteenth century with a combination of public school (16 per cent) and locally-educated (grammar school and civic university) businessmen in later nineteenth-century Manchester.[30] Even the sons of businessmen who experienced the full delights of Oxbridge were often successful, as well as polished, businessmen, for example, Sir Alan Sykes, Orielensis and bleacher.[31] Arguably, it was a real disadvantage for the cotton industry that more sons did not go to public schools and Oxbridge, for this may either have diminished the cycle of hereditary recruitment, or broadened the outlook of the leaders of an industry whose 'parochialism' has been deemed a crucial factor in its subsequent decline.[32]

Nor perhaps did the bucolic charms of land-ownership cause a sufficiently great 'haemorrhage' of capital from industry. For wealthy first-generation entrepreneurs such as the Peels, Arkwrights, and Sir George Philips, land had acted as a magnet for the socially and politically ambitious but subsequently only a minority of cotton men could afford or wished to abandon industry for land.[33] Thus out of a sample of 351 masters, only 39 (or their heirs) ended up as owners of gentry-size estates (1,000+ acres). In some ways, this is a sizeable and impressive figure, over 10 per cent of the total, and so well illustrates the enduring attractiveness of land within English society.[34] Yet its attractions were by no means irresistible and the majority of cotton lords remained permanently attached to urban, industrial society, often owning extensive 'small' estates, farms and pleasure parks but without seeking permanent detachment from cotton and Lancashire. Nor, of course, in some cases did landownership mean complete separation from cotton, with some families such as the Bazleys and Houldsworths able to reconcile business efficiency with rural society. Yet the absentee industrialist was a rare phenomenon, with one survey of 904 partners (in 550 mills) revealing only 29 examples (3 per cent).[35] More typically, businessmen retreated to the suburbs, or to the Lakes, readily reached by train from Manchester on Friday evenings, with fishing rated well above fox-hunting as a recreational pursuit. The cotton bosses provided more prototypes for Beatrix Potter's Mr Jeremy Fisher than for Thomas Hardy's Alec D'Urberville.[36]

While therefore a portion of Lancashire's businessmen were ready to become 'gentrified' or 'feudalised', this was far more a question of choice of lifestyle than a decisive criterion of entrepreneurial success or failure. For most, that choice favoured an affluent bourgeois gentility, with close proximity to factory, warehouse and Exchange. A thriving business community increasingly supported its own cultural institutions, above all the Manchester Literary and Philosophical Society (1781), the Royal Manchester Institution (1823) and the Manchester Statistical Society (1833). Such societies offered both a form of social status and also fields of endeavour peculiarly fitted to an emerging urban-industrial civilisation and its discontents.[37] They were joined later by institutions such as the Manchester Geographical Society as the merchants of 'Cottonopolis' avidly followed the African exploits of Livingstone and Stanley in the nascent age of empire.[38]

A growing number of institutions also offered mercantile leisure pursuits, for example, the Portico Library, set up in Mosley Street, and later joined by the Theatre Royal and the Gentlemen's Concert Hall, prefiguring the importance of drama and music in Manchester's middle-class culture. Manchester also sported its gentlemen's clubs, offering both political and social sustenance. The well-established John Shaw's Club brought together Tory-Anglican professional and business men, while the Union Club (1825) included many solicitors and merchants active in municipal politics. The Manchester Reform Club (1871) offered a much more overtly political venue. Other Lancashire towns also provided similar social institutions, offering genteel recreation for the business community. For example, in Blackburn, a Union Club had been established in 1849, uniting both Tory and Liberal, Anglican and Dissenting employers, in the pursuit of newspaper reading, billiards, cards and refreshment. In Preston, Dr William Shepherd's Library had from the mid-eighteenth century offered more intellectual amusements, to be joined later by the Guildhall Newsroom ('for commercial gentlemen') and the Palatine Library.[39]

Local residence therefore generated its own cultural rewards as an alternative to rustic escape. Both contributed important elements to the social identity of the millowners, helping to maintain 'face to face' relationships within the factory communities and stimulating the philanthropy which was so marked a feature of the business community in nineteenth-century Lancashire.

A further useful index of the social foundations of the business community is provided by the pattern of marriage, although this aspect of entrepreneurial behaviour has been much neglected compared with the study of aristocratic marriage and divorce. From the limited information

available, the pattern is one of strong local and class endogamy, with
81 per cent of wives of cotton masters born in Lancashire or its periphery
and 45 per cent the daughters of cotton masters.[40] This well defines
the circle of eligibility, with acceptable partners also coming from
mercantile, professional (especially clerical) and minor gentry families.
Only very rarely was marriage for the entrepreneur an avenue to 'the
best circles', although Joseph Ridgway moved in this way from Bolton
bleaching to Kentish landed society. At the other end of the scale,
factory lasses were among the wives of some early marrying but rapidly
mobile masters, for example, John Mayall. But the general pattern
reinforced a strong occupational and social solidarity among the business
community. The ceremonial of marriage also acted as a *rite de passage*
within factory communities, the occasion for operative accolades and
paternal festivity, part of the display of wealth and status through the
'outward sumptuosity' scorned by social critics but serving to enhance
the wider sense of community both among the elite and between
employers and employees. For wives themselves, marriage occasionally
led to an important role in firms on the death of husbands, but more
usually, implied the provision of heirs, supervision of education, management of considerable domestic budgets, entertainment on an expanding scale, the introduction of gentility and culture, and the fulfilment
of philanthropic duty.[41]

   Marriage was often closely linked to associations based on religion,
with partners sought and found within church and chapel networks, a
pattern which helped to reinforce the important division of the business
community along the lines of orthodoxy and dissent. For religion was
undoubtedly for many the strongest non-business 'loyalty', with
Quakers, Unitarians and Congregationalists in Lancashire all closely
identified with the economic elite, and with Nonconformity the hall-
mark of that distinctive capitalist breed beloved of nineteenth-century
journalists and transmitted by them to twentieth-century historians.[42]
There is much evidence to support the remarkable cultural contribution
of particular sects, above all that of Manchester's Unitarians.[43] Yet
contrary to many sociological assumptions linking business success with
Nonconformity, Lancashire businessmen were most marked in their
Anglican allegiance. This was by far the largest single denomination
among industrialists, and an important factor in sustaining both the
vitality of the Church of England and 'the Tory party at prayer'. For
example, in the administration of the parish, and later diocese, of
Manchester, and in church-building, the business community played a
leading part within the 'National Church', directly comparable to the
better known part played by businessmen in the 'voluntary' sects.[44]
Religion remained a vital component of entrepreneurial behaviour,
with only rare avowals of secularism, while many continued to be

influenced by strenuous debates on commercial morality, to see in the conduct of their firms the opportunity for 'salvation' as well as profit and to be directed in their giving by scriptural injunctions.[45] The Anglican George Harwood of Bolton was unusual in combining the roles of clergyman and cotton spinner, but religious identities were undoubtedly as central to the business community as to that of the working-class in nineteenth-century Lancashire.

Harwood perhaps illustrates the difficulties of isolating a 'typical' member of the business community and it may be that individual examples can only illustrate the variety rather than a typology of businessmen. Yet such examples may usefully sketch out the types of link we are seeking between the whole and the part. For example, among the most successful of the first generation of Manchester's industrialists was George Philips, cotton spinner, Methodist by upbringing, first chairman of the Royal Exchange, a founder of the *Manchester Guardian* and of the Royal Manchester Institution. As a borough-mongering MP in the unreformed House of Commons, he was known as 'the member for Manchester' and acted as an effective conduit between provincial business opinion and Parliament. Yet in the 1820s he had been driven by the smoke of Manchester to the pastures of Warwickshire, acquiring an estate of some 6000 acres, underwriting settlements for his children's aristocratic marriages, enjoying the friendship of the Whigs of Holland House, and receiving a baronetcy. He ended his political career as MP for South Warwickshire, ready out of deference to his constituents, to support the Corn Laws against which his fellow cotton spinners, including his relative Mark Philips, now MP for Manchester, were staunchly protesting.[46]

Foremost as well as richest among the subsequent generation of Manchester men stands John Rylands.[47] Rylands was undoubtedly Manchester's premier business leader, remaining Mancunian by residence at Longford Hall, Stretford, munificent in his lifetime as a fervent Congregationalist, and most famously commemorated by his third wife in the John Rylands Library. Yet arguably he contributed little to the business community beyond the powerful example of his own success. On the other hand, if we take Sir Thomas Bazley, we have at first sight a prototype for the declining industrial spirit, with Bazley already sending his son to Cambridge in the 1840s and soon to become a considerable landowner in Oxfordshire and Gloucestershire. Yet Bazley, unlike Rylands, was pre-eminent in the business community, the epitome of Manchester man, as well as Matthew Arnold's prototype of the bourgeois 'Philistine'.[48] How did Bazley earn such prominence? Partly as MP for Manchester, but his role as such was based on decades on activity in public life, as a supporter of the Anti-Corn Law League and Liberal politics, a pillar of the Anglican

FIGURE 40. Thomas Bazley, MP for Manchester, as depicted in *Vanity Fair*, 21 August 1875.

FIGURE 41. William Henry Houldsworth, MP for Manchester, 1883–1906, as depicted in *Vanity Fair*, 3 October 1885.

Church, Commissioner of the Great Exhibition, 1851, promoter of the Manchester Art Treasures Exhibition in 1857, activist for cotton supply, President of the Chamber of Commerce, advocate of national secular education, of a Manchester University, of temperance, and an opponent of the Nine Hours' Movement in the 1870s.[49] Here was an endless series of links between Bazley, the partner of Robert Gardner in Dean Mills, Bolton, and Arnold's correct, if critical perception of Bazley as an emblematic figure, a true representattive of a class and a community. Aptly, Bazley personified 'Manchester' in *Vanity Fair* in 1875 (figure 40).

Ten years later (Sir) William Henry Houldsworth succeeded him, embodying 'all the characteristics of the best kind of Lancashire lad.' Houldsworth, like Bazley, a strong Churchman, had however abandoned familial Liberalism for the rebuilding of Toryism in Manchester, based on strong ties with 'democracy'. Houldsworth in his creation of Reddish Mills, Stockport, had already shown that philanthropic entrepreneurship was no Liberal monopoly. As a businessman, he combined an active role locally, including the Chamber of Commerce, with the promotion of industrial causes at the national level, including bimetallism and imperial expansion, a 'Minister of Commerce' in waiting for a department which was never quite created. Yet Houldsworth was no hidebound traditionalist and went on to play a leading part in the formation of the Fine Cotton Spinners' Association, ready to recognise the end of the old family firms and the necessity of collective organisation for the future of the cotton industry.[50] For contemporaries, Philips, Rylands, Bazley and Houldsworth were all emblems of Manchester, itself a synonym for the cotton industry. Yet they were enormously diverse in temperament and achievement, embracing the social-climbing rakish Regency plutocrat, the austere, single-minded, and introverted Liberal Nonconformist business enthusiast, the many-sided landed Liberal Anglican 'Philistine' and the prototype of the 'democratic' Tory Anglican businessman of later nineteenth-century Lancashire. Manchester man had many faces.

## Markets, men and institutions

Given such widely-differing individual characteristics and backgrounds within the business community, its common character stemmed essentially from the very market within which individual entrepreneurs competed with each other for raw materials, customers and labour. In a way, therefore, the Manchester Royal Exchange provides the best symbol of the cotton trade, the central institution to which most sizeable firms belonged, the one irreducible locus of common activity, linking firms and the market, yet combining competition with a form of collegiality.[51] Established in 1804, it numbered 1,543 members in 1809,

H.E.Tidmarsh

3,068 in 1852 (a second Exchange building had been enlarged in 1849 to accommodate *c.* 3,300 members), and 4,209 in 1860. A third building was erected in 1871 and 1874, the massive neo-classical presence surviving today, albeit shorn of its portico in 1890 in the interests of further accommodation of its members, 7,485 (4,600 firms) in 1894.[52] While the home trade to a large extent still centred on Manchester's warehouses, the Exchange expressed Manchester's fundamental dependence upon foreign trade, uniting spinners, merchants, agents, brokers, waste dealers, bleachers in what was described as 'the parliament of the lords of cotton'.[53] Not only did the Exchange bring together manufacturers from all over Lancashire but it could act as a forum for opinion, with impromptu meetings, like that called by John Bright in 1840 to petition Parliament against William Ferrand's slandering of the cotton lords, or that in 1917 to protest against the Indian Cotton Duties.[54] As 'one of the largest rooms in the kingdom', it also served as the venue for Manchester's reception of Queen Victoria in 1851. Conveniently near railway stations, the Exchange acted as the pivot of Manchester's central business district, with its huge number of warehouses and offices,

FIGURE 42. The Royal Exchange – the heart of the business life of Manchester's and Lancashire's cotton industry. Source: W. A. Shaw, *Manchester Old and New* (Cassells & Co., n.d.), vol. 2, p. 25.

its Corn Exchange, its banks and shops, and with easy access to a ever-widening range of services directed towards businessmen.

If cotton dominated the Exchange, it was no less conspicuous in the composition and activities of the Manchester Chamber of Commerce, always the most public face and vocal expression of the business community. Yet numerically the Chamber was much less impressive than the Exchange, with only 229 members in 1825, 484 in 1860 and 1,108 in 1900.[55] More so than the Exchange which never faced effective competition from local markets, the Chamber, while still extending well beyond Manchester, suffered from the rise of local chambers, as formed at Warrington (1876), Oldham (1882), Bolton and Blackburn (both 1892). Moreover, the representativeness of the Chamber perhaps diminished over time, with an increasing weight towards merchants rather than producers, and towards larger rather than smaller firms. Yet even within these limits, it remained the regional embodiment of industrial and commercial opinion, second to none as an influence on government policy-making, and as such the standard-bearer of Lancashire's devotion to free trade, the most obvious ideological face of the business community.[56]

Nevertheless, free trade was a much more divisive issue than is sometimes suggested. For in the 1820s and 1830s, as recent research has suggested, economic views in Manchester were no more uniform than in London or the nation as a whole.[57] Within the Chamber of Commerce itself it was much easier to secure united support for campaigns such as that against the excise duty on printed calicoes or the duty on raw cotton than on the export of machinery, the Copyright of Designs, or most famously, the Repeal of the Corn Laws. This last bitterly divided the Chamber. It occasioned a formal split in its ranks in 1845 with the formation of a rival Manchester Commercial Association, led by moderates such as Richard Birley, J. A. Turner and William Neild. Only in the calmer mood of the 1850s did the two Associations reunite as a serviceable instrument of the business community, or as Cobden liked to think of it, 'the only power in the State possessed of the wealth and political influence sufficient to counteract in some degree the feudal governing class of this country'.[58] As such it supported the completion of the edifice of free trade, for example, the Anglo-French Commercial Treaty of 1860, while promoting a wide variety of causes of primary interest to the merchants and producers of Lancashire. Above all, it successfully informed government, at every point, of the market needs of the cotton industry, particularly with regard to India, acting as a vital collective organ of economic self-defence. In many ways, the Manchester Chamber remained well into the twentieth century the most influential of provincial business associations, with easy access to Whitehall and Westminster.[59]

If the Manchester Chamber acted as the interface between the industry and the government, equally vital to the business community was the local interaction between capital and labour. To some extent, of course, this was a relationship between master and men, the workplace examined in chapter five below. In some ways, employers guarded no right more jealously than that to manage in their own factories, repudiating any interference by the state, workmen and fellow masters. Yet the ideal of an individual wage bargain between master and worker was to be progressively eroded in the cotton trade after 1830, as both groups engaged in collective associations, at first for purposes of conflict yet gradually as the basis of the impressive regime of co-existence. Undoubtedly, businessmen in the 1830s abhorred in theory combinations of both masters and men, yet in no sphere was the orthodoxy of political economy so rapidly displaced as in labour relations. Already in the 1830s millowners were ready to form collective associations to resist the usurpation of their 'authority' by trade unions, with the Preston Masters' Association the model for other towns. The Preston Strike of 1853–54 not only reactivated the local masters' associations but led to the creation of an industry-wide body, the 'Lancashire Master Spinners and Manufacturers'. By the 1860s, masters' associations had been active at Ashton, Blackburn, Bolton, Burnley, Hyde, Manchester, Oldham, Stockport and Wigan. The Wigan masters failed to sustain the legality of the bond by which it held its members together (it was dismissed as a restraint of trade) but masters' associations remained both numerous and formidable.

Yet, most importantly, associations among masters and men were not simply battalions engaged in industrial warfare. By the 1840s they had already turned to peaceful bargaining, the instruments by which joint lists of prices and earnings were agreed.[60] Such conciliatory purposes also encouraged the tendency towards district organisations, signalled by the formation of the North and North-East Lancashire Cotton Spinners' and Manufacturers' Association in 1866, the model for a whole series of regional associations in the later nineteenth century. Despite therefore the hankerings of some employers for 'Free Labour' and despite the recurrence of violent industrial conflict in parts of Lancashire in the 1870s, it was the readiness of masters to combine and to negotiate collectively with men which so impressed late nineteenth-century observers of industrial relations.

The Royal Exchange, the Manchester Chamber of Commerce and the numerous employers' associations provided, therefore, the most permanent structures by which the business community was formally organised in its relations with the market, the state and the working class. Nevertheless, there also emerged a variety of temporary and *ad hoc* associations, supported by and indicative of the interests, aspirations and ideals of the business community. These were by no means confined to Manchester and its central business district. Thus, in the 1840s, growing dependence upon Indian markets for the products of the towns of north Lancashire, encouraged in Blackburn the formation of 'an Association for effecting the Abolition of the East India Company's Monopoly of Salt', and one for 'Effecting a Reduction of the Duty on Tea', *ad hoc* groups which merged in 1846 into a more permanent Blackburn Commercial Association, designed on the model of the Manchester Chamber, as a 'means for centralising and giving adequate expression to the opinions of the manufacturers of this district, with respect to the questions of foreign policy and commercial importance'.[61]

Among such questions, none was more important for the future of the cotton industry than the supply of raw cotton, already a concern of the far-sighted in the 1840s but made obvious to all by the Cotton Famine of 1861–65, with its dire economic and social results.[62] In 1857 Thomas Bazley, as we have seen, one of Manchester's leading citizens and then President of the Manchester Chamber, called for the setting up of a 'Cotton League', from which the Cotton Supply Association resulted. It aimed to encourage the growth of cotton throughout the world, but with its eye most clearly on India and, to a lesser extent, Australia. The failure of India to meet Lancashire's needs was ascribed in part to the maladministration of the East India Company, and strong advocates of *laissez-faire* at home, such as Henry Ashworth, were driven to propose state intervention in India to remove the effects of bad government. The Cotton Supply Association failed to attain the stature of the Anti-Corn Law League, raising only small funds (£2,890 *p.a.* 1861–69), and most masters took comfort in the expected short duration of the Cotton Famine. Even so, the government of India made real concessions to the needs of Lancashire on this issue, marking the greater impact on policy which the industrial interest could now exert.[63] From the 1860s, Indian issues continued to command the greatest interest among the business community, above all the issue of Indian Cotton Duties. Against this infraction of the openness of the Indian market, the Manchester Chamber spearheaded, from 1874 a campaign which eventually succeeded in 1882, although this battle was to be replayed in the 1890s.[64]

Intimately connected with India too was the complicated issue of the bimetallic standard, a proposal increasingly supported in the 1880s and 1890s as a solution to falling prices and the effective devaluation of the Indian rupee, the most obvious symptoms of the sense of economic malaise known as the 'Great Depression'.[65] The notion that a joint gold and silver standard would increase prices and restore markets was attractive to many in the cotton industry, although not to a consistent majority. Manchester was never a 'Silver Citadel', save by comparison with the even weaker degree of support elsewhere, with her main allies found among Liverpool merchants, City of London financiers and disgruntled agrarians. For most cotton men, the 'depression', in so far as it existed at all, had real, not monetary, explanations and for most, the solution lay in cost-cutting and technological modernisation.

Interestingly, in the 1880s and 1890s, the Bimetallic League competed for popular attention with a second movement, which in some ways undermined its premises. This was the movement for the creation of the Manchester Ship Canal, which, while it by no means united the business community, attempted to provide an economic response to the problems of costs of production in the cotton industry. For example, Rylands, one of its leading business supporters, expected to save £5,000 *per annum* on his imports of raw cotton alone.[66] But the projecting of the Canal was, as recent research has helped emphasise, both an attempt at 'popular capitalism' and a classic example of provincial self-assertion within the business community, stressing the values of voluntarism, civic pride and free trade.[67]

The Manchester Ship Canal, the Bimetallic League, and the Cotton Supply Association all in different ways illustrate the collective interests, ideals and aspirations of the business community. None of them secured unanimous support, none, that is, served to organise businessmen into a complete collective entity, for already by the 1840s, the business community had been too large, too diverse and too fragmented to be mobilised behind single issues. Even so, each of these campaigns had constituted an important joint effort to regulate the market conditions within which individual enterprises would continue to compete. As such they formed an effective complement to the more permanent institutions which linked employers, merchants and the market. Yet in many ways the unique character of Lancashire's businessmen was to be best revealed by the part they played beyond the firm, the factory and the counting-house.

## Businessmen, politics and the nation

The impact of industrial change in Lancashire and the emergence of her distinctive business community was to be most vividly proclaimed to Victorian Britain by the activities of the Anti-Corn Law League (1839–1846), the greatest of nineteenth-century pressure groups. For not only did the League cast a long local shadow as an example of Radical organisation and business pressure but it acquired national eminence for its part in the Repeal of the Corn Laws in 1846, the supposed victory of 'the lords of the loom' over 'the lords of the soil'.[68] This 'myth' of the League's influence has been widely debunked by

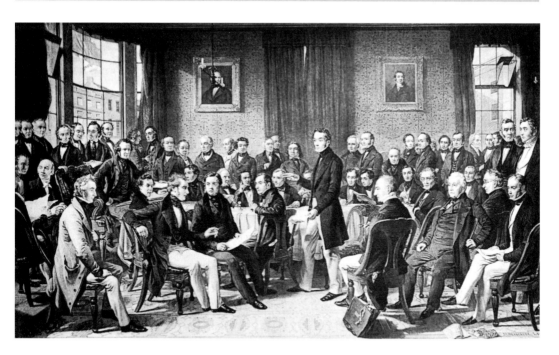

FIGURE 43. Cobden addressing the Anti-Corn Law League Council. In the 1840s the League became the most effective embodiment of the collective power of Lancashire's cotton-ocracy. Source: E. W. Watkin, *Alderman Cobden of Manchester* (Ward, Lock, Bowden & Co., 1891), facing p. 101.

modern historians, but the apparent success of the League in influencing the Repeal of the Corn Laws typified for the nation and the locality the collective power of the 'cottonocracy' and its ideological expression by the 'Manchester School'. This term, coined by Disraeli, became synonymous with the self-interested pursuit of free trade, *laissez-faire* and a non-interventionist foreign policy, ideals promoted by League leaders such as Cobden, Bright and Ashworth. Such supposedly typical beliefs of the 'Hard Times' variety of entrepreneur were satirised by Dickens, and were later central to the attack launched on 'Manchesterism' by the German Socialists of the Chair, and their English *epigoni*, the Tariff Reformers. But in Victorian England, there was perhaps no more powerful political myth than that of Lancashire's millowners waging successful war against the nation's territorial elite. This view had been persuasively generated by contemporary chroniclers such as Prentice and Dunckley, and the League seemed widely to typify the successful class politics of the cotton industry, a collective repudiation of aristocratic government and the assertion of moral values of the industrial elite.[69] Commemoratively and symbolically, J. R. Herbert's painting of the Council of the League provided an ideal image of the serious-minded, respectable and powerful 'sturdy burghers' of mid-nineteenth-century Lancashire. Here was no revolutionary body but one which sought a degree of power and influence commensurate with its economic authority.

The benefits of this symbolism and mythology were considerable in nineteenth-century Radical politics and, undoubtedly, the League did

FIGURE 44. Born in Sussex, Cobden's business career in Lancashire (in Manchester and Sabden) was relatively unsuccessful. But his foremost role in municipal politics, in the Anti-Corn Law League and in national politics established 'Manchester Man' as 'International Man'. Source: E. W. Watkin, *Alderman Cobden of Manchester* (Ward, Lock, Bowden & Co., 1891), frontispiece.

express a class-based 'pride of order', rooted largely in economic interest but suffused with religious, moral and cultural overtones. But the League was more successful as myth than as reality and, while it was largely sustained by the subscribers, organisers and leaders from Lancashire, it never wholly united the business community. As we have already seen in the case of the Manchester Chamber, the Repeal campaign divided the commercial elite, even if the disagreement was more over the means of achieving, than the end of, free trade. Many, too, were anxious to repudiate the Radical political ambitions of Cobden and Bright and were too closely identified with local Tory politics to take up Repeal. In Preston, for example, millowners, to the disbelief of Cobden, petitioned in favour of the retention of the Corn Laws, 'led by the nose by the neighbouring squires into whose pockets the bread tax goes'.[70] Yet despite this unrepentant 'class' treachery, the League was emphatically the creation of Lancashire's cotton lords and was, as Cobden believed, 'the greatest of modern combinations'.[71]

The class overtones expressed in the Corn Law struggle had also been evoked by the long controversy over the Factory Acts.[72] In particular, although some masters as early as 1830 were ready to accept legislative regulation, the threat of a Ten Hours Bill led to sustained and orchestrated opposition. A Manchester Committee to oppose this was more or less permanently in operation from 1833 and, even after the passing of the Ten Hours Act in 1847, it remained in being as the Factory Law Amendment Association and, later, the National Association of Factory Occupiers, a body still active in the 1870s. These groups aimed to bring collective pressure to bear on government, to

FIGURE 45. John Bright, of Rochdale, and MP for Manchester, exemplified the creed of the 'Manchester School', yet turned increasingly towards national, rather than Lancashire politics. Source: R. B. O'-Brien, *John Bright: A Monograph* (Smith, Elden & Co., 1910), frontispiece.

influence the shape of legislation and to challenge it in the courts. Many opponents of legislation were 'benevolent' employers, who rejected state intervention in favour of voluntary regulation, and only slowly learnt to value the role of factory inspectors in ensuring uniformity of regulation. They also held that 'ignorant' legislation represented a clear economic threat to an industry dependent upon foreign trade, as well as a stigma uniquely visited on the mill-owning class. 'It is,' the masters declared, 'the duty of Manufacturers, as a body to sustain the right estimation of the class to which they belong'.[73]

Such arguments were sufficient to produce a solid stand against the Ten Hours Act, with, for example, two petitions against in 1847, one signed by 353 firms, employing 123,226 hands, one in May by 483 firms employing 129,256 hands. Against this the number of masters avowedly in favour was small. Nevertheless, as with attitudes to trade unions, the remarkable factor is the speed with which cotton men came to accept and positively appreciate the benefits of the Factory Acts. Thus by the late 1850s, when it was proposed to apply the Factory Acts to bleaching, although the bleachers themselves opposed this extension, it won the backing of leading cotton spinners. Factory legislation could now to some extent be regarded as self-imposed regulation and no longer the revenge of a defeated body of landed squires, smarting from the Repeal of the Corn Laws. Interestingly, the ideal of the voluntary regulation of industry survived but within the strictly limited field of steam boilers, where the Manchester Steam Users' Association was a successful attempt at collective self-regulation, originating 'among the manufacturers themselves . . . surrounded by evils which they themselves could remove'.[74]

No subsequent political issue generated the same passion and collective *angst* in Lancashire as the Corn Laws and Factory Acts. These were issues which served to define, and to resolve, the tension between the new industrial elite and the traditional aristocratic state. Later issues lacked this resonance, partly as the cotton masters became accepted within the state, and partly because no issue encompassed to the same degree the interests of an increasingly complex and diverse business community. There was not, therefore, an exclusive politics of business in Lancashire and a 'party of the cotton manufacturers' did not emerge. Instead the business community was divided along the existing party lines, defined more by religion than by class or economic interest. To some extent, well before the Reform Act of 1832, businessmen had been integrated into the political nation, at the level of county and urban politics, despite the absence of many parliamentary seats open to their direct control. The eruption of the issue of the Corn Laws never really threatened this pre-existing party division within the business community and hence the recurrent attempts to mobilise the

FIGURE 46. W. H. Hornby was not only an 'active citizen' as Mayor and MP for Blackburn, but also a leading Tory paternalist employer. This photograph shows Hornby's statue in Blackburn town centre. (Photograph courtesy of Lancashire County Library, Blackburn Local Studies Collection)

cotton industry behind the Radical aims of the Manchester School, for example, peace, land reform, and financial reform repeatedly failed.[75] Cobden regularly bemoaned this decline in entrepreneurial activism, with the cotton masters readily 'bamboozled' by aristocrats such as Palmerston and Russell. As is well known, the 'Manchester School' suffered badly in the rallying of the bourgeoisie to Palmerston, losing several seats including those of Cobden and Bright in the election of 1857.[76] Yet this defeat was not as complete as is sometimes thought and left in place a continuous body of Radical opinion, which would reassert its presence in the National Reform Union, the Cobden Club and the structures of the Liberal Party after 1867.

WILLIAM HENRY HORNBY
1805 – 1884
FIRST MAYOR OF BLACKBURN
1851
MEMBER OF PARLIAMENT
FOR THE BOROUGH
1857 – 1869

ERECTED 1912

On the other hand, the 'Conservative opinion, disguised as moderate Liberalism' which Lord Stanley had discerned in Lancashire's towns came into the open after 1867. This drift towards 'the politer faith' helped the Conservative Party to dominate Lancashire electorally until the Liberal revival of 1903–06.[77] But this dominance was also sustained by the Toryism of the working-classes, aided in some cases by the social practices of paternalistic employers, such as W. H. Hornby of Blackburn. Yet both parties were able to benefit from the mobilisation of the factory as a political unit, and there was never to be any simple identity between the business community and the political community.[78] In so far as businessmen presented a collective political profile, commentators in the later nineteenth and early twentieth centuries looked to Manchester's North-West constituency, with its sizeable number of plural (business) votes, as the barometer of commercial opinion.[79] More widely, however, as the pre-eminent leaders of local society, members of the mercantile and industrial elite laid strong claim to parliamentary seats well into the twentieth century, while contributing amply to local and national organisations.

## Business in the community

The business community in Lancashire overlapped not only with the political elite but it provided in many spheres 'public persons and social leaders'. This was widely true in terms of county government, with employers and merchants active as justices of the peace, and willing to take on more honorific roles as deputy lieutenants and high sheriffs in Lancashire and its surrounding counties.[80] Yet to a considerable extent businessmen were also the most active citizens in municipal governance. This was particularly so before 1870 as is clear from even the most cursory glance at the rosters of civic dignity and is confirmed by more detailed study both of unreformed and reformed municipalities.[81] Thus the most 'feudal' of bodies, Sir Oswald Mosley's Court Leet in Manchester drew upon the willing service of leading businessmen as did the Court Leet of the Earl of Stamford at Ashton.[82] The administration of the Poor Law in its old and new forms also attracted businessmen, as did the growing number of Improvement Commissions and Local Boards, whose chairmen in particular were drawn from the wealthy. Most importantly, the town councils gradually established under the Municipal Reform Act of 1835 were, at least between 1838 and 1875, consistently dominated by cotton masters and merchants, with an even greater number of alderman and mayors drawn from their ranks. Businessmen were not, of course, necessarily men of broad municipal vision and some critics feared that the interests of cotton rather than the well-being of the community might predominate. But albeit irregularly by the 1860s, there was a prevailing tone of municipal improvement and civic pride, embracing not only drains, paving and gas works but libraries, art galleries and public parks. 'The duty and dignity of municipal action' had become an important part of the identity of the business community, exemplifying an ideal of citizenship and not simply a prudential check on rising rate bills.

Municipal endeavour was, however, always tempered by the anxiety not to forestall or deter voluntary efforts. In this field lay a further pre-eminent contribution of the business community to Lancashire society. For it patronised a vast array of philanthropic and cultural endeavours, no doubt merely a few crumbs compared with the total wealth generated by the cotton industry but substantially more than many other comparable centres of wealth and business. The total universe of private philanthropy was immense, ranging from doles for the poor, hospitals, town halls, parks, churches, missions, schools, libraries, mechanics institutes, housing to art galleries. To take just two examples of the last, T. C. Horsfall in promoting the Manchester Art Museum hoped through art to regenerate the working classes of

Ancoats, while the Whitworth Art Gallery was founded in 1889 as 'a perpetual gratification to the people of Manchester' in memory of the engineer Sir Joseph Whitworth.[83] This philanthropic effort can neither be quantified nor assessed for its contribution to social welfare. Yet it most effectively contributes to an understanding of the business community's perception of itself as a collectivity, ready to accept the duties of wealth, and to set out an ideal of welfare and citizenship. This was a combination, as Henry Ashworth put it, of 'self-interest and social reforms' which reinforced the class pride of Britain's cotton lords, a partial moralisation of the capitalist which was ultimately more significant for British society than the vaunted 'gentrification of the industrialist'.[84]

Yet this voluntary activity did not, of course, neglect the economic interests of the business community. This was particularly the case with regard to technical and commercial education, where businessmen had not only originally been concerned to promote mechanics' institutes but later contributed importantly to technical schools.[85] There was also an important overlap between businessmen and Manchester's lively scientific community which was expressed above all in support for Owens' College, set up with funds from John Owens, Manchester merchant, and where the needs of local business were met by attention to science and technology as well as modern languages and political economy.[86] Yet the college was also designed to provide a classical education for the sons of local men, some excluded by religious tests from Oxbridge. Hence, traditional 'liberal' pursuits were by no means neglected, enabling Sir Thomas Bazley, when pressing for the college to become Manchester University, plausibly to deny that it was 'secretly devoted to calico'.[87]

### Conclusion: *Fin-de-siècle*: change and decline in the business community

The cohesion and identity of the business community which had dominated Lancashire between 1830 and 1880 were to be undermined and transformed in several important ways in the decades before 1914. Firstly, changes in business organisation diluted the individualistic and familial character of the industry. From the 1870s, a growing number of firms adopted limited liability, for example, the Brights of Rochdale and Potters of Dinting Vale.[88] This did not immediately result in a separation of ownership from control but it heralded the transformation of the firm from a dynamic profit-maximising centre into one designed to provide a *rentier* income for burgeoning family members. Ultimately one of marked features of Lancashire cotton industry, compared for example with that of France, was the failure to sustain a dynastic tradition into the twentieth century. Here the amalgamations and combinations of the 1890s were the most potent solvent of the old business individualism, for with the 'combining' of up to a hundred family firms in associations such as the Bleachers, Calico-Printers, and Fine Cotton Spinners, there was a conscious recognition that the reign of the 'cotton kings' (as individual rulers) was over, to be succeeded by the collective sovereignty of the 'trust'.[89]

Such changes both expressed and further encouraged the growth of a *rentier* class sustained by the cotton industry. The industry had always shown a marked tendency to invest in other sectors of the economy, with dozens of cotton lords becoming directors of home and overseas companies, especially in railways and minerals. But arguably, in the age of empire such investments were to be increasingly remote from the business needs of Lancashire. In particular, the City of London, often charged with neglecting the needs of industry, now acted as the conduit of industrially-generated funds to the peripheries of the world economy.[90]

These changes may also have deepened the 'fracture' of the business community between those 'who looked to protect their interests by investment at home and stimulation of the local economy' and 'those merchants and manufacturers whose business horizons were international in scope' suggested by the historian of the financing of the Manchester Ship Canal.[91] Yet such a clear distinction lacks conviction both analytically and empirically. For not only was the Canal itself conceived as part of the international economy, but it was sustained by investment from the City of London and found key local supporters among those such as Sir Joseph Lee who had been among the most internationally-minded of Manchester's business elite.[92]

Such 'internationalisation' had been a marked feature of the business community since the mid-nineteenth century. For this was a necessary part of an industry whose prosperity depended on the world market (however much some firms might distinctively look to the home trade) and which by the early twentieth century was evolving world-wide bodies, such as the International Cotton Federation, formed in 1904.[93] Manchester had also been in the forefront of the world-wide revolution in transport and communications led by men such as Sir Edward Watkin and Sir John Pender, with the former ready to build the Channel Tunnel as part of his mentor Cobden's cosmopolitan message of free trade and peace.[94] By the 1880s, some businessmen had been ready to set up mills abroad, partly as the result of the very failure of that Cobdenite message, and of the need to get behind growing tariff barriers. Thus J. H. Gartside, of Ashton, the founder of Gartside & Co., controlled mills not only in Ashton but Malaunay in Seine-Inferieure. He was also engaged in mining enterprises in Mexico, British

Columbia and South America. Yet this new generation had discarded much of the Cobdenite message and Gartside combined direct investment overseas with the advocacy of military drill in state-aided schools, in order to improve physique and to instil the military spirit he believed to be an essential source of national strength.[95] Gartside was no doubt unusual in the extent of his international commitment, yet few Lancashire businessmen were able to shelter their fortunes from the fluctuations of the world economy.

Other changes in the business community both weakened links between families and firms while strengthening its collective organisation. Thus the continued tendency towards associations among masters and men led to almost industry-wide agreements, which immensely simplified the tasks of the entrepreneur and permitted the emergence of a new type of businessman, concerned not only with the profits of his own firm but with the collective good of the industry as a whole.[96] This change informed the activities of men such as Sir Charles Macara, and led to the emergence of important bodies such as the Cotton Employers' Parliamentary Association. Above all, quite unusually among heavily-unionised industries, union leaders in Lancashire were closely linked with the employers, with whom they often, by the 1890s, sat on the bench, and both sides held to beliefs in arbitration and conciliation. Here was almost a solidarity of producers, masters and men together, based on technical knowledge of industry and its problems, a world apart from the ideas of the solidarity of labour which were stirring in the metropolitan world of new unionism in the late 1880s.[97]

These changes in economic and industrial organisation necessarily affected the lifestyle of the employers. Firstly, residence near factories, or even in Lancashire, became less essential with the growth of professional management and with accelerated means of transport. By the later nineteenth century, residential drift towards southern England was accelerated, although the leafier suburbs of Manchester and its Cheshire borders remained more typical, while the Lakes grew in appeal.[98] Secondly, this trend helped to undermine the local focus of the social, cultural, and political life of the business community. This strongly affected the practice of citizenship, with a growing abstention from municipal government and the dissolution of 'local patriotism' by the 1880s. Thirdly, and most emphatically, the decline of employer-based Toryism and the rise of 'Progressivism', Labour, and the New Liberalism removed the political landmarks familiar to the old cotton bosses.[99] Finally, the First World War itself proved a watershed, for it led to a greater degree of collective organisation within the industry at the behest of the state while undermining many cherished business beliefs, including that in free trade.[100] War also accelerated the challenges of

Indian tariffs and Japanese competition which would preoccupy businessmen struggling for survival in the interwar years.[101] As a result, the business community in twentieth-century Lancashire was simply that, a community of businessmen; it had lost the unusual degree of social, political and civic identity which the cottonocracy had achieved in Victorian Britain.

CHAPTER 5

# The Factory Workforce

MICHAEL WINSTANLEY

BY the 1830s and 1840s, as the magnitude of the changes in cotton manufacture became manifest, the world beat a path to Lancashire's door, hungry for information. The factories and the towns which they spawned were alien worlds, unimaginable to those not personally acquainted with them and capable of engendering both amazement and despair among those who visited them. Admiration for unprecedented technological advances and mechanical ingenuity was matched by fears that the factory system was alienating and debasing, threatening to undermine the foundations of civil society.

Some commentators were unashamedly eulogistic. 'If a spinner can now produce as much in a day as he could last century have produced in a year', observed Edward Baines junior, 'and if goods which formerly required eight months to bleach, are now bleached in two days, surely these are the very causes of the amazing extension of the manufacture, and are therefore, subjects of rejoicing, not of lamentation . . . The factory system is not to be judged as though it were insusceptible of improvement', he admitted, but this could safely be left to the intelligent, humane manufacturers.[1] Andrew Ure wrote in a similar vein in 1835 of the benefits which mechanisation had brought to workers.

> On my recent tour . . . through the manufacturing districts, I have seen tens of thousands of old, young and middle-aged of both sexes . . . earning abundant food, raiment, and domestic accommodation, without perspiring at a single pore, screened meanwhile from the summer's sun and the winter's frost, in apartments more airy and salubrious than those of the metropolis in which our legislative and fashionable aristocracies assemble. In those spacious halls the benignant power of steam summons around him his myriads of willing menials, and assigns to each the regulated task, substituting for painful muscular effort on their part, the energies of his own gigantic arms, and demanding in return only attention and dexterity to correct such little aberrations as casually occur in his workmanship.[2]

To others, however, these new towns appeared rootless, impersonal, brutalising, devoid of social cohesion. No-one had prepared Charles Mott, Assistant Poor Law Commissioner, for what he was to encounter when he was posted to these 'manufacturing districts' in 1838 to assist in the implementation of the Poor Law Amendment Act. He was shocked at 'the pitiable condition' of this 'extraordinary district', inhabited by people 'scarcely removed from savages' who lived in a 'state of moral degredation' and whose children were 'reared to habits which totally annihilate every moral and social obligation'.[3] A similarly depressing picture was painted by Engels in his portrayal of the working class in Manchester in the 1840s and by Charles Dickens in his unsympathetic portrayal of Coketown in his novel *Hard Times*.

This 'first industrial society' was intensely scrutinised and aroused strong passions. Its possible effects on the family, gender relations, children, public health, social structure, the distribution of wealth, political conflict and power were widely discussed. It also attracted the attention of government. Select Committees and Royal Commissions sought to ascertain if regulatory intervention was necessary and, if it was, whether legislation could be introduced without damaging the profitability of industry or eroding the 'proper' responsibilities which

FIGURE 47. An early spinning team at work on a long mule, unusually showing women acting as piecers. The strength needed to return the mule is implied by the man's forward-leaning stance; a young scavenger or little piecer is shown under the mule carriage on the left. (Photograph courtesy of Manchester Public Libraries)

individuals, private enterprise and voluntary agencies had for maintaining and enhancing the quality of life.

This chapter seeks to describe the society of these new cotton towns, how it changed over the course of the century and how this affected people in their daily lives. It is important to bear in mind throughout that generalisations about textile Lancashire can mask significant differences between districts. Cotton towns were as varied as the yarns and cloths which they produced. Life within them was closely woven and finely textured, its pattern and qualities dependent on a complex series of processes. Furthermore, not all of their working populations were directly engaged in cotton (table 5.1). Many were employed in ancillary trades which supplied the industry or in service sectors of the economy. What was common to all of them, however, was the dominating presence of the factory. Work within it was the primary determinant of most individuals' and families' lifestyles and fortunes. Any attempt to understand the broader social fabric, therefore, must begin with an appreciation of just who the factory workforce were and what they did.

Table 5.1  *The relative importance of cotton manufacture in Lancashire boroughs, 1911*

| | Cotton workers as % of all employed workers | | Total female employment as % of all females over ten |
|---|---|---|---|
| | *Males* | *Females* | |
| Blackburn | 36.41 | 74.14 | 59.19 |
| Bolton | 24.99 | 61.86 | 43.93 |
| Burnley | 40.06 | 76.84 | 56.29 |
| Bury | 22.63 | 61.69 | 50.19 |
| Manchester | 4.01 | 12.42 | 39.40 |
| Oldham | 31.20 | 69.12 | 46.08 |
| Preston | 25.42 | 68.16 | 54.32 |
| Rochdale | 28.02 | 60.03 | 48.37 |
| Salford | 7.29 | 22.99 | 38.63 |
| Warrington | 0.69 | 18.89 | 29.80 |
| Wigan | 3.81 | 46.66 | 37.19 |

Figures including bleaching, dyeing and finishing trades
Source: Census 1911, Lancashire Table 26.

## The workforce

As Geoff Timmins has explained (chapter 2), by the 1830s mechanisation and steam power had been applied to virtually every stage in the process of transforming raw cotton into finished cloth. As Ure's remarks suggest, this had three major implications for the workforce. First it created an extreme division of labour. Workers were far from being an undifferentiated mass of 'hands'; they were engaged to perform specific tasks, whose large number defies detailed description. Secondly, it reduced most processes to routine machine minding and tending, the pace of which was largely determined by the speed and reliability of the technology. This required operators to be alert and vigilant, but it apparently demanded little in the way of skill and removed the need for formal apprenticeships. Thirdly, it eliminated most heavy manual labour, enabling children and women to be employed to a degree which was unparalleled in non-textile industries. What it did not change, however, was the method of payment. Piece work, through which wages were related to the individual worker's output rather than daily or hourly rates, remained the norm for most adults in spinning and weaving, although not for their young assistants whom they paid out of their earnings, or for men engaged in the manual jobs which remained. Until the hesitant and limited application of ring spinning and automatic looms in the late nineteenth and twentieth centuries, no further major technological breakthroughs occurred to disturb the basic pattern and organisation of work which had emerged by the 1830s. Productivity gains came rather from the diffusion of technology and from refinements to existing machines which enhanced their efficiency by improving reliability or permitting faster running.

Within the mills, the jobs which individuals undertook were largely determined by their age and gender. Men dominated jobs which involved physical strength such as the preliminary cleaning and sorting of raw cotton, the preparation of cloth for dyeing and printing, warehousing, haulage and transportation, and stoking boilers. In comparison to spinning, much of this work was poorly paid, low status and undertaken in unhealthy environments. The unpleasant working conditions of strippers and grinders, responsible for cleaning and maintaining the carding machines, deteriorated still further as revolving flat cards replaced the earlier fixed card and cylinder in the 1890s, increasing the dust and floating cotton fibre in the atmosphere. This contributed to high incidences of tuberculosis, bronchitis, asthma and byssinosis amongst such workers.[4] Much of the poorly paid, physically arduous work in bleaching and dyeing was also dangerous because it involved exposure to strong poisonous chemicals, often in poorly ventilated rooms.[5]

Tacklers, mechanics, tapesizers, engravers and calico printers, all relatively skilled workers, were all men, as were mule spinners, from the second quarter of the century. Women, however, were recorded as operating short mules prior to this period and why they were not more extensively employed thereafter has remained something of an enigma. Theoretically, the application of steam power to hand mules should have reduced the need for manual labour, while the new self-actor seemingly transformed previously skilled operators into mere overlookers or minders. These developments should have allowed employers to dispense with expensive male labour in favour of cheaper women and juveniles, as indeed promoters of the new technology had promised.

Several factors probably account for employers' continuing willingness to employ male spinners. Not least of these is the fact that the hand mule's efficiency was substantially enhanced in the 1820s and 1830s by increasing the number of spindles per machine or by doubling up two shorter mules and operating them in tandem. Both of these practices increased rather than decreased the manual effort and dexterity required, but they also had the effect of substantially increasing the male operators' productivity. This contributed to the periodic crises of over-production and widespread unemployment, weakening the ability of spinners to resort to industrial action to resist drastic reductions in piece rates and manning levels. Edwin Butterworth described in 1842 the consequences of this for workers in his native town.

> About 1825–6 the price paid to spinners for work at one of the largest mills in Oldham was 5s. 10d. per 1000 hanks clear; the price now offered on the same size of mules and same counts is but 2s. 2d. per 1000 hanks. The wages of the spinners at the same place were 23s. per week, in 1842 their wages with double the number of spindles to work are but 19s. to 20s. . . . . Thirteen times the quantity of work is now produced by some spinners individually than was produced by the same parties in 1821 at a reduction of five pence per hundred hanks.[6]

Employers, therefore, were able to reduce both labour requirements and piece rates considerably without the need to employ women. Demand for female workers was, in any case, increasing in other sectors of the industry, especially in the powerloom weaving sheds which were expanding rapidly in south-east Lancashire from the mid-1820s. They were also extensively employed in the process of preparing cotton prior to spinning, and this sector must also have increased its labour requirements to sustain the output of rovings to keep the longer mules and self-actors in production. These developments diluted the threat which female labour posed to male spinners, therefore, reducing the pool of females on which manufacturers could draw, just as the incentive to employ them declined because of increases in male productivity.

The extent to which conditions in the labour market continued to work to the advantage of the male spinner during the rest of the century

is less clear, as is the question of whether mule spinning or minding self-actors could be considered a skilled trade. Although spinners succeeded in maintaining customary work practices, they did so only by further conceding to employers' demands for increased productivity and by sacrificing some of the pay differential they enjoyed over other workers. The number of spindles per mule increased on average from 109 in 1850 to 234 by 1890 and mule speeds increased from 5,000 revolutions per minute in 1839 to 11,000 by 1890, raising the amount of yarn produced per man-hour of spinning from just 0.8 lbs in 1845 to 2.3 lbs in 1892.[7]

FIGURE 48. The drawing process straightened the fibres and equalized the thickness of the cotton cardings into slivers prior to roving. Women and children, supervised by a male overseer, dominate this preparatory process. (Photograph courtesy of Manchester Public Libraries)

Some authors, therefore, have suggested that the mule spinners and self-actor minders were a contrived labour aristocracy whose enhanced pay and craft status were artificially maintained rather than dependent on skill.[8] The continued viability of their unions' exclusionary rules and practices depended on the collusion of employers who perceived advantages in retaining an hierarchical division of labour in which the spinners acted as supervisors, keeping order and control within the workplace. Spinners' recognition of their vulnerable position arguably made them compliant workers, overtly acknowledging the validity of their employers' free market philosophies. But mule spinners themselves would have disputed this portrayal, seeing themselves as independent, skilled operatives. Mary Freifeld has argued that they were right to do so. As long as variability in production could not be scientifically and technically rationalised or eliminated, spinners possessed a skill which

GAN MILL GIRLS, WARPING ROOM.

FIGURE 49. The warping room at Rylands Mill, Wigan, c. 1908. By this time all stages of textile production in the Wigan area, including spinning, were dominated by women, since men and youths were attracted to the mines and heavy industry by higher wages. (Photograph, Lancashire County Library Headquarters, Local Studies Collection)

gave them power because they 'retained their roles as keepers of the knowledge of production and managers of the labour process'.[9] Furthermore, Harold Catling, an ex-spinner himself, has vividly described how even self-actors were temperamental beasts requiring constant adjustment and tuning to perform reliably since the quality of the cotton rovings, the humidity and temperature of the workplace all fluctuated. 'Every operative spinner was firmly of the opinion that no two mules could ever be made alike. As a consequence he proceeded to tune and adjust each of his particular pair of mules with little respect for the intentions of the maker or the principles of engineering.' Inevitably, 'before very long, no two mules were ever alike'.[10] Skill, in other words, is relative and could be artificially constructed.

Male domination of mule spinning, however, was exceptional. Females over the age of thirteen comprised the majority of employees and the figure rose gradually over the period as weaving expanded and women increasingly replaced adolescent males on intermediate processes. Card and blowing room workers such as drawers, slubbers and rovers were invariably females, predominantly in their teens and twenties. Winders and warpers, employed in preparing yarn for use in weaving were also largely female. Unlike mule spinning, where each group of male workers enjoyed a degree of autonomy, these ancillary processes were supervised by overlookers who were invariably male, thus serving to emphasise women's subordinate position within the workforce. Once the cloth had been dyed or printed, the finishing stages, such as stitching pieces into continuous lengths, sewing on borders, ribboning, embroidery, light washing, folding and parcelling were also carried out by women, as too, of course, was much of the making up of cloth into garments and household linen. Irrespective of any skill involved, all these processes were devalued in terms of status and pecuniary reward. The widespread belief that female labour was intrinsically worth less, the argument that male wages had to support a family while women's work was part of the life cycle restricted to a relatively short interlude between leaving school and getting married, and women's socialisation which led them to accept subordinate positions in society, all contributed to this situation.

These rigid gender divisions were particularly characteristic of the spinning towns of south-east Lancashire. Weaving in these districts was also essentially viewed as women's work from the time powerlooms

FIGURE 50. Cotton operatives during the Cotton Famine (*Illustrated London News*, 22 November 1862, p. 564). This stylised representation of the workforce vividly depicts the differences in age, gender and social status of workers associated with most, but not all, of the processes involved in cotton manufacture.

| REELER | HOT–WATER WOMAN | | OVERLOOKER TO SELF–ACTING MULES | WEAVER | THROSTLE–DOFFER | |
|---|---|---|---|---|---|---|
| | HAND–MULE SPINNER | WINDER | | POWER–LOOM WEAVER | SELF–ACTING MINDER | JACK–TENTER |
| KNOCKER–UP | HALF–TIMER | SCAVENGER | THROSTLE–SPINNER | CARDER | POWER–LOOM WEAVER | |

were first introduced in the 1820s and 1830s. Adult males, generally able to obtain relatively well-paid employment in spinning or other trades in these towns, were unwilling to remain in a trade which offered nothing in the way of promotion prospects beyond the slim chance of becoming one of the limited number of overlookers, posts which were often passed down through families. The position of women in weaving consequently mirrored that in spinning; it was low status, poorly paid and recruitment was controlled by employers or overlookers rather than by the workers themselves.

Further to the north-east, however, where the majority of the expansion in the coarse powerloom weaving occurred from mid-century, rigid, gendered status hierarchies were less evident. The majority of the adult weavers were still women but the relative paucity of alternative employment meant that many adult males also remained in the industry and worked alongside them. The female workforce was also older than that in spinning and carding and contained a relatively high proportion of married women, who remained at work until the 'double shift' of domestic duties and employment made it impossible for them to continue, even with assistance from their

FIGURE 51. A group of young Burnley mill girls. One wonders what the objective of the photographer was in taking such a photograph. All the girls are wearing aprons to protect their clothing and have their hair tied back. (Photograph courtesy of Lancashire County Library, Burnley Local Studies Collection)

husbands (table 5.2). Recruitment and training largely remained the preserve of the workers rather than employers or their representatives, and consequently family ties and social networks were important determinants of an individual's chance of obtaining a job within a mill. The higher proportion of adult men and women, combined with weavers' relative autonomy at work, meant that both sexes had a common interest in raising the status and remuneration of the trade, a shared commitment which was noticeably lacking elsewhere in the industry. The more egalitarian and less patriarchal culture of weaving settlements of north-east Lancashire was also reflected in the wage structure. Men and women were paid on the same piece rates and wage differentials narrowed noticeably in the late nineteenth century as more women graduated to become four loom weavers.[11]

Table 5.2 *Women's employment in 'Cotton Lancashire' boroughs, 1911*

|  | Females as % of cotton workforce | Married women as % of female cotton workforce |
|---|---|---|
| Blackburn | 61.72 | 36.50 |
| Bolton | 58.67 | 13.06 |
| Burnley | 58.01 | 36.75 |
| Bury | 63.90 | 30.20 |
| Manchester | 60.99 | 18.00 |
| Oldham | 55.70 | 24.00 |
| Preston | 66.91 | 30.19 |
| Rochdale | 57.64 | 27.66 |
| Salford | 60.65 | 19.93 |
| Warrington | 90.26 | 9.14 |
| Wigan | 84.64 | 8.13 |

Source: Census 1911, Lancashire Table 26.

Weaving and spinning towns, therefore, exhibited very different patterns of employment (table 5.3). These affected not just the nature of trade union activity and industrial relations, but contributed to the creation of very different set of values and attitudes.

Table 5.3 *Percentage of cotton workforce (male and female) employed in specific processes*

|  | Spinning | Weaving | Bleaching* |
|---|---|---|---|
| Blackburn | 6.44 | 67.60 | 0.65 |
| Bolton | 38.44 | 21.21 | 2.59 |
| Burnley | 4.09 | 75.84 | 1.11 |

|            | Spinning | Weaving | Bleaching★ |
|------------|----------|---------|------------|
| Bury       | 15.63    | 44.66   | 11.96      |
| Manchester | 19.35    | 17.00   | 28.79      |
| Oldham     | 46.99    | 12.54   | 0.25       |
| Preston    | 12.80    | 63.67   | 0.23       |
| Rochdale   | 33.02    | 20.29   | 4.89       |
| Salford    | 13.31    | 19.80   | 35.80      |
| Warrington | 17.22    | 54.39   | 0.24       |
| Wigan      | 32.91    | 27.65   | 1.28       |

Remainder accounted for by intermediate processes
★ Bleaching, Dyeing, Printing, Finishing: this census category is not exclusively cotton.
Source: Census 1911, Lancashire Table 26

## Child labour

All stages of production, apart from the initial handling of raw cotton and the finishing trades, relied to varying degrees on child labour. Unlike most adult workers, children were not generally paid on piece rates; they received weekly wages. In much of spinning and throughout the weaving towns of the north-east, they were not employed directly by the manufacturer but by operatives who engaged them to undertake a variety of menial tasks associated with the tending of machines. 'Little piecers' assisted spinners with the repairing of broken threads, helped to clean and oil the machines, swept up, replaced or 'doffed' bobbins or just ran general errands. Weavers relied on tenters to perform similar menial tasks related to the smooth running of the loom, thus increasing their ability to mind additional machines and enhancing their earning capacity. Juveniles in their late teens could be given more responsibility. In spinning, a youth could aspire to be a 'big piecer', supervising the operation of one of the pair of mules for a spinner, but still receiving only a daily wage paid out of the latter's piece-work earnings. In weaving, adolescents could be given their own loom or pair of looms to mind. Many of the relatively unskilled, intermediate stages of production in the cardroom or prior to weaving were also heavily dependent on relatively young workers.

The proportion of the workforce who were children under thirteen fluctuated dramatically over the century. After an apparent fall between the mid-1830s and 1850 to just 4.6 per cent, it rose to a peak of 14 per cent in 1874 and then dropped away steadily until the mid-1890s when there was a further marked reduction to around 5 per cent.[12] To some extent this reflected variations in the demand for child workers. As early as the 1840s it had been pointed out that, with the self-actor, 'the greater rapidity of the motions and complexity of the machine' made 'the employment of an older hand more advantageous', since he could take sole responsibility for minding one of the pair of machines.[13] The self-actor's greater reliability and productivity also provided the wherewithal for the spinner to pay the extra wages involved in employing an older juvenile. In weaving, however, technological developments, the increasing pace and labour intensity of work, lower wages and worker control of recruitment, all contrived to maintain the demand for child labour. It was widely believed that proficiency was enhanced by early training, so weavers preferred to hire children as young as possible, especially if they were members of their own families. As the weaving sector expanded from the 1850s it increased its share of the children employed in the industry from just 1 per cent to 43 per cent by 1890, and the numbers employed in it eventually surpassed those in spinning in 1885. By 1911, the absolute numbers of children under fourteen were much higher in weaving and, unlike spinning, the majority were girls (table 5.4)

Table 5.4  *Occupational breakdown of children under fourteen employed in 'Cotton Lancashire', 1911*

| | Males | % | Females | % | Females as % of sector |
|---|---|---|---|---|---|
| Card and Blowing Room Processes | 256 | 1.96 | 1,795 | 11.00 | 87.52 |
| Spinning Processes | 4,097 | 31.35 | 2,188 | 13.41 | 34.81 |
| Winding, Warping, etc | 1,106 | 8.46 | 1,201 | 7.36 | 52.06 |
| Weaving Processes | 4,757 | 36.40 | 9,852 | 60.37 | 67.44 |
| Other Processes | 1,195 | 9.14 | 397 | 2.43 | 24.94 |
| Workers Undefined | 883 | 6.76 | 756 | 4.63 | 46.13 |
| Bleaching, Printing, Dyeing | 774 | 5.92 | 131 | 0.80 | 14.48 |
| Total Workforce | 13,068 | 100.00 | 16,320 | 100.00 | 55.53 |

Source: Census 1911, Lancashire Table 22B.

FIGURE 52. Spinner, big and little piecer. This spinning team, lightly clad, barefoot and oil-stained, became the standard workgroup in mule spinning in south-east Lancashire. There was an above average incidence of cancer of the scrotum among spinners since the oil used to lubricate the spindles and shafting regularly penetrated their work clothes. (Photograph courtesy of Oldham Metropolitan Borough, Leisure Services, Local Studies Library)

By then, however, legislation had removed very young children from the workforce and regulated the labour of those in work.[14] Early attempts by the state to regulate the hours and conditions of children and juveniles in textile mills would appear to have been largely ineffective because they lacked adequate enforcement mechanisms. In the early 1830s, however, as longer mules increased spinners' demands for young assistants, a variety of groups pressed the government to take more effective action. It responded with the Factory Act of 1833 which prohibited the employment of any children under the age of nine and restricted those under thirteen to nine hours per day while requiring them to attend a school a minimum of two hours per day. Enforcement would appear to have been relatively successful, not just because of the appointment of inspectors but because of the insistence that parents and children provided documentary proof of age and school attendance.[15] The Factory Act in 1844 established what became known as the 'half-time system'. This Act did not seek to abolish child labour; in fact it lowered to eight the minimum age from which children could be employed. It limited the hours which under thirteens could work to six and a half per day in order to require them to attend school for three hours daily between Monday and Friday. For over a quarter of a century educationalists and social reformers regarded this as an ideal compromise and its principles were extended to encompass a range of other industries by the 1860s.[16] However, after the extension of elementary education provision and the gradual introduction of compulsory schooling for all children in the 1870s, the half-time system was increasingly viewed as an anachronism. The age at which half-timers could began work was raised to ten in 1874 (to be effective from 1876), eleven in 1893 and finally to twelve by an act of 1899, while local

authorities were given powers to stipulate conditions of educational attainment or attendance which had to be met before children could qualify to go part-time or undertake any full-time work before the age of fourteen.

Clark Nardinelli has argued that legislation was not primarily responsible for the decline in child labour. Rather it was parents' increasing earning capacity which removed the need for them to send their children out to work while providing the wherewithal to support them at school.[17] However, there is little evidence that parents approved of any restrictions on child employment, and Douglas Farnie is probably correct to conclude that the numbers of half-timers 'would have increased even faster if the minimum age for half-timers had not been raised in 1874'.[18] Well into the twentieth century, workers and their unions opposed every attempt to raise the age at which children could go part-time or to increase the educational requirements they had to meet to do so. They defended their right to send their children out to work and argued that such restrictions amounted to legislative tyranny which deprived poor families of income.[19] The majority of children left school as soon as they were able to, especially in the weaving districts, causing despair amongst their teachers whose attempts to construct a coherent curriculum were largely destroyed. Local education authorities, aware of strong parental support for the half-time system, were reluctant to stamp it out, although there were isolated instances, as in Bury, where they were largely effective in doing so, by introducing what amounted to a means test whereby families had to prove economic need.

But the cotton industry was increasingly anomalous by the end of the century in finding a useful role for young children in the workplace and in retaining such a degree of worker autonomy in recruitment. The cotton operatives were no match for the educationalists, socialists, reformers and the rest of the labour movement, who sustained a vigorous campaign throughout the 1890s and 1900s for the abolition of half-time. Their ideas were clearly in the ascendant in the years immediately preceding the First World War and were increasingly subscribed to by manufacturers. Proposals to abolish all forms of partial exemption before the age of fourteen, including half-time, were only delayed by the pressure of other parliamentary business and the outbreak of war in 1914. They were all swept away by the Education Act of 1918.[20]

## Trade unionism and industrial relations

Children were not alone in having their hours controlled by legislation. Early Factory Acts prohibited night work for juveniles in textile mills, laid down the maximum number of hours they could work each day,

FIGURE 53. The weaving shed, John Butterworth & Sons, Dale Mill, Waterfoot c. 1900. This crowded workplace provides a stark contrast to the deceptively spacious and airy interiors portrayed in early nineteenth-century prints. Vivid though such photographs are, they cannot convey the noise, humidity or fluff-laden atmosphere associated with mill work. (Photograph courtesy of Lancashire County Library, Rawtenstall Local Studies Collection)

introduced statutory meal breaks and imposed minimum safety regulations. These provisions were extended in 1844 to encompass women workers. A series of acts in 1847, 1850 and 1853 fixed the times of day during which women and under eighteens could be employed, and their hours were further restricted in 1875 to fifty six and a half per week.[21]

In an age where state intervention was generally regarded not just as unnecessary but as counterproductive, such legislation was justified on the grounds that these groups were not 'free agents'. They were deemed unable to determine their individual destiny independent of familial pressures, as adult males allegedly were. Nor were they viewed as capable of bargaining directly with employers. Male workers were well aware, however, that such restrictions had the effect of shortening their own working week and they were always active in campaigns which called for further state intervention. These initially appeared in the early 1830s in the form of Short Time Committees, re-emerged in the 1840s as the Ten Hours Movement and were reconstituted in the 1870s as the Factory Acts Reform Association.[22] But the precise distribution of rewards between capital and labour was regarded purely

as a matter for negotiation between masters and men. As Anthony Howe has demonstrated (chapter 4), employers gradually organised collectively to defend their interests, but they were also increasingly willing to establish formal negotiation procedures with their men. Their actions were matched by increasing unionisation on the part of the workers.

Despite some attempts in the early 1830s to form general unions which embraced workers from a variety of trades, cotton unionism was characterised by fragility, sectionalism and localism until the last quarter of the century.[23] It was primarily concerned with establishing piece-rate lists which ensured parity of pay for comparable work, whether it was for spinning yarn of different counts or for weaving cloth of specified width and quality.

During the 1830s technological advances and unco-ordinated, individual business decisions on the part of the manufacturers resulted in major cyclical crises of over-production. Not surprisingly these depressions were the occasion of particularly acrimonious disputes about piece rates and were especially bitter in 1836–7 and 1842.[24] Spinners' unionism only slowly recovered from the defeats of these years. By the 1850s, however, as the industry stabilised, disputes became less frequent and bitter and semi-permanent local organisations re-emerged. Union leaders also increasingly adopted a conciliatory stance and were often at pains to stress that 'it would be suicidal and dishonest in us to ask for any concession not warranted by the state of trade'.[25] Recognising their vulnerability to employer reprisals, they preferred to negotiate during recessions about the depth of proposed cuts in rates, although the rank and file were not always willing to accept the implications of this. It was during this decade that the new district lists were negotiated for different qualities of yarn, the forerunners of the Bolton and Oldham lists which came to govern the fine and coarse sectors respectively.[26] But, into the 1860s, spinners' unionism only aspired at best to a partial federation of poorly organised local associations.

Weavers in Blackburn were successful in obtaining a list which governed piece work in their district as early as 1853 and the East Lancashire Amalgamated Power Loom Weavers' Friendly Association, sometimes referred to as the First Amalgamation, was formed in 1858 to campaign for its wider acceptance. Like the spinners, its leaders tried to win the confidence of employers to establish formal negotiation procedures, but the rank and file often put their faith in industrial action. Bitter, extended strikes and lock-outs continued to characterise weaving, especially when employers proposed reductions in piece rates, most notably in 1878 when Blackburn weavers struck for twelve weeks against a 10 per cent cut. These stoppages invariably ended in defeat or an unsatisfactory compromise and led to drops in membership, over

FIGURE 54. Blackburn District Weavers, Winders and Warpers Association banner, now housed at Blackburn Museum. Banners celebrating workers' organisations or proclaiming the various causes which they championed were an integral part of public campaigns in textile Lancashire long before this elaborate example from the late nineteenth century was made. For a detailed study of the subject see John Gorman, *Banner Bright* (Allen Lane, 1973). (Photograph courtesy of John Gorman)

50 per cent in the last case.[27] Other workers found it even more difficult to sustain permanent organisations. A Cardroom Operatives' Association of the Northern District emerged in the boom years of the mid-1840s. In 1845, the radical *Manchester and Salford Advertiser* reported that 'scarcely a day passes without short-lived turnouts, chiefly on the part of the piecers and cardroom hands for the purpose of obtaining an increase in wages'.[28] Similar bursts of activity characterised subsequent booms but invariably collapsed in less auspicious times.

For the majority of cotton workers, therefore, union membership was sporadic. The pattern of industrial relations followed a predictable pattern. 'Demands for wage increases were made in good years, and wage reductions enforced during bad years'.[29] This process was frequently accompanied by industrial action, or threats to resort to it. The failure of the majority of cotton workers to achieve permanent or industry-wide organisations before the 1880s can be attributed to a variety of factors. The large numbers of juveniles and women in many sectors of the industry viewed their participation in the workforce as temporary and saw little need to commit themselves. Relatively low wages restricted the level of subscriptions which comparatively unskilled adult workers could afford and therefore restricted unions' abilities to offer such benefits as sickness or accident insurance, or to sustain unemployment pay during extended stoppages. 'Functional and locational specialisation' within the industry placed considerable barriers in the way of effective inter-district co-operation or agreement on piece rates; there was 'very little co-ordination and identity of interest', apart from exceptional instances such as the Preston lock out of 1853–4.[30] Last, but not least, employers' antagonism to any form of unionism only subsided slowly. 'Hands have no rights except for services rendered', observed the *Manchester Guardian*, the voice of the liberal manufacturing interest in 1853; 'any decision as to the mode of management must arise with the master and be controlled by him'.[31]

Employers' increasing recognition of the benefits of collective bargaining by the 1870s was matched by the formation of amalgamated unions which represented workers throughout the industry. The Amalgamated Association of Operative Cotton Spinners was formed in 1870, although it was only from the mid-1880s that it could claim to represent the bulk of the workforce throughout the county and that permanent officials were appointed at district level.[32] Only after deteriorating promotion prospects had encouraged big piecers to consider forming their own union in 1892 did spinners' unions generally encourage these subordinate workers to join them. The Amalgamated Weavers Association was formed in 1884 and the Amalgamated Association of Card and Blowing Room Operatives, restricted initially to strippers and grinders, was created two years later. The Twisters'

Amalgamation followed in 1890, the Warpdressers in 1894, and Cloth-lookers (warehousemen) in 1895.[33]

By 1914 cotton workers had become one of the most organised and powerful sectors of the British workforce. Approximately 10 per cent of all male trade unionists in the country and half of female union members were in cotton.[34] Over 90 per cent of spinners, 85 per cent of weavers and 50 per cent of bleachers and dyers were members.[35] The Cardroom Workers' Union was the sixth largest in the country. Cotton unions' potential power in the union movement had been substantially increased in 1895 by the introduction of block voting at the Trades Union Congress, and several of their leaders were elected to the post of T.U.C. chairman, including William Mullin of the cardroom operatives in 1911.[36] Their unions were not only among the largest in the country, they were also among the most centralised and bureaucratic. Their leaders did not conform to the popular image of fiery political orators but were more likely to be arithmeticians versed in the technical intricacies of their respective trades to enable them to appreciate the financial implications of the complex wage negotiations which centred around fine adjustments to piece rates. Success in competitive examinations became an important prerequisite for a union post at whatever level. To outsiders not acquainted with it, the cotton industry was an alien, impenetrable world whose inhabitants spoke a foreign language replete with technical jargon and mathematical calculations.

Despite this development of mass unionism from the 1880s there was not a complete break with what had gone before. As might be expected, strike action, membership levels, workers' influence and demands continued to be influenced by the state of trade, and the rank and file remained consistently more militant than their leaders. The majority of stoppages were still linked to local and immediate issues and employers still resorted to lock-outs. The prosperous years of 1888–1891 in particular were marked by offensive strikes over wages and compensation for having to work with poor quality cotton which involved all sections and districts. The strike of spinners and piecers in Stalybridge in September 1891, the employers' subsequent lock-out of 60 per cent of the workers in south-east Lancashire and north-east Cheshire in April 1892, and an even more extensive lock-out in November, marked the end of this phase. Industrial peace was again brought to an abrupt end in 1908 with another employer lock-out to enforce a 5 per cent reduction. The years between 1910 and 1914 saw a new wave of insurgency sweep across the industry.[37] Nor did the massive expansion of female membership lead to any discernible shift in the issues which dictated leaders' agendas. Although 80 per cent of the cardroom union members were females, for example, they remained

very much second-class citizens with male strippers and grinders mo-
nopolising office-holding at every level.

But in other respects there were significant breaks in the pattern of
industrial relations. The Brooklands Agreement of March 1893 between
unions and employers' organisations established industry-wide systems
of negotiation, conciliation and arbitration and ushered in an extended
period of comparative calm which lasted for fifteen years.[38] Levels of
real wages for all workers rose from the 1880s, and the less skilled
succeeded in narrowing the differential between themselves and the
spinners. Union demands also broadened beyond straightforward wage
claims to encompass a variety of other issues. The employers' practice
of 'steaming', increasing the humidity and temperature in the mills in
order to lessen the chance of breakages caused by increasing reliance
on poorer quality of raw cotton, led to mass petitioning in the late
1880s which resulted in the Cotton Cloth Factories Act of 1890.[39] The
next two decades witnessed the gradual erosion of cotton unions'
previous non-partisan stance in politics as they began to sponsor their
own independent political representatives in both local government
and at Westminster. Before we can appreciate the extent and significance
of this, however, it is necessary to review the nature of popular politics
in the cotton towns earlier in the century.

## The politics of cotton

Whether or not they dominated workers' daily lives and social inter-
course, the politics of cotton districts have fascinated historians for
generations. Since the parliamentary franchise was severely circumscribed for much of the century, evidence of workers' political ambitions
and values is often sought from an analysis of their involvement in
protest movements, lobbying, mass petitioning and pressure group
activity.

The troubled 1830s and early 1840s are often portrayed as a 'revolutionary' period in working-class history with radical demands culminating between 1837 and 1842 in mass support for Chartism. This was
a movement which called for root and branch constitutional reform
incorporating universal male suffrage, annual parliaments and equal
electoral districts but it also occasionally included demands for a total
transformation of society which echoed socialist and co-operative ideology in rejecting the liberal political economy's free market theories.
Many textile workers throughout Lancashire were undoubtedly involved in some way in this movement, but the nature and extent of
their participation, and its implications for an understanding of working-class values both remain fiercely contested issues. John Foster, in
his study of Oldham, claimed to have documented the emergence of

a potentially revolutionary working class during the 1830s. In his view, the General Strike of August 1842 was 'clearly a political one' to gain what amounted to 'state power'.[40] But both his Leninist theoretical framework and the accuracy of his account of events in the town have been subject to convincing criticism.[41] At the other extreme there are those who have suggested that workers' political understanding was negligible, that agitation was purely about 'bread and butter' issues and that the strike of 1842 was essentially concerned with restoring wage cuts as the worst of the severe depression passed.[42]

There is no doubt that these were years of severe economic dislocation and that authorities were concerned that the social order would disintegrate. But grievances which fuelled political discontent were not solely economic and those who expressed them were not all working class. Retailers, self employed artisans and small businessmen were often the backbone of provincial radical politics. Often Nonconformist in religion they were opposed to the privileges and power of the Anglican church; economically insecure they were concerned with excessive taxation and restrictions on trade; fiercely independent and anxious to consolidate their status and power in local communities and national politics, they demanded the reform of what they regarded as the unrepresentative, unaccountable and corrupt government from which they were largely excluded. The extent to which they succeeded in rallying workers to their cause is still not clear, although recent studies of both Oldham and Bolton suggest that the Anti-Corn Law League may well have enjoyed rather more support among operatives, and spinners in particular, than has traditionally been thought.[43] If so, then the spinners' acceptance of a modified version of free market ideology, which became more apparent in the 1850s, may not have represented quite such a discontinuity from earlier periods.

But Liberals and Radicals were not alone in wooing mass support. Operative Conservative Associations were being promoted in many towns by prominent local Tories from the 1830s. Although Radicals were active in the movement for factory reform in the 1830s, by the 1840s some larger Tory manufacturers and Anglican clergymen were ardent champions of it, and were able successfully to portray free-trade, non-interventionist Liberals as enemies of working-class interests. In short, workers' allegiances to the two established parliamentary parties may well have been much more developed during this 'revolutionary' phase than was once thought.

The right to vote was, of course, severely restricted for most of the century and the existence of a property qualification for MPs and their lack of salaries also debarred any working men from standing for parliament. Even after the Reform Act of 1832 only adult male householders occupying property rated at £10 *per annum* were allowed to vote in parliamentary borough elections. The electorate was largely comprised of employers, professionals, craftsmen, retailers and some supervisory workers like spinners. Virtually all of the cotton towns of south-east Lancashire returned Liberal MPs between 1832 and 1867. 'Ashton, Bury, Salford and Manchester itself returned none but Liberals, Rochdale returned a Conservative only in the exceptional circumstances of 1857, and Oldham and Stockport returned Liberals without exception after 1852'.[44] It is highly unlikely, however, that this was in any way a consequence of the political power of the unfranchised factory workers influencing the electors by intimidation or exclusive dealing.[45] Individual voters' political preferences over the period, in textile Lancashire as elsewhere, were consistently related to their occupational background. It was the small businessman, rather than the cotton master, who was the backbone of provincial Liberalism during the period.

The right to vote in parliamentary elections in boroughs was extended to all male householders over the age of twenty one by the Reform Act of 1867. Even so, this enfranchised only a fraction of the factory workforce who were largely prevented from voting by their gender or age. Male householders outside the boroughs, an incalculable but far from insignificant number, also had to wait until 1885 when constituency boundaries were redrawn and the distinction between boroughs and counties abolished. The vote was only granted to all adult males over twenty one in 1918.

Nevertheless, after 1867 the majority of the electorate could be broadly described as working class. This transformed parliamentary politics in the textile towns. From the election of 1868 to their disastrous collapse in 1906, Conservatives virtually swept the board throughout Lancashire. Historians have offered a list of possible explanations for this, although their efforts have been hampered by the fact that after the 1872 Ballot Act they do not know precisely who voted for whom, let alone why they did so.[46] Despite the best endeavours of historians, attempts to account for political behaviour are still largely 'unsatisfactory assertion and description of complexity'.[47]

Factory workers' Toryism cannot be seen as attempts to frustrate the political ambitions of Liberal masters. As we have seen (chapter 4), employers were far from being the committed Liberals of popular mythology. Peter Clarke has linked popular Toryism to the dominance, in much of textile Lancashire, of Anglican elementary schools which successfully inculcated an attachment to traditional values.[48] Proof of a link remains elusive, however, and most historians have seriously questioned the impact which the expansion of education had on workers' values. Anti-Irish, or more accurately, anti-Irish Catholic feelings, have also been proffered as an explanation, although the Irish Catholic presence was much more noticeable in Manchester, on Merseyside and in south-west Lancashire than it was in the textile towns.[49] Antagonism towards the Irish was likely to have been especially prevalent in 1868, after a series of Fenian bombings on the British mainland, but it may have re-emerged after the Liberals' commitment to Home Rule in 1886. The Tories have also been viewed as being less critical than the Liberals of the working man's predilection for beer and gambling. Temperance, self improvement and moral reform campaigns may have been particularly evident in cotton Lancashire, but they were far from universally popular and appealed to specific elements of society, especially the socially aspiring middling ranks. Pubs and beer houses, on the other hand, were not merely drinking establishments; their premises occupied a central role in the community, both informally and as venues for societies. The Liberals' close association with temperance provided the Tories with plenty of electoral ammunition.[50] They were also successful in establishing working-men's clubs, while the Primrose League, established in the 1880s to induce political loyalty through the provision of social activities, achieved very high membership levels in some Lancashire cotton towns.[51] Furthermore, Tories were more closely associated with the cause of factory reform and some individuals, like Robert Ascroft, solicitor and MP for Oldham, offered considerable practical assistance to the cardroom workers' unions. James Mawdsley, secretary of the spinners' union, was also a Tory, although he was unusual in this respect.[52]

Patrick Joyce has sought to reintegrate work and politics arguing that 'the factory was at the centre of political life'. In his view, workers were essentially proletarians, lacking real control over work processes which were now dominated by machinery, and they were thus totally subordinate to the authority of capital both in the mill and in the wider community. Their dependency and vulnerability meant that they 'internalised' and deferred to the values of their masters. Work dominated operatives' daily lives making them incapable of forming alternative associations and preventing them from articulating any views other than those which were adhered to and propounded by their employers. The culture of the factory permeated their leisure hours through paternalist employers' promotion of a variety of social facilities and activities: the provision of houses, schools and educational institutions; patronage of sporting and social clubs; holiday excursions; the erection of civic buildings; and celebrations associated with their family or mill. Using evidence of voting behaviour drawn from 1868 poll books for Blackburn, Joyce showed that the electorate in streets surrounding a mill tended, on balance, to vote the same way as its owner. 'More often than not, the tie of employer and worker was one of emotional identification, in which the worker acquiesced in his own subordination'.[53] The picture which is often painted of cotton workers stoically enduring the hardships occasioned by the Cotton Famine seemingly supports this view of a workforce who accepted and did not question their fate.

Compelling though this thesis is, it fails to address other aspects of textile Lancashire's experience during the period. The endemic industrial conflict over wages which raged throughout the period, and which was especially acrimonious in Blackburn in 1878 (see above pp. 136–8) undermines the image of peaceful worker-employer relations. As we have seen, this one town cannot be taken to represent the experiences of very different textile towns elsewhere.[54] Nor was it the case that workers unquestioningly accepted whatever relief was offered to them during the Cotton Famine on their employers' terms. There were riots and threats of disturbances when poor law officials and dispensers of charitable funds attempted to discriminate between applicants on the grounds of respectability, or to replace cash payments with tickets which could only be exchanged for certain goods.[55] Furthermore, it was far from the case that all social life was dominated and controlled by employer initiatives. Workers during this period were developing a vigorous, autonomous, associational life beyond the reaches of their employers which embraced friendly societies, co-ops, sporting and cultural societies and holidays. It is quite possible, then, that the late nineteenth-century working-class electorate, like early Victorian voters, were politically informed and were capable of perceiving where their own self-interest lay and of casting their votes independently of any outside pressure. Significantly Conservative dominance of parliamentary representation in Lancashire evaporated in 1906 when the party nailed its colours to the protectionist mast. However successful Tories may have been in wooing electors on cultural and emotional appeals over the previous forty years, it had clearly been conditional upon them remaining attached to the cause of free trade. Well aware of the importance of the export market, workers did not need to be persuaded that the imposition of tariffs would inflict a damaging blow to the cotton industry.

It is against this background that trade unions' growing involvement in popular politics in the textile towns around the turn of the century needs to be viewed. Not content with lobbying for specific pieces of legislation, they began to express a growing interest in putting their own candidates forward for political office and, in some instances, even flirted with socialism.

The United Textile Factory Workers' Association (UTFWA) was formed in 1889–90, with James Mawdsley as its secretary, to campaign for further legislative controls on the working week and the factory environment. This reflected the newer unskilled unions' relative lack of industrial muscle and their tendency to turn to the state for redress

FIGURE 55. Robert Ascroft (1847–99) was an Oldham solicitor who championed the cause of labour. Like his father William before him, he defended workers in courts; he was also active in settling local disputes in his home town, in drawing up the Brooklands Agreement in 1893, and in supporting the Cardroom Workers Union. As Conservative MP from 1895 he took a special interest in labour legislation. This statue in Alexandra Park, Oldham, was erected by public subscription and unveiled in 1903. (Photograph courtesy of Oldham Metropolitan Borough, Leisure Services, Local Studies Library)

of grievances or for improvements in working conditions. In 1894 the UTFWA decided to seek the opinion of its constituent members on the question of sponsoring its own political representatives, but the outcome was indecisive. However, developments elsewhere in the trade union movement meant that the issue of independent labour representation did not fade away. Mawdsley himself unsuccessfully stood for parliament as a Conservative in the Oldham by-election of 1899 which had been occasioned by the death of Robert Ascroft. Although spinners and cardroom workers both remained decidedly hostile to any dalliance with socialism, elsewhere in the union movement socialists were actively promoting the idea of independent political representation.[56] Predictably, it was in north-east Lancashire, and Burnley in particular, that this took deepest root under the tutelage of H. M. Hyndman, the national leader of the Social Democratic Federation, who narrowly failed to be returned for the constituency in the general election of 1906. The Independent Labour Party, founded in 1893, also made headway in the region, its campaigning *Clarion* newspaper and associated recreational clubs appearing particularly successful.[57] Although the cotton unions did not initially affiliate to the Labour Representation Committee, the forerunner of the Labour party, when it was formed in 1900, they did so two years later after the Taff Vale legal judgement had threatened to undermine the finances of unions by making them liable for employers' losses which were the result of industrial action.

Unions and local Trades Councils also began to put forward candidates for election to local authorities during the period.

A further symptom of this growing political activism was the suffragist campaign for women's voting rights. This was particularly prominent in the weaving towns of north-east Lancashire where, as we have seen, women enjoyed more respect and authority within the workplace.[58] The campaign originated outside the district and was orchestrated by middle-class women like Esther Roper, but it attracted ardent support from a number of operatives like Selina Cooper who began her working life as a winder. A deputation of Lancashire cotton workers travelled to London in March 1901 to present a mammoth petition to David Shackleton, the newly elected MP for Clitheroe. The campaign continued throughout the decade gradually winning over the grudging support of some male-dominated organisations within the region as part of a wider commitment to universal adult suffrage. As the chroniclers of the campaigns, Jill Liddington and Jill Norris, point out, it was symptomatic of something much deeper – 'the pride they [women] took in their work and in their status as skilled workers'.[59]

The extent to which the emergence of Labour undermined workers' political loyalties to established parties and the involvement of women in popular politics should not be exaggerated. Peter Clarke has argued vigorously that a newly invigorated Liberal party wedded to a progressive platform of social reform was the chief beneficiary of the Tories' collapse, and the number of working men who were elected, at local as well as national level, remained tiny. Industrial action, even in 1911, remained restricted to matters related to wages and working conditions. Nor did affiliation to the Labour Party represent a 'fundamental change in the nature and objectives of cotton union politics'. The party was seen as a 'necessary, even essential, medium for trade union politics, [but] it was not seen as exhaustive'.[60] Sectional and narrowly defined economic concerns remained the defining characteristics of their involvement in politics. Even in 'Burnley, Nelson and Colne, socialism remained the often ill-defined creed of a small if eager minority'.[61]

Most women textile workers' support for the suffragist movement was passive rather than active. It made very limited inroads into the spinning towns, or even weaving towns like Preston, where women's reduced autonomy at work restricted their ability to mobilise effectively or to engage in independent action.[62] The movement did not achieve any results before the First World War. Indeed, even in 1918 only women over the age of thirty were initially granted the vote. National political citizenship for women cotton workers over twenty-one was effectively only granted in 1928 and it was only in the inter-war years that women gained any significant influence in local government, even in the weaving areas.

But none of these qualifications should mask the broader significance of what had taken place. They mirrored significant developments in the culture of the textile towns and represented, in Joyce's words, 'the passing of the old order'.

## Community and culture in the factory town

To some observers of the 1830s, the new factory towns lacked any form of social organisation. What they failed to appreciate fully was that people were integrated into the expanding urban settlements and the rituals and routines of factory life through familial networks and community ties. Over the course of the century these largely informal personal networks, allied with a shared work experience and, from the 1880s, rising living standards, became the basis of a highly sophisticated associational and commercialised culture which was distinctive to the cotton towns.

Where the factory workforce came from provides the key to understanding the social cohesion which characterised textile towns. Apart from early pauper apprentices (chapter 1), very few of the workers travelled any distance to work in the mills. Agricultural enclosure and improvement did not drive despairing labourers from the land and through the portals of the new mills. Indeed, an attempt by the poor law authorities in 1834–5 to transport pauper families from corn growing areas in the south, where agricultural 'improvement' and social distress were inseparably linked, to alleviate a temporary labour shortage in the textile districts, proved ill-fated and unsuccessful. London or the Midlands were the main destinations for such people. Nor did Ireland, which lost an estimated 2.5 million people through migration between 1815 and 1851, provide the bulk of the factory labour force. The Irish were heavily concentrated in the cities of Liverpool and Manchester and, to a lesser extent, around Preston and Wigan; relatively few ventured into the textile towns further east and those that did ended up in relatively unskilled jobs.[63] Unlike skilled artisans, who tended to be extremely mobile in their search for work, the vast majority of cotton workers were born in Lancashire and they were already likely to have had experience of textile manufacture as outworkers in the flourishing domestic industry which preceded, and in many areas survived alongside, the factory system.

As areas which had once relied on domestic industry stagnated or declined, the young left to find work in the urban mills. The towns, therefore, grew not just because of natural increase, but by a process of short distance, in-migration, especially of single males and females in their late teens and early twenties. Michael Anderson's pioneering census-based analysis of Preston found that 83 per cent of residents in

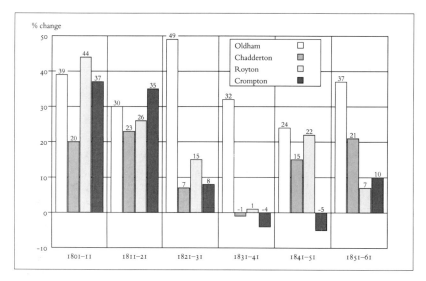

FIGURE 56.
Decennial rates of
population change,
Oldham, 1801–61.

1851 had been born in the town or within thirty miles of it. Nearly a quarter of them came from other textile towns like Blackburn or the less successful Lancaster to the north, but the majority were from surrounding rural areas.[64] John Foster's random sample of Oldham's census in the same year arrived at similar figures; 61 per cent were born in Oldham and a further 27 per cent within twenty miles.[65] The contrasting demographic trajectories of townships in this latter district vividly illustrate what was happening. Up to the 1820s the expansion of handloom weaving had sustained substantial population growth throughout the area. Smaller townships like Chadderton, Royton and Crompton matched neighbouring Oldham's growth rate until the 1820s. However, as steam-powered factories became concentrated in Oldham in subsequent decades, its neighbouring townships went into dramatic declines which were only partially checked in the 1840s when the pace of industrial expansion in Oldham itself faltered.

The textile towns, especially those in north-east Lancashire, continued to attract young migrants into the twentieth century, although urban population growth was progressively fuelled by natural increase. Migrants were integrated into these towns through their family, both nuclear and extended, and informal close-knit communities. These were the adhesives which bonded society together. In Anderson's words 'most people managed to maintain relationships with their family, both the current nuclear family and the family as a web of wider kinship relationships', while 'non-familial primary networks' provided communal identities and support.[66] The importance of extended family and neighbourhood support networks did not diminish over time. Oral evidence from the twentieth century confirms that both 'were of great importance in working-class lives, giving social and material support, and providing a strict system for establishing and maintaining social mores. They were operated largely, but not exclusively, by women.'[67] We should be careful not to romanticize the mutual support offered by families or the community. Much of it was clearly initially a response to shared difficulties and the lack of alternative formal systems of state support outside the hated poor law. But their existence meant that urban Lancashire did not experience the social anomie and dislocation which is often associated with modernisation and rapid industrialisation.

The family also remained important as an economic unit. Although most children and adolescents were unlikely to have worked directly under their parents in the mill,[68] jobs were often obtained through personal contacts with extended family or neighbours rather than through formal channels. Where skilled workers like spinners and overlookers enjoyed the privilege of controlling recruitment to well-paid jobs, positions were often passed down through families.[69] Individual members of the same family were frequently employed in different processes within the same mill, while most employees worked alongside neighbours from their community. All this may well have counterbalanced the sectionalism which characterised cotton unions, helping to explain the relative lack of bitterness on the part of workers laid off as a result of industrial action by other sections of the workforce, for example big piecers' apparent reluctance to act as blackleg labour when spinners went on strike.

The importance of the family unit was further consolidated by its dependence on the earnings of several members of the household, as opposed to a male 'breadwinner's wage'. As we have seen, cotton manufacture offered few opportunities for adult males to earn what might be considered a 'family wage'. It was household income, therefore, the characteristic of domestic industry, which continued to be the crucial element in the increasing prosperity and cohesion of factory towns, rather than notions of dependence on an adult male. Low wages for men in the weaving towns combined with the availability of relatively well-paid work for women also undoubtedly contributed to the comparatively late age of marriage in north-east Lancashire and to the large proportion of married women in the workforce. But throughout textile Lancashire, and in marked contrast with agricultural districts or the commercial districts, it was this plentiful, regular, relatively well-paid work for family members, male and female, which determined a family's prosperity.

Family and neighbourhood ties, allied to shared experiences of work, contributed to the development of a strong communal and associational culture. As one commentator of the 1860s noted approvingly, 'the discipline of the cotton mill has spread its influence beyond the workshop, and regularity and punctuality have become essential parts of

Lancashire life . . . The habit of working together has taught them to associate for other purposes, and the necessity of submission to strict rules with the mill has led them to make rules for their own guidance in matters which seem to concern themselves more immediately.'[70] Temperance, building and friendly societies, savings clubs and educational groups all made early appearances in the mill towns, supported in some cases with middle-class patronage. The most spectacular example of early formal collective activity, however, and probably the most significant, was the Co-operative movement. Reconstituted in Rochdale in 1844, it spread rapidly through the cotton districts of east Lancashire over the next two decades.[71] Local societies owed their origins and success almost entirely to working-class initiative, organisation and custom. Throughout its long existence the movement has remained closely associated with the local communities which it served, offering a range of educational and leisure facilities as well as adhering closely to its founding principles and remaining democratically accountable to its shareholding customers.

As with trade union development within the workplace, however, the viability and vitality of such formal associations was not fully assured until the 1880s when longer leisure hours, settled residential patterns and higher wages greatly extended their scope. Despite its early origins in the textile towns, it was only in the last quarter of the century that the Co-operative movement effectively became a 'universal provider',

capable of furnishing all household needs. The same period also witnessed the emergence of an enormous array of societies and clubs catering for all tastes and interests, encompassing such diverse activities as rambling, cycling, fishing, football, cricket, photography, pigeon racing and athletics. These years also witnessed the emergence of a more materialistic home-based and commercial culture. As housing bye-laws improved the quality of accommodation, the domestic interior environment was transformed. The parlour or 'front room' became a hallowed sanctuary, often containing that household god the piano, decorated with fashionable patterned lino on the floor and shielded from prying eyes by lace curtains at the window. Purely commercial leisure activities like music halls and professional football also developed more rapidly in the textile towns than they did elsewhere.

Just as factory work cemented rather than undermined communal cultures and family values so, too, did this increasing commercialisation of leisure serve to consolidate the distinctive identities of the cotton towns. The expansion of cheap publications, in particular the provincial press and dialect-based literature, served to reinforce local associations and values.[72] Music hall turns were unequivocally 'Lancashire' in flavour well into the twentieth century and the genre promoted local artistes, many of whom appeared in Blackpool during the season and some of whom later achieved national fame through the medium of cinema.[73] Football was a professional sport, watched by thousands, but it also generated interest in local leagues centred on church, workplace, neighbourhood or pub teams, as did other sports like cricket.[74]

But the undisputed symbol of this prosperity and the values of textile Lancashire was Blackpool, the textile workers' entertainment Mecca, dependent almost entirely on custom from east Lancashire for its rapid growth and prosperity from the 1870s. It was the manifestation of a widespread commitment to shared values. It partially depended for its success on the persistence of the Wakes. These were local festivals, originally religious holidays but almost overwhelmingly secular by the nineteenth century, which had survived despite the new, mechanically-dictated work discipline and attempts to suppress them. Initially they were celebrated in the local community with fairs, processions and the giving of hospitality.[75] The coming of the railway broadened their scope and the rise of Blackpool completely transformed them. Dispersed throughout the summer months from June to September, they provided the resort with a viable season. Increasing prosperity, based on rising real wages and family employment, linked to many channels through which savings could be accumulated, including the co-op 'divi', provided the financial wherewithal for extended holidays. The expansion of the railway network and companies' willingness to lay on excursions enabled the entire population of an area to decamp to the coast.[76] Here

FIGURE 57. By the end of the century virtually every community in textile Lancashire had its own co-operative store, owned by worker-shareholders. Through the Co-operative Wholesale Society (CWS), founded in Manchester in 1863, the societies were able to obtain regular supplies of basic products. This shop with its elaborate window displays, adverts for CWS products and local events, and an all-male staff, was typical of many. (Photograph courtesy of Lancashire County Library, Nelson Local Studies Collection)

FIGURE 58. Celebrations for Queen Victoria's Jubilee, Oldham Edge, 1897. Sixty years earlier, in June 1837, Victoria's accession had been celebrated by a procession of public officials through the town, spectators flooding out of the mills to watch. Oldham Edge itself, however, was also the scene of mass rallies associated with radical or trade union capaigns during the 1830s and 1840s; over 20,000 workers were reported to have attended a meeting in April 1834 to discuss a general strike. (Photograph courtesy of Oldham Metropolitan Borough, Leisure Services, Local Studies Library)

they lodged with landladies, who themselves frequently hailed from the textile districts, while continuing to socialise with people they knew from home.[77] Blackpool was effectively a different textile-town-by-the-sea each week throughout the summer season.

All this undoubtedly contributed to and fed off the growing sense of working-class identity during the period which, as we have seen, was evident in the factory. But it also served to consolidate a sense of community which was distinctive to the cotton towns and which mitigated some of the potential class conflict inherent in industrial relations.[78] If this existed elsewhere it did so only in a diluted form, and life in the textile towns contrasted markedly with places like Liverpool, where poorly paid casual labour and lack of work for women and juveniles created a culture of poverty and alienation.[79] Increasing prosperity and the patterns of work associated with cotton were clearly important in its creation, but so, too, was local tradition and a sense of the past, the survival of kinship networks, a strong pride in communal identity. As Douglas Farnie concluded of textile workers, 'their culture had been overlain but not destroyed by the upsurge of an economic civilization'.[80]

## Conclusion

Octogenarians in 1914 looking back to when they were children would no doubt have pointed to much that had changed over the course of their lives. It would have been impossible to take issue with them. But

FIGURE 59. 'Philosophic Lancashire'. The cotton operative, unruffled by financial and political crises, economic depression and technological advances, was a popular image by the 1900s, although within a few years Sam Fitton's cartoons were depicting the conflict between capital and labour. (For an excellent analysis of these cartoons and the paper in which they appeared, see A. Fowler and T. Wyke, 'Tickling Lancashire's Funny Bone: the gradely cartoons of Sam Fitton', *Transactions of the Lancashire and Cheshire Antiquarian Society*, vol. 89 (1993), pp. 1–53.) Source: *Cotton Factory Times*, 22 October 1909.

PHILOSOPHIC LANCASHIRE.

the changes which they had experienced had been incremental rather than dramatic, gradual rather than sudden. By then, the cotton districts were dominated culturally by the workers as the business elite had gradually retreated from active involvement in the local community. An aura of social stability, order and permanence pervaded them which would have astounded the apprehensive observers of the troubled 1830s. With the benefit of hindsight, however, we know that the foundations on which all this depended were, even then, being undermined. The cotton industry was already under threat from external forces, while new technology in the form of ring spinning and the automatic loom were about to transform the established order of work. International capitalism, commercialisation and mass communications were poised to effect another social revolution. Well within the next eighty years the distinctive lifestyle associated with factory Lancashire would almost entirely have disappeared.

CHAPTER 6

# Clothing

SARAH LEVITT

E VERY YARD of cotton ever woven was created for a specific purpose,
yet surprisingly little has been written about the end products of
this vast industry, which ranged from bandages and belting for machinery, to sheets and pillowslips, to exquisite ballgowns. This chapter looks
at clothing manufacture, one of the most important industries to develop
as a result of the revolution in cotton production.

The importance of cotton as a clothing fabric was two-fold. It
transformed fashionable dress, firstly through its seductive prints, and
later through the diaphanous white fabrics of the neoclassical era. Even
more importantly, cotton, being cheap, plentiful and washable, enabled
the majority of the population to be decently clad. The Victorian era
saw more people than ever before entering the ranks of the lower-
middle classes. Cotton gave the possibility of a starched white shirt and
collar to the poorest clerk, and cotton lace, satin and velvet brought
the appearance of luxury within reach of many for Sunday-best.

About a million people were involved in the clothing trades in Britain
in the nineteenth century. Many depended on Lancashire's cotton mills
for their livelihood and a substantial proportion were employed by
firms in Manchester, the hub of the cotton industry and a growing
centre of commerce and communications.

The clothing industries in Manchester continued to flourish, and
even grow, despite the decline in the cotton industry from the end of
the nineteenth century. Disused mills provided instant premises for
clothing factories and unemployed female cotton workers provided a
pool of labour. The industry that had grown out of the cotton trade
found little difficulty in adapting to man-made fibres and wholesale
tailoring.

In the twentieth century ready-made clothing was worn by almost
everyone. Sophisticated marketing and manufacturing techniques and
large-scale distribution methods led to a close partnership between
manufacturers and retailers, which largely cut out the traditional wholesale warehouses. However, the tendency towards ever larger and more
standardised production runs, evident in the 1950s and 1960s, was

checked by the fragmentation of the market. A more flexible approach developed to meet the needs of consumers for leisurewear, individual expression and rapidly changing fashions.

## The impact of cotton

Cotton was cheap and plentiful. It could be gossamer-fine for ballgowns or strong enough for navvies' trousers. It could be dyed or printed, bringing gaiety in the place of the 'drabs' and 'sads' of woollen cloth. Its absorbency gave comfort on the hottest day, and in midwinter there was no better protection than stout corduroy or velveteen. Unlike silk, it need not be spoilt by a grease-spot, and unlike wool, mud was easily removed. Above all, cotton was washable, and at a temperature high enough to destroy bacteria. Indeed, the more it was washed the whiter it got and starching and ironing made it crisp and smooth. Even more starch created rigid shiny bands for collars and cuffs and undulating corset-shapes.

Many of these properties were shared by linen. The essential 'look' of fashionable dress from the fifteenth century onwards was of rich outerwear set off by the plain white of clean linen undergarments at the neck and cuff. However, linen was expensive, and wealth and status were signalled by its cleanliness, quality and condition.

Cotton had been enjoyed only by the very rich until the first chintzes were unloaded from the East India Company's ships in the early seventeenth century. This 'upmarket' image helps to explain its immediate popularity. The company quickly realised the potential of cotton for the mass market and shipped lower- and middle-priced goods as well as luxury ones.

By the late seventeenth century cotton was commonly found in the humblest pedlars' packs and its place as a cheap alternative to linen was firmly established.[1] Its introduction and manufacture in this country were two elements in the wider social and economic revolution that transformed Europe, but cotton, perhaps more than any other innovation, gave visual expression to this change. Cotton enabled more than just the rich to display clean shirts and, through its ability to imitate different fabrics, brought the appearance of satins, velvets and lace within reach of millions.

Recognition of the importance of individual expression has been one of the key elements in modern society. For a few pence a yard, printed cottons brought choice and the concept of changing fashion to almost everyone. Even scraps used for patchwork could be arranged creatively.

Washable cotton clothing and domestic textiles helped to raise standards of hygiene and may have been a factor in improving life-expectancy, for instance, by helping to keep infants and invalids clean.

Homes became more comfortable, as curtains, table linen, towels and sheets became common.

Cotton transformed lifestyles in other ways. Whereas the rich paid others to wash their linen, this was not an option for most of the population. All those cotton shifts and sheets had to be laundered, and so the chore of washday became a dominant feature of women's lives.

## Cotton as a fashion fabric

Cotton was used in clothing in the eighteenth century in four ways: as a cheap alternative to linen for underclothing, to wool and silk for hosiery, to wool and leather for heavy outerwear and as a printed fabric for light outerwear. Prints were used instead of brocaded, painted or embroidered silk, but they had their own specific attraction.

Cotton garments were becoming known in 1663 when Pepys recorded a gift to his wife of 'a very noble parti-coloured Indian gowne'.[2] Little is known about the appearance of cotton clothing of any kind made before 1760, since so few examples survive. This was probably due to cotton's usefulness and democratic appearance. Most eighteenth-century clothing in museums belonged to the wealthy, the most typical survivors being silk gowns and lace lappets, put away for 'best' then forgotten when they went out of fashion. Cotton clothing was worn until it was worn out, cut up for the children, or sold by the owner or a servant to whom it had been given as a perquisite. A substantial proportion of the nation's clothing was bought second-hand and there was no stigma attached to this practice. The finest lady's informal chintz made a best gown for her maid, or someone passing the used clothes dealer's stall where the maid sold it. When little more than rags, the chintz gown could be turned into patchwork, or ripped up for fertiliser or paper.

There is plenty of evidence to show that cotton was increasingly widely worn before 1760. During the period leading up to the 1721 Act banning printed cottons, many hapless citizens were attacked in the streets for wearing it. Elizabeth Price was looking for lodgings in Shoreditch when 'some People sitting at their Doors, took up her Riding Hood, and seeing her Gown, cry'd out Callicoe, Callicoe; Weavers, Weavers. Whereupon a great Number came down and tore her Gown off all but the Sleeves, her Pocket, the head of her Riding Hood, and abus'd her very much'.[3]

By the second half of the eighteenth century cotton clothing held an increasingly dominant position in many wardrobes. The fabric scrap book of Barbara Johnson, a middle-class vicar's daughter, in which she kept a record of all her clothes from around 1750 until 1825, vividly illustrates this. One of her first purchases of British cotton was a length of fustian twill for a riding dress, bought in 1757. This cost her 5s. 6d. per yard as opposed to 20s. per yard for a comparable woollen fabric. She generally paid between 4s. and 7s. per yard for silk gowns, and 3s. to 5s. for cottons. She acquired thirty-one silk gowns before 1780, but only six between 1779 and 1800, plus one woollen one, no linen ones and seventeen made from cotton.[4]

Printed cotton dresses survive in increasing numbers from the 1760s onwards. In cut and construction they are similar to silk dresses and at first they followed the same trends as fashions changed. In the 1750s large patterns were popular on heavy fabrics. Over the course of the next three decades the bold overall patterns broke up into smaller motifs, often interspersed with stripes (colour plate 1).

By the 1780s, cotton printers had taken the lead and silk weavers copied their designs. Fashionable silk dresses had tiny spots and stripes, no more than a hint of pattern across pale, soft drapery. This spelt disaster for the industry since the simpler the pattern, the less weaving was needed and the cheaper the price. These were grim years too for lacemakers, since dense patterns were replaced by little more than gauze. Thousands of silk and lace workers were thrown out of work.

In 1783 a completely new kind of dress was launched in fashionable French society, which took full advantage of the properties of fine cotton. The *chemise à la reine* was made of unstructured white muslin, gathered at the neck and sleeves and held at the waist by a sash. In 1784 the Duchess of Devonshire wore one to a concert, and in 1787 the *Lady's Magazine* noted 'all the sex now, from 15 to 50 and upwards . . . appear in their white muslin frocks with broad sashes'.[5] The *chemise à la reine* paved the way for the diaphanous white, high-waisted, low-necked, short-sleeved dress, inspired by the costumes of ancient Greece and Rome, which was to dominate fashion until the 1820s. Rich ladies wore imported Indian muslin, whose delicately woven spots and stripes created texture and interest in the plain white. The most daring cast off their stays, damped their underclothes, oiled their hair and went barefoot. Lesser mortals wore Lancashire muslin, indistinguishable from the real thing, over petticoats and stays of calico and jean and cotton stockings.

Hand-spun and knitted cotton goods had been produced since at least 1698 when Celia Fiennes saw stockings, gloves, waistcoats, petticoats and sleeves being made in Gloucester. However, it was not until after 1775, when Arkwright developed a machine-spun thread suitable for the knitting frame, that cotton stockings became widespread. They were considered superior to silk in their whiteness and fineness, and perfectly suited to neoclassical fashions.[6]

It should not be assumed that the neoclassical colour scheme was insipid. Those white dresses were set-off by accessories in strong ochres and patterned shawls, imported from the near East at vast expense or made in cheap cotton mixtures in this country. A considerable number of printed cotton dresses also survive from this period with dense patterns in rich palettes, their dark grounds often enhanced by a shiny glaze. These must have been worn by females who, through

FIGURE 60. A photograph of an unidentified woman in a fine muslin afternoon dress, Croston, Lancashire, c. 1910. (Photograph courtesy of Lancashire County Library, Chorley Local Studies Collection)

conservatism, age or occupation, chose not to spend their days in white muslin.

Theoretically it had always been possible for very rich ladies to buy gauze-like linen or silk dresses in white or pale colours. In practice such delicate and expensive fabrics were generally restricted to trimmings and the main dress was of more robust material. Suddenly, at the close of the eighteenth century, complete dresses in extremely fine fabrics became practicable, not just for the wealthy, but for a substantial section of the population. This was made possible by Lancashire cotton.

Whereas women's dress owed much to the ancient world, men drew the line at tunics and togas. Direct influence of classical art was limited to carefully curled hairstyles. However the classical appreciation of the male form was shared by the period and men's dress was characterised by a figure-hugging outline. This was achieved by means of tailored woollen coats and buckskin breeches inspired by the country wear of the English gentleman.

The trend away from highly decorated silk garments to plainer woollen ones encouraged the development of tailoring. This not only involved stretching and moulding cloth, but also using specialised fabrics for padding, linings and interlinings. A significant proportion of the cotton industry was involved in making these products, which is often overlooked.

The neoclassical male look depended on the contrast of dark colours with a white starched linen shirt and neckcloth, tied in an elaborate knot. Immaculate linen was evident round the neck of anyone with pretensions to fashion. The greatest dandies wore, and wasted, vast quantities. The story is often told of Beau Brummel's valet, seen carrying a pile of neckcloths, with the explanation 'those, sir, are our failures'. Cotton neckcloths enabled the ordinary man in the street to share the luxury of a pile of 'failures' in pursuit of this rather difficult style.

The male image developed in the early 1800s dominated mainstream fashion for a hundred and fifty years. As it gradually evolved, the accepted view of respectable dress became rigidly defined by an ever-widening section of the population. Without cheap cotton it would have been impossible for many to maintain this look.

Whilst the rich preferred linen at the start of the nineteenth century, cotton was almost universal by 1900, not only for shirts, but also for women's shifts, petticoats and nightwear. The voluminousness of underwear and shirts meant that calicoes and similar fabrics were an important part of the Lancashire industry's output. The industry was further helped by the custom of keeping a dozen or so of each undergarment, and far more sheets, towels and tablelinen than could ever be needed.

Whilst cotton allowed the very poor to have a new dress before the old one was in rags, for the better off it meant owning several dresses rather than two or three. The nineteenth century brought conspicuous consumption to a fine art. Women's clothing made an extreme contrast with menswear in its complexity and specialised outfits were developed for different occasions and times of day. Acquiring and caring for one's wardrobe was a major headache for many middle-class women of limited means and books with titles like *How to Dress Well on a Shilling a Day* abounded.[7]

As a dress fabric, cotton was used in countless ways throughout the nineteenth century. The tradition of high-quality prints lasted until the 1840s, after which time the fashionable emphasis moved towards surface texture. Lightly patterned delicate fabrics were preferred for 1850s crinoline dresses, and fashions in subsequent decades often depended on trimmings rather than fabric patterns. Printed cottons were relegated to a more utilitarian market. Late nineteenth-century printed dresses are often of humble origin and made from cheap, if memorably patterned, material.

White muslin dresses retained their appeal, especially as summer and evening wear for young women. 'Sewed muslin dresses' were particularly popular until the 1860s, being fabric lengths embroidered with whitework ready to make up. Sewed muslin collars and cuffs were also popular, but only until they became too common. *Perkins' Treatise on Haberdashery and Hosiery* of 1853 described them as 'lately a leading article in the retail trade . . . but less worn since the trimming work has been offered at its present moderate cost'.[8] Such collars, caps and morning wraps were often elaborately frilled. The ability to 'get up muslin', starching and pressing it with tiny irons, was a highly prized attribute in a lady's maid.

From the 1860s it was acceptable for women to be more physically active and outfits were developed for different pursuits. Strong cottons were particularly appropriate, for instance, for bathing dress and other seaside clothes, and cotton was much used for waterproofs.

In the 1880s clothes tended to become darker and heavier. Satins and velvets were essential formal wear for the rich, cotton sateens and velveteens for the less wealthy. The velveteen department at Lewis's store in Manchester made an immense profit selling locally made material at 2s. per yard. Cotton machine-lace added the final touch. 'Chemical lace' became popular at this time because of its rich effect. Dense raised patterns were embroidered in cotton on silk, the silk was dissolved in acid and the 'lace' was left behind.

The number of women in further education and careers became noticeable in the 1890s and much was made of the ideal of the strong, capable 'new woman'. More practical clothing became fashionable, reflecting this interest. The woollen skirt and tailored jacket began its long reign, worn with a cotton blouse, often cut on masculine lines.

## Raising standards of dress

Cotton not only transformed fashionable dress, but also raised standards of clothing for the whole population. Working-class clothing was traditionally made locally from homespun wool, linen and leather. It was expensive and made to last for several generations. Each person owned very few garments. Washing one's only shirt meant a day spent indoors whilst it dried, and this was an obvious disincentive. Wool and leather were not washable and only the rich could afford to have wool cleaned by professionals.

Francis Place's recollection of the wives of journeymen tradesmen and shopkeepers, looking back from 1824 to his youth, was probably typical of many generations before.

> [They] either wore leather stays or what were called full-boned stays . . . These were never washed although worn day by day for years. The wives and grown daughters of tradesmen . . . wore petticoats of camblet lined with dyed linen stuffed with wool and horsehair quilted. These were also worn day by day till they were rotten . . . Formerly the women young and old were seen emptying their pails or pans at the doors or washing on stools in the street in summer time without gowns on their backs or handkerchiefs on their necks, their leather stays half-laced and black as the door posts, their black coarse worsted stockings and striped linsey-woolsey petticoats standing alone with the dirt.[9]

These women may have been noticed by Place because the standard of cleanliness of working people in general had already begun to rise by the late eighteenth century.

Cotton enabled quite humble people to afford several changes of washable clothing, such as the country girls described in Smollet's *Sir Lancelot Greaves* of 1762, 'in their best apparel, their white hose and clean, short dimity petticoats, and their gawdy gowns of printed cotton'.[10] The extent to which cotton was used by the very poor in the mid-eighteenth century is shown by records of babies left at Coram's foundling hospital from 1741 onwards. Careful descriptions of clothing were kept, together with samples, so that children could be identified and reclaimed. Research into babies accepted between 1757 and 1760 has shown that cotton caps, shirts and biggins (forehead cloths) were common, whilst gowns included one of 'dimity and diaper cufed with blue and white dimity' and another of 'striped cotton cuffed with a flowered lining'.[11] Most printed cotton cost less than 1*s*. 6*d*. per yard in the late eighteenth century and a dress length could be bought in the 1770s for 6s. to 8s.[12] This was a week's wages for many, which would not be impossible to save.

Printed cottons were used not only for dresses, but also for bedgowns, loose hip-length jackets which crossed over in front and were held in place by the apron strings. They covered the stays and shift, but revealed the petticoat. They remained popular until the 1840s.

Roller-printing brought down the price of prints still further, and tiny patterns in pinks and lilacs could be had for a few pence a yard (plates 2 and 3). Mrs Gaskell's Mary Barton wore an everyday gown described as 'Hoyle's print you know, that lilac thing with the high body'.[13] A Miss Stanley visited a school for unemployed factory girls at Stockport in November 1862, and saw that 'most of them had the usual factory girl's dress on, print gown and shepherd's plaid put over their heads and pinned under their chins'.[14]

Such prints were good standbys for the armies of country ladies who spent their lives teaching village children to sew. Books published to help them give a valuable insight into working-class dress. One from 1854 stated that

> aprons for elderly people are best made of a breadth and ½ of deep blue or dark lilac yard wide print . . . Young women and servants often wear the same, but generally prefer them of a lighter lilac or deep pink, made of only one breadth.
>
> [Neckerchieves of] lilac print will wear longer [than scotch gingham] and suit the farm labourer; dark for weekday, lighter for Sunday. Cut ½ long, price 2d.–3d.[15]

The garments would be sold at cost or at a discount. Such philanthropy was widespread, but cheap cotton may have made it possible. In an early work of 1789, *Instructions for Cutting out Apparel for the Poor*, checks, duck, Lancashire cloth, dowlas, diaper and printed cotton were among the fabrics used.[16]

Such activities not only clothed the poor, but made sure they were suitably clad for their station. Parishes commonly used clothing and fabric distribution to manipulate behaviour. In 1832 the Farthinghoe clothing club published its results. Each member paid 2d. to 3d. per week, topped up by local worthies, and after a while they could choose from a range of textiles. The rules were stringent. Female servants must be in a post in order to receive anything. Payments were only accepted after attendance at church. Any depositor becoming pregnant whilst unmarried or having an early birth after marriage would be expelled, as would anyone charged with theft, drunkenness, poaching or other misdemeanour. The organisers claimed a drop in illegitimate births and 'improvement with respect to morality, parochial relief, and employment . . . [in] a parish distinguished in 1826 for disorder, pauperism and lacemaking'.[17]

Heavier cotton and cotton mixtures were used for outerwear. Drugget had a cotton warp and woollen weft, and was used for working women's skirts. Fustians were more widely used when heavy, densely woven fabrics were needed. Lancashire was first known for fustians in the seventeenth century when they were made entirely of linen. Cotton–linen mixtures were usual in the early 1700s, but fustians were all-cotton by 1800. In chapter one, Mary Rose has discussed Lancashire's importance as a centre for fustian production and the role of fustian manufacture in developing the early factory system.

Fustians fell into three categories: heavy, unnapped twill cloths, which in the eighteenth century included jean, nankeen, ticking and herringbone; raised corded patterns, such as dimity and diaper; and napped and corded fabrics, with names like pillow, barragon and thickset, but perhaps the best known being moleskin and corduroy.

Many names are still familiar to older people today, but no longer generally used, such as ticking, a stout casing for featherbeds and pillows, and dimity, a favourite for bedspreads. Other fabrics, such as jean, are so closely associated with modern times that it might come as a surprise to find they have such a venerable pedigree.

Fustian was the ideal fabric for hardwearing outerclothing. The Old Bailey records for 1715 include a report of a theft of coats, including a fustian 'frock', a loose garment with a turned-down collar. 'It appear'd that the 3 Persons who lost the Goods were Dust-men; and being at Work in the Street, hung their Cloaths upon the Pales, from whence the Prisoners took them.'[18]

Descriptions of highwaymen on Hounslow Heath mention fustian. In 1751 Ambrose Maynard was attacked by two highwaymen 'well mounted (one on a Bay gelding, the other on a Black one, both dressed in Fustian Frocks, with Ruffles and Silver laced Hats)'.[19] Fustian coats were waterproof and warm and this must have appealed to highwaymen. This particular combination says something about their image problem, since it suited them to pass as gentlemen. A more usual outfit for a working man would be a fustian coat with a dimity waistcoat, worn over a check cotton shirt.

Corduroy and velveteens, such as moleskin, were popular materials for working-men's breeches and later trousers. Francis Place, who had been apprenticed as a leather breeches-maker in the 1780s, saw his master reduced to making cheap ready-made breeches to sell at the fair, but even 'the rag fair breeches trade was rapidly declining in consequence of the increase in cotton manufacture; corduroys and velveteens were now worn by working men instead of leather'.[20]

Nevertheless, the quality of eighteenth- and nineteenth-century working-class clothing should not be exaggerated. It certainly failed to impress Frederick Engels in the 1840s.

> The clothing of the working people, in the majority of cases, is in a very bad condition. The material used for it is not of the best adapted. Wool and linen have almost vanished from the wardrobe of both sexes, and cotton has taken their place. Shirts are made of bleached or coloured cotton goods; the dresses of the women are chiefly of cotton print goods, and woollen petticoats are rarely seen on the washline. The men wear chiefly trousers of fustian or other heavy cotton goods, and jackets or coats of the same. Fustian has become the proverbial costume of the working-men, who are called 'Fustian Jackets', and call themselves so in contrast to the gentlemen who wear broadcloth, which latter words are used as characteristic for the middle-class. When Feargus O'Connor, the Chartist Leader, came to Manchester during the insurrection of 1842, he appeared, amidst the deafening applause of the working-men, in a fustian suit of clothing.[21]

Fustian made a striking contrast to the tailored woollen garments of establishment fashion. Whereas the tailored coat fitted closely, fustian clothes were more loosely structured because of the nature of the fabric and the needs of consumers. Instead of greys and blacks, fustian ranged from white and buff to rich brown and bright blue, with different garments and colours worn in different trades.

White was the only colour thought possible for a gentleman's shirt, but the working man's heavy cotton shirt could be checked, striped or patterned in any colour. The previously mentioned instruction book for parish ladies recommended

> for those made of stout Croydon, at 4d and 4½d. a yard designed expressly for the poor, use metal buttons at 8d. the gross . . . Those made of pink and blue shirting at 6d., and worn by young farmers and mechanics on Sunday, require collars of different shape, fronts put in and fancy agate buttons, which are 4½d. the gross white, and 6d. coloured to match the shirt . . . For agricultural labourers and their sons, brown calico at 5d. or 6d. . . . Observe that working men wear their shirts of greater length than gentlemen, and that the sleeves must be wider and the binder broader, to give them the room and the strength where required.[22]

Wages doubled in the second half of the nineteenth century whilst the proportion of working-class income spent on clothing rose from 6 per cent in 1845 to 12 per cent in 1905. This reflected a growth in skilled trades. At the same time the professional sector grew over twice

FIGURE 61. A photograph of a working-class family, *c.* 1895. Father wears bib and brace cotton overalls, which became popular as awareness grew of the need for proper protective clothing. Washable cotton had transformed childcare. Babies had adequate supplies of diaper napkins (giving rise to the American name for that garment). Terry towelling nappies were still in the future, as were waterproof pants. Babies were handed to visitors with a small cotton quilt to put on one's knee. (Photograph courtesy of Lancashire County Library, Chorley Local Studies Collection)

as fast as the population as a whole and the lower-middle classes increased from 0.8 per cent to 4 per cent of the total labour force.[23]

From the 1840s onwards outfitters aggressively marketed tailored woollen clothing for the working-class man. In *The Clothing Workers of Great Britain* S. P. Dobbs recalled how

the workman who had hitherto been content to pass his life in corduroy or moleskin now took to buying a new suit of tweeds 'off the peg' once a year or oftener. The new suit was, to start with, only worn on Sundays, but soon it came into everyday wear, until today corduroy has been relegated to the use of navvies and tramps.[24]

The proud new owners of woollen suits needed white cotton shirts with stiff fronts and collars to keep up a respectable appearance. Many chose a cotton shirt with a linen front and cuffs, or a linen collar. Others were reduced to paper or rubber collars, or just a shirt front, worn over a dirty shirt, a work shirt or none at all. Robert Roberts remembered how, in his Edwardian childhood, 'the tradesman took pride in wearing stiff collars even in the "workshop" . . . A child's weekly chore was to have his neckwear at the laundry and returned home in time for father to choose the best out of the frayed collection and go off, "dressed up to the nines", on his Saturday evening booze.'[25]

Vests and drawers had not been widely worn; shirt flaps were made long enough to be tucked between the legs. Now knitted cotton and wool vests and Long-Johns were common. Whilst some men slept in their underwear, nightshirts were spreading, creating a new market for cotton.

Women's standard of underclothing also rose (plate 4). Heavy-duty cotton stays replaced leather ones and by the 1880s aggressive advertising promoted fashionable new shapes. The number of shifts and petticoats owned by ordinary women increased and an extra garment, drawers, came into use among all classes around 1860, as a necessary response to the crinoline. Women, too, stopped sleeping in their shifts and bought nightdresses.

FIGURE 62. A design for a chemise, registered by Mrs Hornblow of 12 St Ann's Square, Manchester, in 1867. These were worn underneath the corset and drawers. Originally a wide garment, this one had shaping. Chemises became shorter, closer-fitting and lighter towards the end of the century. (Public Record Office, BT45 4867. Re-drawing of Crown Copyright material, used by permission of the Controller of H.M. Stationery Office)

## The nineteenth century:
## a mass clothing industry develops

The emergence of ready-made clothing as a mass industry met the needs of a society in which, by 1800, one-fifth of the population lived in towns. For the rural poor, spinning and weaving cloth and making it into clothing had been traditional. The new urban poor, working long hours in a cash economy, had no time to make clothes, so had to buy them. The growth of the skilled artisan and lower-middle classes created further new markets.

Traditionally the cost of fabric was substantially greater than the cost of turning it into clothing. The availability of cotton and cotton mixture fabrics reduced the price of the 'raw material' and undoubtedly stimulated the growth of the ready-made clothing trade. A marked increase in clothing production in the 1830s and 1840s coincided with a sharp fall in the price of cotton.

Another factor was the growing sophistication of retailers, who added value to their wares through presentation, packaging and processing. Drapers were the first to show this tendency, installing gas lighting, plate-glass windows and brass fittings. 'Slop-shops', selling coarse, ready-made work clothes, traditionally known as slops, also went 'upmarket' at this time, rechristening themselves 'outfitters'. Clothing was vigorously advertised at marked prices and sold for cash. Prices were kept down by low profits and high turnovers.

Certain garments were particularly suited to professional production and the trade in these was established early. These included items such as heavy fustian outerwear, which were difficult to make at home, being hard to stitch.

Ready-made clothing was in demand when large quantities were needed at short notice. This particularly applied to the army. Forces were constantly being raised and disbanded in the eighteenth century and every recruit had to be clothed. Manufacturers were commissioned to produce vast numbers of uniforms. The production methods and sizing systems developed in this way led to mass production in its truest sense. During the Napoleonic Wars such contracts gave a significant boost to the clothing trades.

Ready-made clothing was produced for markets where clothing could not be made. Work clothes were exported to the fisheries of Newfoundland and slave plantations.[26] Exports to Australia supplied familiar clothing to expatriates, whilst low-quality goods were shipped, as luxuries, to indigenous peoples. Much large-scale clothing manufacture originated in ports because of this and to meet the needs of travellers and sailors. Complete outfits, designed to last years in the outback, were widely advertised.

Hats, shoes, stays and hosiery, which needed specialised equipment, could be produced ready-made to a high standard, and such items were accepted by all classes well before 1800.

Whilst London was the centre for many clothing trades, specific industries were associated with different parts of the country. Gloucestershire and Stockport produced felt hats; Northampton made shoes; gloves came from the west country; Derby, Leicester and Nottingham made hosiery, and ports such as Liverpool, Bristol and Portsmouth supplied the slop trade.

Some country manufacturers set up wholesale operations in the City of London, such as the hosiers George Brettle & Co. of Belper in Derbyshire, who opened their premises in 1801. Such warehouses grew and diversified, eventually supplying clothing to every corner of the world. Stanley Chapman gives further analysis of the growth of the wholesale system in chapter three.

At the start of the nineteenth century, Lancashire, like any other county, had its bespoke tailors, dressmakers and shoemakers in most towns, whilst drapers, pedlars, markets and fairs supplied fabrics, trimmings and ready-made clothing. Lancaster had tailors and dressmakers capable of producing clothes for the London 'season'. Liverpool was another major centre; its tailors were rated second only to the best London houses.

Liverpool had a sizeable ready-made clothing industry but it was to be overshadowed by Manchester; by 1900 there would be 10,000 clothing workers in Liverpool and 40,000 in Manchester.[27]

In the 1830s about 6,000 people in Manchester and Salford worked in the clothing trades.[28] The most obvious reason for this was cotton, but Manchester was also a centre of population, a market for all kinds of clothing, with good trading links throughout the country.

One of Manchester's first clothing success stories depended on wool rather than cotton. Benjamin Hyam came from a Jewish pedlar family which settled in Ipswich in the late 1700s. In 1832 Hyam went to Manchester to seek his fortune.

> Out of his family expertise, considerable energy and organisational skills, a flare for invention and advertisement, and a modicum of capital, Hyam created modern mass-tailoring in Manchester. He relied not upon high prices for each article sold but upon bulk sales at a low margin of profit, fixed but competitive prices, cash on delivery, economy in manufacture, and speed in production, probably in workshops attached to his retail premises. His first advertisements offered to make a complete suit at six hours notice.[29]

By 1841 he had branches in Birmingham, Bristol, Colchester and Bury St Edmunds and his stock in Manchester alone was worth £25,000.

By 1851 there were thirteen branches, three of them in the West End of London, 'their operations co-ordinated by regular April meetings at his warehouse in Pall-Mall Manchester, of managers, salesmen, travellers, collectors and cashiers'.[30]

Felt hat-making had been an important Stockport industry since the seventeenth century. In 1826 Christies, the London hatters, opened a large factory in Canal Street. The industry was threatened by the fashion for silk top-hats rather than felt ones, but recovered with the advent of the bowler, trilby and homburg.

In 1823 Charles Macintosh, a Glasgow chemist, patented his waterproof fabric. Rubber was liquidised with naptha and sandwiched between cloth. He went into partnership with some Manchester cotton manufacturers and in 1824 they started trading as Charles Macintosh & Co. from a Chorlton on Medlock cotton mill. It was found that tailors stuck pins in the cloth, then complained that it let in the wet, so the firm made garments themselves. The industry later diversified into rainproof garments, made from closely-woven water-repellent cottons based on Burberry and Aquascutum fabrics, but rubberised mackintoshes maintained their popularity.[31]

The products made by Manchester firms are illustrated in the registered design sample books preserved at the Public Record Office. This scheme was set up in 1839 to protect products from piracy. A picture or sample of the object was glued into a book and allocated a number, and the date and manufacturer's details were noted.[32] Few designs were registered from other parts of Lancashire, thus showing the importance of Manchester as a clothing centre.

Several designs were for tailored garments, such as Elias and Reuben Levy's 'Leviathan vest', a waistcoat registered in 1849. These merchant tailors operated from Market Street and Shude Hill. Benjamin Hyam registered a coat in 1847 and in 1851 a pocket made from double fabric so that money would not escape through a hole. Thacker & Radford of Hodson's Square registered a 'demi-shirt' in 1846, which passed over the head like a tabard. Flusheim & Hesse of Back Piccadilly registered a collar in 1845, the 'Imperial shirt' in 1846, which gathered at the neck with cords, and a combination collar and necktie in 1848.[33] Their first registration led to a law suit, reported in the *Manchester Guardian* on 18 January 1846.

Yesterday, Messrs Flusheim and Hesse, Stock and Shirt Makers, Back Piccadilly, were summoned to the Borough Court to answer an information laid against them by Messrs Welch and Margetson, a firm in the same trade, for infringing the design for a shirt collar, which the complainants had registered . . . The defendants had also registered a design for a collar, about twelve months after the defendants had registered theirs, and that was the design complained of as a piracy . . . Mr Green, contended upon behalf of the defendants . . . that the collar differed from that of the complainants in being made all in one piece, and having a horizontal line at the band part of the neck, whereas the complainants appeared to have registered their collar in consequence of the novelty which a curvature at that part produced. He then called three witnesses . . . all of whom were practically acquainted with the making of collars, and who gave it as their opinion that the two designs were perfectly dissimilar . . . Mr Mander said that the magistrates had come to the conclusion that the defendant's design was not a piracy.

The Jewish community was becoming a significant force in the clothing trades of Manchester. David Hesse came to England from Cologne in the 1830s and started a drapery business which was transformed into a manufacturing empire with the aid of a succession of partners. By the 1850s he had a factory in Ireland and was importing goods from France and Germany.

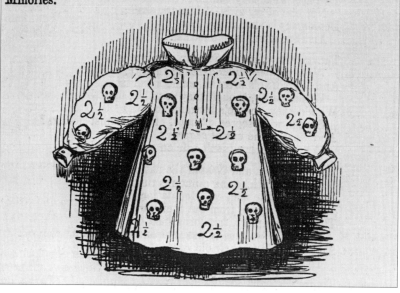

> ## "A SHROUD AS WELL AS A SHIRT."
>
> MESSRS. MOSES AND SON have disclaimed the disgrace of being the employers of the unfortunate shirt-maker EMMA MOUNSER.
>
> We are glad to find that kind-hearted THOMAS HOOD did not write the "Song of the Shirt" altogether in vain, since some of the task-masters of the poor needlewomen are alive to the discredit of paying 2½d. for ten hours' labour.
>
> By the kindness of the pawnbroker we are enabled to furnish a pattern of the "Twopenny-ha'penny Shirt," which can be had ONLY (it is to be hoped) of MESSRS. HENRY EDWARD AND MORRIS MOSES of the Minories.

FIGURE 63. Cartoon from *Punch*, vol. 15 (1848), p. 76, campaigning against sweated labour. *Punch* had attacked Moses & Son, a well-known firm, mistaking them for Moses Brothers, who took a widow to court for pawning the shirts she was making in order to feed her children.

The Jewish population of Strangeways and Cheetham was 610 in 1861 and 1,419 in 1871. The number continued to rise as thousands fled from persecution in Eastern Europe. Jewish refugees became the mainstay of the clothing industry, setting up workshops in hundreds of converted houses from Strangeways to Ardwick and working long hours for little pay in their effort to survive in a new country.

Working conditions in the clothing trades had given concern ever since the first Children's and Young Person's Employment Commission of the early 1840s. In fashionable houses, work was almost continuous for days on end during the season, whilst big shops and warehouses had garments made by outworkers, paid a pittance by subcontractors.

In 1864 the second Children's and Young Person's Employment Commission looked again at the clothing trades and interviewed employers and employees in Liverpool and Manchester.[34] Establishments ranged from Miss Faulder's, milliners and dressmakers, in fashionable St Ann's Square, Manchester, where indoor hands scarcely ever worked less than sixteen hours per day from March to September, to Mrs Rogers, wholesale milliner of Rochdale Road, where girls worked in a room so overcrowded that the fire could not be lit. Other wholesale trades in Manchester included staymaking, crinoline making, millinery, mantles, ladies' underclothing, children's clothing and cloth caps. The scale of the industry was indicated by an extract from a paper by a 'medical gentleman'. 'I was not previously aware of the great number of women who find employment in our warehouses at frill-making, cap-making, and the like, amounting, I am credibly informed, to several thousand.' He looked at ten warehouses, employing between them eleven hundred women, of which 'only two could be said to be commodious and well aired. Nearly all the buildings in Manchester in which women work were originally erected not for warehouses but as dwelling-houses'.[35]

The Commission noted a trend for silkmercers to open dressmaking departments. Mr Kendal, of Kendal Milne & Co. of Manchester, stated that theirs had opened around 1850, 'almost of necessity, as otherwise we should be unable to dispose of some of our best goods to our best customers, private houses liking to make up only their own'.[36] Kendal Milne's employed forty people working a twelve-hour day in this department, of which about twenty slept on the premises. All received three weeks' paid holiday per year.

The trend was also noted in Liverpool, where the Commissioners interviewed six large dressmakers and 144 small ones. It was generally thought to be a good thing, since it would diminish the number of small dressmakers. The larger staffs gave more regularity in working hours, and what six would submit to, fifty would not.

Such shops sold fashionable ready-made dresses, known as 'costumes', from the 1860s. In 1883 G. H. Lee & Co. of Liverpool even registered two exclusive designs from Paris.[37] Lewis's, the other great Liverpool department store, was founded in 1856 as a boys' outfitters, but by 1880, when its Manchester branch opened, it was clothing all the family, specialising in the working-class market. Both this and its Birmingham branch were supplied through its own factory in Liverpool.

The ready-made clothing trade was stimulated by the development of the sewing machine in the 1850s, which was itself invented as a response to the industry's rapid growth in the 1830s and '40s. The Commission heard evidence of its widespread use. Mrs Wilson, a shirtmaker of Egypt Street in Liverpool, worked from a small dwelling-house parlour not more than eleven feet square, with three other people.

> I employ women in making up fine shirts etc., which I take out from shops, and use a sewing machine. I have had as many as twelve women in this room. The regular day in houses, where shirt work is done, of which there are a great number in the town, is 12 hours for all, girls as well as women . . . In a shirt room a girl can earn 5s. a week on plain work, but we do a rather superior kind.[38]

FIGURES 64, 65. Photographs of Nelson mill girls, c. 1893–5, in work clothes and formal outfits. Working-class living standards were rising at the end of the century, and unmarried working girls could dress well. They wear fashionable full sleeves and stiff collars, but their curled fringes were becoming out of date, and their strong boots give away their social background.

Machines were operated by treadle or steam power. Messrs Guthrie & Jones of Back George Street in Manchester, wholesale staymakers, who employed ninety-five people, said that they paid their machinists from 10s. to 15s. per week, whereas girls doing coarser work were

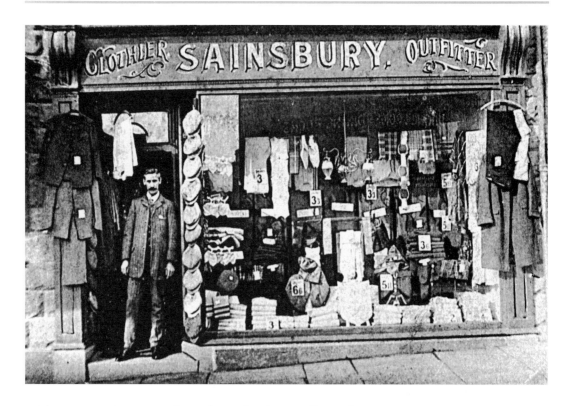

paid 7s. to 8s. 'Some of the girls prefer the treadle, and some steam power for working the sewing machines. The former may have the advantage, as some consider it, of standing instead of sitting.'[39]

Elias Howe, an American inventor, produced the first workable lock-stitch machine in 1846. He sent the prototype to England with his brother, who sold the British patent rights to William Thomas, a London staymaker. Another American, Isaac Merit Singer, improved the mechanism and in 1856 set up an agency for his own machine in Glasgow. As a result of these developments sewing machines were widely used by large manufacturers in Britain from the mid-1850s onwards.

Adoption of the sewing machine in England was hampered by Thomas's patent. Nevertheless by 1862 nearly 400,000 American and European machines had been sold in the United Kingdom. Machines were first made in this country in 1852 by Bradbury & Co. of Oldham. The Jones Sewing Machine Company was set up in 1859 and moved to Guide Bridge near Manchester in 1870. The location of these concerns highlights Manchester's importance as a clothing centre.[40] The speed of the sewing machine had to be matched in cutting out garments before its potential could be fully exploited and in the late 1850s numerous patents were taken out for bandknives to cut multiple thicknesses of cloth. Subsequent expansion in production of sewing

FIGURE 66. A photograph of Sainsbury's clothiers and outfitters, Moor Lane, Clitheroe, Lancashire c. 1900. Garments were often hung outside such shops from the 1700s until the 1940s. Cloth-cap making was a staple Manchester industry. (Photograph courtesy of Lancashire County Library, Clitheroe Local Studies Collection)

machines in the late nineteenth century led to continued and rapid diffusion. In 1886 the Singer Sewing Machine Company built a new factory in Scotland which could produce half a million machines a year. By 1900 it dominated the market.

One by-product in the evolution of the sewing machine was the Swiss embroidery machine, invented in Mulhouse in 1828. Henry Houldsworth of Portland Street Mill in Manchester bought the British patent rights and produced machine-embroidered fabrics from the 1840s. Some examples were registered by his son James in 1851, in the form of shaped silk panels for skirt fronts.[41]

By the second half of the nineteenth century clothing manufacture was a significant Manchester industry specialising in light clothing for the cheaper markets, such as shirts, underwear, nightwear, dresses and millinery. The mackintosh trade also flourished. By the end of the century Manchester made a third of the world's mackintoshes.

The Manchester industry was dominated by Jewish immigrants, typically working from converted houses. The clothing 'quarter' curved round the northern edge of the city from Ardwick to Ancoats, behind Piccadilly to Strangeways. Shude Hill was, and still is, the heart of the industry.

In contrast, several vast, well organised factories employed a significant proportion of Manchester's clothing workers. Rylands & Sons Ltd, Manchester's largest textile wholesaler, had been involved in clothing manufacture since the 1840s. They employed 1,200 workers making all kinds of garments at their Longford works and had several other factories in different parts of the country. A wholesale catalogue from the 1880s survives in the Central Reference Library, Manchester. It is embellished with prints of their warehouses and factories, such as Medlock Mills, where they made ladies' and children's underclothing, and the range of garments listed is extensive. Whilst 'Gentlemen's' ties and scarves, or 'Alma shape' dressed and boxed white shirts were available, the choice of stout working clothing was more extensive, such as 'dowla', 'calicoe', serge and union shirts. Duck, drabbet, velveteen, mole and cord figured largely in the men's outerwear section. Interestingly, all the trousers were available with 'falls', a square flap with buttons along the top, which had been replaced in establishment fashion by flies over a generation before. The men's hosiery department offered a wide range of underwear, from white, brown or fancy cotton vests, at 8s. to 12s. per dozen wholesale, to spun silk at 60s. to 70s. Women's underwear included corsets in jean, coutille and sateen, plain or fancy, with names like the 'Slap Bang', the 'May Queen', or the 'Little Beauty'.

By the 1880s some of Manchester's largest clothing concerns were mackintosh manufacturers. Joseph Mandleberg began making rubberised garments in Shude Hill in the 1850s. His products had led the field in style and lightness. His trade mark, F.F.O., meaning free from odour, alluded to the unpleasant smell associated with most mackintoshes. In a pattern typical of many late Victorian companies, Mandleberg & Co. moved from the city centre as they expanded. In the 1860s they went to Cheetham and in the 1880s a showpiece factory, the Albion Rubber Works, was built in Pendleton.

## The twentieth century

In the twentieth century ready-made clothing became almost universal. There was also a significant reduction in the cost of clothing, the quantity worn, its weight and complexity. This was due to changing lifestyles, but also to changes in the industry. Improved transport enabled regional shopping centres to develop, with department stores and chain stores. These big retailers increasingly dealt directly with manufacturers, rather than wholesalers, and lorryloads of garments were sent across the country on the new trunk roads.

Production methods and marketing became more sophisticated; sales patterns were manipulated, reducing fluctuations in demand and promoting profitable lines that were easy to make, competitively priced and preferably wore out quickly, or were subject to changing fashion and so needed to be replaced.

A good example was the shirt. Before the First World War they were expensive, voluminous and heavy. Two or three would last a lifetime. In the 1920s manufacturers began to make lighter-weight, lighter coloured and less bulky shirts. Men took to buying several, which wore out more quickly than the old ones. This represented, for the same amount of cotton, an increase in shirtmaking and more work for weavers.

The two world wars stimulated trade, as other wars had done before, bringing lucrative contracts for uniforms. In the 1940s rationing and the utility scheme were accompanied by strict manufacturing regulations. New companies could not be set up and existing firms were helped to update production methods, for instance by introducing conveyor belts. In this way the clothing industry was supported and strengthened.

By the 1930s many clothing factories had electricity, and used equipment such as overlockers, the Deerborn blind-stitch machine for hemming, the Hoffman press and the Eastman band-cutter, which could be pushed round a table.

Clothing was transformed in the 1920s by the introduction of artificial silk, known as rayon. This suited the unstructured look of women's fashions and gave a luxurious appearance. The 1935 census of production revealed that the women's clothing industry consumed £5,473,000 of

FIGURE 67. Photograph of the Co-operative Retail Society's window display, Hammerton Street, Burnley, 1929. The days before the annual mill holiday were busy, but then the town emptied as everyone headed for Blackpool or Morecambe. Even the shops stayed shut. The Co-operative Wholesale Society had shirt factories across the country and their success led the Society to acquire cotton mills, such as the Springs Mill in Bury. By 1933 60 per cent of co-op shirts and pyjamas were made from its own material. (Photograph courtesy of Lancashire County Library, Burnley Local Studies Collection)

rayon and £3,168,000 of cotton.[42] Cotton was relegated to the cheapest garments. Cotton manufacturers were badly hit, as were the old underwear factories, undercut by new concerns at home and abroad, which used unskilled women on semi-automatic machinery to overlock knitted rayon tubes.

Many cotton manufacturers diversified into rayon, but John Maden & Son of Bacup went one step further when in 1928 they also began garment production. Within twenty years they were solely clothing manufacturers. Their first knitting attempts were laid aside until one of the factory girls offered to make up the fabric. The managing director recalled

> this seemed a good idea, but it was a trade of which I had no knowledge or training, but the girl herself was full of confidence, so I purchased one sewing machine, and asked her to make some samples. Much to my surprise she rolled a piece of cloth down the table and proceeded to cut out garments without the use of paper patterns, and to my utter amazement the garments sold!

The buyers pointed out however that they were a little crudely made-up, and that special machines should be used for overlocking the seams, and for inserting elastic. These were obtained, and we were in business, and without the assistance of any expert knowledge![43]

The company supplied Marks & Spencer for thirty years, their first contract being for 100 dozen lock-knit blouses at 18s. 6d. per dozen, to retail at 1s. 11d.

Whilst the bulk of Lancashire's clothing workers were found around Manchester, it was increasingly common for factories to be set up elsewhere, particularly in Liverpool, Blackburn, Wigan and Preston. However, the advantages of premises in Manchester were still obvious. A huge choice of fabric was instantly available and firms could respond rapidly to orders. It was noted that 'the manufacture of wearing attire has become a staple occupation of the commercial centre. Further, it is possible to say that the industry is growing'.[44]

*An Industrial Survey of the Lancashire Area*, produced by the University of Manchester for the Board of Trade in 1932, gave the following breakdown of clothing industries:[45]

FIGURE 68. Holidaymakers from Colne visiting Selside, c.1905. The women's cotton blouses, which could be bought ready-made for a few shillings, are the only informal element. The men wear stiff collars even for a day out. (Photograph courtesy of Lancashire County Library, Colne Local Studies Collection)

FIGURE 69. Mill girls celebrating the 1937 coronation at Horrockses Crewdson (?) Mill. High fashion had no place for printed cotton, but it was still used for cheap clothing such as their gaily patterned overalls. (Lancashire County Library, Preston Local Studies Collection)

Table 6.1 *The clothing trades*

| Trade | Workers | % of national total |
|---|---|---|
| Tailoring | 24,950 | 12.4 |
| Dressmaking and millinery | 9,120 | 9.0 |
| Hats and caps | 11,830 | 33.7 |
| Shirts and underclothing | 17,980 | 21.2 |
| Others, e.g. corsets, gloves, umbrellas | 2,730 | 9.9 |
| Boots and shoes | 10,280 | 7.6 |
| Total | 76,890 | 13.1 |

Tailoring was centred on Manchester, but a Co-operative Wholesale Society factory employing 1,200, and Brown & Haig with 400 on its books, were based in Wigan. Lewis's also employed considerable numbers in Liverpool. Bespoke tailors were becoming less common. This was put down to the effect of the depression on middle-class incomes.

Six years ago a typical well-established Manchester tailor had 80 employees in the best shopping centre of the town; now he has none. This type of business is still carried on in the highest-class trade but by far the largest part of the demand for less expensive suits and overcoats is met by factory-made clothes – either bespoke or ready-to-wear . . . intense organisation, specialisation and continuous production have reduced the costs so that prices are tempting more customers to wear this type of clothing, with the consequence that the demand for the bespoke journeyman tailor has declined.[46]

In the 1920s Crook's Tailors and Clothiers for Man and Boy, founded in 1857, had ten Manchester branches and thirty from Darwen to Stockport, supplied by four factories in Manchester.[47]

The wholesale bespoke system emerged around 1900. A shopkeeper could measure a customer, post off the details and have the suit back in forty-eight hours. Burton's were the market leaders in this with a country-wide chain of shops. In 1935 they took over part of a disused mill in Walkden to train ex-cotton workers to sew whilst a new factory was built for them. They were encouraged by Lancashire Industrial Development Council, which was seeking new sources of employment to compensate for the cotton industry's decline. A prominent site, well placed for distribution, was bought on the East Lancashire Road at Worsley. Burtonville was an *art deco* fantasy, with an eighty-foot tower, neon lights and a searchlight visible for miles. It had air-conditioning, welfare and sports facilities, and a canteen for 2,000.[48]

Burton's suits were cheap and fashionable. Their shops had a uniform image, down to the last detail of window displays and salesmen's patter. Their formula was ideal for its time and sales continued to soar. The Walkden works were expanded and in 1939 Halliwell Road cotton mill, one of Bolton's largest, was turned into yet another Burton's factory.

Raincoats, classed with tailoring, remained important, employing around 5,000, mainly in Cheetham, Strangeways and Salford. Unrubberised rainproof garments were widespread by the 1930s. In Manchester there were hundreds of back-street firms employing between ten and a hundred people, a handful with over a hundred and just one with a workforce of over one thousand.[49]

Mackintosh production also flourished. A fleecy-lined waterproof to double up as a winter coat had been a best-seller according to Manchester University's report, which also noted that

women's waterproofs are manufactured in a great variety of colours and styles so that a fashionable mackintosh is almost as important as a fashionable coat. Many waterproof manufacturers also make

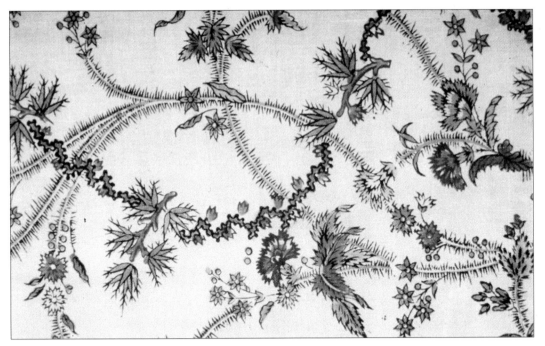

PLATE I. Detail of a woodblock-printed fabric of a printed cotton day dress, 1775–85. Blue was 'pencilled' in by hand over yellow to produce green. (Photograph courtesy of The Gallery of English Costume, Manchester City Art Galleries)

PLATE 5. Swatches of linen hooping from the Holker manuscript, c.1750. These coarse and relatively inexpensive cloths became a feature of Manchester manufacture in about 1735 and were used for ladies' paniers, or petticoats. The left sample has *chiné* or warp-printed stripes. (Musée des arts décoratifs, Paris) (Author's photograph)

PLATE 2. Day dress, c.1833–5, in green and white striped roller-printed muslin. Inset: PLATE 3. Detail of fabric. (Photographs courtesy of The Gallery of English Costume, Manchester City Art Galleries)

PLATE 4. All this underwear from the 1860s could have been made out of cotton. The stockings are a wool-cotton mixture. (Photograph courtesy of Leicestershire Museums, Arts and Records Service)

PLATE 6. Block-printed Manchester cotton velvets in a sample book prepared in 1783 by Thomas Smith to facilitate orders from American merchants. (Photograph courtesy of Winterthur Museum Library: Joseph Downs Collection of Manuscripts and Printed Ephemera)

PLATE 7. Produced at Bannister Hall for the London linen-draper Richard Ovey and in-scribed 'The Black Gro[und] Demy. False Pink & White Run[ning] Gum Cistrus. R Ovey 24th March 1803. 30 P[ieces] on Super 7/8 Cloth.' 'Demy' refers to the limited colour range. (Photograph courtesy of Stead McAlpin & Co. Ltd, reference c/124)

PLATE 8. Muslin with woven check, block printed by Watson, Myers Fielding & Co., Catterall 1792. With a clear white ground and three dyes used to create a full colour range, its high quality made it equal to prints produced in London. (Author's photograph)

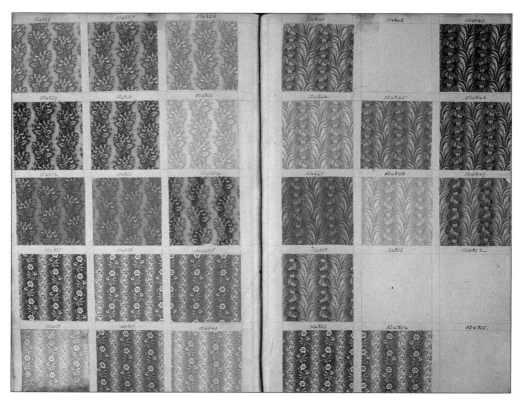

PLATE 9. The vivid colours shown here date from about 1825, although the patterns are older, as indicated by this volume's inscription, 'Ros[sen]dale 1795–1800' (samples 024826–855, CPA volume. Photograph courtesy of The Museum of Science and Industry, Manchester)

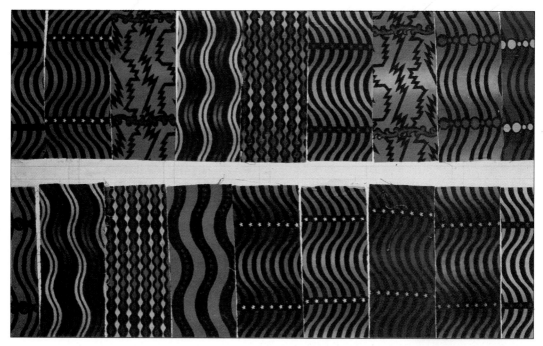

PLATE 11. Cotton velvets continued to be a Lancashire speciality. These, of 1845, have all but one in the right-hand column overprinted with the same 'vermicelli' pattern and are also good examples of mineral-dye colours. (CPA 1968.1.5. Photograph courtesy of The Museum of Science and Industry, Manchester)

PLATE 10. By an unidentified Lancashire printer, c.1848, for the American market. The bold delineation of the pattern derives from the highly contrasted colours. (Photograph courtesy of Manchester Central Reference Library)

PLATE 12. A 'golding' produced for the Indian market at Abbey Print Works, Whalley, on 11 October 1888. This expensive cotton was so named for the addition of a printed gold pigment. (Photograph courtesy of Lancashire Record Office)

PLATE 13. The Gregson & Monk 'Ideas for New Designs FC' volume of *c.*1906–8 contains a wide variety of printed cloths, including these handkerchief borders, one for children. (Photograph courtesy of Harris Museum and Art Gallery, Preston)

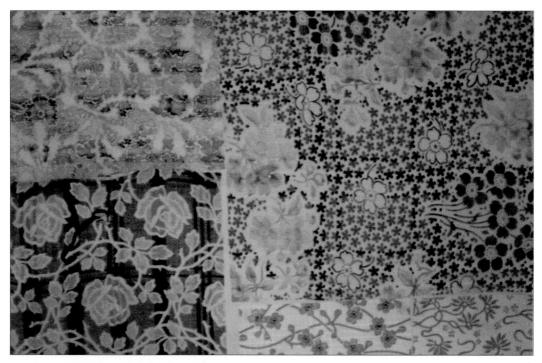

PLATE 14. Roller-printed plaid muslins and plaid cambrics, from a volume compiled in 1901 by Gregson & Monk Ltd, Preston, entitled 'Ideas for New Designs FC'. (Photograph courtesy of Harris Museum and Art Gallery, Preston)

leather and leatherette coats for women. All these clothes are within reach of working-class incomes and have been sold in great quantities.[50]

As with raincoat manufacturers, most firms were small, with only a few employing over one hundred people.

The number of dressmakers' shops was declining, whilst factories were increasing. Two-thirds of Manchester's dressmakers worked in 353 factories. Some of the largest producers also made cloth, such as Tootal, Broadhurst, Lee & Co. Tootal's gained a reputation for quality ready-made garments and were one of the first to launch a trade-name for dresses. A new factory was opened in Bolton in 1930 to produce their *Chesro* range.[51]

The 1932 survey noted the benefits of factory production.

Frocks are cut out in bulk so that far less cloth is used than when a single frock is made up; the cloth is bought wholesale, or direct from the manufacturer, and the cost of converting it into a frock is a matter of a few shillings – a frock which can be made up for 1s. to 3s., according to style, could not be made by a dressmaker for less than 25s. Actually, factory-made dresses can often be sold in the shops for less than the cost of the cloth bought in the retail stores. This has brought ready-made frocks within the reach of the majority of women and has compelled numbers of local dressmakers to go out of business.[52]

The pull-on hats of the 1920s were also more cost effective to make in a factory. Many cloth cap firms opened millinery departments, and whilst the trade overall was growing, traditional milliners had to seek work in factories.

The women's clothing industry still fluctuated, with Christmas and Whit week producing surges in demand. Rather than lay off hands in the summer, they made children's party frocks, overalls, blouses and underclothes, and tea-cosies and handkerchief cases for the Christmas trade.[53]

Forty-one firms made felt hats in Stockport, Denton, Hyde and Bury. This represented 80 per cent of all the country's felt-hat workers. Some firms, such as Christies, employed over a thousand, but most were small. The stitched fabric caps so common at this period were made by 211 firms. Most were based in Manchester and Salford.

The hundred or so shirt firms in Manchester tended to be larger than the dressmaking factories. Trade was expanding rapidly. About half used the sectionalised method rather than workers 'making through' garments. One factory estimated that with this system 400 girls turned out 1,750 shirts per day, as opposed to 1,250 with the old method.[54]

Many cotton manufacturers diversified into clothing production. Henry Bannerman & Sons Ltd, founded in 1805, developed a successful shirtmaking business at Brunswick Mill in Ancoats. They also spun cotton there and at mills in Stalybridge and Dukinfield.

> There is a huge workshop here full of sewing machines operated by girls and women who work under healthy conditions in a clean and well-lighted factory. By means of special attachments, some of the machines concentrate on certain parts of the work, for instance, one will stitch on a button in about a second, and another will in little more time make a complete buttonhole, cutting the hole and sewing the edges at one operation. In adjacent rooms are the cutting, making up and packing departments. In the making of a shirt the cloth is first cut into the required length. Then a bundle of about thirty pieces is taken, the top one being stencilled for the guidance of the cutter who is in charge of a machine with a bandknife running at a high speed. This blade cuts the thirty pieces up into the component parts of the shirt, the operator manipulating the bundle until the cutting is complete . . . The operations into which the making of shirts are divided are cutting, sewing, examining, folding, making-up and packing.
>   The main production of the factory is the famous 'Banner' shirts, but a considerable quantity of overalls, nightwear, aprons and other garments is also made.[55]

Pyjamas were a new line. It was noted that 'manufacturers of shirts and pyjamas have benefited more than any other of the clothing manufacturers from the higher standard of life of the working classes. There has been a great increase in the demand for pyjamas in recent years because of a change in the normal night attire of working men'.[56] This made up for lost trade in women's cotton underwear, although increasing quantities of rayon underclothing were produced. In 1926 the Co-operative Wholesale Society opened the Belmont Garment Factory in Store Street. Its telegraphic name was 'Undies Manchester' and it brought together lingerie production from Kettering, Birmingham and their general factory in Broughton.

Boot and shoe making meant the slipper industry of the Rossendale valley, centred in Bacup, Rawtenstall, Haslingden and Bury. Felt making was introduced from Leeds in 1854 and slippers were made for workers' use in the process. By the 1870s local entrepreneurs were selling their wares in Manchester, taking advantage of its distribution network. Large-scale production developed in the 1880s, during the depression in the cotton industry. From that time onwards cotton mills were frequently turned over to slipper manufacture, which flourished on the cheap premises and labour created by the cotton industry's decline.

FIGURE 70. Advertising sheet for 'Hawkins Guarantee Sale', published by John Hawkins & Sons Ltd, Greenbank Mills, Preston, in June 1931. Hawkins' garments were available direct from their mills, by mail order and through their shops. All goods were British-made. (Illustration courtesy of Lancashire County Library, Preston Local Studies Collection)

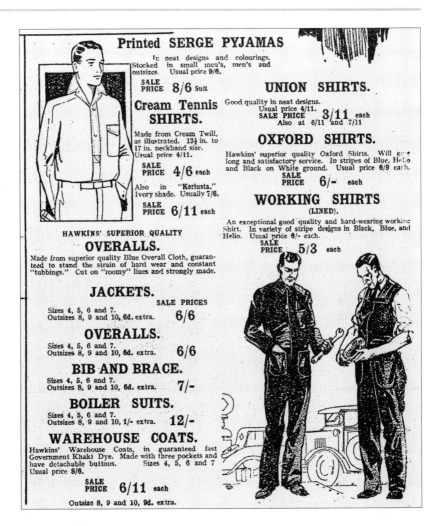

By the 1920s the industry had diversified into women's boots and shoes and men's plimsolls. In 1923 twenty-five firms produced 450,000 pairs of shoes between them each week.[57] Shoe manufacture was also carried out in Preston and Rochdale.

Whilst the cotton industry steadily declined, clothing production expanded until the 1960s. Many manufacturers emerged from the war years in a stronger position than ever before, producing quality clothing using up-to-date methods. The tendency for firms to move out of cramped inner-city premises to development areas now became a stampede, as recruitment became harder faced with competition from more attractive occupations.

The workers filling new factories in places like the Wirral were called 'green labour'; unskilled teenagers trained for just one or two processes. They saw themselves as general hands, not clothing operatives, and tended to disappear if something better turned up. Armies of school-leavers always had to be trained afresh, but this kind of workforce, in the hands of professional managers and work-study departments, was capable of a massive output.

The need for variety and the texture of fabric meant that 'product engineering' to the extent practised in other industries was impossible. Cotton lends itself to mass-production methods because of its more standard texture and simplicity in making up. In *The Women's Outerwear Industry* of 1957 Margaret Wray commented, 'it is in the large, post-war cotton dress factories that the application of production engineering techniques have resulted in biggest economies of scale'.[58]

When Christian Dior launched his New Look in 1947, with its crisp lines and full skirts, cotton was acknowledged as the perfect fabric and the industry was ready. In 1940 the Cotton Board had established its Colour, Design and Style Centre to encourage good design in the industry. The Centre generated considerable interest in British manufacturers and designers through its exhibitions and fashion shows, which were often televised.

Dresses from the Centre's shows, many of which were presented to Platt Hall Gallery of English Costume in Manchester, sum up the look of the 1950s, a decade of spots and stripes, bold prints and rustling organza. This was a 'sharp', starched look, in contrast to the draped styles and muted colours that had reigned supreme for so long. Big manufacturers, such as Tootal's and Horrocks's, became household names for their crisp cottons that laundered so beautifully.

The next decades saw a revival in cotton. Man-made fibres were uncomfortable on their own and mixtures, such as polyester–cottons, became popular, combining the comfort of cotton with easycare qualities. The rise in leisurewear at the expense of tailored woollen garments brought a return of stout cottons for everyday clothing, such as denim, corduroy and poplin, worn with cotton jersey 'T' shirts and sweat shirts.

In the mid-twentieth century the market changed. The middle classes no longer demanded such high quality products whilst the working classes, with new spending power, bought more and better clothes. Clothing was less an indicator of class and more one of age, interests, individual expression and occasion. Spending on clothing increased in comparison with other products, whilst it became cheaper, with the emphasis on novelty and value for money.

This checked the tendency towards bigger factories and more standardised products. Small, flexible suppliers were needed, able to respond quickly with short runs. Large concerns had to adapt to the new, retailer-dominated climate.

The British clothing industry survived the changes of the 1960s and '70s, protected from foreign competition to some extent by international

FIGURE 71. Publicity photograph showing a printed cotton dress designed by Alan Boyd, against a backdrop of Carson and Berry's map of Manchester and Salford of 1741. The dress was modelled as part of the Manchester Cotton Board's contribution to the Brussels fair of 1958. (Photograph courtesy of Manchester Public Libraries)

agreements on export quotas. Its workforce was considerably reduced, yet in the 1970s around 6,000 clothing workers were still employed in Lancashire [59] and over 30,000 in Greater Manchester.[60] These represented just over 13 per cent of the total industry, the same proportion as in the 1932 survey.

A survey by Lancashire County Planning Department in 1988 described the British clothing industry as 'potentially one of the largest and strongest in Europe',[61] with the north-west producing one-third of the country's weatherproof outerwear, over one-quarter of all work clothing and jeans and one-fifth of all men's shirts, underwear and nightwear.

These figures might suggest a reassuring continuity with the traditional clothing industries of Lancashire, but for one difference. Whereas the old factories thrived alongside cotton mills and bustling warehouses, most manufacturers complained that home suppliers were unable to meet prices and deadlines or just did not exist, so they were forced to turn to Europe. One commented, 'whenever we can we buy locally but this is seldom possible – it is a wicked situation – there are no UK producers at all'.[62]

CHAPTER 7

# 'Shewey And Full Of Work':[1]
# Design

MARY SCHOESER

T HE MASSIVE SCALE of the Lancashire cotton industry at its peak
has made it an important field of study for historians, who have
made a thorough examination of their subject from virtually every
angle except one – design. The very success of Lancashire cotton
manufacturers contributed to this state of affairs by producing massive
quantities of cloth, suited to a wide range of tastes and pockets. Very
little survives today and, given the tendency of the industry towards
specialisation, these cannot be used to draw general conclusions.[2]

What can be said of the existing designs, strike-offs (record prints
on paper) and cloth samples is that they were often kept for their
potential value for re-use and therefore lean towards the decorative.
For the same reason, and as companies amalgamated, they have over
time more often than not also been separated from written production
records which would indicate quantities produced of a particular pattern
and amplify references to customers. This means that little is known
about the origins of orders for specific designs and with it the burden
of financial risk represented by each design choice. However, it is clear
that from the late eighteenth century to the present day, large numbers
of patterns emanating from Lancashire were made on request (or commission) and thus do not represent the personal tastes of the majority
of Lancashire manufacturers. How the textile was eventually sold
(for example, as yard goods or made-up garments or furnishings) and
to whom is also difficult to ascertain. Only educated guesses are possible
regarding the eventual cloth price, and thus the consumer's own
economic status, based on the printing method together with the
number and type of colouring agents used. And it does not always
follow that several colours were preferable to one.

Designs and cloth samples in public collections are almost always
separated from production records. So while they certainly help to give
an indication of changes in taste over a given period, they too, have
inherent limitations with regard to estimating actual production. They

also chart a very limited, although influential, category of design, for both museum collecting policies and studies emanating from these holdings have, for most of the past century, concentrated on 'fine' design and, more specifically, on furnishing fabrics. The latter never accounted for more than about one-fifth of Lancashire production. The remainder – utilitarian and commemorative textiles, Western dress fabrics and cloths carrying designs specifically for export markets (with the exception of furnishing fabrics destined for America) – have hardly been studied.

Lacking samples, our perception of design in Lancashire is coloured by the writings of both contemporaries and historians. One reading of such evidence suggests that the industry gained a reputation for ambivalence towards 'good' design which it did little actively to refute, in part by failing to create records of its own products. As late as 1852, when Edmund Potter estimated a total of twenty million pieces printed annually in the whole of Great Britain, the majority being of Lancashire production, he confessed that he had been forced to 'arrive at this estimate with considerable difficulty, owing to the absence of any very authentic statistics'.[3] Mid-nineteenth-century criticism might have been rebutted by a public-spirited gesture such the proposed Museum of Calico Printing, of which the sole legacy is an account by John Graham, who compiled an important manuscript on printworks in the Manchester area from 1790-1846.[4] In the pioneering studies of printed (and mainly furnishing) textiles undertaken in the 1950s by Peter Floud, the condemnation of Lancashire was latterly legitimised by his decision to end his most widely available survey of English printed textiles at the point when 'unpleasant' Victorian examples appeared.[5]

This essay attempts to shed a different light on the subject. It lays particular stress on the contemporary meanings of terms such as fustian and style, as opposed to pattern, and on the impact of the scale and nature of the export market. It also attempts to provide a context against which the motivations of critics of Lancashire design can be more fully understood.

## 1750–1820

Dyeing and bleaching had been established in Lancashire in the seventeenth century. Lancashire manufacturers also understood the use of blocks, whether for printing pigments (which did not impregnate the cloth) or impressing un-coloured patterns. The latter process evidently found a good market, for 'a mid-seventeenth-century Robert Peele rose to wealth as a woollen manufacturer selling cloth stamped with patterns cut into elm blocks'.[6] Patchy evidence makes it difficult to establish the precise pattern of developments in these trades until about

1750. However, it seems certain that until this date the printing and bleaching of high quality cotton and linen goods was done only in London, where the process of producing a 'true' print had developed in the 1670s. This involved a complex series of processes based around printing a mordant, which made the pattern areas receptive to colour in the dye-bath; it also required efficient bleaching. Thus the development of the finishing trades in Lancashire from 1750–1820 are partly the result of the introduction of London-style printing and partly the further development of its own established traditions.

The key to understanding the early history of printing in Lancashire is the distinction between chintz and printed fustian, terms which have altered their meaning over time. In the mid-eighteenth century, chintz meant a printed flat cloth. Surviving samples confirm a contemporary description of high-quality chintzes as following the taste in silks; their thoroughly bleached-white ground and glazed finish further heightened this comparison.[7] These were the full-colour prints made in London, where the high-quality silk industry was also to be found. Formerly all-cotton, chintzes often had linen warps and cotton wefts from 1721–1774, when printing on all-cotton cloth (except for export) was banned. Fustian, on the other hand, had been introduced into England in the early 1600s as a linen warp, cotton weft cloth. It had several forms, the earliest of which was a 'false' fustian, with a brushed surface. All variants had a texture of some description and by 1674 true fustians, with a looped or cut pile, were being made in the district around Bolton, which had become the centre of fustian manufacture.[8]

Confusion arises because the flat linen and cotton cloth originally made for printing chintzes also became known as fustian. This was undoubtedly the result of the act of 1736, which clarified the 1721 prohibition of the sale, use and wear of all British printed calicoes to allow the printing of fustian. The legislation was intended to continue to curb the London printers' competition against the weavers of silks, half-silks, worsted and fine woollens. The 1736 act was dubbed the 'Manchester Act', which suggests that it took fustian to mean a textured or pile-woven cloth, but the term was taken by London printers to mean the fibre content rather than the cloth's weave.

Whatever the intentions of the 1736 act, the effect was that Lancashire replaced India as the source of much of London's print cloth. The first documented evidence of the appearance of Lancashire cloths printed in London appears in a manuscript of about 1750. It was compiled by John Holker, who intended to secure a prominent place for himself in the French textile industry by revealing the secrets of English textile production. This folio, in the *Musée des Arts Décoratifs*, Paris, contains just over 115 samples (plate 5). It shows the wide variety of woven fabrics for which Lancashire was already known; most come from

Manchester and a few come from outside Lancashire altogether. It includes thirteen chintzes, the patterns block-printed on a linen warp, cotton weft flat cloth of a type now

> made in the Manchester district, especially at a small town called Blackburn. The output is so large that scarcely a week goes by without a thousand rolls being sold and sent to London unbleached. The merchants of that great city turn them over to bleachworks. The printing is done as soon as they are returned from the meadows . . . The volume of business done with foreign countries is infinitely greater than with the domestic market, although this is very extensive.[9]

Without making direct reference to it, Holker's manuscript does not rule out printing in Lancashire. On the last pages are samples including several thought to have been made under Holker's direction in Rouen; all save one demonstrate his interest in corded and pile-woven cottons, which he began to manufacture in his own Rouen factory in 1752, having recruited eight English master-workers in the previous year. According to Holker, the secret of making cotton velvets was so closely guarded that he risked his life obtaining the un-printed samples contained in the main part of the manuscript. It is therefore also possible that the supplementary samples represented cloths he knew how to make but had not obtained samples of in Manchester. If the latter is true, it is significant that the extra samples included two printed velvets (one a warp print, the other block printed and noted as made in Tours). The importance of these is the light they shed on what is thought to be the earliest reference to printing in the north-west, contained in an article on Manchester in the *London Magazine* in 1750, which notes that the town 'has been for long a manufacture of fustians called Manchester cottons, much improved of late by dyeing, printing, etc. . . .'[10] Judging from Holker's twelve samples of fustians, the cloths referred to by the *London Magazine* were not chintzes but velvets, of which, Holker noted, 'many patterns and qualities were manufactured in Manchester and its environs'.[11] Since Holker was employed in Manchester from 1740–45, the printing of fustians must have begun in the late 1730s at the latest.

'Manchester velvets', as these fustians were subsequently called, were often plain-dyed. But a weaver's pattern book kept by J. Fielding of Manchester from 1775–8 includes the notation, 'printed', adjacent to the draft for cotton velvet − and only cotton velvet − suggesting that the block printing of cotton velvets in Manchester was the norm at that date. Such cloths were known by continental buyers as well as in the home market, and Manchester velvets were said to compete with Utrecht velvets − a linen backing-cloth with a goats' hair or mohair pile – which were fashionable upholstery fabrics also embossed or printed with patterns. Examples survive in American collections in quantity as small swatches in pattern books and on long folding pattern cards prepared in Manchester.[12] Those dating from 1783 show small, busy, block-printed patterns, often arranged in or over narrow stripes and in colour combinations that seldom exceeded three; the grounds are not a true white, but unbleached or tinted ivory or tan (plate 6). Such patterns were most often used for fashionable men's clothing until the 1820s, when the proletariat connotations of cotton were no longer either useful or *soingé*.

Holker's reference to the thousands of rolls of flat print-cloth being made in Lancashire, and to the importance of the export market, highlight the logic of setting up local chintz printworks, particularly as Liverpool gained ascendence as a port. However, the production of printed Manchester velvets offers one explanation why calico printing *per se* – that is, on a flat cloth – was not widely practised in Lancashire in the 1750s and '60s. Holker's comment that Manchester velvets were dyed in all colours except scarlet, which would not 'take' on cotton, also suggests a local lack of understanding of printing mordants and the highest grade of bleaching, which was so fundamental to producing good reds on vegetable fibres that in the twentieth century it was still called 'madder bleach'.[13]

The desire to improve local bleaching skills only emerged in 1756, when Dr Francis Home, employed by the Board of Trustees for the Improvement of Fisheries and Manufactures in North Britain, published his *Experiments on Bleaching*. This introduced oil of vitriol (sulphuric acid) in place of buttermilk during the penultimate process, known as souring. Despite such local attempts to improve bleaching and dyeing (and thus printing), it seems certain that much vital information was obtained from London. Graham recorded that Edward Clayton, who was listed as a calico printer in the Walton-le-Dale parish register of 1753, had brought his workers from London, and family tradition credited Jonathon Howarth's several years' residence in London with the instigation, in 1764, of what was to become the Peel printing empire. On the other hand, Livesey, Hargreaves & Co., founded in 1776 by the Livesey brothers (who by the 1750s were manufacturing vast quantities of fustian, mainly destined for printing), gained dyeing skills in 1778 by bringing in a partner John Anstie, a Wiltshire clothier with an interest in dyeing.[14]

The Liveseys also recruited workmen from London in 1783 and an account of Manchester in the same year noted the 'succession of capital artists' who had left London for Lancashire. The same report also described a local contribution to a new fashion in printed textiles, commenting that the newcomers not only instructed others, but also added to their former experience by printing upon grounds, which the dyers followed with other shades, and hence there was a communication of nostrums and chemical secrets between printers and dyers, to the advantage of both branches in the further perfecting of grounds, and giving a firmness and clearness to colours. These improvements soon left the London printers nothing to rival us with but the light airy patterns, upon which we are making a considerable progress, with the advantage of darkening [that] which is deficient, or pencilling and grounding them afresh . . . .[15]

This undoubtedly refers to the fashion for 'dark-ground' prints that appeared in the late 1770s, unique not so much for their coloured backgrounds (which had also been fashionable in prints of the 1740s), but because these grounds met the pattern without leaving a large area of uncoloured surround, as had been the case earlier. Some of these may have been created by eliminating areas of mordant prior to dyeing, which did not require a strong bleach. The implication is that the traditional divisions found between London printers, bleachers and dyers were not duplicated in Lancashire. The writer also implies that Lancashire had embarked on the printing of true chintzes, that is white ground, highly glazed cloths (now all cotton). By the 1780s, then, the London monopoly on high-quality printing was being challenged, but not without retaliation, for dark-grounds were printed in the London area from at least the 1790s. Richly coloured grounds – including the tea-coloured grounds that became fashionable in the 1810s – remained popular into the 1830s and continued thereafter as an important option for designers (plate 7).

Black, blue, red and brown grounds provided a means by which Lancashire printworks could demonstrate their increasing prowess. Improvements in bleaching and dyeing were promoted by the Manchester Literary and Philosophic Society (founded in 1781) and included the introduction of chlorine bleaching, discovered by the Frenchman Claude Louis Berthollet in 1785. In use in Lancashire within a few years,[16] chlorine was made easier to use by Tenant's patent of 1799, but it was not until the 1810s that its production began to increase dramatically and its price fell. This process reduced the bleaching time from months to days and contributed to significant improvements in the dark-ground style. It also allowed the introduction of its variant, which could be termed the discharge style, in which bleach was printed in dots onto an already-dyed ground, leaving a flickering white pattern. In the years between 1800 and 1820 it appears that large amounts of these were produced in a number of variations, three of which are recorded in price lists of 1806 and 1817 from the Peel's Church Bank printworks near Accrington. The second cheapest price

(129 pence per piece of twenty-eight yards), quoted in 1817, was for 'black ground and white', the simplest of the discharge styles. Listed in 1806 at 176½d. was a 'Choc[olate] ground discharge pad'd Yellow' (costing 188½d. in 1817),[17] a colour combination created by dyeing in yellow after discharging.[18] Larger areas of pattern amid the dots could also be left white and printed with one or more colours. Resists, or printing of paste which kept the pattern area white during dyeing, were also improved. It was also used to create another type of design initially based on dots – the lapis style, in which the resist paste (called resist-red) contained a mordant for madder; dyeing blue and then madder-red gave accurately juxtaposed areas of both colours. Church Bank probably called this style 'Marine Blue and Red', entered in their price lists at 190d. and 189d. Reds themselves had been improved in 1786 by the introduction to Manchester of Turkey red (an involved process creating brilliant, very fast reds) by Louis and Abraham Henry Borelle, who received £2,500 from Parliament for importing this technique from Rouen.

Turkey red, often referred to in this period as 'morone', was later to become a noticeable feature of many handkerchiefs and export cloths, but as with all the styles just mentioned, was used to supply both the dress and furnishing trades.[19] The design distinctions between the latter two was minimal in this period; the cloth itself was also often the same, whether gauzy muslin, cambric made from the fine cotton yarns developed in Lancashire in the 1780s (and often glazed), or cotton velvet. There was also a fashion for printing on 'welted quilting', marcella or piqué, all terms for loom-woven cottons imitating hand-quilting, and a Lancashire speciality from the 1780s. The demand for these for printing was brisk by the early 1800s. They were recommended for summer waistcoats by Ackermann in 1809 and this fashion continued until 1820, when William Nash wrote to his supplier, 'I regret no quiltings, as dandies do not suit . . .'[20] Distinctive patterns such as the 'pillar' prints (with, as their name implies, a design incorporating a column) and 'drab' style designs such as those commissioned by Manchester 'furniture printer' Bateman & Todd in the early nineteenth century, or those containing exotic birds, block printed at Church Bank and Bannister Hall in the 1810s, were clearly not intended for dress. Nor were the well-documented scenic prints, produced initially by flat copper plate (in use in Lancashire from the 1780s to the 1860s, but latterly used for commemorative items) but mainly by engraved rollers from about 1815.[21] However, these were rare patterns and, throughout this period, the majority, for whatever use, were small designs, such as geometrics, 'cashmere' motifs, or florals arranged as spots, stripes or in connected, all-over networks; simple weaves such as pinstripes were also imitated.

Such patterns were block printed until the 1820s and beyond but were particularly well-suited to machine printing, introduced into Lancashire at Livesey, Hargreaves & Co. in 1785. By the time of their bankruptcy in 1788 they had six to seven hundred cylinders cut or pinned. The latter were probably like those used on the machines installed by Peel in 1788, which had wooden rollers inserted with pins. These rollers allowed a maximum of about 12 inches downward repeat and were ideal for the dot-resist style. The mule, combining wooden relief rollers and engraved copper cylinders, was invented by James Burton in 1805 but direct printing (printing the mordant for colour on a white ground) by either mule or engraved copper rollers alone was not widespread until around 1810. Once introduced, these machines served many printers extremely well.[22] At Newton Banks Print Works, built by Benjamin Ashton in 1816, the annual production soon reached 2.5 million yards, all for home consumption and most in 'small black, purple and chocolate styles, by machine'.[23]

Ashton's single-colour styles were all based on an iron mordant and madder dye; iron alone resulted in purple, a stronger iron concentration gave black and iron mixed with alum gave chocolate. Iron mordants were hard to control, and some printers made their reputations by doing so, most notably Thomas Hoyle (founder of a large dye- and printworks at Mayfield in the 1790s), who was an early pioneer of chlorine bleaching. Hoyle's name through much of the nineteenth century was synonymous with reliable purples. Among the successful printers were others who were themselves chemists or had close links to people who were. Prominent among the former was James Thomson, chemist and manager at the Peels' Church Bank printworks until 1811, when he set up his own printworks at Primrose Mill, Clitheroe. Thomson took out patents for discharging Turkey red in 1813 and 1815 (giving his name to this colour) and for a printed indigo discharge in 1826.

The ability to control colours was crucial to the printer's success, since the capacity to produce a substantial volume of wash-fast dress prints was vital. Moreover, until the late nineteenth century, colour rather than pattern was more important in dress prints (and to a lesser extent in furnishings). Indeed as late as 1951, the author of the *History of the Calico Printing Industry of Great Britain* assumed his readers would understand that the term 'style' meant the manner of dyeing.

Many of the surviving samples sent as inspirations for the pattern drawer at Church Bank referred to colours by name or simply requested work 'in this style'. The Peels also copied patterns, a practice which became the subject of debate in the period preceding the passage, in 1787, of the first British copyright act for printed textiles, which gave protection for a period of three months. It was a debate which crystallised the north-south divide. On behalf of London printers, designers and some wholesale and retail linen-drapers, William Kilburn (the most successful London designer and calico printer of his day) claimed that the copying of designs in northern manufactories drove quality customers away, since Lancashire copies at 4s. 6d. per yard – as opposed to 6s. 9d. for London calicoes – were available in London after a lapse of only ten days. The Lancashire printers admitted their dependence on London fashions, but also reiterated their intention, as laid out in the previous year, to exploit the fact that 'three parts out of four of printed goods are consumed by the lower classes of people'.[24]

However, the timing of the Londoners' protest suggests that there was far more at stake than the possibility, observed by O'Brien in his thinly disguised anti-Lancashire publication of 1790, that 'cut-price methods would lose the custom of "persons of taste, fashion and opulence" who would not want for five or six shillings what their servants could buy in imitation for two or three'.[25] Judging from Peel's later prices, such Lancashire copies could only have been one- or two-colour prints. It seems more likely that it was fear of Lancashire's ability to produce *high* quality prints and the growing realisation that 'they have & will command all the trade which used to be carried on near London'[26] (plate 8). The 1787 copyright act also followed by one year upon the enactment of the Eden Treaty, which established free trade with France (silks excluded) and resulted in a flood of exports of good quality low-priced prints (and was thus a boon to the Lancashire printers). In addition, it coincided with a change in taxation, substituting a flat rate of 3½d. per yard for duties weighted according to the cost of the finished cloth (and therefore favouring printers of more expensive goods). These three themes – the export trade, France and duties – were to underpin the design debate of the nineteenth century.

## 1820–1890

In 1842 the copyright on dress fabrics was extended to nine months (with furnishings protected for three years), but only after a Select Committee met on the subject, which had been raised in 1820 and 1833. The debate regarding design, which surrounded this legislation and so coloured perceptions of Lancashire printed cottons, persisted to the end of the nineteenth century. However, the criticism of English (and now predominantly Lancashire) printed textiles ceased to illuminate the competition between printers in London and the north. Instead it came increasingly from outside the industry and thus often represented a perspective less familiar with market forces and more inclined towards political, ideological or nationalistic goals. This dichotomy became more apparent as exports increased both in proportion to home consumption and in real terms, rising from over 136 million yards in 1820 to more than ten times that amount in 1890. Thus while the critics strove to define appropriately English design, the industry had its eyes on distant shores.

By 1820 it was clear that Lancashire printers and merchants had an accurate understanding of foreign tastes. In the home market, except for trends in furnishing prints, they were also independent of London.[27] France, both by virtue of its lead in fashion and its recent and dramatic rise in production of printed textiles, now replaced London as the focus of Lancashire interest, particularly when French fabrics (banned at the outbreak of war in 1793) returned to the British market in 1826. The availability of French prints in both home and export markets under-pinned many of the stylistic changes in English printed textiles of the subsequent sixty-five years. However, of equal importance was the way in which French design altered the expectations and perceptions of both consumers and critics.

Wallis, speaking in 1849, saw a radical decline in standards soon after French prints entered the British market, describing the period from 1828 to 1838 as

> just as barren of originality, beauty or even excellence of execution as the period from 1816 to 1826 had been prolific in these qualities. There appeared no purpose whatever in the design of the period. For instance, perspective representations of geometric solids studded the dresses of the ladies, and box-lids, card cases, books, and many sided object[s], from a prison to a Church spire, appears to have been pressed into the service of patterns produced . . .[28]

He represented the trend among critics to condemn such designs as inappropriate for their purpose, with such purpose defined, by and large, by the establishment rather than the merchant, manufacturer or consumer. That aside, it is hard now to perceive from surviving examples such a dramatic and disastrous change in terms of *pattern*; certainly, more hard-edged motifs appeared, but since these can be found in sample books until the 1890s, they cannot have been regarded as distinctive patterns of 1828–38. Further, the approach in terms of pattern continued throughout and beyond these ten years; the 1842–1870 samples in the PRO are 'predominantly non-figurative (excepting florals as such) . . . stripes, spots, checks, florals and geometrics, and permutations of these. Mostly the repeats are small . . . the standards of printing were rarely poor, often excellent and the fabrics used were usually of good quality.' In fact, some firms prospered by remaining faithful to small milled patterns produced in a single or two closely-ranged colours; Hoyle's improved purple, patented in 1831, accounted for the bulk of their production and was described some twenty years later as 'superior in brilliancy, fastness, and utility for domestic wear [and] may be said to have superseded the old navy blue print, in English wear'.[29]

Some elements had changed: 'dark designs were in a minority; many designs used brilliant colours and strong patterns'.[30] These changes, as well as the hard-edged look, began to dominate printed fashion fabrics in the early 1820s and are essentially about *style*, as understood by the industry, rather than *design*. They can be accounted for by the use of new dyes (begun around 1813 with the introduction of steam-fixing) and better control of established ones – both resulting in stronger contrasts – in tandem with increased use of multi-roller machines and new methods of engraving copper cylinders (plate 9). (Block printing continued throughout this period as an alternative method of adding colours to a one-colour machine print.)

Furnishings, which in this period were for the first time produced *en masse* by machine, were characterised by the addition of ornamental scrollwork grounds and realistic depictions of flowers, birds, lace, and 'landscapes'. The church spires that offended Wallis may well have been gothic arches, such as those arranged as a dark green stripe on white and printed in this colourway from 1827–1830. However, this print was commissioned by Miles and Edwards, fashionable London 'furniture printers' (1821–47) and produced by John Lowe of Shepley Hall from rollers engraved by the leading engraver of the day, Joseph Lockett. Therefore patterns such as these obviously had enthusiasts, a great number of them in the export trade.[31]

With regard to the home market, what seems to lie behind such criticism of Lancashire prints was that the highly ornamented was not thought suitable for the ordinary classes. This is best revealed by Richard Redgrave, whose disapproval of the French printed textiles shown in the 1855 Paris exhibition was based on the fact that a Parisian of middle or lower class who 'cannot afford realities . . . will obtain the appearance of them by gaudy finery and over-decoration'.[32] The relevance to England of Redgrave's remarks rested on the widely held view that Manchester was entirely dependent on Paris for its designs and 'even then they managed to select the most hideous examples'.[33] A new twist on the age-old fear of servants dressed as masters, such remarks were increasingly aimed at furnishing rather than dress fabrics. The provision of cottons provided real betterment in both comfort and cleanliness, but by providing inexpensive ornamentation as well, printers, whatever their personal views, were encouraging people to get 'above themselves'. Simplistically put, by focusing on French design, British design critics could obliquely condemn France and its *petit-bourgeois* culture (the English equivalent representing the real threat to the British establishment) and at the same time respond to the new commercial threat posed by France. In the home market competition from French prints increased with the repeal of all duties in 1831 (including the 7d. per yard on imported prints). That French textiles remained much more expensive than home-produced goods until the Cotton Famine (1861–65) and were always produced in smaller amounts, only served to increase their *caché*.

In export markets, such as America, French textiles also provided a commercial threat, based on their higher degree of ostentation which was setting the pace in both pattern and style: 'before . . . women can dress perfectly, they must have the taste of the French, especially in colour'.[34] The latter was becoming an important factor in America, which in this period dramatically increased its capacity to produce low cost (single dye) goods in direct competition with those of Lancashire. There, perhaps as late as the 1870s, 'Hoyles' purples, chocolate chintzes, 'Potter's plate work', and other familiar English prints supplied the larger part of the goods consumed.[35] But these were the very styles which formed the basis of American production. Given what is known of the other comparable situations, it is likely that many enterprising dry-goods sellers sold American prints as English, a fact that must have galled the Lancashire firms who first created them, including Thomas Hoyle, whose apprentice, John Dynley Prince, set Merrimack Manufacturing Company (Lowell, Massachusetts) on its way to success as its superintendent from 1825–55.[36] Aside from the popularity in the lower end of the market of 'English' prints (largely based on one dye), the Americans expressed an open preference for 'French' designs (more realistic and highly coloured), and it made sense to provide them (plate 10). Doing so meant that they were available in Britain too.

Strong connections certainly existed between France and Lancashire between 1820 and 1890; but they were far more complex than the supposed absolute dependence which so disheartened critics, not least because there were some 500 designers recorded in Manchester in 1841.[37] The links were principally with Alsace, which was transformed between 1830 and 1860 from an area with numerous small firms to eighteen large ones, relying largely on technology perfected in Lancashire. In exchange, France continued its tradition of excellence in textile chemistry and, as a result, the most noticeable evidence of change. Even new dyes such as manganese bronze, introduced in 1823 by Thomas Mercer (1791–1866) and popular until about 1880, and aniline dye, isolated by William Henry Perkin (later Sir, 1838–1907) in 1856 but not applied to cottons until the 1860s, were based on or improved by French techniques; the lapis style used by Thomson, for example, was developed in Mulhouse. Both there and in Paris, designers worked for Lancashire printers from 1828, when Jean Baptiste Roman Lebert set up an *atelier* exclusively for MacNaughton & Thon of Manchester.

Studios specialising in English designs include those of Adolphe Braun (from 1848, customers including the merchants Butterworth & Brooks and the printer James Black) and Edouard Schultz (from 1841, associated with Edmund Potter of Dinting Vale in 1865). James Thomson also retained a Parisian designer in the late 1830s and early 1840s. Some firms, including MacNaughton's, employed French designers in their own studios. Similarly, French printers also benefitted in some cases from training in Lancashire, as did Charles Steiner, nephew of Frédéric Steiner, who purchased the Peels' Church Bank works in 1836.[38] Such evidence suggests the existence of a spirit of collaboration that deserves further study.

There is also little doubt that the French copied 'English' patterns, both old and new (that is, made successful by British printers, whatever the origin of the design), as did the English themselves. Particularly noticeable from about 1840 was the revival of late eighteenth-century English patterns which, in furnishings, evolved into what we now know as English chintzes. Opponents of extended copyright told the Select Committee in 1840 that they feared this would give an advantage to the foreigners, who would still be free to copy. It is significant that while Lancashire printers such as Thomson and Potter were generally in favour of copyright, those against were Manchester merchants such as Butterworth & Brooks, whose businesses were more affected by competition in America and other French export markets.[39]

The critics of Lancashire – including Henry Cole in the 1840s and '50s and William Morris from the 1860s until his death in 1896 – particularly disliked the choice of colourings (plate 11). These included rainbow printing (multi-colour in one operation), developed by block printers in the mid-1820s, adapted to roller printing within a decade and fashionable until the mid-1850s. Many of the new dyes were extremely vivid when printed on wool. A fashion introduced by the Alsatians in the 1830s, it was taken up in Lancashire as delaines (worsted weft and cotton warp). Delaines were so often printed with flat ribbon-like floral stripes (and often also rainbow printed) that the pattern itself, popular into the 1870s (together with other wide patterned stripes), became associated with this cloth. From the late 1850s colours also went from sharp to hazy on dress cloths with alternating satin and gauze-like stripes or plaids, and silk, cotton and silk, and cotton muslins were also printed. These increased in popularity as the period progressed, the making of less yarn-intensive cloths no doubt given impetus by the Cotton Famine. This period of changing fibre content, colour combinations and base cloths coincided with both the emergence of a sizeable middle-class market and the American manufacture of single-dye patterns; many Lancashire prints for the Western market thus gradually became less utilitarian. At the same time patterns were beginning to grow somewhat larger and more open, florals became more realistic, and *faux* flounces and military-style braidwork were also printed. Indian and Chinese motifs had been used throughout the period and from the late 1870s, so too were those evoking Japan, Turkey and Egypt, often in two or more tertiary colours (such as aqua, mauve, rust and yellow-ochre).

As the design reform movement gained momentum it was clear that what was wanted, instead, was an English style, something dignified, quietly coloured and, in sum, not 'shewy and full of work'. However, there was little to induce Lancashire manufacturers to change their approach to design. Business was, generally speaking, still booming. Further, during most of this period, the export market accounted for about two-thirds of Lancashire production, much of which required variations on a theme rather than innovation *per se*. Successful patterns (in which the colour style was often culturally determined) could run for decades, some – it transpired – for a century; for example, a number of patterns printed for the African market in the second half of the nineteenth century were still being made by the CPA in 1969.[40] Much work was also done in topical scenic styles for furnishings, handkerchiefs, traycloths and commemorative items. For example, the now dispersed pattern books (1849–1957) of Lockett, Crossland & Co. show numerous such engravings specifically for several countries, including Russia (where the royal family had also developed a taste for English chintzes).[41]

Attempts to improve design had begun in July 1836 with a grant from Parliament to the National School of Design in London. Thereafter Government Schools of Design were set up in the regions. The Manchester school (established in 1838), despite support from the likes of Thomson (who campaigned for good design right up to his death in 1850), was not an immediate success; it was criticised – as these schools generally were – for generating better copyists but few innovators. The general belief remained that good design originated outside Lancashire, whether at the instigation of a fashionable shop or influential tastemaker, and this is partly because, for a good part of the nineteenth century, the source of most fabrics was not disclosed. Thus while the description in May 1850 of a print for Liddiards (a well-known London draper), as 'one of the most lively and tasteful chintzes issued this season' was not unusual, the addition by the *Journal of Design* (an important forum for discussion and criticism of mid-nineteenth-century decorative arts) of acknowledgement of Hargreaves as the manufacturer was rare. However, which of the firms originated the design is not known – nor, of course, is the designer's name. As department stores increased in number and influence they were happy to perpetuate this situation.

The emergence of architect-designers in the mid-nineteenth century only gradually altered perceptions regarding who should make design choices. The entire working career of Owen Jones (1809–1874), the first prominent architect to engage extensively in designing for mass-produced decorative arts, was 'a time when there was a strong professional feeling that it was *infra dig* for an architect to descend to such "minor details"'.[42] In furnishing textiles this trend bore fruit when William Morris (1834–1896) designed his first printed textiles in 1873. In 1878, in the revised fourth edition of his *Hints on Household Taste*, Charles Eastlake could note that 'happily a great improvement has taken place within the last few years in the character of almost every kind of textile fabric used for curtains and upholstery . . . in many varieties of material, and produced at a price which is quite within reach of ordinary means', adding that he himself had supplied designs to Cowlishaw, Nicol & Co. of Manchester.[43] Consumer-led from the outset, the Lancashire industry served popular taste around the world (plate 12). It was not until the 1880s that the need to show itself as an instigator of 'English' design trends was finally signalled by the increase in British and American retailers selling 'artistic' products.

## 1890–1955

In 1890 the passage of the McKinley Tariff made British and French textiles almost equivalent in price in America. As a result, Lancashire printed cottons could no longer compete in the market for which they had been designed. This year also marked the general downturn in fortunes for the Lancashire finishing industry. Although not as dramatic as the decline in spinning and grey-cloth weaving, it was a trend that placed design in a more significant position as successive markets for low- and then medium-priced goods eroded, in effect following the American model. The response to increased competition was a demand for shorter print-runs, more patterns in four or more colours and high-quality printing on lower quality cloth. As a result, although Lancashire printers began in reality to produce fewer 'standard lines', it seemed that they dramatically increased their manufacture of high quality, well-designed ones. This was for two reasons. Between about 1910 and 1938 three-quarters of the export trade was lost,[44] so that the dominance of specialty design for the export markets decreased and attention focused on fashionable goods to regain western markets (in 1938 the home trade nearly equalled that for exports). In addition, as methods of reaching the consumer altered, printed textiles benefitted by being more photogenic than weaves.

In the years around 1880 Lancashire firms began to announce their use of well-known designers, such as Christopher Dresser (1834–1904), who supplied a number of designs to Barlow & Jones (for weaving into fine-cotton coverlets) in the late 1870s and 1880s, when the notion that a textile designer *could* be well-known was in its infancy. In 1881

Lewis F. Day (1845–1910, from 1870 designer of a wide range of decorative arts and from 1878 a prolific writer on the subject) was invited to become artistic director of Turnbull & Stockdale (founded in that year by William Turnbull at Stubbins, with William Stockdale, a skilled chemist, mechanic and businessman, becoming partner two years later). Thereafter, linking the name of a designer with particular printed pattern increased, aided from the 1920s onward by the inclusion in popular magazines of photographs, rather than sketches, of fashions and interiors. The same phenomenon provided a significant increase in information regarding the appearance of a wide range of fabrics, the identity of the retailer and, very occasionally in dress fabrics and often in furnishings, the name of the designer and manufacturer. As a result, from this point onwards Lancashire printers can be divided into two distinct categories from the historians' point of view: those who actively courted such coverage and those who would or could not. This roughly coincides with those who had independent sales operations and those commission printing only. The firms selling printed fabrics under their own name often also manufactured to commission, which was the dominant practice.

In the years up to the First World War printed fabrics for furnishing were much more fashionable than they had been in the mid-nineteenth

FIGURE 72. Tray cloth, commissioned for the Russian market, engraved by Lockett, Crossland & Co., 1912. (Photograph courtesy of Christie's, London)

century and can be divided into three types. A very limited number of large-scale block printed floral chintzes were made exclusively by commission printers acting on orders from wholesale merchants. A new form of chintz – highly glazed and roller printed with delicately engraved, relatively small, sweetly coloured patterns – were so often produced by Lancashire commission printers that they came to be known as 'Manchester chintzes'. Finally, a fair amount of fashionable Arts & Crafts and Art Nouveau patterns (the former often printed on a textured base cloth) were produced at the instigation of both retail and wholesale merchants, as well as merchant-printers. The lessened dominance of wholesale merchants in the provision of up-to-date patterns not only provided them with competition, it also engendered a perception of activity in design terms, even if the specifics of designer, design-instigator and manufacturer were not known to the consumer. Far more research is needed to ascertain, for example, to what extent designs by C. F. A. Voysey and Christopher Dresser, produced by both the printer-merchant Turnbull & Stockdale and F. Steiner & Co. (which continued to supply a good proportion of its roller prints to France), were promoted by the use of the designer's name and were, in addition, merchant-printed. Nevertheless, at least in retrospect, it was firms such as these that finally brought Lancashire credit for contributing to design developments in furnishing textiles.[45]

In dress textiles there was no equivalent renaissance in the years up to 1920. With the exception of white and pale plain-dyed gauzes for summer wear, cottons were no longer fashionable in and of themselves (as they had been in many circumstances until the 1820s and '30s and thereafter for summer gowns), although there was a growing market for printed shirtings as a result of the development of tailor-mades and fashions suitable for sports. For much of the period, patterns for these were single-colour essays based on dots or fine lines, arranged to form stripes, sprigs and conversationals. Increased informality in attitudes towards children was catered for with suitable patterns (including pre-printed cut-out doll shapes, ready for sewing and stuffing) (plate 13).[46] In general, however, the main trend in summer dress fabrics was the imitation of lightweight *chiné* silks (or printing on lightweight silk itself) and printing on gauze-striped or -plaid cloths (plate 14). Although present in the early 1890s, this fashion seems to have increased towards the turn of the century and then gradually declined. (Muslins were also printed to use for 'draping purposes', curtains and bedspreads.) The many discharged indigo, black or deep purple/maroon patterns surviving in sample books were presumably for winter.[47] Those with very detailed patterns on very fine, firm cottons also offered a fair alternative to silks and were undoubtedly for the middle-class market; those on coarser cottons were a cheaper option.

The decade prior to the First World War was the last in which large numbers of single-colour dress prints were produced for the western market. It is at this point that, in retrospect, the significance of the Lancashire printers' reputation for fast colour work became clear. After 1914 the supply of dyestuffs, largely controlled by the Germans since the 1880s, was no longer straightforward.[48] Costs increased dramatically and the only alternative – to lower standards – was often requested. As the price of high-quality printed cottons rose in the 1920s and '30s, they came into competition with printed silks, particularly after about 1931, when hand-screen printing was introduced in Macclesfield. During the same period, printed man-made fibre fabrics were introduced, initially for use as undergarments and only later, as dyestuffs for these fibres improved in the 1930s, for women's clothing. By this time the distinction between high and low fashion was largely a matter of detail – the quality of cloth and cut of the garment. This phenomenon arose from the inter-relationship between changes in society and access to information about the latest styles, provided by the media boom which began in the late nineteenth century. Whether in magazines, mail-order catalogues or advertising brochures, images were predominantly in black and white. So too, were films, and these two media together promoted pattern over colour. The move away from colour-led fashions in western markets should have been a boon to Lancashire printers during a period when dyestuff supplies were unreliable. But it was not to be

FIGURES 73, 74.
W. Fielden Royle's design for a dress fabric, *c.* 1938; and Sidney M. Plaskett's design for beach wear, *c.* 1939.
Source: W. G. Hayes Marshall, *British Textile Designers Today* (Lewis, 1939), pp. 239, 225.

so, for in its wake came the expectation of multi-colour printing and, of course, more emphasis on design.

The education of designers locally had undoubtedly improved, at least in the opinion of Walter Crane, who became director of design at the Manchester Municipal School of Art in 1893.[49] Nevertheless, such training was still not taken seriously even in the 1930s; 'no matter how large an Art School – as in Manchester, for example – it is never recognised as a College of Further Education. Large or small, independent or otherwise, an Art School is just an Art School, and there's an end on't!'[50] The Design and Industries Association, founded in 1915 to improve standards of British industrial design, was also received with little interest.[51] As in so much of British industry, technical skills remained much more highly valued throughout this period. Despite this, evidence of the presence of designers was reflected in the trend in dress fabrics towards casually placed florals and other motifs composed of marks that looked hand-painted as opposed to sharply engraved. Such designs reflected the impact of artist-designed printed textiles, which became available (and on the whole were hand-printed outside Lancashire) in the 1920s. These were associated with France, where the International Exhibition of 1925 once again brought comparisons unfavourable to the English. In 1926 Basil Ionides praised French manufacturers for their support of present-day designers and claimed that

> in England the creative spirit is left to be imported, and the makers content themselves with the steady favourites of the past, some originally designed as chintzes and prints, and some originally as papers, damasks, brocades, and needlework, but now adapted to chintz and cretonne designs.[52]

Ionides refers to printed furnishing textiles – which after about 1910 became predominantly traditional in style. Nevertheless, it was a Lancashire firm that was possibly the first to make mass-produced artist-designed furnishing prints; Tootal Broadhurst Lee Co. Ltd (which exhibited at the 1925 Paris exhibition), were in 1928 advertising cretonnes at 3s. 6d. and 2s. 6d. (for fifty- and thirty-inch wide cloth, respectively) by ten British artists.[53]

Tootal's promotion of artist-designed fabrics seems to have been a short-lived policy, but in 1931 it was the founding principle of Allan Walton Textiles, which was set up by two brothers, Allan and Roger. The firm received extensive and favourable editorial coverage for their designs. By Allan Walton himself, as well as Helen Simpson, Winning Read, Barbara Pile, Duncan Grant, Vanessa Bell, Frank Dobson and others, these were produced by 'a new and secret process' which was undoubtedly screen printing. The same reports studiously avoided mentioning the location of their printworks, but the family owned a Manchester cotton mill, John Walton, in Collyhurst.[54] Walton's, together with Turnbull & Stockdale and F. W. Grafton (founded 1782), were among the handful of firms included in the influential 1934 Dorland Hall exhibition, which excluded 'any article whose designer has mistaken vulgarity for Modernism; or any article in which a cowardly spirit of compromise has produced an historic hybrid'.[55] (Grafton's was the only CPA company to sell fabrics under its own name until the 1920s, when furnishing prints began to be issued as designed by the CPA, a marketing tool that was transformed into the brand-name Cepea, under which Grafton and other fabrics were sold from the early 1930s.) Walton's and Turnbull's also exhibited at the 1937 International Exhibition in Paris; Turnbull's included designs by Hans Tisdall, one of a number of *émigré* European designers who were to transform British textile design in the years after 1930. The Guild of British Textile Designers, founded in Manchester in 1938, had asked 'buyers of designs to give preference to all-British productions whenever possible'.[56] However, by 1948, when David Whitehead Ltd (a subsidiary formed in 1937 from the Whitehead Group, founded 1815) began to produce the well-designed inexpensive furnishing prints for which they remained well known until 1969, the use of foreign designers, resident or not, had ceased to be a source of concern.

With so much publicity given to artist-designed fabrics, it seemed that the best designs came from sources outside Lancashire, or outside Britain, although the designers actually working in Lancashire have yet to be studied and were rarely acknowledged. In 1937 an unnamed dress fabric firm was recorded as using over 800 designs annually (200 for ties, 100 for shirting and 50 for handkerchiefs), 200 of which were created by un-named members of their own studio.[57] Nevertheless, in the 1935 British Art in Industry Exhibition, among the dress fabrics section, in which designers were rarely credited, the CPA had at least acknowledged its *atelier*.[58] Two years later the index of *British Textile Designers Today* contained thirty-four entries for Lancashire, the majority in Manchester. Many were studios such as those of I. De Coutére, whose designs were produced by Graftons; Newbold & Houghton, whose clients included Kahn Textiles and Langworthy Brothers; W. E. Currie & Company, who are known to have provided designs for Nahums Fabrics Ltd; and Neville Headon, who specialised in designs for menswear, both printed and woven.[59] Within the city, design was put in the spotlight in 1940 by the creation of the Cotton Board's 'Colour, Design and Style Centre', which established a reputation for 'startling and original' exhibitions, numbering about five a year.[60] Among the designers of Whitehead prints – who included Pat Albeck, Terence Conran, Jacqueline Groag and Henry Moore – was Anne

FIGURE 75. Miss D. E. Ashworth, designer in the CPA's cretonne department, in front of part of the East and West Africa stand, 1949. In the far left background are the 'old faithfuls' (i.e. fifty years old). (Photograph courtesy of the Museum of Science and Industry, Manchester)

Ashworth, a member of the design studio from 1951–59, trained through day release to Manchester School of Art.[61]

While the Western market was moving away from colour-led sales, the African, Indian and South Sea Island markets did not, as a description of this trade in 1947 indicates.

In West Africa the printed designs must conform to certain con-
ventions, but within these they can be changed, and indeed *must*
be changed, as often as possible. But the range of colours in which
the patterns are printed must always remain within a certain
well-defined range, or the native buyer will have none of them.
This colour range is chiefly made up of deep indigo blue, dark
maroon, heavy dark greens, ochre yellow and all tones of brown
and cream . . . the type of colouring used necessitates the very
finest kinds of resist and developed dye printing . . . In East Africa
the demand is for something quite different; . . . bright primary
reds and yellows, brilliant magenta-pinks and sharp blues being
the favourites . . . For the South Sea Islands the Manchester trade
departments make 'pareo' cloths – again lightweight plain-woven
cottons in continuous lengths. These are printed with very large
and florid single colour designs, almost always deep blue or scarlet
on white grounds, or white on blue or scarlet grounds. Some
other colours are sometimes used, but they are always of extreme
brilliance.[62]

The combination of increased prices and unreliable supplies of appropriate dyes must have considerably aided the Japanese penetration of
these markets. And it was not easy, as no doubt had happened in the
nineteenth century with cloths printed for America, to off-load such
export cloths in Britain. However, this did occur, the most notable
examples being the selling of export cloths by Omega (1913–1919,
founded by Roger Fry), production of Europeanised batik cloths by
Graftons in the 1920s and the introduction immediately after the Second
World War of beach wear, house coats, dressing gowns and furnishings
made from trade goods. In 1939 at least one Manchester design studio,
that of Sidney M. Plaskett, had survived from twenty years before,
when 'British designers were mainly engaged in shipping styles for
markets which unfortunately have since been lost . . . [and did so] by
catering for the Home Trade and Colonial markets which formerly
had been left almost entirely to the Parisian designers'.[63]

## Conclusion

The decade after the Second World War could be called an optimistic
interlude, during which prints were highly fashionable for dress and
furnishings. However, in about 1955 restructuring began which resulted,
some ten years later, in an industry barely recognizable as descending
from the old Lancashire empire built on the roller printing of its own
grey cloth in styles tailored to export markets. The voluntary liquidation
of Steiner's in 1955 seemed to mark the end of an era. Looking back
over a period of two hundred years, it is clear that design leadership

was incompatible with the structure which made Lancashire cottons so successful, for even in the 1950s it was said that 'the question of obtaining . . . trade is not, of course the business of the calico printer, who is dependent entirely on the merchant to obtain the orders'.[64] Ironically, it was the strength of the industry – its ability to supply vast quantities of well-made inexpensive goods – that by definition made it open to criticism from those whose standards of design were based on exclusivity. Only in the years of decline was Lancashire deemed a suitable source of up-market textiles. As with block prints since the advent of roller printing, this was not through improvement in quality, but by virtue of relative scarcity. The catchphrase for the 'Britain Can Make It' Exhibition of 1946 was 'Good design means good business'; if, on the other hand, good business means good design, then there could be no designs better than the 'purples' and 'chocolates', the pareos and batiks, on which the trade in Lancashire printed textiles was built.

# CHAPTER 8

# Lancashire and the International Diffusion of Technology[1]

DAVID J. JEREMY

## The early nineteenth-century contest for technological leadership in cotton manufacturing

WHEN A COPY of the *Lowell Statistics* for 1836 was pinned up in the Manchester Exchange, it hung there for some months without occasioning comment.[2] This carelessness was not surprising. Lancashire manufacturers had developed an arrogant cast of mind, based on a shortened vision, which assumed that past triumphs guaranteed future conquests. Lowell was three thousand miles across the Atlantic and even further from Britain's great and growing Asian markets. Furthermore, the *Lowell Statistics* showed that Americans still relied on waterpower, which the best-informed men of Lancashire knew was far less reliable and less efficient than steam. In any case, Americans were basically preoccupied with primary production: running a plantation economy in their southern states (indeed growing cotton for Lancashire), concerned with farm and forest products in their middle and western states and territories. How could a clique of capitalist cotton manufacturers in the north eastern states, New England, possibly match Lancashire? Lancashire men had knowledge and reputation. Above all, they could tap the networks which stretched from Europe's most advanced workshops and nurseries of engineers on their doorstep, to the mercantile and trading networks and services which lubricated the movement of raw materials and finished goods between semi-tropical plantations and the sophisticated markets of European towns and cities. Lancashire men had been engaged in factory production for over half a century. They had built up an unequalled industry and knew the cotton business inside out. It was scarcely thinkable that erstwhile colonials would ever be other than marginal competitors in marginal markets.

By the late 1830s Lancashire was clearly established as the largest and most technically advanced cotton manufacturing district in the United Kingdom. In 1841 the district's 975 firms employed over 188,000 people.[3] With the inclusion of handloom weavers this figure would rise to an estimated 394,000 in the industry in 1839.[4] However, any impression that the leading district in the leading sector of the leading industrial economy had no international rivals before the 1850s is as misguided now as it was in the 1830s. France by 1843–5 had 705 installations for cotton spinning (462 water-powered, 243 steam-powered), nearly a third of England's 2,315 (674 water-powered and 1,641 steam-powered).[5] The USA, closer on the heels of Lancashire, by 1840 had some 1,240 cotton factories and 129 printing establishments, as many as those in Lancashire (where they were much more geographically concentrated and therefore reaped greater external economies).[6]

Impressionistic knowledge of American competition reached Lancashire via Liverpool merchants and their agents who encountered New England cotton goods in South American markets. Harder data appeared in 1833 when a Scottish cotton mill manager, James Montgomery, reprinted statistics assembled by a leading Boston capitalist. These reported that United States manufacturers in 1831–32 ran 800 cotton mills with a total of 1.2 million spindles and 33,500 looms, which Montgomery compared to Britain's 16.6 million cotton spindles. That same year a Parliamentary Select Committee investigated the state of Britain's trade, partly in response to falling profit margins in cotton. 'Witnesses from manufacturing and trade, from the USA as well as Britain, affirmed the spread of American competition and attributed it to America's comparative advantages, cheaper raw cotton and power, and also to artificial costs borne by British manufacturers, like import duties on flour and cotton or variations in British wage levels'.[7]

The USA's largest and leading cotton mill town, Lowell in Massachusetts, accounting for about a tenth of the American cotton industry, was not as modest in size as supercilious Lancastrian competitors might assume. In 1836 its eight cotton manufacturing firms operated 141,508 cotton spindles and about 4,500 cotton powerlooms in twenty-two mills, employing 6,777 people: an average of 17,688 spindles, 562 powerlooms, and nearly 850 people per firm. The largest of the eight Lowell firms was the Merrimack Manufacturing Co., with 35,704 cotton spindles, 1,253 powerlooms, 1,321 women and 437 men working in five mills and a printworks.[8] With over 1,750 employees in a vertically integrated firm, the Merrimack matched or even exceeded in size most of the biggest cotton spinning and weaving firms in Lancashire in 1841. Numbering eighteen, they employed on average 1,066. The largest Manchester cotton spinning firm in 1833, M'Connel & Kennedy, employed 1,545 hands, while one of the largest integrated firms outside Manchester in the 1830s, the Gregs, had over 2,000 employees.[9]

The USA's record of catching up with Lancashire's cotton industry was repeated by France, Germany, India and Japan during the course of the nineteenth century. For them, the adoption of cotton manufacturing technology marked one of the first steps by which an agrarian economy moved into factory-based manufacturing and fully-fledged industrialisation. Initially the transfer of the technology was based on learning about the new processing machinery. Knowledge was then backed by investment in cotton manufacturing. Investment created opportunities to modify the imported Lancashire technology to suit local social and economic circumstances. Once new techniques, like the ring frame or the automatic powerloom, were developed abroad, Lancashire had the chance to adopt them. The whole process is known as technology diffusion and the purpose of this chapter is to present some of its themes in outline: some theoretical perspectives; barriers raised in Britain against the international diffusion of technology; the spread of Lancashire's new knowledge to Europe, Russia, the USA, India and Japan; foreign transformations of Lancashire's textile technology; and, last, the implications of neglecting foreign innovations.

## Theories of technology diffusion

Sharing technology[10] is widely recognised as a principal means of achieving the onset of industrialisation, economic growth and the relief of global poverty. However, the hard fact that technology transfer does not occur evenly or smoothly across the international economy raises questions that have troubled and challenged both academics and policy makers. The largest question of all informs both students of technology transfer in general and of textile technology in particular: is there a reliable model (i.e. general explanation that fits the observed historical evidence) of technology diffusion? For answers, economists have turned to the supply and demand of factors of production (land, labour, capital) and of products, in international markets; sociologists, to patterns of non-economic group behaviour. Historians have shown that it is a very complex process which often defies economic prediction.

Among economists, David Ricardo's early nineteenth-century theory of comparative advantage (demonstrating that economies benefit by specialising in activities at which they are relatively better than their neighbours) explained why all might profit in a free trade international economy. Hecksher and Ohlin in the 1930s and 1940s traced the sources of comparative advantage to relative proportions of the factors of production in differing countries.[11] Most recently Michael Porter has given Ricardo a new twist by analysing the kinds of advantages that competing firms can create, one of these being a technological 'competitive advantage'.[12]

Raymond Vernon related international investment and trade to the product cycle (and hence an historical process).[13] In an advanced economy (like Britain in the early-nineteenth century) there were unique opportunities to market innovations meeting wants at high levels of income and produced by high labour costs – for example, luxury textiles in Britain. At the first stage, labour costs are high because of the lack of standardisation. As demand grows, so products and production methods become more standardised and labour costs fall. Knowledge of the new goods and methods spreads internationally and foreign demand emerges in advanced economies, met at first by exports from the pioneer economy.

A second stage develops when pioneer manufacturers (like those in early nineteenth-century Lancashire) find that average costs of production abroad are lower than the marginal costs of production at home plus transport costs of exports from the pioneer manufacturer.

A third stage arrives when fully standardised products and production methods are transferred to less developed countries, again in pursuit of low labour costs, import substitution and exports to capture world markets.

Vernon's model assumes that there are no barriers to the international flows of knowledge, labour and capital, which was not true of Lancashire before 1843. It does not adequately explain why technology transfer has failed or been delayed. Nor does it throw much light on the actual process of diffusion. Finally, nothing is said about the adaptation of new technology to suit foreign conditions, economic or social. For these matters further understanding has come from empirical work by economists, sociologists and historians.

Nathan Rosenberg, another economist, has probed interactions between economic growth and technical change.[14] For example, he raised the possibility that technical change could be much slower and more far-reaching than economists allowed. And he has emphasised the gradual, cumulative aspects of inventive activity (in contrast to Schumpeter's leaps forward), the importance of machine-making skills and 'complementarities' (technical constraints on the primary innovation).

From a sociological standpoint Everett Rogers and Floyd Shoemaker found numerous reports for and against many of the generalisations about the transfer of innovations made by anthropologists, agricultural economists, educationalists, geographers and many other specialists.[15] However, some propositions found wide support. From these Rogers and Shoemaker produced a typology of the diffusion process. Summarised as S–M–C–R–E (source, message, channel, receiver, effects), this model emphasised the role of channels of communication, change agents and the S-curve of adoption over time.

How did this fit with the economists' models? Kenneth Arrow, another economist, argued that 'the economists are studying the demand for information by potential innovators and sociologists the problems in the supply of communication channels'.[16] But was it possible to unravel the two that easily? What if, for instance, social systems (like the patent system) helped to alter demand, or differing standards of living (shaped by both economic and non-economic factors) contributed to the international migration flows carrying skilled technical migrants and bearers of new technology?

Historians like John R. Harris, A. E. Musson, Eric Robinson, Kristine Bruland and this author have examined numerous cases of technology transfer and concluded that it is a very complex process. Rational models do not fit it easily. 'It is simultaneously a cyclical, a spatial and a multi-dimensional phenomenon. It is *cyclical* in several senses. In the long term it is contingent on the comparative advantages between nations and the competitive advantages developed by firms across them. The models of Vernon and Porter have explanatory power at this first level. There are other dynamics feeding into the cyclical, however. One is the changing scientific and technological paradigm which has shifted "normal science" and "new technology" from eighteenth-century mechanical engineering empirically discovered to modern science-based information and bio-technology. Another movement within the large international economic cycle is a rough stages-of-diffusion process, starting with the artisans and professionals who take new knowledge, then find backers in the host economy and, finally, see modifications made and transmitted back to the originating economy. International transfer of technology is also *spatial*. There is a physical movement of skilled people, hardware, software and services between countries and organisations. Differences in geology, climate, time, language, organisation, political system, culture, have to be taken into account. Technology transfer increasingly happens because it is engineered by business organisations but the international scale and the capitalist setting mean that it is also a *multi-dimensional* phenomenon. Economic and ideological contexts provide motivation for transfer. Cultural systems (government and politics, law, education, language, underlying values, for example) facilitate the movement of new technical knowledge. Technological knowledge, generated for the most part within firms, but also in academic settings, imposes its own limitations on ease of transfer. Paradoxically, while the complete process of successful technology transfer requires a set of layered and interdependent conditions, like the fibrous strands in a rope, it is still possible (as cases of military and industrial espionage testify) for a single individual to take the crucial steps that will lead to effective technology transfer'.[17]

## British barriers against diffusion, before 1843

### 1. *Geography and war*

Geography and international relations protected Lancashire manufacturers during the period 1780–1810, years when the industry was becoming established, when its chief inventions were spreading, and when (according to Rostow) the economy was experiencing 'take-off' in economic growth.[18] Cut off from its European rivals by the Channel and from its assertive former colonies in America by the Atlantic Ocean (which took over a month to cross in the 1790s, a time not much reduced until 1840 and the advent of steamship services),[19] the industry was further shielded from the swift international movements of men and machines by war. During the thirty-five years between 1780 and 1815 there were twenty-four years of war against France and her allies and prolonged uneasy relations with the USA, culminating in war, 1812–14. In a westerly direction this reduced flows of skilled artisans to a trickle. In the five years 1809–14 only 806 textile immigrants are recorded as having arrived in the USA (though some may have abandoned their trades after arriving; also the evidence is not perfect). By comparison in the eight years 1824–31, some 4,999 textile workers arrived in the USA. That is, in wartime the flows of skilled immigrants were reduced to a quarter of peacetime levels (160 as opposed to 625 *per annum*).[20] Presumably the aggregate movement of textile workers to continental Europe was similarly affected by war, though as yet data are only impressionistic. Of course, peace or war was not the only factor explaining the pushes and pulls of immigration to America.

### 2. *Industrial secretiveness*

Industrial secretiveness was the prevailing attitude awaiting foreign visitors nosing around Britain's early industrial districts. Since the Middle Ages novitiate craftsmen had been sworn to keep secret the 'mystery' of their masters' crafts and among manufacturers this attitude persisted, even intensified, when there were technical improvements to be guarded, machine-breaking mobs to be feared, patent application procedures to be observed and labour piracies to be checked. Sharpest watch against intruders was kept where the technology was most recent. In the 1780s and 1790s Robert Owen recalled that cotton mills regularly kept their outer doors locked against strangers. And many a mill resembled a medieval fortification with perimeter walls and gatehouse.[21] In the mid-1830s Manchester manufacturers and merchants were so secretive that they moved goods in and out of warehouses by back doors and at night. Curious visitors admitted to Manchester factories had to be careful what questions they asked for fear of arousing suspicions.[22]

As late as the 1820s the Manchester manufacturers tried to suppress the publication of technological information which might convey their new knowledge to foreign rivals. The first thorough description of the new cotton manufacturing technology was not published until 1812 when the article on 'Manufacture of Cotton', by James Thomson, a calico printer of Clitheroe, and John Farey Jr, appeared in the latest instalment of Abraham Rees' monumental *The Cyclopaedia: Or Universal Dictionary of Arts, Sciences and Literature* (45 vols, London: Longman et al, 1802–1820); and a set of cotton processing rules, specifying sizes of gears, relative speeds of rollers &c, did not become available until James Montgomery published his *The Carding and Spinning Master's Assistant* (Glasgow: John Niven Jr, 1832).[23]

However, as new 'best practice' technology spread and became representative technology, familiar to foreign rivals, there was less foreign inquisitiveness and domestic protective measures relaxed somewhat. The reported openness of the Glasgow cotton manufacturers in the 1820s stemmed from their use of what had become a widely known technology for spinning coarse yarns (mules). Another reason why some manufacturers seemed open to foreign rivals was because the locus of their technology lay not in the line of machines in their mills but in the workers who worked with or in conjunction with those machines. Thus production methods still requiring heavy inputs of human skill, like those in the finishing trades, could be displayed to visitors without fear of easy espionage. Workers would have to be seduced, and not just individuals but whole teams whose skills had been acquired by lengthy apprenticeships (three to seven years).[24]

British machine makers were far more open to foreign customers than were the manufacturers. They had capital equipment for sale and foreign manufacturers were as much potential customers as domestic manufacturers. James Nasmyth, one of the larger machine makers in Manchester in the late 1830s, gladly exhibited his works and designs to visitors, confident that the advantages of secretiveness were far outweighed by the augmented trade gained by openness.[25] This openness on the part of machine makers was widespread throughout the capital goods industries, as MacLeod has recently shown.[26]

### 3. *The prohibitory laws*

Industrial secretiveness was also imposed by the state. Whether embodied in the 'dead' (implements or machines) or 'living' instruments of trade, the new technology and much of the old, would have been theoretically halted at Britain's ports by severe prohibitory laws. That at least was the legal position. In reality these laws, which were enacted between the 1690s and the 1780s chiefly in response to manufacturers' pressure groups, were far from effective. They threatened severe consequences to violators: agents faced a £500 fine for each worker enticed abroad and twelve months imprisonment; the export, or attempted export, of textile, metalworking, clockmaking, leatherworking, papermaking and glass manufacturing equipment incurred a £200 fine (£500 for printing equipment), forfeiture of equipment seized and twelve months' imprisonment. During the French Wars procedures were tightened up. An Order in Council of 1795 obliged captains of foreign vessels to submit a list of passengers' names, ages, occupations and nationalities before clearing. The Passenger Act of 1803 limited the number of passengers British vessels could carry. And packet captains were instructed to offer free passages to artisans willing to return to England. However, with the advent of a free trade ideology after 1820 the prohibitory laws were drastically modified. All restrictions on emigration were lifted in 1824. Machinery exports came under a licensing system which continued to check exports of new manufacturing technology until it, too, was abandoned in 1843. Since the machine tool makers – one section of capital goods manufacturers – expressed relatively little concern about machinery exports, their equipment (lathes, planers and the like) was more often licensed for export than was manufacturing equipment capable of being immediately installed in a textile production line.[27]

In Britain, the European war led to the tightening up of the restraints on the emigration of skilled workers (like textile manufacturers) and the export of machinery. The Board of Trade was informed in December 1811 that the Commissioners of Customs had received 'a letter from a Person at Bristol, representing that a Mechanic had left that Place by Coach with intent, as is supposed, to embark on board one of the Packets at Falmouth, taking with him a Trunk suspected to contain Tools, Brasses and Iron Work used in the construction of Machinery employed in the Cotton Manufacture of this Kingdom.' The Board was told that the Collector of Customs at Falmouth had been alerted and directed to intercept and detain the aspiring conveyor of the 'high tech' of the day.[28]

### 4. Technical traditions

There were yet other barriers in the path of foreign spies, prying into the structure and nature of Britain's 'high tech' industries of the early nineteenth century. Interlacing both machine building and manufacturing processes was a maze of technical traditions. In machine building, for example, the cutting of screws conformed to no single standard until the 1860s, with the widespread adoption of Joseph Whitworth's average dimensions of pitch, depth and form which he had formulated in 1841. Before the 1840–60 period each machine shop had its own screw and bolt contours and these were not easy to copy, being the product of craft and labour-intensive conditions and skills. Even the Whitworth compromise standard screw thread needed three kinds of cutters and two lathes in its manufacture.[29]

In manufacturing, the localised structure of the pre-industrial economy had likewise created an undergrowth of technical practices whose standards and nomenclatures can only have bewildered the intruding foreigner. In cotton textiles, systems for expressing the tightness of cloth structure varied from district to district. Thus in 1808 a Bolton cotton manufacturer testified that 'what would be a sixty reed at Bolton would be a hundred one at Stockport; in Preston they are still worse, for almost every Manufacturer has a particular way of counting his own reed'.[30] Everywhere the thicket of craft practices on which industrial technology was imposed gathered further obscurity from local dialects (or languages in the case of Scotland and Wales) and regional or local systems of weights and measures.[31]

### 5. *The pace of technical change*

Because in the eighteenth century technical improvement was increasingly seen as an engine of economic growth, since invention was becoming more related to economic change, foreign industrial spies needed a rising level of knowledge before they could even understand the new technologies they found in early industrial Britain. The well-known measure of technical change is patent registration and a brief reminder of British rates and conditions provides a rough idea of the size of this barrier to industrial espionage.

In the 1750s about a dozen patents, for all kinds of invention, were registered each year in England. From the 1760s a long-term rise began. By the 1790s the level stood at about 90 a year. Between 1800 and 1830 it moved up from 100 to 200 and in the 1830s the rate doubled to over 400 a year.[32] In cotton manufacturing, the high tech area of the day, some 168 patents for mechanical devices were taken out between 1790 and 1830. Another 27 were obtained for cotton and woollen machine making.[33] This may not sound like many patents. However, it should be noted that some patents covered several devices; that the rate of registration was rising; that (as Dutton confirmed) patenting was becoming more economic (i.e. more closely related to the market); that there was a shift towards more, rather than less, complex capital equipment (as well as a more capital-intensive technology), designed to produce high quality goods; and that patents, being so expensive in Britain, were but the public manifestation of many localised technical modifications some of which might eventually be recorded in patents.

Certainly not all *major* cotton textile inventions were patented but most were by the 1790s. (Crompton's mule is one of the oft-cited exceptions.) This assertion is based on a reading of the 303 cotton and woollen textile patents of 1790–1830 and on the comparative cost of British patents of invention in the early nineteenth century. At £70 in 1815 and at least £150 in 1829, they were around three times the annual wage of a British cotton factory overseer – a rise incidentally which contrasted with the general fall in prices of 1815–47.[34] In comparison American patents cost only $30 to register, about a fifth of a skilled American artisan's annual wage. British patentees therefore needed more confidence and stronger expectations of commercial returns from their patented inventions than American counterparts.[35] It may be that British patents were longer in moving from the workshop to the preliminaries of patent registration, so that winners more frequently emerged in Britain than in the USA. At any rate, foreign acquisitors (themselves or their agents) needed to consult British patent lists and the patents in their area of interest.

Not knowing which technical improvements were protected by a patent and which were not, foreign borrowers were therefore obliged both to search the London patent offices and patent journals and also to ferret around the machine makers and manufacturers in the industrial districts. Only about a quarter of British textile patents were reported in the *Repertory of Arts*, the main patent journal, from its foundation in 1794 until 1830, though the journal did print a list of titles, identifying the subject of each patent. To obtain copies or make summaries of patents, enquirers had to make costly searches in London. The rolls of vellum on which the patents were recorded were scattered between three offices (the Petty Bag, the Rolls Chapel and the Enrolment Offices) and were neither adequately nor reliably indexed before the 1830s (indeed, no proper indexes were published until Bennet Woodcroft produced his in the 1850s). Searches demanded time and money. By 1829 it was costing between two and forty guineas to secure a patent copy. A final point: since the struggle over Arkwright's patents in the 1780s, patent case law required that the specifications be comprehensible only to mechanics familiar with existing machines. This meant that as the knowledge frontier advanced so it would become increasingly difficult for the uninitiated to understand patents.[36]

Extending markets, as Adam Smith taught, led to increasing divisions of labour. With them came fresh specialisations that necessitated the formation of teams of trades and skills in the production of industrial goods. In textile machine making, for example, more than six trades were needed to make a spinning frame or throstle (itself simpler than the mechanically complex mule) in the 1820s: spindle maker, roller maker, turner or bobbin maker, founder, tinman, flyer maker, and others.[37] Recruiting teams of skilled workers such as these would not have been easy.

## Timings and carriers

### 1. Carriers and costs

The impression left by contemporary evidence is that Britain's protectionist laws and customs against the outflow of men, machines and technical knowledge were soon breached by international emigration and the efforts of foreign borrowers. Knowledge, embodied in people, machines and drawings, seeped abroad within just a few years of its introduction in Britain. The creation of rival industries abroad, however, took much longer to accomplish. On the other hand the prohibitory laws did raise industrial espionage costs. In 1825 smugglers' premiums for insurance against Customs' seizure were reportedly 30 to 45 per cent of the value of the equipment; by 1841 they were 10 to 25 per cent for small machine parts.[38] From the perspective of the foreign customer this was not much of a deterrent. In the long run it could well be worth paying this excess if the equipment were entirely new, for it could then be 'reverse engineered' to introduce some new product or processing technique, or adapted to local conditions.

Illegal emigrants incurred the personal costs of anxiety about breaking the law and, when caught, imprisonment. Writing from Delaware in 1821 an English handloom weaver (who had emigrated alone in 1817) asked his brother living near Shrewsbury to 'write to my son John [in Manchester] to make a bag and put his shuttles and bobbins in, and put them in his bed till he gets out to sea. If he has a side engine [drop box presumably] he may take it and conceal it under his berth. Tell him to keep on good terms with the Customs House Officer. But if you are in any way afraid to risk it, do not attempt to do it'.[39]

That such fears were not imaginary was illustrated by the experience of two Manchester cotton spinners in 1811. Arrested on board a ship waiting off Liverpool to sail to America, one of them (David Wooding) was revealed as a spinner by a marriage certificate found in his chest; the other (Denis Manion) Wooding betrayed as his father-in-law and another cotton spinner.[40] How much the pair were fined is unknown. That they paid some penalty for their offence is almost certain. That the laws leaked is even more evident. Manion next turns up as a spinner working in the Globe Mill, Philadelphia, in September 1814, at which date he recorded that he had been in the USA for three years and three months, i.e. he had reached the USA in June 1811, three months after being arrested by the Liverpool magistrates.[41]

Both in the early industrial period and later, when the Japanese came to acquire western technology, it is evident that skilled workers, managers and engineers (rather than unaccompanied machines, models, drawings, or written descriptions) were the prime conduit through whom Lancashire's textile technology percolated abroad.[42]

## 2. *Timing and carriers to Europe*

The exchange of technical knowledge between continental Europe and Britain had an earlier pedigree, as A. E. Musson showed.[43] Now, in the eighteenth and early nineteenth centuries, Britain became more originator than recipient. Britain's first major cotton inventions of the eighteenth century, the fly shuttle (1733) and the drop box (1760), which between them increased the productivity and versatility of the handloom, were taken to France by their inventors, John Kay and his son Robert, in 1747 and *c.* 1760 respectively.[44] Kay senior was a waspish inventor of genius, not a solid man of business.

Others were left to transport across the Channel the jenny, the water-frame, the spinning mule and the powerloom. The first jenny taken to France reached there in 1771–2, within one or two years of its UK patent. It was smuggled by John Holker, junior, son of John Holker (1719–86), the Manchester master callenderer and Jacobite soldier who fled England after the 1745 rebellion and thereafter industriously im-ported the latest English improvements to France. The jenny was set up in the Holkers' works at Saint Sever, in Rouen, and Oissel, also in the Seine basin. Holker junior established a factory to make jennies and they became common in Normandy, one of the country's three main cotton manufacturing districts (the other two being Lille and Alsace), by 1780.[45] However, despite efforts to popularise the machine following the crisis induced by the Eden Commercial Treaty of 1786, there were only 900 jennies in the whole country in 1790, according to one official estimate.[46] The technical and managerial secrets of waterframe spinning which Arkwright, towards the end of Kay's life in the 1770s, was per-fecting, arrived within a decade of its UK patent date (1769). 'John Milne [from Stockport] and his three sons (John, James and Thomas) smuggled one of Arkwright's machines into France and successfully erected it at Oissel' *c.* 1779–80.[47] Morgan and Massey set up a mule-jenny at Amiens in 1789.[48] Finally, drawings of a powerloom (presumably a primitive one) and a spinning mule were smuggled to Strasbourg by John Heywood, a Manchester man, in 1806.[49] The first French steam-driven cotton mill was set up near Paris in 1810 by Francois-Charles-Louis Albert, a native of Strasbourg. Albert visited England in 1791, was arrested for industrial espionage in 1792 and languished in Lancaster gaol until 1796. He married an English lady and eventually settled in Mul-house where he smuggled English machinery for the Alsace manufac-turers.[50] By 1834 large mills had appeared in the French textile districts: one of 44,000 spindles in Normandy and one of 100,000 in Alsace, for example.[51] In all of these transfers skilled artisans played a key role, some-times as machine builders, sometimes as operators (in the case of the jenny, an English maiden lady was recruited to teach spinning skills).[52]

'The first German cotton-spinning mill, using Arkwright's water frame, was established in 1794 in a village appropriately named Krom-ford, east of Dusseldorf. In Saxony, the frame and mule came in just before the turn of the century; in the Low Countries (Verviers and Ghent) slightly later'.[53] In Norway a mechanised textile industry was transplanted from Britain's textile districts from the mid-1840s.[54]

Although the data on aggregate size are blurred, it is clear that by the 1830s and 1840s the French and Saxony textile industries were sufficiently established to be interested in the latest technology coming out of Lancashire. This was hardly surprising because so much know-how had moved to the continent. A parliamentary committee was told in 1824 that over 16,000 British artisans had gone across the Channel during the years 1822 and 1823, when the British economy was still suffering from a cyclical trough and high unemployment. Another witness put the figure at 14,000 to 15,000.[55] (These numbers sound like scaremongering claims.) Even if there were no more than hundreds of such migrants, many would have gone to France with some know-ledge of new machines and techniques in Lancashire. Given their number this human tide surely surmounted the difficulty facing foreign promoters and investors, of assembling teams of immigrant workers possessing appropriate and complementary skills. Indeed John Lee Bradbury, a Manchester calico printer with experience in cotton spin-ning, had seen British workers in all the trades needed to make a spinning machine in the Paris factory of the textile machine maker, Callas, in 1817-18.[56] This represented a passive approach to the ac-quisition of Lancashire's technology.

Rival economies and aspiring hosts of Britain's new textile technology could adopt a more aggressive stance towards the task of borrowing. Johann Georg Bodmer, the Swiss engineer and inventor, who toured British industrial districts in 1816 and 1817, demonstrated one method. First, he came to Britain in person. Second, he made forays into the manufacturing districts.[57] Third, he relied on a chain letter system, collecting letters of introduction in one district to open doors in the next on his itinerary.[58] Having gained access, sketches might be made, parts or models obtained. Later he settled in England and took out important textile patents (see figure 76).

Contemporaries were unsure whether workers were more valuable than machines in conveying technology abroad. Bradbury (noted above) firmly believed that good machinery was more important than good workmen. He had seen fine models collected by the French government in the Conservatoire des Arts et Métiers, some of them (he referred to machine tools particularly) superior to their British counterparts.[59] By the 1820s British textile machinery was as available in France as it was in Manchester; the only difference was price, according to the engineer Alexander Galloway.[60] (Indeed, Norman calico printers in

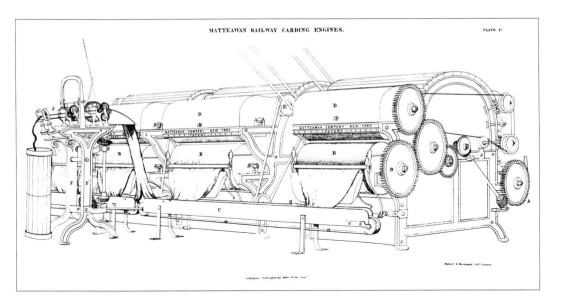

MATTEAWAN RAILWAY CARDING ENGINES. PLATE I

FIGURE 76. Railway carding head, patented in England by Johann Georg Bodmer (1786–1864) in 1824 but used much more in the USA where it was patented on 16 September 1833 by William B. Leonard of the Matteawan Manufacturing Co. of Fishkill, New York. Source: D. Jeremy, *Technology and Power in the Early American Cotton Industry* (American Philosophical Society, 1990), p. 80

1834 reckoned their costs were two-and-a-half times those of Lancashire counterparts.)[61] On the other hand, Adam Young, a Manchester carder who left Birleys in 1818 to work for Nicholas Schlumberger et Cie at Guebwiller, Alsace, reported that the French did not maintain their machinery so well and that its design was twenty years behind that of England. Half-a-dozen Englishmen worked for Schlumberger, out of 700 French employees: a carder, a stretcher, a spinner and a spindle-maker among them.[62]

Certainly Lancashire mechanics played an important role in establishing a machine-making capacity on the continent before 1840. Among them were the Milnes in Paris in the 1790s; Job Dixon, who built spinning machinery in Alsace for Schlumberger at Guebwiller and in the 1820s for Risler Frères at Cernay; Aaron Manby, founder of an ironworks and engineering establishment at Charenton near Paris in 1822.[63]

Russia, eventually to possess Europe's third largest cotton manufacturing industry, presented a variation of the foregoing picture. From the start the government closely promoted cotton manufacturing and for over four decades relied on its own model works, the Alexandrovsk State Textile Mill, to make some of the machinery needed by the private firms. When that fell short of requirements, machines were imported from France and Belgium.[64] Immigrant British workers were actively recruited throughout the second half of the eighteenth century, initially to transplant steam engine, machine building and metallurgical technologies.[65] Centred on the Baltic region and the Moscow area, the infant Russian cotton industry struggled to survive against competition from imported English yarns. By 1828 the state-owned Alexandrovsk Mill with its 35,496 spindles was larger than the nine private cotton spinning

FIGURE 77. Flat-top finisher card used by Samuel Slater (1768–1835) in Rhode Island, where he introduced it in 1790. (Photograph, author)

mills combined. The breakthrough came after 1843 when all British prohibitions on the export of machinery were lifted. One enterprising merchant, the Bremen-born, Manchester-trained Ludwig Knoop, seized the opportunity to export Lancashire equipment to Russia. Between the early 1840s and his death in 1894, Knoop (supported by his two sons) reportedly set up 122 spinning concerns in Russia. Chief of these was the great Krenholm Mill on the River Narova in Estonia (built in 1857–8) which ran 389,000 cotton spindles and 2,100 powerlooms by 1891. Most of the textile machinery Knoop (based on St Petersburg and Moscow) and his trading companies (Knoop Brothers of Bremen and De Jersey & Co. of Liverpool and Manchester) supplied to the Russian cotton firms (in many of which he took a shareholding) came from a handful of Lancashire manufactuers. Platt Brothers of Oldham received all orders for cotton spinning and weaving machinery (and in turn gave Knoop exclusive distribution rights in Russia); Mather & Platt of Salford, orders for bleaching, dyeing and printing equipment; Hick, Hargreaves & Co. and John Musgrave & Sons, both of Bolton, orders for steam engines. The Knoops also recruited English artisans, mechanics and manager-directors to key appointments in the mills in which the Knoops had an interest. While Knoop's success aroused the chauvinistic envy of some Russian merchant-manufacturers, it was noticeable that the Russian textile industry, fourth largest in the world in 1913, was, with its average dividend of 9 per cent, more profitable than Russian industry as a whole.[66]

### 3. *Timing and carriers to the USA*

Between the 1770s and the 1790s Americans were eager to build up their manufacturing capacity as part of the drive towards, and consolidation of, nationhood. Consequently they actively sought the new technical solutions that were emerging in Lancashire. This entailed various recruiting measures to attract those with knowledge of the new textile technology and examples of the technology. Their first success was the spinning jenny, two versions of which were built in Philadelphia in 1774–5. However no carding machine design seems to have crossed the Atlantic until 1783 (and then it was in parts and, along with a disassembled spinning mule, was sent back to England four years later). Mechanics, managers, and machine makers from Britain's textile districts, most of all from Lancashire, were the American recruiters' main target. Richard Arkwright's carding machine and waterframe technology were introduced by Samuel Slater, pupil of Jedediah Strutt of Belper and one

FIGURE 78. Warp spinning frame (64 spindles) of English design, built by the Locks & Canals Co. of Lowell, Massachusetts, USA, in the 1830s. (Old Slater Mill Museum, Pawtucket, Rhode Island, USA) (Photograph, author)

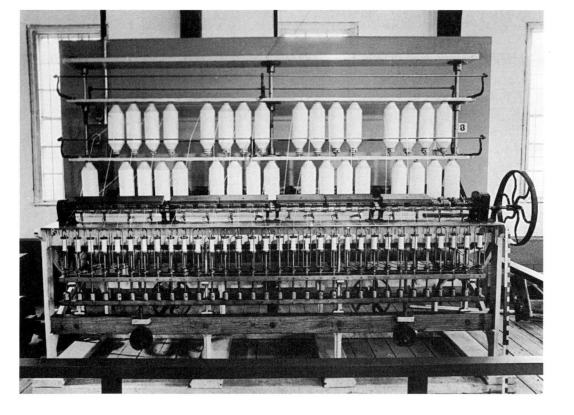

of Arkwright's partners (see figures 77 and 78). He was not the only immigrant textile mechanic in the USA ready to advertise his knowledge of Arkwright's system. He was, however, the first to find American capitalists whose commercial resources and skills would enable him to get on with building and operating a cotton spinning factory in the difficult stages of an infant industry. Slater in 1790 moved from New York (where he had arrived a few months earlier) to Providence, Rhode Island, attracted by the promise of the patronage and investment of Quaker merchants, William Almy and Smith Brown. Between 1790 and 1793 Americans at over half-a-dozen places between Boston and Philadelphia secured the small-scale capacity to build and manage both Arkwright and mule spinning technology. One of the best documented was William Pollard (see figure 79).[67]

FIGURE 79. Arkwright-type water-frame patented in the United States by William Pollard of Philadelphia on 30 December 1791. Source: *William and Mary Quarterly*, 3rd series, vol. 34 (July 1977), p. 412.

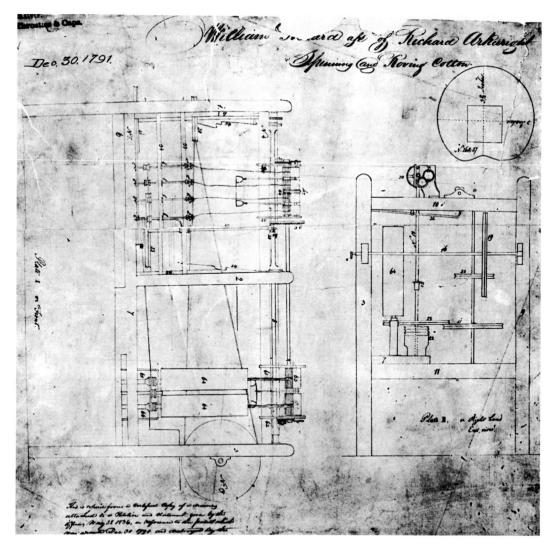

FIGURE 80. Plain cotton powerloom, iron-framed with wooden accessories, illustrated in the United States patent of William Howard, dated 12 February 1830. Source, D. Jeremy, *Technology and Power*, p. 128.

Industrial espionage conducted by Americans in Britain secured other triumphs. Francis Cabot Lowell, visiting Britain in 1810–11, obtained designs for the first American powerloom.[68] In 1822–5 Timothy Wiggin, another Boston merchant, recruited John Dynley Prince, a leading Manchester printworks manager, who became responsible for building up one of the largest and most advanced printworks in the USA, the Merrimack Printworks at Lowell, Massachusetts.[69] In the 1830s American recruiters made one of their biggest catches when they attracted James Montgomery from Glasgow to Saco in Maine. Through his publications (which introduced the world to Lancashire's textile technology in the 1830s and 1840s), through his practice as a cotton mill manager and through his migrations from New England to New York and then South Carolina, Montgomery contributed to and was part of the diffusion of textile technology across the Atlantic and then from New England to the American south.[70]

Over 350 new American cotton mills or firms were started between 1820 and 1831, using increasingly improved technology (see figures 78 and 80). The workforce in the US cotton industry rose from 12,000 to 62,000 over this period. A proportion of these new positions was filled by new immigrants from Britain, perhaps by as much as 25 per cent in the case of slots for skilled adult males.[71] Some of the most skilled – those with managerial or special technical experience – were recruited in England and then despatched along the networks set up by American manufacturers. The experiences of one set of American mill managers in New Hampshire during the 1820s provides a revealing if unflattering view of Lancashire workers in a host society intent on extracting new knowledge from the Lancashire immigrants.

The Dover Manufacturing Co. of Dover, New Hampshire, used an agent in England named Swan who proved valuable in the mid-1820s when the Dover management competed against managements at Lowell and Taunton, Massachusetts, in the race to capture the latest British calico printing technology (figure 81).[72] The correspondence between the Dover agent (factory manager) in New Hampshire and his treasurer (executive director) in Boston discloses how their recruiter's efforts with English (presumably Lancashire) workers led to hopes raised and hopes dashed. Looking back in 1827 over the problems of two years of trying to operate vertically integrated cotton manufacturing at Dover, the agent analysed the causes of impeded expansion in a long and informative letter to his Boston treasurer. One cause was the defects of the skilled workers sent out from England.

Of the six sent out by Mr Swann, the spinner was a worthless wretch, who had neither character nor knowledge of his profession except on mule spinning; the carder was well versed in part of his business but knew nothing of double speeders or stretchers, when not in such a state of intoxication as not to know the difference between day and night, which was not often the case, and was altogether so useless that his mysterious disappearance was a relief to us. The dresser or sizer [who] had been accustomed to work on a frame as one of our females do here, of course could 'handle yarn' well, and with the experience he has gained here, I think him qualified to take charge of the dressing room in No. 4 [mill] when it goes into operation. Of the three weavers who had been overlookers in England and who were qualified to become immediately overseers with us, it may be said they understood individually on handlooms and their overlooking amounted simply to their having had charge of three or four looms in their houses or cellars. They had no knowledge of the discipline of a room, keeping the accounts or anything connected with it and not one of them would have been competent the charge.[73] [Two eventually became second overseers.]

The point the Dover agent was making was that the English workers were largely inappropriate for his American needs. If their intemperance did not conflict with his industrial discipline, the puny scale of their workshop overlooking experience made them wholly unfitted for the factory management positions they had been recruited to fill. Plainly, had the Dover agent been able to tour Lancashire, as others did, he would have diminished the blunders of his recruiter.[74]

### 4. *Timing and carriers to India and Japan*

The transfer of British textile technology to India and Japan, Lancashire's other great rivals, came long after the British restraints on the emigration of artisans and the export of machinery had gone. In both India and Japan, therefore, entrepreneurs were free to hire mill managers and engineers and to buy textile machinery from Lancashire and thus to convey the new textile technology abroad. This they did, but with several major differences. First, with respect to timing, India (under the British Raj) secured the technology between the 1850s and the 1880s; Japan, in the 1860s and 1880s. Second, in Japan the government played a much larger part in the process of diffusion. Third, while Japan secured both a textile manufacturing and a textile machine making capacity, India remained dependent on European machine makers, almost all of them in Lancashire.[75] Fourth, Japan overtook India in switching from mules to rings between the 1880s and 1913.[76]

The first successful cotton spinning company in India, the Spinning

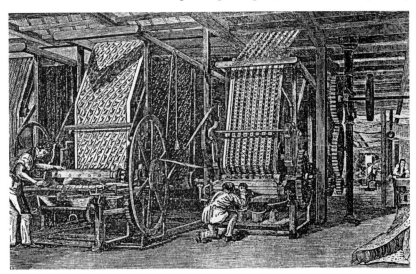

FIGURE 81. (*Top*) Calico printing in the USA in the 1830s. (From George S. White, Memoir of Samuel Slater, the Father of American Manufactures (reprinted A. M. Kelley, 1967), facing p. 395). This illustration is clearly derived from the British illustration (*bottom*) in Baines, *History of the Cotton Manufacture*, facing p. 267, the only difference being that while British operatives were depicted wearing knee-length breeches, American workers were given trousers – a symbol, perhaps, of American democracy?

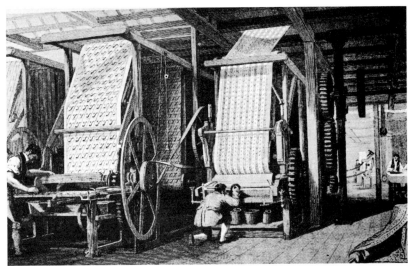

& Weaving Co., was formed in Bombay in 1854. Its mainspring was the Parsee merchant and financier Cowasjee Nanabhoy Davar. Located at Tardeo, Bombay, and opened in February 1856, the mill was designed by Sir William Fairbairn and equipped with 17,000 throstle-type spindles built by John Hetherington & Sons of Manchester. Erection and management were in the hands of six men with British names, most presumably from Lancashire.[77] By 1870 Bombay had thirteen factories with 291,000 spindles and 4,100 powerlooms, employing 8,100 workers.[78] By 1914 India had 271 cotton mills, 95 of them in Bombay, the major cotton manufacturing district.[79]

Pioneered in the USA (see below), the first ring frames in India were set up by Jamsetji Nusserwanjee Tata in his Empress Mill at Nagpur, near Bombay, after 1883. Tata learned about rings from his English mill manager, Brooksby, who returned from leave in England with a cut-down set of Rabbeth ring spindles. Satisfactory experimental results led to the adoption of ring spinning. When Platts of Oldham refused to build them, Tata got his frames from Samuel Brooks (later Brooks & Doxey), of Manchester.[80] By 1895 nearly half of Bombay's 2,124 million spindles were rings.[81]

For thirty years the Indian mills were reliant on British immigrants for mill management and engineering knowledge. In 1895 in Bombay 27 of the city's 55 cotton mill managers were European.[82] Most of these immigrants came from Lancashire and as a result Lancashire's technology, in particular the skill-intensive spinning mule, dominated. It has been argued that this influence retarded the Indian cotton industry by delaying the adoption of the ring frame.[83] However, it has been observed that ownership and control of 85 percent and more of Bombay's cotton mills, 1895–1925, was in the hands of non-European managing agencies, and therefore Europeans cannot be held responsible for the short-sighted policies that lay behind Bombay's reliance on mules.[84] Moreover, between 1895 and 1900 ring spindles surpassed mule spindles in number.[85]

Japan's reliance on Lancashire was more short-lived. The arrival of American steam-driven warships in Yedo Bay in 1853 and the subsequent humiliating treaties with western powers led to a political struggle in Japan between conservatives and modernisers which the latter eventually won. Whilst that was in progress in the 1850s and 1860s one of the modernising clans, the Satsumas, took the first steps in transferring western technology – seen as the key to economic growth, military strength and parity with the West. In autumn 1865 they sent two of their samurai to Oldham to buy a line of cotton spinning equipment from Platt Bros. Platts recommended a 5,200 spindle mill (2,640 mule and 2,560 throstle spindles) and this was duly installed at Kagoshima at the south end of Kyushu, southernmost of the four main islands of Japan, with the help of six workers from Platts.[86]

Following the Meiji restoration of 1867–8 (which returned the
emperor to power and committed the state to economic development
and modernisation), the Satsumas imported machinery for a second
mill, this time at Sakai in south Osaka. By 1873 a third, and smaller,
mill (with only 576 spindles) was set up in Tokyo by a merchant,
Manpei Kashima. Partly because the Satsumas fell out with the new
government, these early experiments made little impact. The Meiji
government in the late 1870s made a fresh investment in a cotton
spinning industry. It imported equipment for ten 2,000 spindle mules
and sold them to entrepreneurs at advantageous financial terms. By
1885 there were seventeen cotton spinning mills in Japan. None was
commercially very successful. Two of the first three mills had been
too large for Japan's skill resources. The second wave of investment
was too small to realise scale economies. Only when Eiichi Shibusawa
decided in 1883 to make a large scale investment in a cotton mill
(10,500 spindles), financed by a joint stock company and managed by
Takeo Yamanobe a former samurai trained in textile engineering at
Blackburn, was the first stage of textile technology transfer to Japan
complete. Within three years the Osaka Spinning Co. was running
31,320 spindles.[87] The 1890s saw the Japanese cotton industry switch
from English mules to American rings. By 1913 it had 2,415,000
spindles (and 44 firms), well under a third of the size of the Indian
cotton industry[88] (see table 8.1). However, the much higher productivity of Japanese spindles enabled them to produce 98 per cent by
volume of India's yarn output.[89]

Table 8.1 *Leading cotton industries of the world 1913*

| Rank in cotton spinning | Country | No. of cotton spindles (millions) | % of world | No. of cotton power looms (thousands) | % of world |
|---|---|---|---|---|---|
| 1 | UK | 55.653 | 38.80 | 805.5 | 28.01 |
| 2 | USA | 31.5 | 21.96 | 700.3 | 24.35 |
| 3 | Germany | 11.186 | 7.80 | 286 | 9.94 |
| 4 | Russia | 9.212 | 6.42 | 67 | 2.33 |
| 5 | France | 7.4 | 5.16 | 140 | 4.87 |
| 6 | India | 6.597 | 4.60 | 94 | 3.27 |
| 7 | Austria | 4.909 | 3.42 | 160 | 5.56 |
| 8 | Italy | 4.6 | 3.21 | 133 | 4.62 |
| 9 | Japan | 2.415 | 1.68 | 24 | 0.83 |
|  | World | 143.452 | 100.00 | 2,876.13 | 100.00 |

Sources: Mitchell, *European Historical Statistics*; Allen, *Short Economic History
of Modern Japan*.
Data collected by Dr. D. A. Farnie and used with his permission.

### 5. Foreign transformations of Lancashire's technology

The textile technology which developed in Lancashire before 1830 was neither as static nor as universally applicable as the foregoing survey may have at times implied. As the standard historical accounts show, a host of modifications, some major (like the self-acting mule of 1830) and many minor, came out of the English cotton industry.[90]

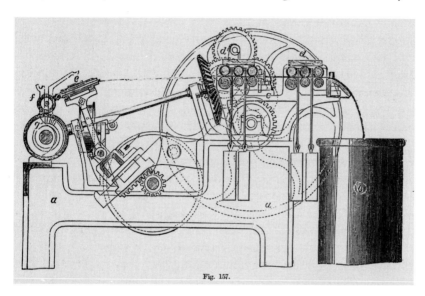

Fig. 157.

FIGURE 82. Tube or Taunton speeder, patented by George Danforth of Taunton, Massachusetts in 1824, and patented in Britain in 1825 by Joseph Chesseborough Dyer. Source: E. Leigh, *The Science of Modern Cotton Spinning* (Manchester; Palmer & Howe, 1873), vol. 2, p. 193.

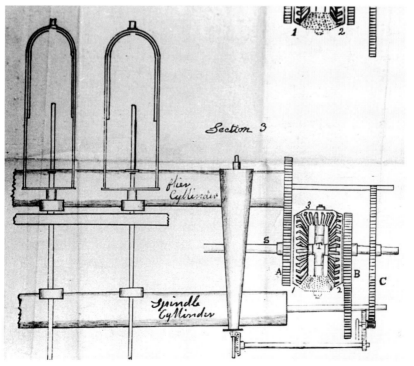

FIGURE 83. A detail of Aza Arnold's differential gear installed in the roving frame, illustrated in his American patent of 21 January 1823. (Rhode Island Historical Society, Zachariah Allen Papers) (Photograph, author)

At the same time, news of this evolving technology was quickly spread overseas where, also, the earlier imported cotton manufacturing technology was being adapted to meet local circumstances. In the mills, machine shops, mechanics' institutes and manufacturers' clubs of the world's cotton industries the latest technical and organisational improvements, their merits and alternatives were under constant discussion and trial. Not surprisingly, it is beyond the limits of this essay to do more than indicate salient landmarks.

Of all the foreign modifications that were made to Lancashire's cotton manufacturing technology in the nineteenth century, the most radical emerged from the USA. Labour scarcity and inelasticity, due chiefly to the enormous supply of land which continually lured new immigrants westwards, drove American manufacturers to seek labour-saving inventions. In cotton manufacturing, three achieved almost universal adoption: the bobbin-and-fly frame with differential gear; the ring frame; and the automatic loom.

The improved bobbin-and-fly frame, a machine for preparing roving, was designed to allow a simple change in the thickness of the roving being prepared. Since roving was very delicate and easily breakable, it had to be laid on the spindle by means of a sensitive mechanism which took account of the increasing diameter of the cop. To secure this variable rotary motion, several devices were invented by American mechanics, like double speeders (pre-1820) or Danforth's tube speeder (1824) (figure 82) Some, including the Lancashire version, utilised one or two pairs of cone pulleys. However, the most effective and mechanically elegant solution was one which incorporated a differential gear to slow down spindle rotation as the roving package increased in diameter. The gear was invented (actually reinvented, given earlier European examples in other mechanisms) in 1822 by Aza Arnold, a Rhode Island mechanic who had served his apprenticeship with Samuel Slater[91] (see figure 83).

The ring spindle seems to have been a response to the shortage of skilled mule spinners in New England in the 1820s and the quest for higher outputs. Two spindles, destined to transform the textile spinning industry, were patented within months of each other in 1828 by mechanics in southern New England. Charles Danforth's cap spindle (figure 84) would supplant the throstle in the worsted industry while John Thorp's ring spindle (figure 85) would carry the day in medium count cotton spinning. John Thorp (1784–1848) was a very active inventor. In the late 1820s two spinning problems occupied his attention: spindle design and winding motions. Between November 1828 and November 1830 he took out seven spinning patents including the one for the ring spindle (20 November 1828). By substituting a ring and C-shaped traveller for the old flyer he resolved the problem of flyer

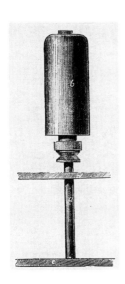

FIGURE 84. The Danforth throstle. Source: E. Leigh, *Science of Modern Cotton Spinning* (Manchester; Palmer & Howe, 1873), p. 208.

arm spread and spindle wobble at high speed. The absence of flyer or cap also reduced doffing time, by as much as thirty minutes a day. Although it took another decade for the ring frame to get a foothold in the American cotton industry, its advantages were well proven by 1840. A series of improvements in the late 1860s and early 1870s in the design of the spindle took its speed above 6,000 revolutions per minute. Foremost were Sawyer, Rabbeth, and Whitin spindles.[92]

Early examples of the American search for labour-saving devices were stop motions (figures 86 and 87) and high speed machines like the tube speeder (figure 82) The search culminated in the automatic loom. In one sense this was the product of a rational pursuit of commercially profitable innovations by a dynasty of machine makers and patent managers, the Drapers of Hopedale, Massachusetts. Before 1830 they specialised in loom temples, beginning with the automatic one patented by Ira Draper in 1816. In the 1850s they commenced their strategy of buying key patents and hiring their inventors as a way of creating a very lucrative patent pool, which they vigorously defended in the courts. Warren W. Dutcher's temple in the 1850s and Jacob Sawyer's spindle in the 1870s were secured in this way. Their last great success was the development of an automatic loom between 1888 and 1892. Prominent among the Draper employees who worked on the loom was James H. Northrop, ironically, an immigrant from Keighley, Yorkshire (figure 88). The major additions to the loom were a self-threading shuttle, a device to grasp the shuttle and another for cutting the weft yarn, a cop changer, a rotating magazine, a filling motion and, later, a warp stop motion. Following further modifications, by 1895 together they enabled an operative to tend twenty-four instead of eight looms.[93] (The automatic, or Northrop, loom is considered further in chapter 9.)

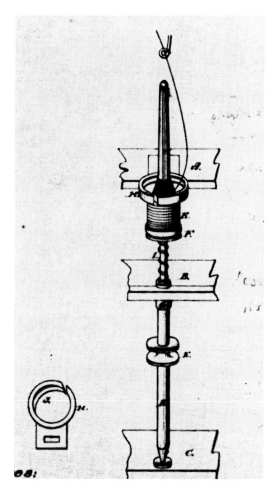

FIGURE 85. One of John Thorp's patents for a ring spindle taken out in the USA in 1828. Source: D. J. Jeremy, 'Invention in American textile technology during the early nineteenth century', in *Working Papers From the Regional Economic History Research Centre*, vol. 5, no. 4 (1982), p. 37.

### 6. *Learning from followers*

Just as foreign manufacturers selected from the shelf of Lancashire's textile technology whatever suited their circumstances, so those in Britain's cotton manufacturing district chose what they regarded as technically and commercially appropriate.

FIGURE 86. American stop motion in the drawing frame. Source: Montgomery, *Practical Detail*, p. 58.

FIGURE 87. American stop motion in the warping frame. Source: Montgomery, *Practical Detail*, plate VI.

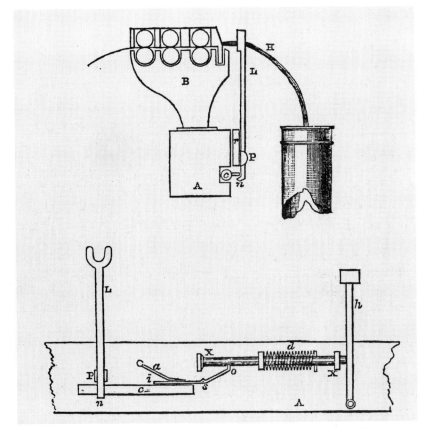

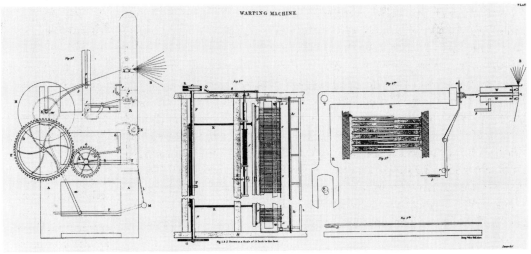

Early in the nineteenth century, Lancashire was seen as a major market for improving and finding sales for foreign inventions. Americans came to England with their inventions and one or two even set up as machine makers. The most successful of these was Joseph Chesse-

borough Dyer (1780–1871), a Rhode Islander who settled in England in 1811. He established a card clothing manufactory first in Birmingham and then in Manchester. Another was Jeptha Avery Wilkinson, a mechanic from Otsego in upstate New York, who settled at Manchester in 1817 and demonstrated his steam-driven reed making machine, another marvel of self-acting labour-saving invention.[94]

FIGURE 88. Model A Northrop (automatic) loom, 1894. Source: Draper, *Labor Saving Looms* (Hopedale, 1904), p. 76.

Production of the ring frame in Lancashire was commenced by Samuel Brooks of Manchester in 1872 and by Howard & Bullough of Accrington in 1878. By the early 1880s all the leading Lancashire machine makers were producing ring frames. However, until 1939 all but a small proportion went abroad. 'Lancashire itself remained loyal to the mule, especially during the last mill-building boom of 1904–8, to the mutual satisfaction of both employers and operatives'.[95]

The same story could be told about the automatic loom, but that belongs to chapter 9.

## Conclusion

One verdict on Lancashire and the international diffusion of cotton manufacturing technology must be that, though she did so unwillingly at first, Lancashire taught the world. Besides the actual technology – the hardware of carding, spinning, weaving and finishing, the techniques of manufacturing and the knowledge of machine making – went also the practices of factory management. Little has been said about this, for the subject is both under-explored and beyond the scope of this essay. However, it was just as important as the purely technical side of cotton manufacturing. From the management of cotton mills, other industries learned the advantages of combining mechanisation with the division of labour.

Although Lancashire's industrial artisans fanned out across the globe, becoming the prime agents of technology transfer, the parent industry was slow to adopt the technical transformations wrought by its foreign offspring. In the short term this may have been defensible. By the late nineteenth century, and in hindsight, it held the seeds of ultimate destruction.

CHAPTER 9

# Indian Summer, 1870–1914

ANDREW MARRISON

L OOKING BACK from the bleak vantage point of the 1920s, Benjamin
Bowker identified the Edwardian years as Lancashire's 'heyday', an
'opulent . . . gold-rush time' when it took little more than 'the trick
of short division' to make a fortune! Small wonder, perhaps, that the
'new Lancashire was arrogant'.[1] In spite of a rise in foreign tariffs after
1870, the second half of the nineteenth century saw a considerable
development of the world economy and a large increase in international
trade. Lancashire, especially Manchester, was inclined to take much of
the credit – here was a vindication of the policies of Cobden and the
Anti-Corn Law League. Manchester and Liverpool, home to thriving
communities of foreign-born merchants, were suffused with a cosmo-
politanism which, though unusual for provincial cities, was unsurprising
when it is remembered that four-fifths of the cotton industry's product
was shipped abroad.

In those vital overseas markets, Lancashire began to meet a certain
amount of rivalry from the cotton industries of the USA and industrialising Europe, but it was mostly limited, and Japan scarcely entered
the international market before 1909–14. At the same time, indigenous
industry appeared even in some of Britain's less-developed markets.
The third quarter of the nineteenth century had seen vigorous developments in India, especially in Bombay, in the Bahia province of Brazil
and in Japan. Thereafter, some degree of factory industry spread
gradually into the underdeveloped world. Such developments elicited
widespread comment in the Lancashire trade press, especially in the
*Textile Recorder* and *Textile Mercury,* where detailed descriptions of the
machinery and products of new mills building overseas constantly
appeared. Cotton consumption in the UK rose from 1,229 m lbs in
1875 to 2,178 m lbs in 1913, an increase of some 77.2 per cent. The
growth of world consumption is more difficult to gauge. Robson
calculated an increase of around 260 per cent between 1882–4 and
1910–13, from 4,000 m lbs to 10,500 m lbs. More recently, Farnie
has estimated a quadrupling in the years 1870–1900 alone, a rise from
1,675 m lbs to 6,767 m lbs. Whichever is correct, both estimates

demonstrate a clear tendency for world consumption to grow considerably faster than British.[2]

## Structure of the Lancashire industry

Those discontented with Britain's Free Trade policy, a policy which had entered the soul of Lancashire many decades before, lamented the faster growth of the industry abroad. But within Lancashire itself, most perceived little threat from the future.[3] The labour force in the British industry increased from 331,000 in 1850 to 577,000 in 1907; spindleage rose from 41.9m in 1874 to 55.7m in 1912; the number of power looms installed increased from 463,000 in 1874 to 786,000 in 1912; and steam horsepower in spinning and weaving rose from 309,000 in 1870 to 1.24m in 1907, water power all but disappearing.[4] The rate of growth of the UK industry had fallen considerably from the dramatic figures of the first half of the century – in 1860–1914 it was only about 2 per cent and cotton's share of total employment was falling. But, as Sidney Chapman, Professor of Political Economy at the University of Manchester and academic defender of the cotton trade, observed, it was inevitable that Britain would lose her effective monopoly of world markets and probably healthy that cotton's rôle in the British economy should shrink, especially if this could be achieved without distress and disruption in the labour market.[5]

Clearly, the UK labour force increased far more slowly than raw cotton consumption, whilst longer and faster self-acting mules in spinning and faster shuttle speeds in weaving meant that the figures for spindles and looms, given above, heavily under-represent the real increase in productive capacity. This suggests a considerable improvement in labour productivity. The UK industry has been criticised for being slow to make the transition to ring spinning and to the automatic or Northrop loom (see chapter 8), and some historians have doubted that the increase in labour productivity was sustained after c. 1885–90. Nevertheless, and in spite of the development of cotton production overseas, Lancashire rose to the height of its exporting power – cloth exported 'in the piece', in value terms some three-quarters of the export earnings of the industry, rose from 3,600 m yds in 1875 to 7,100 m yds in 1913. By some combination of increasing productivity at home and rising demand abroad, in the late nineteenth century some 80 per cent by value of Lancashire cottons were destined for export. Probably never has a major industry in a leading industrial nation been so dependent on the external market.[6]

At the same time, Lancashire's predominance over other regional producers in the UK continued to grow, until by 1911 it employed nearly 90 per cent of the UK industry's workforce. North of the border,

few could match the dynamism and profitability of J. & P. Coats of Paisley, which dominated the sewing-thread trade; in general the Scottish industry declined inexorably from the 1860s. In Lancashire itself, whilst Manchester retained and consolidated its grip on the commercial and merchant functions of the industry (see chapter 3), the gradual movement of manufacturing out of the city continued and there was an increasingly clear intra-regional specialisation between spinning and weaving. The development of firms that combined both spinning and weaving, evident before 1850, was not only arrested but reversed thereafter. In 1914, combined firms comprised only 14 per cent of the total, though their share of spindleage (22 per cent) and loomage (30 per cent) was distinctly larger.[7]

This 'vertical disintegration' in the industry contrasted oddly with trends in other manufacturing industries. In other industries, in Britain and more especially abroad, there developed in the closing decades of the nineteenth century a trend towards large scale, capital intensity, vertical integration and concentration, with large firms taking an in-

FIGURE 89. Advertisement for Horrockses, Crewdson & Co. Ltd, c. 1901. The mill in the centre of the picture is Moses Gate Mill, near Farnworth. The Preston mills are shown bottom left. Source: W. B. Tracy, *Port of Manchester* (Manchester, Hind Hoyle & Light Ltd, 1901), p. 88.

FIGURE 90. Sir William Houldsworth (1834–1917), in 1887. Houldsworth was Tory MP for North West Manchester from 1883 to 1906, and chairman of the Fine Cotton Spinners' and Doublers' Association Ltd. Unusually for a cotton master, Houldsworth was an open supporter of Joseph Chamberlain's campaign for tariffs and imperial preference, and was chairman of the North West Branch of the Tariff Reform League. (Photograph courtesy of Manchester Public Libraries)

creasing share of the industry's market. Such firms sought market power through size, and scale economies through the internal co-ordination of the various stages of production and distribution.[8] In the British cotton industry, giant firms did emerge, but, though durable, they were highly untypical. Average firm size grew more rapidly in the period 1850–1914 than it had in the first half of the nineteenth century, but in context it was still unspectacular, largely reflecting incremental, evolutionary improvements in the self-acting mule and the power loom. What might be regarded as the 'industry standard' in new spinning mills laid down rose from 50,000 spindles in 1870 to 100,000 in 1890, but overall change was less dramatic than this. The number of spindles (excluding doublers) in the average spinning firm grew from 16,872 in 1870 to 36,504 in 1890 according to the Factory Inspectors' Returns, and from 40,732 in 1884 to 75,358 in 1914 according to Worrall's directory.[9] Employment showed a less pronounced rise. Large firms became characteristic of spinning only at the very end of the century and were not typical in the weaving sector even then.

Furthermore, apart from a handful of mergers in the finishing sector, of which the Calico Printers' Association and the Bleachers' Association are the best remembered, and J. & P. Coats and the English Sewing Cotton Co. in thread manufacture, the industry proved relatively immune from the 'combination movement' of the turn of the century. In 1907 there were only two amalgamations in cotton spinning and weaving. Horrockses, Crewdson & Co. was the product of the amalgamation of two Preston concerns and one Bolton firm in 1885–7 (see chapter 3). A combined firm, Horrockses employed 5,300 on 7,000 looms and 250,000 spindles in 1906, and was capitalised at £757,100. Far more prominent was the Fine Cotton Spinners' and Doublers' Association (FCSDA), with a capital of £7.25 m. Formed in 1898, this was an amalgamation of thirty-one firms spinning fine sea-island cotton, a figure which had risen to forty-two by 1902, by which time the FCSDA also possessed spinning capacity in France, including a controlling interest in its main French competitor, and had purchased its own colliery. With some 30,000 employees, the FCSDA was the largest manufacturing employer in the UK, though only seventh largest in terms of capitalisation.[10]

Thus, the industry remained the domain of the small and medium sized firm; even its few

large firms achieved higher outputs from a serial addition of relatively normal-sized mills rather than from the building of one or two giant plants.[11] The industry came to be seen as perhaps the best, and certainly the most well-known, example of 'external economies of scale'. The geographical concentration of the industry, and the wide availability within a small area of independent firms specialising in the import and supply of raw cotton, or in printing, dyeing, and other finishing processes, or in the wholesaling and exporting of finished cloth, or in the supply of banking and financial services for the trade, reduced the need for the spinner or manufacturer to extend his range of activities. Indeed, it probably also reduced his *ability* to do so. From Manchester, the merchant-converter exercised a huge control over the types of products pouring forth from the outlying mills. The export merchant, or shipper, on whom the industry relied for the disposal of some

FIGURE 91. Henry Bannerman and Sons Ltd of York Street, founded around 1810 and one of the most famous and prosperous Manchester merchant houses. By the 1850s the sons of Henry Bannerman were adopting the style of country gentlemen, and in 1880 Charles (later Sir Charles) Macara became managing partner. The Liberal Prime Minister, Henry Campbell-Bannerman, was descended on his mother's side from the founders. Source: W. B. Tracy, *Port of Manchester* (Bannerman version, Hind, Hoyle and Light, 1901).

four-fifths of its product, monopolised the industry's knowledge of its foreign markets – their shifting tastes, their business cultures and business practices, their opportunities and their risks. Direct selling, the employment of travelling sales representatives by the manufacturing firm or the establishment of direct contacts with mass retailers, made some impact on the home trade before 1914. But the appointment of overseas agents in foreign markets remained almost unknown in the cotton trade. The importance of the export merchant, and of his connections with import merchants abroad, was sustained in Manchester and Liverpool as it dwindled elsewhere (see chapter 3). There has never been a definitive count, but around the turn of the century an industry comprising some 2,000 spinning and weaving firms probably supported well over 1,000 merchants. Unfortunately, there is still far too little known about the internal business activities of this critically important sector of the cotton trade.[12]

The lack of integration between spinning and weaving gave rise to a complex dynamic within the industry. It was an industry where 'margins' could be critical in determining profits. For the spinner, buying on the Liverpool Exchange, the critical margin was that between raw cotton prices and yarn prices. For the manufacturer (i.e. the weaver), what mattered was the difference between yarn prices and the merchant's offer price for cloth. Raw cotton prices constituted a high proportion (some 60 per cent) of the value of the industry's final product – the result is that the industry's impressive export earnings tend in some ways to overstate its importance to the British economy.[13] Within the industry, this could result in a fight for the meagre spoils.[14] Spinning and weaving firms tended to benefit unevenly from the different phases of the trade cycle, weaving firms benefiting first from an upturn in demand but then losing ground, as new entrants into their trade bid up the price of yarn and depressed that of cloth. In the longer run, and against the background of declining prices in the 'Great Depression' of 1873–96, margins in spinning probably shrank by a larger amount than they did in weaving. The fall in margins was particularly marked in the years before 1885[15] and was more pronounced for coarse yarns than for fine; as figure 92 shows, the medium-term trend stabilised in the last 15 years of the century, though there were still marked year-to-year fluctuations. That spinning margins fell further than weaving margins should not, however, be taken as an indication of a greater pressure on that sector. Whilst there was a clear loss of foreign markets for yarn due to earlier mechanisation of spinning overseas than weaving, the value of yarn exports peaking in 1872 and the volume in 1884, UK home demand for yarn was rising, so that the deterioration of the spinner's terms of trade with the weaver may in part have reflected faster productivity growth and cost reduction in the spinning sector. Indeed, it is consistent to argue

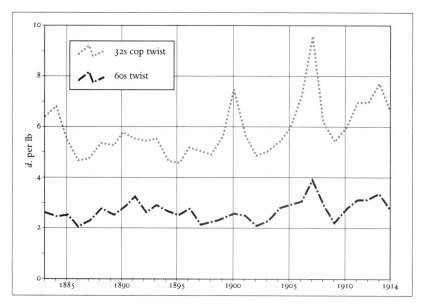

FIGURE 92. Spinning margins, 1883–1914. Source: Robson, *Cotton Industry in Britain,* A3, p. 336.

that, though the spinner's margins *appeared to be* under the greater pressure, the weaver's competitive position was generally weaker and his trade was subject to higher exit rates.

Broadly speaking, southern and eastern Lancashire specialised in spinning, the centre of coarse spinning being Oldham in the east and that of fine spinning being Bolton in the west. As the last handloom weavers dwindled almost unnoticed, weaving sheds multiplied in the towns and villages of the north, again with some specialisation in quality – coarse cloths in and around Blackburn and Burnley, finer cloths in Nelson and the Colne Valley [16] (for the decline of handloom weaving, see chapter 2; for the differences in labour market characteristics between towns, see chapter 5). This geographical separation was never complete – there were important spinning concerns in Preston and Blackburn – but the separation of spinning and weaving between firms was unusually thorough. If its root lay in the high extent to which external economies prevailed within the industry, it was promoted by the spectacular growth of Oldham. Already, in 1870, Oldham had more spindles installed than Manchester, and itself would have ranked as the third largest spinning country in the world, after the rest of the UK and the USA. By 1914 the town housed 29 per cent of UK spindles. Its rapid development has been assigned a central rôle in causing the decline of spinning and the consequent rise of weaving in north-east Lancashire. Oldham was clearly at the centre of the process in which the vertical disintegration of the industry took place. The town's particular advantages in spinning were perhaps central – a fierce local democracy and fluid social structure in which upward mobility was

FIGURE 93. Weaving in the mid-1890s. Thompson's Trafalgar Shed, Burnley. (Photograph courtesy of Lancashire County Library, Burnley Local Studies Collection)

high, the extensive development of the system of renting 'space and turning' within a mill to several small masters who would have otherwise had insufficient capital to enter the trade, local landownership patterns and land values. Almost certainly, however, the dominant factor was the spectacular rise of the textile engineering giant, Platt Bros, which supplied the technical dynamic behind the development of the self-acting mule in the late nineteenth century. Only as Platts rocketed to dominance between 1844 and 1870 did Oldham become a spinning centre of unusual note amongst the towns of Lancashire.[17]

One product of Oldham's democratic structure was the rise of the 'Oldham Limiteds'. Earlier in the 1850s there had been the establishment of 'co-operative' weaving ventures, most notably in Rochdale. In spinning, the prototype of the 'Oldham Limiteds' was the Sun Mill, established in 1858, but the main phase of their creation was the 1870s. Though some hoped that the new 'Limiteds' would herald an age in which the ideals of the Rochdale Pioneers made a transition from the realm of distribution to that of production, the 'Oldham Limiteds' in fact proved merely a medium for floating companies with small share denominations, more accessible to working-class investors. The worker in such concerns fared no better in terms of wages or conditions of service than did those elsewhere, but nevertheless the proportion of Oldham residents holding shares soared from one-twelfth to one-fifth in the company promotion boom of 1873–5. Furthermore, the 'Oldham Limiteds' probably did something to dispel the suspicion of joint stock and limited liability in fiercely individualist Lancashire, so aiding the spread of the new form of company organisation throughout the industry. Indeed, the 'Oldham Limiteds' were inalienably associated with the three pronounced waves of joint stock company promotion in the late nineteenth century, those of 1873–75, 1880–84 and 1889–92.[18]

## Overseas markets

The mill town, with that distinctive culture which still survives in Lancashire's folk memory, was by the late nineteenth century critically dependent on a large number of foreign markets, hugely different in size, affluence and tastes. It was difficult for contemporaries not to take pride in Lancashire's dominance of world trade. Yet, even before the export trade reached its spectacular peak of 1910–13, there were worrying trends. Economic historians are divided over the fundamental origins of the long agony that beset the industry in the 1920s. Was the atomistic and individualistic structure of an industry characterised by a myriad of relatively small firms and jealously independent masters to blame? Or were the strategies of the turn of the century rational, the structures efficient, so that subsequent decline should be seen as the result of a cruel train of events which would have been irresistible even if foreseen? To pursue this question we must examine three related areas – the changing nature of export markets, the Lancashire shipper's response, and the domestic productive processes and strategies which ultimately conditioned his ability to compete abroad.

In most industrialising countries, cotton spinning, then cotton weaving, were the first branches of manufacture to make the transition to factory production. Cotton manufacture involved fairly simple processes and machinery was easily importable, whilst operative skills and managerial talents were relatively easily acquired. The optimum size of firm was relatively small, capital-output ratios low and capital requirements in consequence not a major obstacle.

Development abroad, sometimes state-aided, usually concentrated first upon coarser, lower-quality yarn and cloth. In the USA, protective tariffs initially bit more heavily upon cheap cottons and forced British exporters to concentrate on more expensive goods where the incidence of the tariff was lower. American economist Frank Taussig's early analysis, that in some lines protection may have become superfluous as early as 1830, is almost certainly mistaken.[19] Protection aided 'learning by doing' in the industry, and northern cotton output grew rapidly before 1860.[20] In the late nineteenth century, integrated Massachusetts firms pioneered the introduction of the ring frame, and then the Northrop loom, on a commercial scale. Furthermore, the years after 1880 saw a dramatic rise of the southern mill industry, contesting the national market by substituting cheap labour for organisational maturity.

Perhaps surprisingly, however, the US industry did not emerge as a major exporter on the world market in the late nineteenth century. It has been suggested that US cloth may not have been highly competitive in international markets, its dominance at home still being due to tariff protection.[21] Contemporary British observers acknowledged American advances in technique, but doubted that, price for price, US cloth was of sufficient quality to succeed in foreign markets.[22] The US industry did develop an important but unstable market for heavy pure cloth in China, but otherwise its exports tended to be confined to periods when US domestic demand was slack. This pattern was discerned by several contemporary observers when trying to explain why US cotton exporters did not make a better showing in Latin America, a region where they seemed to possess all the advantages of proximity.[23]

Beyond America, too, tariffs were generally designed, at least in the early stages, to exclude lower-quality goods, the products on which a fledgling industry could most easily be built. By 1860 British exports

FIGURE 94. A Mexican ring-spinning mill, the Rio Blanco Mill, Orizaba, built in 1892. Rapid growth in the 1890s led to Orizaba being described as the 'Manchester of Mexico'. Source: Platt Brothers & Co. Ltd, *Particulars and Calculations Relating to Cotton Spinning* (Oldham, Platt Brothers & Co. Ltd, 1907), p. 342.

to Germany and France, like the USA fairly early developers in mechanised production, were showing a similar tendency to rise in quality. This enabled the British shipper to avoid the relatively heavier tariff on lower-quality goods and distance his product from that issuing from indigenous mills. But he was to find the new cotton masters of Europe less content than their US counterparts to confine their ambitions to their own home markets.

Britain's share of world cotton cloth exports fell from 82 per cent in 1882–4 to 70 per cent in 1910–13, as Germany and France, and behind them Italy and Spain, increased their export-potential in the late nineteenth century. By 1913 continental Europe was contributing 20 per cent of the cotton cloth entering world trade. But the USA still contributed under 5 per cent and Japan, with around 2 per cent, had only just emerged as a significant exporter in the preceding four or five years.[24] From this perspective, the erosion of Britain's position seems relatively undramatic, especially when it is considered that European export rivalry was often limited to particular markets and speciality products. Indeed, Manchester observers often exhibited considerable arrogance when dismissing European attempts to build up export business.[25]

Table 9.1 *Declining growth rate of UK cotton exports from 1869–73*
*(per cent growth per annum by volume)*

|  | Thread | Yarn | Piece-Goods |
|---|---|---|---|
| 1869–73 to 1874–78 | 6.64 | 3.30 | 2.00 |
| 1869–73 to 1879–83 | 6.33 | 2.16 | 2.82 |
| 1869–73 to 1884–88 | 5.85 | 1.81 | 2.38 |
| 1869–73 to 1889–93 | 4.22 | 1.01 | 1.99 |
| 1869–73 to 1894–98 | 4.72 | −0.43 | 1.55 |
| 1869–73 to 1899–1903 | 3.66 | 0.94 | 1.75 |
| 1869–73 to 1904–08 | 4.97 | 0.16 | 1.70 |
| 1869–73 to 1909–13 | 2.92 | 0.26 | 1.69 |

Source: *Annual Statement of Trade of the United Kingdom,* House of Commons Sessional Papers, various years.
Note: The table shows the rates of growth (by volume) of the three kinds of cotton export for which volume data is available in the official trade returns. Yarn exports are shown to have decelerated rapidly over time, their long-term rate of growth 1869–73 to 1894–98 actually being negative. The growth rate of all three categories, however, declined distinctly. Since, in value terms, piece-goods were so heavily predominant in exports, this series most closely represents the overall trend in the growth rate of British cotton exports. It should be noted that rate of growth by value, at constant prices, would look more impressive.

There was also, however, the growth of indigenous industry in markets outside Europe and the United States. World exports increased much more slowly than world cotton consumption, suggesting that, at least before the devastating appearance of large-scale Japanese exports in the 1920s, the more pervasive erosion of Britain's position lay in import substitution as mechanised factory production emerged in less-developed economies. Britain's share of world spindleage fell to less than 50 per cent in 1893. Accurate estimates of her share of world weaving capacity are harder to come by, bedeviled not least by the survival, *and indeed growth,* of handloom sectors in many less-advanced economies. By 1914 there were probably few economies which entered significantly into international trade which did not have at least some rudimentary factory cotton industry,[26] and in less sophisticated markets a handloom weaving sector using domestically-produced or imported yarn could still offer viable competition to British imports. UK mill consumption of cotton fell from 37 per cent of world mill consumption in 1882–4 to 20 per cent in 1910–13.[27] Yarn exports, which grew at 3.3 per cent *per annum* between 1869–73 and 1874–78, decelerated more or less progressively thereafter, so that the overall growth rate between 1869–73 and 1909–13 was only 0.26 per cent *per annum.*[28]

We might expect, therefore, that the upward quality shift we have noticed in the US and European trade would have become more generally applicable to the wider markets of the world. This is certainly what many contemporaries believed. They prided themselves in the knowledge that British ascendancy in production was *most marked* in the finer cloths. Industry observers talked of a trend towards 'finer counts' as British exports, almost contemptuously, soared above the best efforts that indigenous producers could manage. Even Switzerland could not match Britain in producing the highest counts. Some contemporaries also mentioned a trend towards more highly-finished goods, though this was perhaps less dwelt upon than finer counts.[29]

Plausible as it sounds initially, this postulated strategy of response to mounting competition in overseas markets raises problems. Increasingly, in the late nineteenth century, British exports were directed to less-developed economies with lower consumer incomes and a predominant demand for coarse counts. Of course, there was a demand for high-quality cloth even in those markets, but not one sufficient to sustain an export sector *as large* as Lancashire's around 1900. Export quality to such markets might have risen somewhat after 1865, but it is unlikely to have risen to such an extent that it was totally immune from local competition. Indeed, whilst, in the face of export rivalry from India and Japan, the average count of British yarn exports probably did rise, at least until 1907, some contemporary observers doubted that there was any trend towards 'finer counts' in cloth exports at all, whilst others

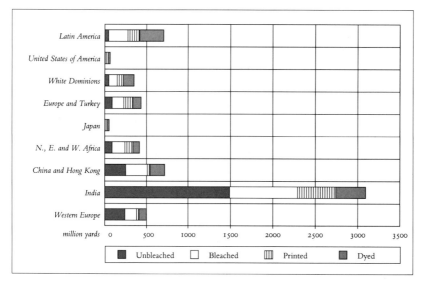

FIGURE 95. Exports of piece goods by volume, 1913. Source: *Annual Statement of Trade of the United Kingdom*, House of Commons Sessional Papers.

doubted that it was pronounced enough to be significant.[30] This is scarcely surprising given Lancashire's heavy dependence on India in the late nineteenth century, an issue to which we will return.

Available statistics on piece-goods exports, three-quarters of UK exports in this period, regrettably shed little light on the question of quality. The Board of Trade collected no information on count, or fineness. Cloth was merely divided into four categories, unbleached grey, bleached white, printed and dyed.[31] If other aspects of quality remained unchanged it could be safely assumed that a shift from grey and bleached cloth towards printed and dyed goods would represent an upward shift. A shift from printed to dyed goods would, however, be less certain in its effect. Furthermore, unrecorded downward shifts in average count could conceivably offset small rises in the proportion of printed and dyed cloth exported.

To overcome such problems, Lars Sandberg used an indirect method to construct an index of cloth quality. In a study which spanned the entire period 1815–1914, Sandberg essentially compared the average unit values of British cloth exports[32] with the prices of a range of cloths which remained unchanged in quality over time. For the post-1845 period he used a price index compiled by *The Economist*, which, with one important change around the turn of the century, continued to appear until 1914.[33]

Most of the considerable decline in the Sandberg index between 1815 and 1914 can be traced to low-income markets – the quality of exports to high-income countries increased slightly during this period. Indeed, without the inclusion of India, the quality-decline of 1815–1914 would have been approximately halved. More relevant for present purposes is the movement of the Sandberg index in the late nineteenth century – a gentle trend upwards over the whole period 1870–1914, broken only by a decline in the 1880s. Interestingly, the improvement in the Edwardian boom was more noticeable in exports to low-income countries than it was to high-income countries such as Canada, Australia and New Zealand.[34]

This is also the pattern discerned by Marrison in a more limited, but more detailed, study of the Latin American market. British exporters were highly aware both of the growing presence of export rivals and, more immediately, of the rising threat from indigenous industry, especially in Brazil and Mexico. Yet, at the same time, they were conscious of the need to accommodate what was predominantly a low-income demand. In consequence, they developed new lines of product, particularly cheaper dyed goods known as 'coloured cottons'. These were woven from dyed yarn rather than dyed in the piece, and were cheaper than vat-dyed cloth. Partly this was because they could be more heavily sized – dyeing after weaving removed the sizing agents and it was uneconomical to re-apply them – so that cheaper raw materials like china clay could be substituted for more expensive raw cotton. Thus, there was an ambivalent character to the quality 'improvement' of exports to Latin America. Intrinsic cloth quality may have improved little, or may even have fallen, as heavy sizing allowed coarse cloths to be disguised, but consumers were attracted by the higher degree of finish that this process allowed on goods which still remained within their pockets. Indeed, it was US exporters to Latin America who suffered in the attempt to sell in low-income markets the high-quality pure cloths and prints that periodically became surplus to their own home market.[35]

There was indeed a general shift towards printed and dyed goods in British exports as a whole. Figures 96 and 97, based on yardage rather than value, show a tendency for the product-mix to the broadly-defined markets to tilt gradually towards printed and dyed goods. In round figures, printed and dyed goods were only about 30 per cent of total piece-goods exports in 1889; by 1913 they had risen to about 38 per cent. The shift was small in the Indian and Chinese cases – a feature which makes the overall trend appear less dramatic in view of the absolute size of those two markets.[36] Some high-income markets, also – the USA at nearly 60 per cent – appeared to have reached a point of *stasis,* whilst the white dominions showed a small regression. But in the majority of low-income markets, printed and dyed goods, especially the latter, had risen distinctly in the product-mix of British exports.

Whatever happened in the world beyond, India dominated, not only amongst Lancashire's low-income markets, but amongst her markets as a whole. The state of the Indian harvest was hugely important to a substantial proportion of Lancashire businessmen. Beyond this, Manchester merchants were little short of obsessed with managing the

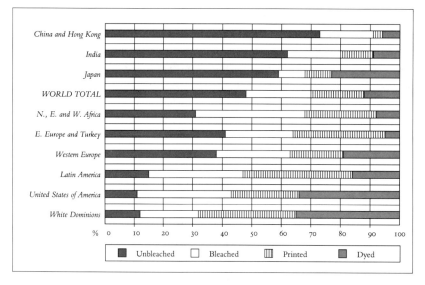

FIGURE 96. Export mix of piece goods, by volume, 1889. Source: *Annual Statement of Trade of the United Kingdom*, House of Commons Sessional Papers.

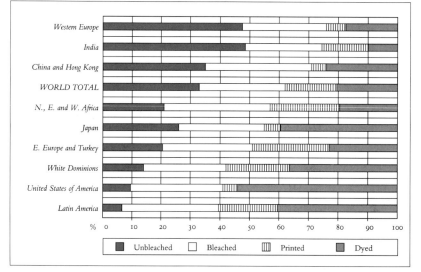

FIGURE 97. Export mix of piece goods, by volume, 1913. Source: *Annual Statement of Trade of the United Kingdom*, House of Commons Sessional Papers.

affairs of the sub-continent in a way which sits curiously with the city's international reputation as the home of economic liberalism. In the 1850s and 1860s, their concern had been with developing an alternative to US sources of raw cotton, a concern that persisted as American supply recovered after the Cotton Famine, despite increasing frustration over Whitehall's inability to effect any improvement in the quality of Indian cotton.[37] By the late nineteenth century, their attention had shifted towards broader aspects of economic policy. Some advocated the re-monetisation of silver to raise the exchange rate of the rupee and expose India even more remorselessly to British competition (see chapter 4). But more widespread and enduring was Manchester's agitation over the

Indian cotton duties. The Indian Administration had to grapple with a vast area in desperate need of public works, many of which – such as railways – were considered by Lancashire businessmen as much to their own interest. In consequence, many within an Indian Civil Service constantly bedeviled by the state of the Indian finances were far from unsympathetic towards nationalist desires for a tariff on India's largest category of manufactured imports. What was protection to some held out the prospect of revenue to others – customs duties were politically acceptable in India and virtually the only elastic source of revenue available to the authorities.

The conventional story has been that considerations of British domestic politics – whether Liberal ideology or Conservative need to retain electoral support in Lancashire – dictated that Lancashire was given a full hearing in Whitehall. The modest Indian revenue duty of 3–5 per cent, dating from before the Mutiny, was described in a memorial to the Prime Minister in 1874 as 'absolutely prohibitory to the trade in yarn and cloth of the coarse and low priced sorts' by the directors of the Manchester Chamber of Commerce! It was reduced in stages from 1875 and finally abolished in 1882. In 1894–5 fiscal needs occasioned the re-imposition of a 5 per cent duty on imported cottons, but pressure from Lancashire forced a reduction to 3½ per cent and the imposition of a countervailing excise duty on Indian domestic production.[38]

Certainly it is true that 'no cotton duty could be low enough or temporary enough to placate Lancashire'.[39] However, recent research has shown that Lancashire's influence was not as central as is often assumed. The reduction of 1875 was in some ways a defeat for Lancashire, part of a broad reduction of the Indian general tariff when Lancashire interests would have preferred the maintenance of duties on other imports and the *total* abolition of duties on cotton. The Indian tariff on cottons was in fact not seen as of critical *economic* importance by many in the India Office and the Government of India, since they thought imports not directly competitive with the products of Indian mills. Tariff policy became a point of conflict between opposing factions within both branches of the dual system of government, and usually revenue considerations or the power struggle between the India Office and the Government of India, rather than the interests of Lancashire, were at its heart.[40] Even so, Lancashire's less-than-wholesome determination to maintain free access to the Indian market was broadly accommodated until the First World War.[41]

## Productivity and Performance

In the last 25 years there has been an intense debate over the performance of the British cotton industry between 1885 and 1914, a debate which has centred upon the Lancashire industry's productivity record and its apparent reluctance to adopt ring-spinning and the Northrop or automatic loom, the most significant changes in production techniques in the period after 1860.[42] The US industry adopted the new innovations rapidly; by 1905, 17.9m ring spindles and only 5.2m mule spindles were installed, whilst in 1914 40 per cent of US looms were automatic. But in Britain, even in 1913–14, only 10.4m ring spindles were installed, compared with 45.2m mule spindles, and automatic looms were only 1–2 per cent of the total.[43] Platt Bros, whose earlier dominance of the textile machinery industry had been based heavily on the production of the mule and the Lancashire loom, found the years after 1895 trying, in spite of the firm's positive attitude towards the new technology and towards exports. In the face of a deceleration in the growth of world demand and intensified competition at home and abroad, employment shrank from 15,000 in 1898 to 10,700 in 1907, and profits shrank from the 10–20 per cent customary since 1870 to under 6 per cent in 1904–13.[44]

In 1933, G. T. Jones derived an index of 'real costs' in which spinning and weaving costs in the Lancashire industry were calculated from weighted indices of raw cotton, wage and other cost components. His dominant finding was that little reduction in 'real costs' (alternatively, little improvement in productivity) was achieved after 1885.[45] For some thirty years, this result was little questioned. Some writers associated it with Lancashire's slowness in making the transition to ring spinning and the automatic loom. The US industry, especially that in Massachusetts, 'regarded [by contemporaries] as Britain's main rival in efficiency',[46] seemed to provide an object lesson of higher output per operative using later and superior equipment.

Nevertheless, Jones' findings raised something of a 'paradox'.[47] The Lancashire industry expanded healthily in the Edwardian years and continued to dominate world markets. Why should Lancashire have had difficulties in making a transition to the newer technologies? To Lars Sandberg, Jones' findings flew in the face of an easily demonstrable increase in labour productivity. Indeed, Jones' own index of output, when modified to reflect improvements in product quality and set alongside employment figures which were adjusted for changes in wages and working hours, could be used to demonstrate an improvement of labour productivity in the order of 40 per cent for the period 1885–1914.

This suggested weaknesses in Jones' original findings on 'real cost'. Sandberg improved Jones' indexes of production costs and revised his cotton output index to reflect quality improvements. More importantly, he also made technical revisions to Jones' cloth price index.[48] His revised findings indicated a decline in 'real costs' (as defined by Jones) of at least 11–12 per cent between 1885–1914. Allowing for the fact that some 60 per cent of production costs were raw cotton, where significant cost reductions were scarcely possible, it was thus valid to argue that efficiency in the use of inputs *other than* cotton increased by 25–30 per cent.

Sandberg's questioning of Jones' findings on efficiency threw into doubt any easy association between observed differences in choice of technique and entrepreneurial failure centred upon technological conservatism and complacency. In an article destined to become the classic analysis of the difference between British and American practice, he explained this largely in terms of the difference in the cost of labour in the two countries and the different raw cotton requirements of the two methods.

The factors involved in the decision to install rings or mules were complex, and varied according to whether the new machinery was an addition to plant or a replacement of existing mules, and whether it was to be employed in the production of weft or warp. It was well-known to contemporaries such as Copeland that the ring frame held the advantage in spinning coarse counts and the mule was more effective in producing finer yarns.[49] But as late as the 1900s the transition point seems to have been different in Britain and the USA. In the USA, the ring was used for warps up to 120s, whereas in Britain the implication of the Universal Ring Spinning List, negotiated in 1912, was that little yarn over 43s (warp *or* weft) was spun on rings (for the wages lists, see chapter 5).[50]

For a given yarn count, ring frames required more expensive (longer-staple) raw cotton than did mules. This was because of the stronger motion of the ring and its tendency to break threads more frequently. The structure of prices in the raw cotton market meant that up to counts of about 40 the cost of raw cotton rose more steeply with ring spinning than with mule spinning – at about 40s the differential was about 2.0 cents per lb, after which it stabilised. On the other hand, the labour cost of ring spinning per lb of yarn around count 40s was similar in both countries. But because of the relative abundance of skilled labour, mule-spinning was cheaper in Britain than the US, so that the labour cost of mules at counts of 40 was about 2.4 cents per lb higher than the labour cost of rings in the USA and only 1.6 cents per lb higher in Lancashire. Given such a difference, argued Sandberg, it was rational for US producers to incur the 2.0 cent cost penalty of the longer staple cotton necessary for production on ring frames, and rational for Lancashire masters to pay the penalty of higher labour costs in order to economize on raw cotton.

What was the situation as yarn count rose? As has been mentioned, the differential cost of the raw material stabilised, but labour costs behaved somewhat differently in the two countries as count rose. In

general, technological considerations dictated that labour costs increased more rapidly with count in mule-spinning than in ring-spinning, because in rings an operative producing higher counts could tend a higher number of spindles.[51] Furthermore, ring-spinners (mostly female) were paid less than mule-spinners (mostly male and unionised) in both countries. But in Britain, mule-spinning labour was both cheaper and less militant than in America. Hence US cotton masters continued to install rings up to counts as high as 100, incurring the raw material penalty to save on labour, whereas in Lancashire increased labour cost still did not outweigh the extra raw cotton cost, and the introduction of rings for counts above 40 remained negligible.[52]

This work, coupled with his own earlier findings on productivity advance in the British industry, led Sandberg to a flat rejection of the 'entrepreneurial failure' hypothesis. There was no technological lag: Lancashire adopted ring spinning as and where appropriate, any apparent neglect of ring-spinning being nothing more than a rational response to the particular market circumstances and factor costs facing the British industry. This position had direct consequences for the analysis of the causes of Lancashire's precipitous decline after 1921. Rather than failing on account of its own internal weaknesses, the British cotton industry

FIGURE 98. Little piecer and self-acting mule, Oldham, around 1900. (Photograph courtesy of Oldham Metropolitan Borough Leisure Services, Local Studies Library)

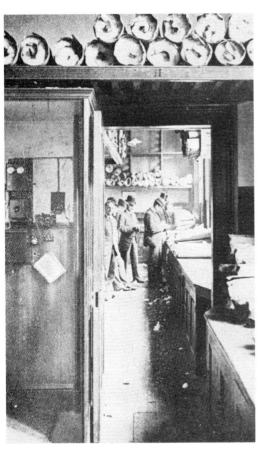

was caught between the hammer of cheap labour in India and Japan and the anvil of increasing world protectionism, factors 'outside the control of British management'.[53]

Sandberg's analysis was widely accepted until the early 1980s, when it was questioned in a series of articles by Lazonick, with his sometime co-worker, William Mass. At the centre of a highly complex issue was a questioning not only of Sandberg's labour productivity estimates, but also, and arguably more important, of their significance.

Lazonick and Mass argued that Sandberg's labour-force figures were overestimates, but more so for 1881 than for 1911, thus exaggerating the increase in output per worker. Their own revised figures suggested an increase in labour productivity of only 15 per cent between 1885 and 1913, improvement in the early period giving way to stagnation after 1900. Though they took these estimates as *prima facie* evidence that it was becoming harder to maintain productivity advances with machinery which was coming to the limit of its technological development, their revision has proved highly controversial.[54]

FIGURE 99. A Liverpool cotton broker's sale room, c. 1894.
Source: *Cotton From Field to Factory* (reprinted from 'the Diary and Buyers Guide', 1894), facing p. 62.

Much more important to Lazonick and Mass than the precise increase in productivity, however, was the *way in which* the increase was achieved. This was done by economising on raw cotton content, using low-grade, short-staple cotton to produce heavily sized goods. In this, ironically, the mule and the power loom were particularly suitable. These were less prone to break threads spun from poor cotton, the mule also producing a soft-twisted yarn that took size better than ring yarn.[55] The strategy of economising in this way was re-enforced by the peculiar structure of the Lancashire market for purchasing raw cotton. Seldom holding stocks of cotton, the spinning firm bought from week to week, thus being able to select the grades most cheaply available at the time. In this the mule was particularly suitable, since its very flexibility could cope with variation more easily than the ring frame.

Inferior cotton also allowed the master to circumvent the wage list agreements. Earlier in the century cotton masters had fostered the evolution of the well-known hierarchy of mule spinner, big piecer and little piecer – a system of sub-contracting which effectively delegated close supervision to the mule spinner and avoided personnel management costs – but by the late nineteenth century this was imposing restrictions on the master's freedom of action. According to Lazonick, the wage lists effectively prevented employers cutting piece-rates if higher-productivity capital equipment was installed, thus blunting the incentive for technical progress. But the lists *also* committed workers to accepting increased effort in order to maintain piece-rate earnings. The result was an intensification of effort against a background of increasing use of inferior cotton. According to Lazonick's calculations, physical productivity in mule spinning reached a climacteric in the late 1880s and stagnated thereafter. To stay competitive in world markets, the Lancashire spinner had to exploit the mule's flexibility by using inferior cotton – that is, by producing yarn of a given count using lower-quality raw cotton than would have been necessary on the ring frame. Friction increased, virtually all the stoppages in the trade between 1890 and 1914 being due to grievances over 'bad spinning', but only in 1913 did the Brooklands Agreement actually break down (see chapter 5). There was a progressive degradation of yarn and cloth quality, often hidden by more elaborate finishing, and broadly acceptable to foreign consumers in view of the predominantly low-income nature of Britain's export markets. A survey of the British export-mix to the main foreign markets revealed characteristics similar to those found in Marrison's earlier study, but was more pessimistic in interpreting them as an unambiguous degradation in product quality.[56]

Lazonick and Mass did not regard this strategy as irrational, nor did they deny that it yielded acceptable profits in the Edwardian years, but they did regard it as short-sighted.[57] Why should British masters have resorted to these expedients to stretch the mule beyond its time, to avoid re-equipment along lines which were to become virtually universal outside of Britain by the 1930s? Whilst labour relations were clearly a re-enforcing factor, the prime reason for Lancashire's limited adoption of rings lay in the vertical disintegration of the British industry. Lazonick and Mass put great weight on a factor which had been included in Sandberg's analysis, but only as a factor of relatively small importance. Ring yarn (more accurately, ring *weft*) had to be transported to the loom on a heavy wooden bobbin, which then had to be returned.[58] This made rings less viable in a vertically disintegrated industry such as the British, since this became a matter of shipping bobbins between firms, not just between departments within the same factory. Rather than *overcome* this 'constraint' by a determined process of co-operation, combination and vertical integration – what in the 1920s would be called 'rationalisation' – Lancashire producers chose to *adapt to* it.

Behind Lazonick's analysis was a fundamental difference with Sandberg over the criteria by which entrepreneurial action and performance should be judged. 'New Economic Historians' such as Sandberg used an essentially static neoclassical framework which limited the horizon to the short term – that is, broadly speaking, they defined entrepreneurial success as the ability to maximize profits in given circumstances. Lazonick adopted the perspectives of Joseph Schumpeter and Alfred Chandler. To Schumpeter, the engine of growth was the *innovating* entrepreneur. To Chandler, vertical integration, the combination within the same firm of production and marketing, and the development of elaborate managerial structures were all central to the emergence of the 'modern' industrial enterprise, the giant corporation. These were striking by their absence in Edwardian Britain:

> British businessmen performed admirably as neoclassical managers – they took the conditions facing them as given and tried to do the best they could, subject to these constraints. As entrepreneurs, however, they failed precisely because as individualistic managers in highly competitive and vertically specialised structures they were powerless to alter the organisational constraints that determined feasible technological choices and profitable opportunities. As a result, they barely even tried, either individually or collectively, to transform their industrial environment. Certainly in the decades prior to World War I, when the German, American and Japanese economies were developing on the basis of modern corporate structures, British capitalists were oblivious of the need to make these institutional changes if Britain was to maintain its position in the world economy in the long run.[59]

Indeed, Lazonick found Lancashire masters even more wedded to the mule than had Sandberg. He made revisions to Sandberg's estimates in three areas. Firstly, he corrected Sandberg's underestimate of the number of spindles tended by a mule-spinner and recalculated Sandberg's factor costs calculations to argue that in Britain mules were competitive with rings at lower counts than Sandberg had estimated – in the region of 20s–40s for warp, and in the region of 20s–40s for weft in *unintegrated* firms. Secondly, applying different assumptions on the output-mix (the ratio of yarn and cloth above and below counts of 40) of the British industry and the rate of replacement of old mules, he concluded that only 56 per cent of new spindles installed for counts up to 40s were rings. This compared with Sandberg's earlier finding that 'a very large percentage of the spindles installed [in *c.*1907–14] for counts up to 40 were rings'. Thirdly, Lazonick sought to demonstrate, partly on direct evidence from Oldham, that virtually all new installations for weft yarn, right down to 1914, were mules rather than rings.[60]

Such revisions were naturally acceptable to Lazonick's opponents, most of whom found it hard to understand why, if the disintegrated

structure of prosperous Lancashire was so crippling to its prospects, there was not a greater trend towards the erection of integrated mills. Saxonhouse and Wright could accept Lazonick's finding that Lancashire's preference for the mule was even stronger than Sandberg had allowed, but still took issue with the importance of the transport cost constraint. The Lancashire industry was not alone in neglecting to follow the US model – of the new spindles ordered by Indian concerns from six Lancashire textile engineering companies, more than half were mule spindles until after 1900, whilst the corresponding figure for Russian concerns stayed above 40 per cent until 1916. None of the countries which led in the adoption of rings – the US, Japan, and Brazil – had an export sector of substantial proportions before 1914[61] Furthermore, the transport of bobbins could not have been of great significance, since the development of paper tubes on which ring weft could be spun was an innovation only slowly taken up in Lancashire even though it would have provided a way for introducing ring frames in unintegrated mills. Indeed, the adoption of paper tubes in the unintegrated industries of France, Germany and Austria suggested that industrial structure did not pose a binding 'constraint' on the introduction of ring spindles.[62]

This led to a complex disagreement over the precise significance and purpose of methods in which paper tubes were used in ring-spinning of weft and the cost of having to rewind onto a 'warp beam' in ring-spinning of warp yarns. More significant, however, were disagreements over the concept of a 'constraint' on a broader level. Lazonick's argument was that the failure to adopt ring spinning and to develop integrated structures within the cotton industry were the result of historical constraints over which the individual entrepreneur had no control. After the First World War they would have unfortunate consequences upon the competitive strength of Lancashire. But Lazonick's critics found it difficult to separate his thesis from the more venerable one of 'entrepreneurial failure'. This became more pronounced as Lazonick appeared willing to dilute his definition of the word 'constraint' (which 'was never meant to be taken literally'), seemingly unable to demonstrate that 'institutional constraints' meant anything more than conservative mentalities and mindsets inherited from the age of Britain's splendid Victorian domination.[63] If there were no concrete constraints and if, as Lazonick agreed, entrepreneurs were rational and profit maximisation still possible in the Edwardian industry, why was there such limited movement towards combined structures? Surely the most plausible reason was that 'external economies' still ruled in the cotton industry and that mule technology was still competitive given Britain's factor costs and product mix? It was pointed out that the Japanese industry was not highly integrated and that the high-throughput,

FIGURES 100, 101. Progress in the Japanese cotton industry. Above: Kagoshima, the first Japanese mill, built in 1866. Below: the famous Osaka Mill, built in 1888. Source: Platt Brothers & Co. Ltd, *Particulars and Calculations Relating to Cotton Spinning*, pp. 338–9.

integrated mills of Massachusetts buckled under the postwar onslaught (in their case not only from Japan but also, and more importantly, from the southern states) even more rapidly than Lancashire did.[64]

Lazonick has always insisted that British masters acted rationally in retaining the mule. If they acted rationally when there was no binding constraint, his argument would seem to reduce to the claim that they were technologically short-sighted and unadventurous, conservative in their attitudes towards changing the industry's structure, in a situation where there was no immediate financial incentive to be otherwise, and when there was no certainty that future innovation would pay. Was this a failure of the Schumpeterian entrepreneur?

In itself, Lazonick's own finding that Lancashire mule-spinning re-mained competitive before 1914 suggests that the cost-advantage of rings in the production of yarn was at that time small even at lower counts. Its importance in the final product price (and attractiveness) of a woven and finished cloth, shipped abroad some thousands of miles on decisions dependent on the skill and knowledge of the merchant converter, the finisher and the shipper, and then, perhaps, subjected to the tender hands of several middlemen, was clearly minimal.[65]

On this basis we might be sceptical of the practical importance of the 'rings *versus* mules' debate. But Lazonick's further argument (more prominent in recent contributions than in his earlier writings) is that the vertical specialisation of the industry which so retarded the intro-duction of rings also prevented the installation of planned and co-or-dinated production using both the ring frame and the automatic loom in conjunction.[66]

The constraint, or at least the 'impediment', was thus a two-stage one. Vertical specialisation impeded the ring and absence of the ring impeded the introduction of the automatic loom. But Lazonick also stresses the importance of the ring and the automatic loom together in enabling management to co-ordinate the two processes, planning the appropriate quality of yarn and setting up of the loom, etc. Ashton Brothers of Hyde is cited as a pre-war example of an integrated high-throughput firm in which ring-spinning provides hard-twisted yarn suitable for automatic looms, and in which the process of production is integrated with the process of distribution.[67] Hence it is not just the absence of strong, ring-quality yarn that is at issue and it is therefore not clear that ring yarn from vertically specialised spinners would have been that much more useful to specialised weavers than mule yarn would have been, since such co-ordination would have been difficult. In this sense the impediment to the rise of the combined firm was apparently the vertical specialisation of the industry! Again, it is legit-imate to raise the question, if there had been a need or even a *desire* for vertical integration, then why did not more firms embark upon it?

Lazonick cites the industry's 'failure . . . to make the transition from the competitive capitalist firm to the corporate capitalist firm' as being 'primarily responsible for this prolonged state of technological back-wardness'.[68] To the extent that he laments the failure of the British cotton industry to develop according to the Chandlerian model of the large-scale company, we have to be clear that the cotton industry did not figure strongly in Chandler's analysis of large-scale business in the USA, a fact which Lazonick accepts. All participants in the debate accept that a large shrinkage of the Lancashire industry was inevitable in interwar conditions and it cannot be certain that it would have been *significantly* more successful in the face of low wage competition from the Far East if it had been vertically organised and equipped with later technologies.

If, on the other hand, Lazonick laments the conservatism and short-termism that stemmed from the persistence of the individual owner and the private company, it is well to remember that shareholders can be as adept at asset-stripping as can owning dynasties. Interesting work by J. S. Toms suggests that Lancashire spinning firms were disinvesting in the period 1885–1914. That is, given their rate of return on capital, they dispensed too much of their profits in dividends and payed insufficient attention to depreciation. This was irrespective of whether the firm was privately owned or a public company – indeed, in the case of the latter, Toms paints a picture of a sort of tyranny imposed by shareholder expectations of high dividends. Whether Toms has discovered a 'financial constraint' to buttress the Lazonick thesis, or whether there was rational disinvestment and switching of funds to projects yielding higher returns, is worthy of further study. But in either case, it cannot always be assumed that the public company will be more immune than the private to short-termism, more adventurous in investment policy, or more active in research and development.[69]

## Conclusion

In absolute size, the Lancashire cotton industry expanded by an amount unparalleled in the rest of the world during the Edwardian period. It also commanded the markets of the globe, at least beyond that small but important group of advanced industrial countries which had long excluded its products by a systematic use of protective tariffs. In their most recent contributions, Lazonick and Mass have shifted the weight of their analysis onto the interwar period, when, under the threat from Japan and the loss of the Indian market, the need for rationalisation and structural change in the Lancashire industry were clearly more pressing, and onto improvements in Japanese weaving productivity through the introduction of the impressive Toyoda automatic loom after 1924[70] (see chapter 10). Of course, Lazonick and Mass are correct in their general assertion that British industry was slow to make the transition to corporate capitalism and the integrated concern, both institutional structures which were to be a prominent feature in the growth of the advanced economies between the 1920s and 1970s. But it is by no means clear that this line of argument is applicable to the cotton industry, and even less clear that it affords particular insights into the *Edwardian* cotton industry. Indeed, current empirical research by Farnie suggests a degree of flexibility in Lancashire; though from a low base in 1890, the expansion of British ring capacity in the period 1890–1913 (5.9 per cent) was faster than that in the USA (5.0 per cent) and in the rest of the world, including the USA (3.95 per cent).[71] Lancashire's problem in 1914 was in many ways *over-development* rather than *under-development*. There was no realistic way in which the cotton industry could be maintained at the size it had achieved. That size was the result of early advances in relatively simple technology, easily emulated; a large expansion of the world economy under conditions which, whilst not exactly liberal, were at least liberal in relation to what was to come in the interwar period; and an unsustainable domination of the world's less-developed markets, a domination which hinged upon a manipulation of Indian politics. Furthermore, Lancashire's success abroad was far more dependent on the success and the practices of the merchant-converter, and less upon the spinner or manufacturer, than is often acknowledged. Indeed, it is even possible that Lazonick and Mass's argument (that sizing and product degradation was a strategy necessary to maintaining the viability of the mule) should be turned on its head – maybe persisting with the mule was necessary to allow a process of heavy sizing which shippers recognised to be vital to the retention of Britain's extensive markets in low-income countries.

Thus, the extent to which a transition to the integrated spinning and weaving firm might have staved off the onslaught from far eastern industries using cheap labour in combination with advanced machinery was probably small. Ultimately, however, that question must always remain a matter of conjecture. The mechanism by which the foundations for such a transition could have been laid in the thirty years before the Great War, and the incentive to pursue that mechanism, remain just as elusive.

## Acknowledgements

I would like to thank Tom Marrison for undertaking the laborious calculations upon which figures 96 and 97 are based. I would also like to thank Theo Balderston, Steve Broadberry, Douglas Farnie, John Singleton, and the Editor for their helpful comments on earlier drafts of this chapter.

# CHAPTER 10

# Foreign Competition and the Interwar Period

## MARGUERITE DUPREE

THE Lancashire cotton industry lost its competitive advantage in the interwar years as foreign competition emerged and export markets declined during and after the First World War. 'The things which in 1914 had appeared to the very discerning as a distant menace, magnified a thousandfold by the wastage of war, had gathered near. Conditions, forces, men abroad were ready for the onslaught on Lancashire'.[1] In 1913 Lancashire dominated the world trade in cotton textiles, supplying two-thirds of the world trade in cotton cloth and exports of cotton goods constituted a quarter of all exports from the UK, making it the largest British export industry. By 1938 the industry was but a shadow of its former self. Output and employment fell to half the 1913 level, Lancashire's share of international trade in cotton cloth decreased to 25 per cent and cotton goods accounted for only 12 per cent of Britain's exports.[2] The industry's decline was dramatic, yet firms, workers, banks, representative organisations within the industry and government responded to changed conditions between 1914 and 1939 and struggled to find workable solutions. The effectiveness of the solutions and why they were not more successful are issues of controversy among historians.

## The First World War

### 1. *Internal*

From within the cotton industry, it seemed that 'the War had, on the whole, managed to get on very well with the Lancashire cotton trade'.[3] There was pressure on the industry's supplies of labour and raw cotton, particularly in the later years of the war, but all mills continued to operate throughout the war, albeit at reduced levels, and profits reached record heights.

Initially in the autumn of 1914 there was high unemployment in Lancashire only partly due to dislocation caused by war. A fall in demand in India, Lancashire's largest market for cloth, was already underway as a result of overstocking and a poor monsoon season. The war caused a financial panic in India and aggravated the slump, but by mid-1915 Lancashire's exports to India had stabilised at about two-thirds of the pre-war level.[4] Employment in Lancashire returned to pre-war levels by Spring 1915 and from the middle of the year there was a shortage of male labour. Patriotism, unemployment or low pay led cotton workers to volunteer for military service in large numbers. In the spinning section in particular, many piecers, who were less well paid and younger, volunteered. In Preston in September 1914 1,131 men enlisted compared with only 3,521 in all of London. After the introduction of conscription in 1916 the military enlistment rate of male textile workers was 31 per cent, about the same as that for all manufacturing workers, and by July 1918 it reached 47 per cent.[5] Prominent employers such as Herbert Dixon, chairman of the Fine Spinners and Doublers Association, and Edward Tootal Broadhurst, chairman of Tootal Broadhurst Lee, were instrumental in raising and equipping the Manchester Pals battalions in 1914 and 1915, units recruited from the locality consisting of cotton workers and those in other occupations.[6] One-third of the 11th Battalion (Accrington) East Lancashire Regiment who were either killed in action or died of their wounds before the end of July 1916 were cotton operatives.[7] By the end of 1917, 470 members of the Burnley Weavers' Association had

FIGURE 102. Accrington 'Pals' drilling at Ellison's Tenement, Accrington, before receiving their uniforms, September 1914. One-third of Accrington East Lancashire Regiment who were either killed in action or died of their wounds and whose occupations are known were cotton operatives. Source: W. C. Turner, *Pals: the 11th (Service) Battalion (Accrington) East Lancashire Regiment* (Barnsley Chronicle, 1992), p. 38.

FIGURE 103. Roll of Honour, India Mill, Darwen. (Photograph courtesy of Lancashire County Library, Darwen Local Studies Collection)

been killed in action.[8] The territorial basis of units meant that some Lancashire towns suffered devastating and disproportionately high rates of military casualties.

Employment in the cotton industry fell by 20 per cent from 620,000 in June 1914 to 500,000 in June 1917, but the industry retained more labour than was necessary to meet military requirements and basic civilian needs for several reasons. First, despite union fears that the introduction of women in the spinning section would lead to an erosion of wage rates, the decision was left to local branches. Encouraged by the series of Acts for the Defense of the Realm and the Treasury Agreement of 1915 which led to the setting aside of restrictive practices in munitions-related industries for the duration of the war,[9] most local branches, apart from Preston, allowed the introduction of women as piecers, with the understanding that the pre-war gender division of labour would be restored after the war. In many areas weaving became an overwhelmingly female occupation with large numbers of men remaining in the industry only in parts of north-east Lancashire.[10] Second, the government reliance on persuasion and high wages was not sufficient to attract many cotton workers to munitions factories. There was no mass exodus from cotton, as workers who had secure long-term jobs and seniority were reluctant to give them up for higher pay. Third, unions were able to acquire exemptions from conscription for overlookers, several grades of skilled preparatory workers, married spinners and piecers and single men born before 1890, though not for weavers who could be replaced by women.[11] Fourth, some employers supported key workers' appeals before recruiting tribunals. Yet, where overlookers and elite male workers were absent, many employers developed new means of acquiring labour by utilising the Labour Exchange.[12] And finally, after mid-1917 when shortages of raw cotton forced the reduction of production, the government was afraid the war effort would be undermined by mass unemployment in the cotton industry; it feared a situation analogous to the Cotton Famine during the American Civil War in the 1860s. At the same time, industrial unrest increased as the cotton unions began to object to the failure of wages to keep up with the cost of living. In June 1917 the government established a Cotton Control Board (CCB) made up of twelve members representing employers, trade unions, merchants and the government which implemented a rota system to maintain employment in the industry by allowing workers to take regular periods of temporary and partially paid unemployment.[13]

The industry's output was not limited by shortages of raw cotton until 1917. Surprisingly, raw cotton prices fell during the early months of the war, as there was no immediate threat to the North Atlantic trade and supplies of American cotton. Throughout the war the industry supplied allied armies with cotton textiles for a variety of uses, including fabrics for airplanes, balloons and airships, as well as army tents, gas masks, underwear and bandages. The French bought their military textiles in Britain to reduce their imports of raw cotton and save valuable shipping space. In April 1918 about a quarter of those employed in the industry were engaged in production for government contracts. Although recently historians have been sceptical, contemporaries, both employers and unions alike, believed the production of cloth for export was essential for the wartime balance of payments. This, together with continued employment to avoid social unrest, justified maintaining production as long as there were supplies of raw cotton.[14]

The shortage of raw cotton became acute in the summer of 1917. The German U-boat campaign successfully isolated Britain by submarine attacks on British merchant shipping. Cotton had a low priority compared to munitions and food for the limited shipping space and the stocks of raw cotton in Liverpool warehouses declined. The government suspended the Liverpool raw cotton market and, as mentioned above, the Board of Trade established the Cotton Control Board in June 1917. This was under an order forbidding the purchase of raw cotton except under licence from the CCB. The Board did not adopt a policy of the 'concentration' of production in a few mills (thereby releasing labour for the military and munitions) as happened in 1941.[15] Instead, it pursued a strategy of 'spreadover', keeping all mills open. This prevented the demand for cotton from outstripping supply by fixing a maximum percentage of spindles and looms which firms could work without licence. To run machinery above this percentage a firm needed to pay a levy and obtain a licence from the CCB. The CCB used the levy to provide unemployment pay for workers (25s. for men, 15s. for women) who were unemployed on a strict rota system. Spinning employers were allowed to work 60 per cent of their spindles without a licence; a licence enabled them to increase the proportion to 70 per cent. The scheme, however, only applied to firms spinning American cotton. Firms using Egyptian cotton could use all their machinery because there was a plentiful supply; troop ships going to Egypt had plenty of space for cotton on the return voyage.[16]

With the fall and subsequent stability in raw cotton prices at the beginning of the war, and with strong demand from government contracts and the elimination of competition from European cotton industries, the price of cotton cloth rose and profits in the industry soared especially after 1916. This continued in the years after the war until early 1920. 'Lancashire rather accepted offers than quoted prices. And in value offers increased prodigally'.[17] The net profit per pound for medium counts of American cotton (32s twist and 40s weft) in the spinning section rose from ½d. in 1912, to 2½d. in 1916, to 10d. in 1917, and continued after the war to 1s. 3d. in 1919 and 1s. 6d. in the first three months of 1920. A similar increase occurred in manufacturers' profits on cloth, rising from 5d. per piece in 1912 (a 38 yard piece of shirting, made from 32s twist and 40s weft) to 5s. per piece in 1919.[18] Large dividends for shareholders reflected the profits. Dividends were relatively stable at 5 per cent in 1915 rising to 7½ per cent in 1917, before climbing to 16¼ per cent in 1918, 21¼ per cent in 1919 and a peak of 40 per cent in 1920.[19]

Before the First World War substantial new capacity was added during booms. For example, in 1907 when dividends reached 15⅞ per cent, the reaction in Lancashire was to expand by building new spinning mills and weaving sheds.[20] Yet, there was also disinvestment as shareholders came to expect higher dividends than the rate of return on the capital of firms warranted (see Marrison, chapter 9, p. 263). In the later years of the war and immediately afterwards, the building and machinery industries could not meet demand rapidly enough for expansion to take place by adding new capacity. As a result the reaction in Lancashire was to speculate in the existing mills and sheds, beginning in mid-1919 and reaching a peak in June 1920, particularly in the section spinning coarse and medium yarns from American cotton. This section accounted for two-thirds of the spindles in the industry.[21]

Speculation took two forms, recapitalisation and re-floatation. A system of finance developed in the spinning section in the last quarter of the nineteenth century in which shareholders paid only a portion, usually about half, of the nominal value of their shares, the rest was 'on call'. The balance of the company's capital was raised in the form of unsecured loans from operatives and from the local public in Lancashire. The system catered for two types of investor. The speculator was attracted to the partly paid-up ordinary shares with their fluctuating dividends, while investors seeking a steady income and security put their money into loans which returned a certain 4½ to 5 per cent on a money-back on demand basis.[22] Directors recapitalised their companies, increasing the share capital by issuing new shares. In cases, where firms were refloated, a syndicate bought the shares of a company at a high price with money borrowed from a bank and repayable from the proceeds which it received from the re-floatation of the company. The syndicate thus formed a new company with a far higher capital value based on the assumption of continuing high profits. When the boom ended in the second half of 1920, some banks were caught with substantial advances, made for the purchase of mill companies which could no longer be re-floated at boom prices. Furthermore, firms had begun to accumulate sizeable bank overdrafts.[23]

Financial reconstruction affected about half of the spinning section and companies owning 14 per cent of the looms in the weaving industry, with, as mentioned above, the section of the industry spinning American cotton most affected.[24] The majority of firms in the section spinning Egyptian cotton followed the lead of the Fine Cotton Spinners' and Doublers' Association, the largest firm in the industry, and resisted re-floatation.[25] When the post-war boom collapsed in 1920, the industry was left with a financial structure poorly suited to meet the difficulties it was to face.

### 2. External

Although 1913 was a record year for production and exports, the cotton industry was vulnerable at the outbreak of the First World War (see chapter 9, Marrison). Eighty per cent of its output was for export and 45 per cent of the exports went to one market – India. Moreover, the Lancashire export trade in cotton piece goods was dependent in general on the bulk production of relatively low-quality cloth – just the kind of product that was most exposed to competition from newly developing local industries in its overseas markets, such as France, Italy, Brazil, India, China and especially Japan.

The First World War accelerated the adverse trends in markets apparent before the war. The need to import war supplies into Britain resulted in a shortage of shipping capacity, so later in the war there was little transport for imports of raw cotton from the United States or for exports of cotton cloth to markets in the Far East. With the supply of British cotton cloth cut off, the demand for cotton goods in markets such as India encouraged the further expansion of the Indian cotton industry and the growth in exports of cotton goods from Japan.

The effects of the war were especially drastic in India. They took place in two phases. During the early years of the war exports of Lancashire piece goods dropped to 66 per cent of the pre-war level, primarily due to problems on the demand side in India. The wartime supply-side problems of increased freight, insurance and cabling costs were offset by a fall in raw cotton prices, but on the demand side in India the Indian market was overstocked with cloth; a poor monsoon season hurt demand and the war aggravated the problems bringing a financial panic and upsetting the delicate credit machinery in India.

In the second phase, from mid-1917, there was a more serious collapse of British exports to India. Three general reasons have been cited for this decline.[26] First, freight became increasingly costly and space scarce. As mentioned above, unrestricted submarine warfare led to the requisitioning of ships and control of imports, thereby reducing the supply of raw cotton and the output of Lancashire mills. Second, the already substantial Indian mill industry expanded its output by 25 per cent between 1913–14 and 1918–19. Although expansion was limited by its dependence on Britain for mill stores and textile machinery, its share of the Indian market rose from a little over 20 per cent to over 40 per cent.[27] In addition, imports from Japan, which had shipping available, increased between 20 and 30 times during the war; its share of imports rose from less than 1 per cent before the war to 21 per cent in 1918, while Lancashire's share fell from 97 per cent to 77 per cent in 1918. Yet, Japan in 1918–19 still accounted for a relatively small share (7 per cent) of the piece goods market in India, compared with the Indian mills (43 per cent).[28] Third, there was a decline in demand in India, as the normal problems associated with the failure of the monsoon were compounded by an influenza epidemic in 1918 and adverse movement in terms of trade when the world-wide movement of prices against agriculture began to reduce the buying power of the rupee. Finally, during the war, duties on imports of British cotton goods into India were raised. Before the war tariffs were kept at 'revenue' levels of 3½ per cent with a countervailing excise of 3½ per cent on Indian exports (see Marrison, chapter 9, p. 253). During the war the government of India made a major contribution to the war effort.[29] It recruited over a million soldiers, its military expenditure rose by between £20–30 million annually and in March 1917 it made a gift of £100 million to help reduce Britain's war debt. The government of India met this massive increase in its expenditure by expanding the currency, contracting large war loans, increasing taxation, and, with the approval of the British government, raising customs duties to pay for the interest on the loans. Thus, in 1917 duties on cotton goods increased from 3½ per cent to 7½ per cent with no change in the countervailing excise on Indian exports of 3½ per cent. Although it was a revenue tariff in name, it was protective in effect creating a 'net tariff' of 4 per cent. The Indian constitutional reforms adopted in 1919 as a result of the war, gave India some fiscal autonomy and allowed the government of India to adopt a policy of protection for local production, raising duties to 11 per cent in 1921. It is hard to isolate the effects of tariffs, but it is likely they hurt Lancashire's trade; especially in the depressed conditions of the 1920s when small differences in prices had most effect.[30]

## The 1920s and 1930s

After the First World War two new elements faced Lancashire – obsolete equipment and heavy loss of markets. Recent commentators argue that 'by and large they were separable developments'.[31] The failure to reorganize the industry and the loss of markets arose from different causes and were not necessarily linked by a simple causal connection. Yet, whatever the causes, the loss of markets led to surplus capacity within the industry which required an adjustment that failed to occur until the 1930s. Thus, what follows below looks first at the internal structure of the industry in Lancashire and responses to its loss of markets, since it is in this period, as indicated in chapter 9, that commentators now locate Lancashire's loss of competitive advantage. The second section examines the loss of markets and the considerable collective effort the industry invested during the 1930s in attempts to alter the 'constraints' facing individual firms with regard to overseas trade and the development of a new relationship with government which had some success in restoring and preserving markets.

   Historians agree that even without Japanese competition in the interwar years, Lancashire would have had to adjust capacity and reorganise in the face of import substitution strategies and protectionism abroad.[32] In addition, there was a fall in world demand for primary products and hence a general fall in commodity prices and consequent reduction of world purchasing power and world trade in cotton textiles (table 10.1). About two-thirds of Lancashire's export losses were due to the development by former customers of their own industries, and one-third was captured by Japan.[33] Also, they agree there were barriers to the reduction of equipment and labour, inhibiting reduction in the 1920s so that adjustment only got under way belatedly in the 1930s despite falling demand, falling prices and intense competition. In the 1930s a substantial reduction in capacity took place via market and non-market forces, but this still left in 1938 capacity utilisation at 75 per cent in spinning and 66 per cent in weaving.[34] There were a number of barriers to adjustment, including not only the industrial structure, but also the post-war recapitalisation of firms and the banks' extension of overdrafts, low profits, the differential impact of the fall in exports which weakened employers' associations and unions, and price cutting.

Table 10.1  *World trade in cotton textiles*

| Country | Years | | |
|---------|---------|---------|---------|
|         | *1910–13* | *1926–28* | *1936–38* |
| UK      | 6,650   | 3,940   | 1,720   |
| Europe  | 1,900   | 2,320   | 1,490   |
| USA     | 400     | 540     | 250     |
| India   | 90      | 170     | 200     |
| Japan   | 200     | 1,390   | 2,510   |
| Other   | 260     | 190     | 290     |
| Total   | 9,500   | 8,550   | 6,460   |

Source: R. Robson, *The Cotton Industry in Britain* (Macmillan & Co. Ltd, 1957) p. 4.

## 1. *Industrial structure*

William Lazonick, in an influential series of articles, argues that the vertically specialised structure of the industry with separate firms specialising in spinning, weaving, finishing or merchanting worked well up until the First World War. But this structure became a constraint when the economic environment shifted (see chapter 9, Marrison). The industry failed to adopt the vertically integrated corporate structures of Japan or the United States which were more appropriate for the new environment after the First World War. Britain's problem was that economic decision-makers, lacking the individual or collective means to alter existing constraints of industrial relations and industrial organisation to meet new conditions, in effect took them as 'given'.

Undoubtedly the difficulty of finding a course of action to adopt in the interwar years was increased by the horizontal organisation of the many small firms within the industry, which made combined general movement by the industry as a whole difficult to arrange. Like the industry itself, the organisations within it were horizontal. There were separate associations for spinning,[35] weaving or manufacturing,[36] and finishing[37]; the merchants and exporters were organised within the Manchester Chamber of Commerce.[38] These groups knew each other only slightly and there tended to be hostility among them. The Secretary of the Manchester Chamber of Commerce commented in 1933 that 'the manufacturers generally do not greatly trust the Chamber of Commerce element'.[39] Moreover, individual owners and managers tended to be fiercely independent. For example, Frank Platt, the Chairman of the Lancashire Cotton Corporation was:

> too much of an individualist to work with any corporate organis-
> ation. He . . . never allowed the Lancashire Cotton Corporation
> to become a member of the Federation of Master Cotton Spinners.
> This has certainly weakened the strength of the spinning industry,
> but he was in such a powerful position that the Federation had
> to kowtow and admit him and his representatives to membership
> of negotiating committees with the trades unions although they
> did not support the Federation with money or loyalty.[40]

Platt, a spinner, would not even attend any lunch that included merchants or a whole group of other people he regarded as his natural enemies.

Yet, important as the vertical specialisation of the industry was for inhibiting adjustment, Lazonick's supply side explanation is too narrow. He pays little attention to the demand side, though clearly, as will be discussed in detail in the second section, the market conditions of the pre-war period were not replicated in the interwar years. Maurice Kirby, for example, argues that the nature of the demand in the Far East encouraged large scale production of long runs of a few standard lines, but carried the inherent difficulty that variety was reduced, making it more difficult for producers to follow profitable changes in demand for securing good margins. When Lancashire's export markets in the Far East collapsed after 1921, world demand for high quality cotton goods was rising and Lancashire still possessed a comparative advantage in the production of these. It was rational in marketing terms, though not in terms of productive efficiency, for producers to move into higher quality goods often outside their normal ranges of production.[41] Also, contrary to Lazonick, in the interwar years the 'position of firms in world markets depended not merely on the classical sources of strength such as organisational structure, productivity, competitiveness or technical know-how, but also on state protection and state promotion'.[42] The structure of demand changed fundamentally as the interwar years were 'characterised by extreme economic nationalism and a massive intervention by governments in the external economy'.[43] Yet, even Lazonick's supply side explanation is too narrow a view of the response of the industry and internal barriers to adjustment in the interwar years. First, the recapitalisation during the post-war boom and the role of the banks in extending overdrafts together with low profits meant the finance was not available in the 1920s for either scrapping or re-equipment. Second, although employers and unions were organised along the lines of vertical specialisation, a significant feature of the two main periods of labour unrest in 1918–1921 and 1928–32 was the industry-wide action. Moreover, the differential effects of the loss of markets meant that divisions between coarse and fine spinners and weavers were arguably more important than vertical specialisation in weakening both unions and employers in industrial relations, and employers in attempts to maintain prices. And finally, there was collective action within the industry in the 1930s and a joint approach with the government to the industry's internal problems.

*Postwar recapitalisation and the banks*

Rather than enforce the liquidation of firms which were incapable of repaying debts incurred in the postwar boom, the banks willingly allowed industrial overdrafts to rise. This made reduction of capacity and reorganisation difficult to achieve either through the bankruptcy of weaker firms or by privately initiated mergers among mill owners. The outstanding example of a merger in the cotton industry in this period, the Lancashire Cotton Corporation (LCC), was an amalgamation of spinning companies forced by the Bank of England in 1928 to save the banking system in Lancashire where the local banks, unlike nation-wide banks, could not offset losses in cotton from profits elsewhere.[44]

> It was in an attempt to resolve the interrelated structural problems of the Lancashire banks and the cotton industry that [Montagu] Norman (Governor of the Bank of England) intervened in the late 1920s, when he marshalled most of the creditor banks into coercing a large number of their debtor mill companies into a new merger, the Lancashire Cotton Corporation (LCC).[45]

Its promoters believed the LCC would automatically produce economies of scale in the short-run and it would lead ultimately to vertical integration throughout the whole industry. But the LCC mills were a random collection of old and inefficient mills unloaded by the banks and scattered all over Lancashire. The LCC had an uphill task to turn its heterogeneous legacy into an efficient horizontal amalgamation. By the later 1930s, under the management of Frank Platt, the LCC managed to scrap a large number of spindles and integrate the rest into a profitable firm.[46]

There were proposals for other amalgamations, mainly horizontal, in the early 1930s but, without the compulsion of the Bank of England or government legislation, they failed to agree on the reductions of capacity needed for sufficient profit to attract finance.

*Profits*

The collapse of exports after 1920 undermined the profitability of the industry. The figures in table 10.2 suggest very low profits from 1927 to 1933, with some recovery from 1935 associated with the eventual bankruptcy of some of the least profitable and most heavily indebted companies and with the provisions of the Cotton Spinning Industry Act of 1936 encouraging the scrapping of capacity. The low profits are not surprising given the continuing excess capacity in the industry for much of the period.[47]

Table 10.2 *Dividends in the spinning section, 1913–39*

| Year | Dividend (%) | Year | Dividend (%) |
|------|------|------|------|
| 1913 | 7.25 | 1927 | 2.73 |
| 1914 | 6.86 | 1928 | 2.19 |
| 1915 | 5.00 | 1929 | 2.07 |
| 1916 | 6.00 | 1930 | 1.91 |
| 1917 | 7.50 | 1931 | 1.46 |
| 1918 | 16.25 | 1932 | 1.55 |
| 1919 | 21.25 | 1933 | 1.50 |
| 1920 | 40.21 | 1934 | 1.57 |
| 1921 | 9.97 | 1935 | 1.75 |
| 1922 | 4.01 | 1936 | 1.91 |
| 1923 | 2.27 | 1937 | 4.28 |
| 1924 | 2.43 | 1938 | 5.53 |
| 1925 | 4.65 | 1939 | 5.39 |
| 1926 | 4.08 | | |

Source: Robson, p. 338.

*Labour and industrial relations*

Lazonick and his collaborators argue that the systems of labour organisation in Lancashire moved, from an important source of Lancashire's competitive advantage before the First World War, to a major contributor to the industry's loss of competitive advantage in the interwar years.[48] In the late nineteenth century employers and unions came to an agreement whereby 'the fragmented employers had been willing to grant workers substantial shopfloor control and earnings stability in exchange for labour peace and uninterrupted production'. After the First World War a change in corporate structure toward the vertical integration of the processes of the industry was required, together with a shift of control over work patterns from workers to management. Unions contributed to restricting the options available for making the industry more competitive. This was because they were able to protect their positions of job control and thwart attempts both to raise productivity and cut costs by redivision of labour on traditional technologies. They could also inhibit the introduction of the new technologies of ring spinning and automatic looms by controlling the level of piece rates and the number of machines per worker.[49]

Yet the interwar years, particularly 1918–1932, were not characterised by peaceful industrial relations. Employers cut wages and intensified production; unions launched industry-wide strikes. At the same time it was not the sectional divisions between spinning, weaving, finishing and merchants that stand out, but the differential effects of the decline in exports within sections that led to the undercutting of lists and to weak employers' associations and unions.

Although in retrospect the loss of trade seems inevitable, the realisation that export markets could not be regained – that the reduced demand was not temporary but permanent and the industry would not return to the conditions of 1913 – spread very slowly. Even in the late 1920s and the 1930s when it was realised that the reduced demand for exports was permanent, the industry was confused and uncertain as to the course of action to adopt. Merchants felt the first effects of the 1920 slump in cancelled orders and a cessation of buying which they quickly passed on to the spinning and weaving sections.[50] The spinning employers' first response was to organise short-time working, but when this failed to improve profit margins, the spinning and weaving federations combined to cut wages in 1921 and 1922, wiping out post-war advances so that real wage levels were the same as in 1914, and ending the first of the two waves of labour unrest in Lancashire in the interwar years.[51]

Labour unrest in the cotton industry began in 1918 when employers attempted to use the CCB to restrict wage increases at a time when they were making uniquely high profits.[52] This provoked a trade union offensive, led by the Oldham spinners, the pre–1914 centre of industrial militancy, which involved in 1919 the first general strike by all cotton operatives. The aim of the offensive was to make good the losses of war, to achieve a 48 hour week and to eliminate the half-time system. In 1921 employers attempted to restore the industry's prosperity through wage cuts. This left the operatives with the 48 hour week as their only lasting gain from the war and post-war boom and the unions weakened by the costs of meeting strike and unemployment pay.[53] Between 1922 and 1928 industrial relations in cotton textiles were quiescent.[54] Some employers however, exploited their increased bargaining power due to recession and a more strident, direct form of management control emerged in the 1920s and 1930s which curtailed traditional craft controls, independence and the authority of overlookers in the workplace. Wage inducement above Uniform Lists, common between 1915 and 1920, disappeared and 'the trend reversed to one of wage cribbing and unofficial undercutting, usually on the grounds of competitiveness'.[55] Thirty-two million working days were lost from disputes in the textile sector between 1921 and 1932, primarily as a result of cotton employers' return to a strident policy of cost reductions and the reimposition of managerial authority. In response to the interwar depression cotton employers' strategies hardened into a policy to slash production costs, but within the limits of existing technology, as an alternative to the more costly process of re-equipment and reorganisation. At the same time, the depression led to a severe erosion of employers' solidarity in the face of intensified competition and the differential effects of markets. A consensus on labour relations strategy became increasingly difficult for employers' federations to formulate because of internal divisions. The initiative in industrial relations policy returned to the individual firm.[56]

The second wave of unrest took place between 1929 and 1932 when the rest of the trade union movement was relatively quiescent. The cotton unions were able to maintain a high level of industrial unrest even after the General Strike of 1926 and in face of the world depression. With low profits, fierce price cutting, recognition of emerging competition from Japan and falling exports, all inhibiting investment, employers attempted in 1928 to increase productivity by cutting wages again and to intensify production by increasing the numbers of looms per weaver from four to six or eight. Designed by Burnley employers to reduce costs, the more-looms-system opened a bitter price war. The system could only be operated by employers in the coarser sections and those with appropriate spacing between looms, due to technical difficulties. Other employers introduced the new wage lists without more looms thus cutting weavers' wages. Cotton workers saw the more-looms-system as leading to unemployment or under-employment and it threatened to undermine the 'family wage', as married women formed the majority of the labour force in weaving. While a ballot in 1931 showed the membership opposed to more looms, the union leadership was prepared to agree a settlement with employers on the basis that the more-looms weaver would be an adult male who would receive adequate remuneration to replace the family wage. Margaret Bondfield, the first woman Cabinet Minister, even suggested that women in Lancashire should leave the cotton industry and work as domestic servants to solve unemployment. Thus, the depression sharpened the sexual division of labour, encouraging the relegation of women to the home.[57] Labour unrest was strongest in weaving because the centres of industrial militance, particularly Nelson, known as 'little Moscow', concentrated on weaving fine cloth which was less affected by the decline in export markets in

FIGURE 104. Weavers' demonstration in Carr Road, Nelson, 1936. (Photograph courtesy of Lancashire County Library, Nelson Local Studies Collection)

the 1920s which hit Blackburn, heavily committed to cheap cloth for the Indian market, especially hard (see Winstanley, chapter 5). In spinning, Oldham was the centre of American cotton spinning, producing coarse yarns for the Indian and Far Eastern markets. The decline of these markets especially in the 1920s dramatically reduced union membership. By 1932 it was Bolton, which produced fine yarns and was traditionally moderate, where union membership held up and leadership against wage cuts originated.

After 1932 the cotton unions increasingly looked to political rather than industrial solutions to the industry's decline. State intervention in labour disputes came with the Labour government insisting on intervention. In 1929 a government arbitrator recommended a wage cut and in 1931 the Cabinet tried to persuade the weavers to accept the more-looms-system. In two disputes in 1932 the National Government continued the pattern of intervention, and even intervened through legislation. The Cotton Manufacturing Act of 1934 legalised weavers' wage agreements reached via the bargaining machinery already established for the industry and effectively stabilised wages.

Union membership halved between 1920 and 1939. Cotton operatives' wages declined. Yet, there was continued resistance in the 1920s and 1930s to employers' cost-cutting policies, due to the long tradition of trade unionism amongst cotton workers and to the operatives' belief that it was the employers' massive speculation between 1918 and 1920 which created the crisis of the 1920s. Also encouraging workers' resistance were the high levels of wage cuts and the threats to the family wage from proposals to reduce married women's employment by the more-looms system and suggestions that women take up domestic service. Furthermore, markets for fine goods held up and workers in these areas, such as weavers in Nelson and spinners in Bolton, were able to maintain militant attitudes toward employers.[58]

In both 1918–21 and 1928–32 the unrest took the form of general strikes affecting both sections of the industry. In 1918–21 it was a response to the growing cooperation of the two employer organisations, to state intervention via the Cotton Control Board during the war and to a wider movement toward industrial unions. Although the disputes in both periods ended in disunity within the unions, it appears to have been the result more of the need of the union executives to avoid a rebellion of their rank and file than of sectionalism – in 1919 and 1921 the Spinners' Amalgamation and in 1929 the weavers were responsible for the break away from the other unions.[59]

Employers' organisations, too, experienced decreasing unity, again not on sectional grounds. Membership fell in towns particularly hit by the loss of exports.[60] The percentage of total spindleage organised in the local employers' associations in Oldham fell from 92 per cent in 1920 to 75 per cent in 1935 and in Ashton from 83 per cent in 1920 to 60 per cent in 1935, while the proportion in Bolton remained stable at 87 per cent in 1920 and 84 per cent in 1935. As will be apparent below, the efforts to shape proposals for the industry in the Joint Committee of Cotton Trade Organisations were handicapped by the inability of representatives to commit their rank and file.

### Price cutting and the failure of price maintenance

Division among employers was not limited to industrial relations. The struggle for orders in declining markets led to price cutting, particularly in spinning, which left no margin for interest and depreciation, and in many cases did not fully cover direct running costs. In all sections attempts to undersell competitors led to product debasement, supplying a yarn, cloth or finish a little lower in quality and cheaper.[61] In the later 1920s employers established loose associations, most notably the Yarn Association, to prevent weak selling by restricting output, fixing prices and other protective measures. But these attempts at regulation failed: first because a large number of producers did not join, and then undercut the prices of members of the associations; and, second, because, with the industry's difficulties due to the loss of exports, attempts to maintain or even raise prices were unlikely to strengthen Lancashire's competitive position.[62]

The failure of the Yarn Association led in the late 1920s to a concern with 'rationalisation' and schemes for amalgamations aimed at securing the closure of marginal concerns and concentration of production in the most efficient firms, and to the realisation that the fragmented nature of the industry meant that any voluntary amalgamation was difficult to secure. It took institutions outside the industry – first the Bank of England, as we saw above, and then the government through legislation (Cotton Spinning Industry Act, 1936, see below) – to promote amalgamation and scrapping.

*Investment*

The pattern of investment behaviour in Lancashire in the interwar years is not surprising. The slowness of the realisation that the industry would not return to the conditions of 1913 and that the reduced demand for Lancashire's exports in the 1920s was not temporary but permanent, together with the very low realised profits and high interest payments, explain the pattern of investment behaviour in Lancashire in the 1920s. The reduction in capacity in Lancashire was limited in the period up to 1930 (table 10.3). Spindles and looms decreased by only about 5 per cent between 1924 and 1930 and there was some investment. In the 1930s capacity fell sharply and investment declined to almost nothing. The number of ring spindles fell by 20 per cent due to their second-hand value abroad, though their share of total capacity rose. The total number of spindles fell by nearly 40 per cent and the number of looms by 30 per cent (table 10.3).

Table 10.3 *Changes in the cotton industry, 1912–39*

| Year | Machinery | | Labour | Production | | Exports |
| | Spindles (million) | Looms | | Yarn (m. | Cloth | Piece goods |
| | Mule | Ring | (000s) | (000s) | lbs) | (m. yd²) | (m. yd²) |
|---|---|---|---|---|---|---|---|
| 1912 | 45 | 10 | 786 | 621.5 | 1963 | 8050 | 6913 |
| 1924 | 44 | 13 | 792 | 572.4 | 1395 | 6046 | 4444 |
| 1930 | 42 | 13 | 700 | 564.1 | 1048 | 3500 | 2472 |
| 1937 | 27 | 11 | 505 | 408.6 | 1375 | 4288 | 2000 |
| 1939 | 24 | 10 | 495 | | | | |

Sources: Robson, p. 339; Board of Trade, *Working Party Report – Cotton* (HMSO, 1946), p. 6.

*Central organisation in the industry*
*and the reluctance of government intervention*

Many leaders of the industry were convinced of the need for a central organisation and a joint approach to the industry's internal problems. The CCB, strictly a wartime organisation, was wound up in 1919, but provided a model and experience of co-operation among the industry's organisations. In 1925 the sectional organisations joined to form the Joint Committee of Cotton Trade Organisations (JCCTO). It included representative employers, merchants and, from 1928, trade unionists and had the vague aim of investigating the causes of the continued depression in Lancashire. The committee had a full-time Director, though in its early years the President of the Manchester Chamber of Commerce was the Chairman. Between 1928 and 1937 the Joint Committee brought forward several sets of proposals for reorganisation within the industry, but its work was severely limited by the fact that the members were not authorised to commit their constituents. Only two concrete measures were accepted: one a scheme for an industry-wide levy to buy up redundant spinning equipment which became the Cotton Spinning Industry Act, 1936; the second, a measure setting up an industry-wide cotton board with committees to operate sectional redundancy, price and quota schemes which became the Cotton Industry Reorganisation Act, 1939. It took years for the sections to agree on them.

Although every government devoted much time to the problem, these were the only two occasions in the interwar years when the government intervened in the internal organisation of the industry with legislation, and on both occasions the legislation was derived from the proposals originally formulated by the Joint Committee and accepted within the industry. Lancashire's experience confirms the view that governments of all parties were extremely reluctant to intervene in the internal affairs of the cotton industry. Government reluctance stemmed in part from a general unwillingness to break with economic liberalism. Also, while the industry had difficulty co-operating in a central organisation to represent its views on internal organisation, the government, too, faced the practical problem of what agency to work through, given the reluctance of the Board of Trade to intervene actively. Only in exceptional circumstances in the interwar years did governments initiate industrial reorganisation policies on their own account, preferring instead to encourage and give sanction to proposals formulated and accepted by a decisive majority in an industry.[63]

Contemporaries faced a circular problem. As competition increased in overseas markets emphasis shifted to the competitiveness and efficiency of the industry. Yet reorganisation at home seemed fruitless without reasonable access to markets. Much time and effort was devoted to attempts first to restore and then to retard the reduction of overseas markets. The Manchester Chamber of Commerce was the acknowledged voice of the cotton industry when the trade wanted to make approaches to the government on these matters. While government intervention in the internal organisation of the industry through legislation was limited to two Acts in the late 1930s, the government's sphere of activity was far greater with regard to tariffs, trade agreements, quotas and overseas markets, and the Board of Trade had a clear remit to act in this area, though, as will become clear, the Foreign Office and the aims of British foreign policy exerted constraints.

## 2. *Decline in exports and attempts to retain markets*

Export markets for Lancashire's piece goods fell first and most massively in India due to problems within the Indian market resulting from low prices for primary products, poor monsoons, import substitution, and tariffs. They also fell first in China and then elsewhere due to Japanese competition. Finally, failure of exports of cotton goods to revive contributed in the later 1920s to Britain's wider problems with the gold standard; in turn, the overvaluing of sterling further disadvantaged exports of cotton goods, although protective tariffs in Britain after 1931 gave the industry a bargaining counter to use to its advantage in bilateral trade negotiations.

### *India*

Trade with India presented particularly complex problems. As noted above, in 1913 80 per cent of the output of the British cotton industry was for export and 45 per cent of the exports went to India. By 1929 exports of British cloth to India were less than half their pre-war level and by 1938 exports to India had dropped to only 10 per cent of the pre-war level.[64] With the advent of a measure of fiscal autonomy for the subcontinent after the First World War, Bombay mill owners successfully pressed for high protective tariffs. The tariff on Lancashire piece goods was raised from 7.5 per cent to 11 per cent in 1921, and the 3½ per cent excise on exports of Indian cotton goods was removed in 1925.[65] In 1930 preference in favour of Lancashire was introduced when duties on imports of Lancashire cotton goods were raised to 15 per cent and those from all other countries (notably Japan) increased to 20 per cent; in 1931 duties on Lancashire goods were raised to 25 per cent with those on cotton imports from other countries raised further reaching 75 per cent in 1933.[66] In addition, the Congress Party made cloth imports a chief focus of its political campaign, with Gandhi leading a boycott of British cotton goods. The issue of British cotton exports to India was inextricably bound up with the question of independence. For example, when Gandhi travelled to London for discussions regarding the Indian constitution in 1931, he also visited Lancashire, meeting workers and employers, explaining the boycott.[67] Also, the Government of India needed revenue from duties to balance its budget. Lancashire, however, was able to exploit conflicting interests within India. Lancashire was a potentially expanding market, for Indian raw cotton and imports of cloth from Lancashire without tariffs were cheaper than cloth produced in Indian mills, so the Indian consumers were losing out because of tariffs.

After 1931 and the introduction of protection for the home market in Britain, two methods emerged for attempting to improve conditions for the export trade in cotton goods: inter-governmental treaty negotiations and discussions at the industrial level between British cotton trade representatives and the cotton textile representatives of certain other countries. The latter was a new technique for attacking the problem of international commercial relations. It received the support and encouragement of the Government in the hope that agreement between industrialists would ease the way to inter-governmental agreements.[68]

The campaign to secure more favourable tariffs in India on imports of Lancashire cotton and rayon textiles used both methods. The Manchester Chamber of Commerce provided a meeting place and a secretariat for committees of British cotton trade leaders who carried out inter-industrial negotiations, and the Chamber helped to co-ordinate

FIGURE 105. Gandhi, in Britain for the Round Table Conference on India held in London, visited Greenfield Mill in Darwen on 26 September 1931. Gandhi also met leaders of the Lancashire cotton trade later that day. (Photograph courtesy of Lancashire County Library, Darwen Local Studies Collection)

the cotton industry's efforts providing information and putting pressure
on the Government during inter-governmental negotiations. Furthermore, the Chamber organised three delegations to India in six years
which contributed to a lowering of the tariff on plain cloths in 1936
and as part of the Anglo-Indian Trade Agreement in 1939.

Lancashire's exports of cotton yarn and cloth to India were not
included in the Ottawa Agreement of 1932. During the next seven
years the British cotton trade put great effort into attempts to resolve
the issue of duties on imports of its goods into India. During 1933 the
Chamber concentrated particularly on discussions between industrialists
to prepare the way for an agreement on cotton goods which would
be 'supplementary' to the Ottawa Agreement. In September the British
cotton and rayon delegation headed by Sir William Clare Lees travelled
to India. After two months of discussion they reached an agreement,
the so-called 'Lees-Mody Pact', with the Bombay Millowners' Association. They also obtained a promise from the government of India
to negotiate with the British government a new agreement concerning
Indian tariffs on British cotton and rayon goods. In addition, the British
delegation agreed to recommend practical steps to increase Lancashire's
purchases of Indian cotton as proof of genuine reciprocity.

During 1933 the Chamber of Commerce took the lead in a related
area of comparable significance. In conjunction with the Federation of
Master Cotton Spinners' Associations it submitted evidence to the Joint
Select Committee on Indian Constitutional Reform. The Chamber
came close to submitting evidence which called for safeguards for
Lancashire trade to be written into the Indian Constitution. Not only
would this have been unacceptable in India, it would have given support
to the 'diehards' in the Conservative Party such as Winston Churchill
who opposed reform in India.[69] The Chamber's evidence was so
important that it led to the Privileges Affair in which Churchill accused
the Secretary of State for India and Lord Derby, both members of the
Committee on Indian Constitutional Reform, of committing a breach
of privilege by putting pressure on the Chamber to change its evidence.
Churchill was ultimately unsuccessful but the episode highlights the
political threat that Lancashire still posed.

The work of the British cotton and rayon delegation in 1933 had
some effect. Late in 1934 the government of India incorporated the
Lees-Mody Pact into the Indian Tariff Amendment (Cotton Protection)
Act which set the duties on cotton goods for a period of five years.
These duties, however, could be reduced if the finances of the Indian
government permitted removal of the 5 per cent revenue surcharge
component of the duties, or if a review of the duties in the light of
conditions at the time of the expiration of the Lees-Mody Pact (31
December 1935) warranted reduction.

These measures aroused the suspicion of business groups and nationalists in India. The powerful nationalist Federation of Indian Chambers of Commerce (FICC), which disapproved of the Ottawa agreement, complained that they had not been consulted and concluded that the 'supplementary agreement' was dictated by British interests to the prejudice of India. The two governments signed the 'supplementary agreement' early in January, but later in the month the Indian Legislative Assembly voted against it. In order to forestall further criticism, the government of India agreed that the operation of the Ottawa agreement as a whole would be reviewed early in 1937, during the next budget session of the Assembly. Lancashire was not happy, either. Although the 'supplementary agreement' had been achieved, duties had yet to be reduced. The Manchester Chamber of Commerce and the British government were waiting for the Indian government to fulfil its promise to reduce the duties on cotton goods from the existing 25 per cent *ad valorem* as soon as finances permitted.[70] There was a surplus in the Indian budget for 1935–6, but the government of India decided to utilise it for purposes other than abolishing the surcharge on cotton duties. This led to great disappointment and increasing discontent in Lancashire.

Yet hope for lower cotton duties remained in the government of India's assurance that when the Lees-Mody Pact expired the duties on UK goods would be fixed after a Tariff Board review of conditions

FIGURE 106. The British textile mission to India on the railway platform at Simla, 1933. (*Left to right*: Miss Seddon, F. Longworth, R. W. Lacey, M. Spilman, E. R. Streat (secretary), Sir W. Clare Lees (leader), A. D. Campbell, S. S. Hammersley, H. L. Aspden. (Photograph courtesy of B. R. and C. R. Streat)

then existing; this review might isolate the 5 per cent revenue surcharge and recommend its removal. The Tariff Board enquiry took place in India in November and December 1935.

A delegation travelled to India to present evidence on Lancashire's behalf, but the Tariff Board's report took months to appear. In the meantime, delegations from Lancashire waited on the Secretary of State for India, urging him to help; delegations met the Lancashire MPs; and the President of the Manchester Chamber of Commerce argued in his speech to the annual meeting in February that the government should do more for Lancashire. The feeling did not diminish, even among 'moderates' on the board of the Chamber, that 'export trade and that of the cotton trade in particular, had too often become a Cinderella at the council table'.[71]

When it appeared at last, the unanimous report of the Tariff Board recommended less than Lancashire expected (it excluded printed goods and rayon fabrics), but it proposed reductions in duties and they were quickly implemented. By mid-1936 the government of India reduced duties on Lancashire's plain cotton piece goods in accordance with the recommendations of the Board, from 25 per cent to 20 per cent *ad valorem*.

Earlier in 1936 the Indian Legislative Assembly voted to terminate the Ottawa and supplementary agreements. It was clear that cotton goods and raw cotton would be at the centre of any new agreement and that this aspect must be acceptable to Congress and Gandhi.

The inter-governmental negotiations for a trade agreement with India were a major pre-occupation for the Chamber during 1937. Throughout the spring its secretary, Raymond Streat, kept in touch with the Board of Trade's preparations for the negotiations which concerned, first, how much of the preferences which imports of British goods enjoyed in India on the basis of the Ottawa agreement should be retained and, second, questions specific to textiles. Lancashire wanted the duty in India lowered on imports of cotton piece goods from the UK and the Indians wanted Lancashire to agree to purchase a specified amount of raw cotton from India.

By the end of March 1938 the negotiations with India reached a stage where all was agreed except for the sections concerning the cotton trade. A Lancashire delegation travelled to India in the spring and attempted, without success, to reach an agreement with the Indian industrialists who were 'unofficial advisers'. In June and July when negotiations between the two governments resumed in London, the Indian delegate offered better terms than those previously approved by the 'unofficial advisers'; and Lancashire agreed.

Despite the complications over details, the disapproval of the 'unofficial advisers' and the opposition of the Indian Legislative Assembly, the British government and the government of India concluded a trade agreement which the Viceroy 'certified' in April 1939. Although the terms covering the cotton trade disappointed Lancashire, the agreement lowered the duties on imports of cotton goods from Lancashire to India.

Thus, in the face of changes brought about by the First World War, the world depression and the ascent of Indian nationalism, the Manchester Chamber of Commerce, and through it the cotton industry, played an active part in trying to alter the new tariff constraints facing the industry in its major market, India. Its leaders were among those who felt it was useless to proceed as if India were not going to have the power to determine matters in favour of the interests of India and the Indian economy. They recognised that, although still backed by sixty Lancashire MPs, the cotton industry representatives were only part of the complex relations between the different factions of businessmen (British and Indian), the government of India, the British Government and the Indian national Congress. Those holding such views were hotly assailed in Lancashire and accused of being 'yes men' for the government. Eventually they received the support of the majority of the industry. Moreover, such local criticism strengthened their position *vis à vis* the government and opinion in India, for they could stress their responsible attitude compared with the negativism of their critics. Their efforts were not without success, for the concessions would not have been won without the Chamber's insistent, knowledgeable but flexible pressure directed at their Indian counterparts and at the British and Indian Governments. As the historian of the Anglo-Indian Trade Agreement of 1939 argues, the relative decline of the Lancashire cotton industry did not lead to a corresponding decline in its political clout, though the claims of Imperial finance had priority in a crisis. 'India might have gained, but Britain certainly had not lost'.[72]

### Japanese competition

A fall in Lancashire's exports to India was inevitable given the growth of Indian nationalism, the central role of fiscal autonomy as a symbol of the nationalist struggle and the development of the factory side of India's cotton industry during the First World War and the 1920s. But, despite discriminating tariffs in India, by 1930 Japanese competition in India and in the British colonial markets in Africa and Asia was taking more of Lancashire's trade than Indian tariffs were blocking. Japanese imports made substantial inroads in Lancashire's market in India. Lancashire's share of imports into the Indian market fell from 97 per cent in 1912–13 to 50 per cent in 1931–2, while Japan's rose from 0.1 per cent in 1913 to 45 per cent in 1931–2, with the largest increase coming in the late 1920s.[73]

In the early 1860s machinery was brought from Lancashire to Japan and yarn production began a year before the Meiji restoration of 1868.[74] The industry expanded and in the early years of the twentieth century it was increasingly dominated by a small number of large-scale, vertically integrated concerns which sought overseas markets for their yarn and cloth. In China by 1914 Japan had displaced the United States cotton industry in the market for coarse fabrics, shirtings, sheetings and drills, and its yarn competed with yarn from Bombay and Lancashire. Yet, its share of world trade was a modest 2 per cent. The war benefited Japan enormously, coming at the right time in the industry's development. Output of cotton cloth increased by 55 per cent between 1913 and 1918 and exports of piece goods increased four times, compared with a fall in Lancashire's output by one-third and exports by one-half. During the post-war boom 1918–20 both Lancashire and the Japanese industry grew, though Lancashire experienced the widespread speculative investment which assumed the resumption of exports at the pre-war level. In 1920–21 both industries slumped.

From 1921 the paths of the two industries diverged. In Lancashire there was stagnation during the 1920s and then decline after the 1929–31 slump. In 1925 Lancashire's piece goods exports to most markets were much the same as in 1913 or better; the substantial exceptions were India where exports of piece goods was one-half of the 1913 amount and China where exports were only one-third of the 1913 yardage. Lancashire saw the problem as lying in the domestic conditions in the two markets. In both markets indigenous cotton industries grew rapidly during the war, and after the war the fall in the prices of primary commodities aggravated the poverty of consumers for coarse, low-price fabrics. In addition, nationalism led to tariffs to protect home industries and to boycotts of British imports, and there was political unrest and instability particularly in China. By 1925 Lancashire recognised that Japanese competition had grown in these markets and in 1926 there was growing pressure from Japanese competition not only in India and China, but also in the East African markets where Japanese cotton goods accounted for 50 per cent of imports.

A severe financial crisis hit the Japanese economy in 1927, as the yen, devalued by 20 per cent in 1924, rose again and depressed export sales

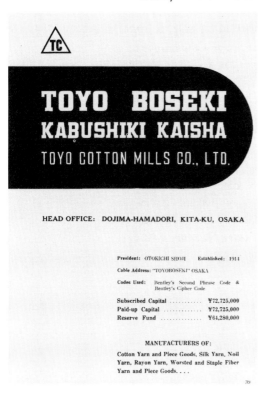

FIGURE 107. A Japanese textile firm's advertisement, 1938. Source: *Japan in 1938: A Symposium of Financial, Economic, Industrial, Cultural Activities* (Tokyo: The Japan Times and Mail, 1938), p. 38.

into 1928. In a key contrast with Lancashire, Japanese cotton firms had large profits in the earlier 1920s and they reacted to the crisis by investing heavily in new plant. Productivity grew at enormous rates (output per worker grew by 32 per cent in spinning between 1929 and 1935, and by 37 per cent in weaving) based on ring-spinning equipment and automatic looms of Japanese design and manufacture. These were adapted to utilize blended cotton, keeping raw cotton costs low.[75]

Japanese expansion was unaffected by the 1929–31 slump. In December 1931 the Japanese government reinforced the industry's expansion by abandoning the gold standard and devaluing the yen by 60 per cent against the US dollar. Sterling, too, fell against the dollar, but the yen fell further. By 1933 when currency markets stabilised the value of the yen compared with sterling was 42 per cent lower than in the spring of 1931 before the abandonment of the gold standard. The impact of the currency policy was felt between 1931 and 1935 as the volume of Japanese cotton goods exports doubled. Furthermore, the boycott of Japanese goods in China over Japanese actions in Shanghai in 1929 and Manchuria in 1931 pushed the Japanese to export increasing quantities to hitherto British markets in East Africa, West Africa, Australia, Ceylon and Malaya. In 1933 Japanese exports exceeded British exports and the gap widened until 1937 when the outbreak of the second Sino-Japanese War disrupted trade.[76]

### Response

In the 1930s the British cotton industry demanded aggressive government measures against Japan including export subsidies, Empire preferences and the denunciation of the Anglo-Japanese Trade Agreement. In September 1932 the Board of the Manchester Chamber of Commerce sent a deputation to the Board of Trade to discuss the Anglo-Japanese commercial treaty and in December the Chamber convened a general meeting of members to consider the problem of Japanese competition. As a result of a unanimous resolution at this meeting the Special Committee on Japanese Competition came into being. It was made up of representatives of all sections of the cotton and rayon industries and was responsible not only to the board of the Chamber but to all the trade organisations whose representatives comprised the committee's membership.

Early in 1933 several conferences took place between the committee and the President of the Board of Trade and his advisers. From these meetings the committee learned that the Government was considering inviting the Japanese for an Anglo-Japanese textile conference rather than denouncing the treaty immediately. During the spring the government issued the invitation and gave twelve months' notice to Japan of their intention to withdraw the British West African colonies from

FIGURE 108. Negotiations between representatives of the Japanese and the British textile industries, 1933. (Photograph courtesy of B. R. and C. R. Streat)

the scope of the most-favoured-nation clause of the Anglo-Japanese treaty. The Japanese government agreed to the conference and in January 1934 negotiations began between the British and Japanese cotton and rayon industries. The Lancashire Committee on Japanese Competition, chaired by Sir Thomas Barlow, represented the British cotton and rayon industries in the talks in London.

Despite long negotiations, the Japanese would not agree to voluntary restraint and negotiations broke down in March 1934. The British government then imposed a system of quotas restricting imports of Japanese goods throughout colonial markets. These quotas against Japanese goods, for which Lancashire had argued over a long period, did more than anything else to slow down the contraction of Lancashire's export trade.[77]

Although they were clearly effective, the quotas raised issues such as the criteria for goods to qualify as 'made in Britain' under quotas; the Chamber strongly advocated the triple criteria of 'spun, woven, and finished'. Also, attempts were made to standardise the procedures for issuing 'certificates of origin' necessary for goods to enter free of quota restriction.

Thus, instead of implementing Lancashire's demands, the government wanted Lancashire to take responsibility for regulating international competition, and it pushed the cotton industry into unsuccessful negotiations with the Japanese cotton industry for a cartel agreement limiting Japanese exports. When the negotiations predictably failed, the British government reluctantly appeased Lancashire, introducing quotas on imports of Japanese cotton goods into British colonies despite Foreign Office and Board of Trade fears that even these relatively mild measures would jeopardize British foreign policy and relations with Japan, and help to shift the balance of politics within Japan toward militarism. As in India, diplomatic and political considerations limited the efforts of the Lancashire cotton industry to preserve its markets.[78]

### Other markets

The failure of British exports to recover their pre-war levels was a major source of weakness in the balance of payments. This in turn meant that the overvaluation of sterling in 1925 when the gold standard was restored clearly aggravated the problems of UK exporters and that maintaining the value of sterling became very difficult.[79] As mentioned above, when Britain left the gold standard in August 1931, sterling, to the dismay of Lancashire, was still at a disadvantage against the Japanese yen.

During the early 1930s the Manchester Chamber of Commerce attempted to influence policy on currency problems through documentation and behind-the-scenes deputations both before the government abandoned the gold standard in 1931 and afterwards when many European and South American countries imposed foreign exchange restrictions to protect their currencies and caused great difficulties for Lancashire's exporters.[80] In neither case did the Chamber's efforts bring tangible results. These frustrations could be taken as evidence for the view that provincial industries lacked influence in the City and on the government.[81] Nevertheless, the Chamber vigorously attempted to alter these constraints facing individual firms and it did not at first see its attempts as fruitless.

During the 1930s the Manchester Chamber of Commerce was concerned not only with specific markets and currency issues, but also with the wider policy and organisation of the government machinery for dealing with tariffs and trade agreements. Early in 1931 the Chamber passed a historic motion in favour for the first time of a protective tariff (see Howe, chapter 4). While giving general protection to British industry in its home market, the Import Duties Act of 1932 enabled Britain to join in the bargaining process that was determining tariff barriers as the world moved from multilateral to bilateral trade relations. The cotton industry through the Chamber urged the Board of Trade to use the protective tariff actively as a bargaining counter in renegotiating trade agreements to the advantage of Lancashire. Although she acknowledges the concern with other goods, one of the Board of Trade officials involved in the negotiations of these trade agreements has testified to the high priority the Board of Trade put on concessions for cotton goods, saying that 'the cotton industry, still "King Cotton" and one of our major industries would be chief candidate for concessions'.[82]

The Chamber not only pressed the case for concessions for cotton but made it easy for civil servants and ministers to comply by supplying them with information and briefs. After the Ottawa Conference in 1932 the Chamber plunged into work on trade agreements between Britain and countries outside the Empire which needed to be negotiated in order to take full advantage of the introduction of a system of protective tariffs. The Chamber, using special representative sub-committees composed primarily of exporters familiar with the markets in question, but also including members of spinners', manufacturers' and finishers' organisations, furnished the Board of Trade with memoranda setting out the kind of tariff adjustments which would be best calculated to assist the cotton export trade in each market and provided technical information at short notice.

By 1933 a new line of economic policy was discernible in the British government's actions in matters pertaining to overseas trade.[83] There was a tendency in government negotiations with foreign countries towards a basis of 'bilateral reciprocity as opposed to multilateral equality'. During 1933 the government was engaged in treaty negotiations with Argentina and with ten European countries (Norway, Sweden, Denmark, Iceland, Germany, Finland, Latvia, Lithuania, Estonia and Poland). Negotiations continued with European countries and Argentina during 1934, and they began with other countries, including Spain, Italy, Turkey, Uruguay, Paraguay, Australia and Egypt, as well as representatives of the French and Dutch cotton industries.

The resulting treaties provided concessions for exports of cotton goods, though there was some disappointment in the trade. In part this was due to the government pressing the claims of other industries and securing reciprocal concessions on their behalf rather than on behalf of the textile trade. In addition, the Board of the Chamber felt that the government was less successful than it might have been, because it remained wedded to the most-favoured-nation clause which was inappropriate in the new conditions.

According to the Chamber the most-favoured-nation clause in trade agreements limited the scope of bilateral negotiations unnecessarily because concessions which might be entirely unobjectionable if confined to a single bilateral agreement, would be impossible to contemplate if they had to be extended generally. The Chamber, however, found the minds of the officials in the Commercial Relations and Treaties Department of the Board of Trade 'all closed to any suggestion that the most favoured nation clause may no longer be the desirable "sheet anchor" of British policy which it has been for so long'.[84]

The Chamber was critical not only of the Board of Trade's attitude toward policy, but also felt its organisation was inadequate for the bilateral negotiations necessary.[85] In 1934 it led a successful campaign for the reorganisation of the Commercial Relations and Treaties Department of the Board of Trade to deal better with the deluge of negotiations.

Thus, in new, complex and changing circumstances, the Manchester Chamber of Commerce during the 1930s forged a new, more flexible relationship with the government in the realm of trade negotiations and agreements. In the end the Chamber's method was more effective than direct political agitation. Ministers and civil servants had to listen to the Chamber because of the industrial and political interests it represented, particularly the implicit political threat embodied in the sixty Lancashire MPs. In addition, the government knew that the alternative to the Chamber would be those in Lancashire with more extreme views which would inflame nationalist opinion abroad. Moreover, the Chamber's extensive documentation made it easy for officials to present informed arguments on behalf of the industry's interests.

## Conclusion

Although contemporaries did not begin to realize until the later 1920s that Lancashire's export trade would not return to its pre-war levels, it was vulnerable in 1913 because a large proportion of its output was low-quality cloths for export markets in poor countries. Once the British government granted its major market, India, tariff autonomy in 1919, the decline of the industry from its position in 1913 was inevitable. This was further reinforced by protective tariffs and import substitution in other former markets, reflected in the overall decline in world trade in cotton textiles. Yet, this still leaves the question of why the industry lost its competitive advantage to Japan during the interwar years.

Industry leaders in the interwar years and more recent commentators argue that Lancashire could not compete with exports from a low-wage economy. However, that does not explain why Japan was so successful rather than India where wages were lower.[86] Moreover with unemployment high in Britain during the interwar years, employers successfully lowered wages in the cotton industry albeit not to the levels of those in India, and labour in the cotton industry could not shift to more productive employment to benefit the economy as a whole.

Mass and Lazonick and others point to the vertically specialised structure of the industry compared with the structure of the Japanese export sector with a few large vertically integrated firms taking advantage of economies from blended cotton using high throughput equipment. Certainly the vertically specialised structure of the industry in Lancashire, with large numbers of separate firms in each section, exacerbated price-cutting and made it more difficult to organise collective action to eliminate surplus capacity. Yet it is hard to agree with Lazonick's characterisation of industrial relations in the interwar years emphasising the collaboration of sectional employers' associations and unions. There were two periods featuring industry-wide industrial action, and both employers' associations and unions were undermined by the differential impact of the decline in exports with coarse goods hit much harder than fine cotton goods.

The recapitalisation boom after the First World War and the banks' extension of overdrafts led to intense price competition, the failure to eliminate capacity, the intervention of the Bank of England to save banks rather than restructure the industry and low profits in the 1920s. It was in sharp contrast to the situation in Japan where profits in the earlier 1920s meant the industry had funds to invest in new equipment after 1928, giving it a competitive advantage. In addition, the overvaluation of sterling after 1931 reinforced Japan's competitive advantage over Lancashire.

It should not be overlooked that the industry tried to respond other than by wage and price cutting. Both its responses and those of the government were confused and uncertain with regard to internal reorganisation. The Yarn Association, for example, tried to maintain prices by price and quota schemes when arguably this worked against the elimination of surplus capacity and a shift toward better quality, higher priced markets. The Lancashire Cotton Corporation was hampered by its origin as a rescue operation for Lancashire banks, but it eventually eliminated large amounts of capacity in the spinning section. Governments in the interwar years were reluctant to intervene where there were serious disagreements among sectors in an industry, but the Joint Committee of Cotton Trade Organisations was able to draw up plans and obtain the industry's agreement for two pieces of legislation in the later 1930s, one to eliminate spindles which reinforced market forces and the other which was not implemented due to the outbreak of the Second World War.

The industry's and government's responses with regard to the preservation of markets were more extensive than those concerned with the internal organisation of the industry. In the 1930s the Manchester Chamber of Commerce forged a new relationship with the Board of Trade, putting much effort into trade negotiations. Yet, nationalism and the political situation in India in the 1920s and 1930s, the interests of British foreign policy in the Far East and the interests of other British industries in bilateral trade negotiations placed severe constraints on their effectiveness.

# The Decline of the British Cotton Industry since 1940

## JOHN SINGLETON

BETWEEN 1940 and 1970 the cotton industry entered its final phase. Each decade had its own unique characteristics. Lancashire, during the 1940s, was largely insulated by the war and by the post-war economic dislocation of Europe and Japan, from overseas competition. The 1950s saw a renewal of the struggle for markets between Lancashire and its old rivals, Japan and India, as well as new competitors, including Pakistan and Hong Kong. This struggle was lost by Lancashire. In the 1960s much of Lancashire's cotton industry was subordinated to the man-made fibre producers and steps were taken to rationalise and modernise the capacity of the cotton sector, in an unsuccessful attempt to restore its lost competitiveness.

Table 11.1 depicts some overall trends in the cotton industry between 1939 and 1980. One glance is enough to show that all was not well. Raw cotton consumption fell by 85 per cent between 1950 and 1980. Over the same period, the output of cotton yarn declined by 80 per cent and the output of cotton cloth declined by 82 per cent. Exports of cotton cloth also fell by about four-fifths between 1950 and 1980. To a degree, mills responded to the decline of cotton by turning to the spinning and weaving of man-made fibres. But man-made fibres were no panacea, and the peak years for their weaving and spinning on the cotton system were 1954 and 1973 respectively. Table 11.2 shows that the number of spindles and looms in use declined in the 1950s and 1960s, as was inevitable, given the downward trend in the industry's output. Mule spindles were more vulnerable than ring spindles, but even the number of rings began to fall after 1954. Finally, employment in cotton spinning and weaving fell by 69 per cent between 1950 and 1970. In table 11.3 some indication is given of the extent of contraction in the ten largest spinning and weaving centres between 1950 and 1962.

Table 11.1 *Summary statistics of the British cotton industry, 1939–80*

| | Raw cotton consumed | Output of cotton yarn | Output of spun man-made Wbre yarn | Output of cotton cloth | Output of man-made Wbre cloth | Exports of cotton cloth |
|---|---|---|---|---|---|---|
| | million lbs | million lbs | million lbs | million yards | million yards | million yards |
| 1939 | 1,317 | 1,092 | – | – | – | 1,462 |
| 1945 | 717 | 605 | 20 | 1,569 | 278 | 469 |
| 1950 | 1,017 | 868 | 76 | 2,207 | 623 | 867 |
| 1955 | 780 | 684 | 87 | 1,876 | 604 | 587 |
| 1960 | 614 | 528 | 112 | 1,380 | 531 | 344 |
| 1965 | 506 | 426 | 101 | 1,090 | 550 | 205 |
| 1970 | 379 | 328 | 111 | 780 | 435 | 143 * |
| 1975 | 234 | 237 | 90 | 557 | 436 | 140 † |
| 1980 | 152 | 176 | 69 | 399 | 327 | 172 |

* 1969     † 1976

Notes: Output of cotton yarn excludes waste yarn. In 1939, output of cotton yarn and cloth excludes mixtures. From 1945 onwards, mixtures are allocated between cotton and man-made fibre yarn and cloth, according to which fibre predominates. Cloth output is in linear yards. Cloth exports are in linear yards 1939–60, and square yards 1965–80; a linear yard is approximately 1.05 square yards.
Source: B. R. Mitchell, *British Historical Statistics* (Cambridge University Press, 1988), pp. 332–3, 353–5, 357.

Table 11.2 *Productive capacity and employment, 1945–70*

| | Running mule spindles | Running ring spindles | Running looms | Spinning operatives | Weaving operatives |
|---|---|---|---|---|---|
| | millions | millions | | thousands * | thousands |
| 1945 | 9.24 | 5.20 | 216 | 72 | 96 |
| 1950 | 15.22 | 8.16 | 304 | 107 | 137 |
| 1955 | 9.68 | 8.33 | 253 | 91 | 118 |
| 1960 | 2.83 | 6.22 | 149 | 64 | 81 |
| 1965 | 0.6 | 4.1 | 113 | 45 | 65 |
| 1970 | 0.2 | 3.1 | 68 | 33 | 43 |

* excluding doubling
Sources: B. R. Mitchell, *British Historical Statistics* (Cambridge University Press, 1988), p. 371 (spindles and looms); J. Singleton, *Lancashire on the Scrapheap: The Cotton Industry 1945–70* (Oxford University Press, 1991), pp. 115–16 (employment).

Table 11.3  *Falling capacity in the main spinning and weaving centres,*
*1950–62*

(i) Spinning

|  | Spindles in 1950 ★ | Spindles in 1962 ★ | Percentage fall |
|---|---|---|---|
| Oldham | 8,316,862 | 2,875,306 | 65 |
| Bolton | 5,988,633 | 2,120,030 | 65 |
| Manchester & Salford | 2,778,680 | 330,436 | 88 |
| Leigh | 2,338,648 | 863,658 | 63 |
| Rochdale | 2,178,786 | 1,021,566 | 53 |
| Stockport | 1,300,900 | 203,782 | 84 |
| Farnworth | 1,200,094 | 168,628 | 86 |
| Middleton | 1,175,532 | 160,918 | 86 |
| Preston | 1,091,296 | 479,532 | 56 |
| Ashton-under-Lyne | 625,800 | 193,212 | 69 |

(ii) Weaving

|  | Looms in 1950 | Looms in 1962 | Percentage fall |
|---|---|---|---|
| Burnley | 50,959 | 13,345 | 74 |
| Blackburn | 38,539 | 9,483 | 75 |
| Nelson | 38,174 | 15,488 | 59 |
| Preston | 36,665 | 13,055 | 64 |
| Colne | 34,196 | 13,973 | 59 |
| Bolton | 16,801 | 6,573 | 61 |
| Accrington | 16,006 | 6,693 | 58 |
| Darwen | 13,757 | 3,496 | 75 |
| Chorley | 12,761 | 4,990 | 61 |
| Manchester & Salford | 11,403 | 4,132 | 64 |

★ mules plus rings
Notes: all figures refer to installed capacity, not necessarily running.
Source: J. Worrall, *The Lancashire Textile Industry* (1950, 1962)

Broadly speaking, there are two interpretations of the experience of post-war Lancashire. Lazonick, and to some extent Dupree, take the view that the cotton industry could have been saved, had the correct strategy been adopted. Lazonick argues that the reorganisation of the cotton industry into large, vertically integrated – or multi-process – combines could have restored it to prosperity.[1] Dupree suggests that Lancashire's prospects would have improved, had the government implemented the plans for minimum price regulations and managed trade, which were advocated by the Cotton Board to restore confidence and induce firms to re-equip with modern spindles and looms.[2]

Alternatively, Singleton maintains that, in the absence of rigid import controls and extravagant state subsidies, it would have been impossible to avoid a large-scale contraction in the cotton industry after 1945. Cotton was a relatively labour intensive industry in the mid-twentieth century, in which developing countries enjoyed a competitive advantage, resulting from their lower wage costs. Observed from this second perspective, Lancashire's decline was not a tragedy; rather it was a signal to transfer factors of production into more promising sectors of the British economy.[3]

## The Second World War

No detailed thought had been given to preparing the cotton industry for war. The brand new Cotton Industry (Reorganisation) Act was suspended in September 1939. This legislation had been designed to stabilize the industry in a period of weak demand, but wartime problems were likely to be of a different nature. An official Cotton Board, composed of employers and union officials, was established to advise the government on how to organize the industry's war effort. The immediate crisis was a fall in export orders because world markets were shaken by news of the outbreak of war. At home, the armed forces required large quantities of textiles to clothe their recruits, supply their hospitals and meet numerous other needs. A Cotton Controller, responsible to the Minister of Supply, was appointed in November 1939 and given powers to regulate the price and distribution of raw cotton, yarn and cloth. At the same time, the Cotton Board was put in charge of promoting exports, encouraging R&D, collecting statistics and discussing general issues concerning the industry's development.

During the early months of the war, the accent was on maintaining exports of consumer goods to earn foreign currency to pay for imports of munitions. After the fall of France, the government adopted a different strategy. This entailed running down non-essential industries and releasing labour, factories and transport, for use in the arms drive. By early 1941, raw cotton supplies were dwindling due to the lack of shipping, and it was decided to ban private trading in cotton at Liverpool. In 1941, the government ordered the concentration of production in the cotton industry. Instead of allowing every mill to operate a proportion of its machinery – which would have been wasteful of coal and buildings – selected factories were closed down, while a nucleus of mills continued in full production. Closed mills were compensated for loss of trade, by charging a levy on the nucleus mills. About one-third of the cotton industry was shut down for the duration of the war.

Under the auspices of the Cotton Controller, raw cotton rationing and production controls were enforced. Mills were not allocated raw

*They look forward*

TO
DOULTONIAN
TABLE
CLOTHS

Gone for the moment are the pleasures of the home. No time to indulge in peaceful reflections. It's Service now, not self. But the time will come when once again you will be able to enjoy the quiet, tasteful yet gay atmosphere which surrounds the table graced by Doultonian Cloths.

**HIGHAM-TONG LTD**
113 PRINCESS ST., MANCHESTER, 1

THE 'BOUQUET' DESIGN

**DOULTONIAN** *Printed Table Cloths*

FIGURE 109. An example of Lancashire pride in a Second World War advertisement. Source: 'Photography', war-time series, vol. 1, no. 4 (summer, 1944), p. 55.

cotton unless the Cotton Controller approved of their production plans. Priority was given to firms with military contracts and to mills spinning and weaving under the Utility clothing scheme, which had been introduced in September 1941 to ensure that the public had access to sturdy and cheap clothing. Prices were controlled at each stage of production in the fight to contain inflation. As labour became scarce, married women and retired operatives were asked to return to the mills on a part-time basis, sometimes working evening shifts.

For the remainder of the war, the cotton trade was working under strict orders from the Cotton Controller in Manchester. Raw cotton consumption and employment in the industry were halved during the war and the volume of exports fell by about two-thirds. The government successfully avoided a repetition of the upheavals experienced by the cotton trade between 1914 and 1918. Despite operating the cotton industry at a lower level than that of 1914–18, the country was supplied with enough textiles and clothing to see it through to peace.[4]

## The export drive, 1945–51

'Britain's Bread Hangs by Lancashire's Thread' was the slogan of the early post-war years. It reflected the contribution the government expected cotton to make to economic recovery. During the Second World War Britain sold about one-quarter of its overseas assets to pay for arms and other necessities. By 1945, Britain's annual income from overseas assets was considerably reduced. It was estimated that British exports would need to rise to a level 75 per cent above the pre-war level simply to maintain equilibrium in the balance of payments – yet exports had been halved between 1939 and 1945. Cotton, cars and coal were selected as the spearheads of the nation's export drive. On the performance of these industries, it was believed, rested the fate of Britain and the living standards of its inhabitants.[5]

Sir Stafford Cripps, the austere President of the Board of Trade, in the Labour government elected in 1945, was the minister responsible for the cotton industry and its export drive. On the demand side, Lancashire had a great opportunity in world markets in the late 1940s. Its main competitor, Japan, had been temporarily knocked out of contention and continental European textile industries also needed time to recover from the war. On the supply side, the picture was far less rosy. Almost two hundred thousand operatives had left the cotton mills during the war. Recovering these lost souls was the government's most urgent problem. But it would not be easy to persuade people to return to an industry with a reputation for low wages, poor working conditions and frequent bouts of unemployment. Nor would it be easy to obtain sufficient inputs of raw cotton for the export drive. Britain's traditional supplier, the United States, wanted dollars for its cotton and these were strictly rationed in post-war Britain. Given the shortage of raw materials, the fear of inflation and the need to channel production into export markets, it is not surprising that the government retained the Utility clothing scheme and many wartime controls over the allocation of raw cotton and the price of textiles.[6]

How was the labour shortage to be tackled? In accordance with its anti-inflationary policy, the government would not countenance offering everyone a large pay-rise with no strings attached. Instead, ministers concentrated on a plan to reform Lancashire's arcane wage lists and archaic work practices. They argued that the labour shortage could be partially relieved by improving the efficiency of existing workers. Under a piece-rate system, higher labour productivity would lead to increased earnings, thereby attracting new workers. Some operatives were suspicious of the government's proposals, which reminded them of the hated more-looms system of the 1930s, but most union leaders trusted their comrades in Westminster and accepted the need for reform. Three commissions were set up to revise the wage lists: the Evershed Commission for mule spinning, the Aronson Commission for ring spinning and the cardroom, and the Cotton Manufacturing Commission (CMC) for Lancashire loom weaving. Provision for flexibility in workloads already existed in automatic weaving and further investigation of this area was deemed unnecessary. Mule spinning was the first section to reach agreement and the new Evershed List was introduced in all mule rooms in 1946. The main change in mule spinning was the abolition of the labour subcontracting system, under which piecers had been exploited by minders for over a century. But mule spinning was a dying craft and little could be done to improve productivity on the mules. In ring spinning and the cardroom, however, more substantial changes were made to working practices, but it took until 1948 for the unions in these sections to agree to the new Aronson List. In weaving, the CMC proposals were quite radical and involved the introduction of standard timings for units of work. The CMC List was not finalised until late 1949 and, unlike the new spinning lists, its introduction was optional, requiring the agreement of workers at individual mills. By Christmas 1950, only 4 per cent of looms were on the CMC system. In parallel with the work of the three wage commissions, the Cotton Board conducted experiments with the use of time study techniques in spinning; in 1950, 104 mills were trying out these alternative methods of regulating workloads and setting wages.[7]

The new wage lists contributed to an increase in earnings of between 25 and 50 per cent, depending on the type of operative, between 1945 and 1950.[8] The tendency of the new lists was to narrow the pay differentials between older and younger workers and it was hoped that this would make cotton a more promising career for school-leavers. But the Evershed and Aronson systems had no observable impact on labour productivity in spinning, which was stagnant. Labour productivity in weaving was creeping up at the rate of 1.8 per cent *per annum* between 1948 and 1952, but this improvement cannot have been due to the CMC system, since it was not yet in widespread use.[9] The wage commissions had been forced to tread warily in order to avoid alarming the operatives and therefore their recommendations were too little and too late to boost the export drive.

What else was done to increase the supply of labour? In 1946, the cotton unions won a cut in the working week from 48 to 45 hours. Shorter hours helped to make the mills more attractive to potential recruits, but ministers regarded this reduction in the working week as irresponsible and urged operatives to make up for the lost hours by doing more overtime. Evening shifts were introduced for married women and there was a programme to encourage firms and local authorities to build mill nurseries. Some towns, such as Nelson, were the focus of dramatic production campaigns, with prizes given to the hardest workers. At one point in 1948, the government's Economic Planning Board even considered conscripting women into the mills, but this idea was dropped when thought was given to its likely effect on the Labour Party's electoral prospects. The most imaginative attempt to increase the labour force was the shipping in of migrants and displaced persons from central and eastern Europe and Malta, including ethnic Germans from the Sudetenland in Czechoslovakia. About fifteen thousand Europeans worked in Lancashire's mills in the late 1940s. Migrants were warned that they would be the first to be laid off in a recession and in 1952 this promise was kept.[10]

How well did Lancashire perform during the period of the first post-war Labour government? By a mixture of shifts and expedients, the government was successful in meeting its export targets for the cotton industry. But ministers had been careful not to pitch their targets at levels which were too ambitious. Only about eighty thousand operatives returned to the cotton mills between 1945 and 1951, or less than one-half of those who had left during the war. Cloth exports in 1951 remained below pre-war levels and cotton textiles' share of total British exports hovered at about 9 per cent in both 1946 and 1950. Cotton's contribution to the post-war recovery of Britain's trade, while not insignificant, did not measure up to the industry's billing as an export spearhead.

## Planning Lancashire's future in the 1940s

Market conditions in the 1940s were abnormal and could not be expected to last indefinitely. Everyone knew that the Japanese and other competitors would be trying to expand their textile exports as soon as possible after the war. How could Lancashire avoid a crisis similar to that experienced in the 1920s and 1930s? One solution would have been to lift the suspension on the 1939 Cotton Industry (Reorganisation) Act, but this did not happen because the war provided interested parties with plenty of time for the formulation of other strategies.

First, Frank Platt, chairman of the industry's largest firm, the Lancashire Cotton Corporation, persuaded the wartime President of the Board of Trade, Hugh Dalton, that the main obstacle to progress was Lancashire's dependence on small firms. Platt recommended the establishment of an official agency to encourage and, if necessary, to compel, spinning firms to amalgamate into larger groups. He believed that big firms would be in a better position to buy expensive new machinery because they could keep it fully occupied on standardised orders. Large firms would replace incompetent family capitalists with professional managers, who were better equipped to cope with the challenges of the future. Platt's faith in the large capital intensive firm was reinforced during his leadership of a wartime mission to study the American cotton industry. In the USA, Platt found evidence which confirmed that big American firms were far in advance of Lancashire in terms of technology, management and labour practices, and productivity.[11]

Secondly, the Cotton Board's Committee to Enquire into Postwar Problems reported, in 1943, that the key to Lancashire's future was the control of competition. Firms would not invest in new equipment unless they were confident that they could find secure outlets for their production at reasonable prices. The British government, it was argued, must take action at an international level to restrict Japanese textile exports after the war. The system of Imperial Preference would have to be strengthened to preserve colonial markets from a renewed Japanese onslaught. At home, price-fixing schemes, overseen by the Cotton Board, would be required to prevent any return to the cut-throat competition witnessed in the past.[12]

FIGURE 110. Sir Raymond Streat, Chairman of the Cotton Board. (Photograph courtesy of Manchester Public Libraries)

Thirdly, the unions, while agreeing with the Cotton Board that the Japanese needed to be held in check by the Allies, indicated that, in the long term, nationalisation was the best solution for Lancashire. Nationalisation of the cotton industry, said the 1943 Report of the Legislative Council of the United Textile Factory Workers' Association, would lead to considerable improvements in efficiency. A state-owned cotton corporation would be able to maximize the advantages of large-scale organisation, by appointing professional managers, investing in the latest technology and enjoying long production runs. But a nationalised cotton industry promised an additional benefit: the wages of male operatives could be raised to the point at which their wives no longer needed to go out to work. If this meant higher production costs, then consumers would just have to pay more for their clothes. By the late 1940s, however, the unions were beginning to see nationalisation in a different light. If public ownership of the mills resulted in faster re-equipment, there was a danger that female ring spinners would soon replace male mule spinners. This was a chilling prospect for the union patriarchs and they advised the Labour Party that the time was not yet ripe for nationalisation.[13]

Lancashire's strategy was still being debated when the Labour Party came to power in May 1945. State ownership of the mills was not mentioned in Labour's manifesto, but after the election the employers were warned that, unless they co-operated with the new government, the question of nationalisation might resurface. In the event, only the Liverpool cotton market (in 1948) was nationalised, and it was soon privatised by the incoming Conservatives in 1952–4.[14]

Sir Stafford Cripps believed in planning by consensus. He wanted to set up a new tripartite cotton board, representing the interests of

FIGURE III. Sir Stafford Cripps, Chairman of the Board of Trade, 1945–47. A portrait by I. M. Cohen. (Photograph courtesy of the National Portrait Gallery)

labour, capital and the nation. This organisation would draw up plans for the industry, which would then be implemented in a public spirited manner by firms, unions, civil servants and ministers. As a first step, Cripps appointed a Board of Trade Working Party, consisting of employers, union officials and experts, to reconsider the industry's problems. This initiative was not well-received. The existing Cotton Board thought that it had been snubbed. Even worse, the Working Party was divided over some key issues. All accepted that the industry should re-equip with new machinery, scrap redundant capacity and reform its labour practices. But there was disagreement about how this should be done. A majority on the Working Party advocated statutory schemes, financed by a mixture of levies on firms and government grants, to purchase and scrap excess capacity and to subsidise investment in spinning. This group hinted that there might have to be compulsory mergers, should firms prove unwilling to amalgamate of their own accord. A smaller group, led by Professor John Jewkes of Manchester University, recommended doing nothing and leaving market forces to decide the industry's fate. Finally, the trade union members added that, in their hearts, they would prefer to see the industry nationalised.[15]

Cripps was dismayed by the squabbling on the Working Party. Even so, he decided to press on with the creation of his tripartite board. He now decided to base this on the old Cotton Board and in 1948 the Cotton Board was transformed into a Development Council, although it acquired no new powers of significance. Relations between the Cotton Board and the Labour government were relatively cordial after Cripps had made this concession.[16] The government also followed up the Working Party's recommendation that assistance be given to firms installing new machinery. A Cotton Industry (Re-equipment Subsidy) Act was passed in 1948, making £12 million of investment subsidies

FIGURE 112. The Cotton Working Party in session. *Left to right*: A. V. Symons, A. Knowles, A. Naesmith, T. Griffin, Professor J. Jewkes, C. B. Clegg, Miss A. G. Shaw, Professor E. L. Hirst, W. M. Wiggins, Sir G. Schuster and C. McMahon (secretary). Source: *Textile Recorder Year Book, 1946–47*, plate 4.

available to spinners. To qualify for help, companies had to be of a certain size: 400,000 spindles for spinners and 250,000 spindles for vertically integrated firms. This encouraged some amalgamations, but not as many as the government had hoped for, and only £2.6 million of aid was actually claimed by firms. Why were firms so reluctant to invest despite the offer of a 25 per cent subsidy? Singleton argues that the cotton masters understood that the day was approaching when Lancashire would be struggling to keep its overseas markets. In the absence of adequate protection in the colonies and dominions against competition from countries with low wages, firms doubted whether new spindles and looms could ever be made to pay.[17] The Cotton Board continued to call for permanent restrictions on the Japanese mills and visited General MacArthur, the Allied commander in Tokyo, to plead for his support. But both the British and American governments concluded that Japan must be allowed to export more textiles, otherwise it would remain an economic burden on the Anglo-Saxon powers and become a prey for communist and militarist agitators.[18]

No clear long-term policy emerged during the intensive discussions of the 1940s. Tripartism did not produce the wide-ranging change in attitudes that its sponsors had anticipated. The Cotton Board and the unions maintained that imperial protection and international agreements ensuring orderly marketing were preconditions for Lancashire's revival. But the government and its American allies were committed to freer trade, as part of their strategy for encouraging growth and stability in the world economy. Given this fundamental disagreement about policy, the cotton industry was allowed to drift.

### The pattern of decline, c.1950–c.1965

A collapse in demand hit the world cotton textile industry in 1952–3. Cotton was traditionally a boom and slump industry, and this pattern was now reasserting itself. Lancashire suffered more from the slump in demand than did most of its competitors. In the summer of 1952, 33 per cent of spinning operatives and 22 per cent of weaving operatives in Lancashire were either unemployed or on short time, and some feared a return to the conditions of the 1930s. But demand picked up in 1953, and more or less full employment was restored to the cotton industry.[19] The following years, however, saw a gradual contraction of the cotton industry in Lancashire, as mills were picked off one by one by the competition. Lancashire was defeated in a war of attrition rather than a *blitzkrieg*.[20]

Lancashire's remaining markets were slipping away. In 1950, Britain's most important overseas customers for cotton cloth were British West Africa (121 million yards), South Africa (117 million yards) and Australia

(105 million yards). By 1965 these three markets combined took a mere 57 million yards of cotton cloth from Lancashire. Table 11.4 shows what was happening to British exports in a range of markets. In Australia, between 1953 and 1959, Britain's share of the import market for cotton fabrics fell from 71 per cent to 24 per cent, while Japan's share rose from 10 per cent to 53 per cent. Despite facing higher tariffs under the Commonwealth Preference system, Japanese cloth cost Australians only between 40 and 80 per cent as much as British cloth of the same quality.[21] Even exports of cloth woven from man-made and mixed fibres started to decline after the mid-1950s. British imports of cotton cloth more than doubled during the 1950s and by the end of the decade the UK had become a net importer of cotton cloth for the first time since the industrial revolution. Imports of Japanese textiles were tightly restricted in the UK market, so that India and Hong Kong posed the main threats in Lancashire's backyard. Textiles from India and Hong Kong enjoyed duty-free entry into Britain under the Commonwealth Preference regime and they were produced with very cheap labour. Hong Kong's cotton mills, unlike India's, were also very modern and technically efficient. They were

FIGURE 113. Halstead's Mill, off Colne Road, Burnley, in the process of demolition. (Photograph courtesy of Lancashire County Library, Burnley Local Studies Collection)

owned by textile capitalists from Shanghai, who had fled the mainland during the political crises of the 1940s. Using funds held in overseas bank accounts, these families built new factories in Hong Kong, where the British colonial governor was anxious to encourage economic development.[22] In the 1960s, British weaving mills also faced new competition from firms at home. Advances in warp knitting and man-made fibre technology enabled firms in the midlands to market cheap knitted fabrics in direct competition with cloth woven in Lancashire, especially in shirtings, lingerie and women's nightwear.[23]

Table 11.4 *British exports of cotton cloth to selected markets 1938–69*

|  | 1938 | 1950 | 1960 | 1969 |
|---|---|---|---|---|
| Argentina (quintals) † | 95 | 6‡ | — | — |
| Australia | 138 | 105 | 36 | 10 ★ |
| British East Africa | 6 | 12 | 6 | 1 |
| British West Africa † | 66 | 121 | 61 | 2 |
| Canada (quintals) | 41 | 16 | 7 | 2 |
| Ceylon | 19 | 11 | 5 | — |
| Egypt | 42 | 4 | — | — |
| India | 216 | 5 | — | — |
| Indonesia | 36 | 9 | — | — |
| Ireland | 29 | 25 | 11 | 13 ★ |
| Jamaica | 13 | 6 | 2 | 1 |
| New Zealand | 18 | 43 | 25 | 7 ★ |
| Pakistan | — | 70 | — | — |
| Rhodesia | 26 | 38 | 20 | — |
| Malaya and Singapore | 49 | 36 | 4 | 1 |
| South Africa | 152 | 117 | 57 | 11 ★ |

† One thousand quintals is approximately equal to one million square yards
‡ 1948
★ 1970
— zero or negligible
Note: unless stated, figures are in million square yards
Source: J. Singleton, *Lancashire on the Scrapheap: The Cotton Industry 1945–70* (Oxford University Press, 1991), p. 118.

Workers drifted from the mills into more buoyant industries and the service sector. Whereas in 1951, 9 per cent of the male workforce in Lancashire had jobs in textiles, the proportion had fallen to 5 per cent by 1971; and whereas in 1951, 22 per cent of women in employment in Lancashire were textile workers, only 6 per cent were in textiles in

1971.[24] Fortunately, these were prosperous times for the British people and other industries were growing in cotton's place. The overall rate of unemployment in the north-west rarely approached 3 per cent. Low unemployment rendered cotton's plight less newsworthy than it had been before 1939. Only the most elderly textile operatives had difficulty finding alternative employment. Full employment, and a recognition that workers and bosses were in the same boat as regards overseas competition, no doubt accounted for the amiable labour relations enjoyed by the post-war cotton industry. During the 1950s and early 1960s, the cotton unions and the employers signed a number of agreements governing the introduction of shift-working on new equipment. The unions also co-operated with the employers' associations in further moves to reform labour practices, by relating pay more closely to work done at the individual mill.[25]

The number of active mule spindles fell from over 15 million in 1950 to 0.6 million in 1965, while the number of active ring spindles declined from 8.16 million to 4.1 million over the same period. Running looms totalled 304,000 in 1950, but their numbers fell to 113,000 in 1965. The number of automatic looms in place rose slowly from 34,300 in 1952 to 42,500 in 1965. Over the course of the 1950s, the rate at which automatic and semi-automatic looms were being installed was actually falling. In July 1952, 2,400 automatic and semi-automatic looms were due for introduction over the next twelve months; but in January 1958, only 1,000 such looms were awaiting installation. Britain continued to lag behind its rivals in the deployment of ring spindles and automatic looms. The United States, for example, had virtually no mules or non-automatic looms left by the early 1950s. Some developing countries also outpaced Britain: in 1964, 85 per cent of Hong Kong's looms were either automatic or semi-automatic.[26]

## Survival strategies, 1950–65: modernisation or protection?

What strategies did the cotton industry adopt during the 1950s to try to counteract its decline? A number of options were open to firms: meeting the competition head-on by purchasing new equipment; establishing plants overseas to utilize cheaper labour; seeking niche markets; diversifying into new products; restricting competition through collusive agreements; lobbying the government for import controls and subsidies; or just hanging on for as long as was possible before quitting.

Lancashire chose not to pursue a vigorous policy of re-equipment. In searching for an explanation, we must re-examine the debate about the cotton industry's structure. Lazonick says that, in the 1950s, Lancashire was still suffering from a shortage of strong, vertically integrated combines, and suggests that this was the main factor inhibiting modernisation.[27] As late as 1955, only 36 per cent of the spindles and 33 per cent of the looms in the British cotton industry were owned by vertically integrated firms.[28] Lazonick argues that a higher degree of vertical integration would have made it easier for the industry to co-ordinate the re-equipment of its spinning and weaving capacity. For maximum efficiency, ring spindles and automatic looms should have been installed simultaneously. Large orders were required to keep these machines busy, therefore firms should also have integrated forwards into marketing. Unless new ring spindles and automatic looms were run flat out, costs of production could not be reduced to the level at which British cloth became competitive with Asian textiles. Lazonick laments the fact that most firms in Lancashire were reluctant to sacrifice family control. Such loyalties, he admits, were understandable, but they were not in the best interests of the industry as a whole.[29]

Higgins questions Lazonick's claim that vertical integration was a precondition for modernisation. In a study of Lancashire between the late 1940s and late 1950s, Higgins finds that single process spinning companies were not inhibited from replacing their mules with rings. Spinners switched from mules to rings for several reasons, including the post-war shortage of mule labour and purchase tax regulations which made mule yarn very expensive to buy.[30] On average, in the 1950s, vertically integrated firms were less profitable than single process spinners equipped with either rings, or a mixture of rings and mules. In some years, even mule-only mills enjoyed a higher rate of return than integrated firms.[31] Higgins also finds that some spinners developed semi-permanent alliances with weavers. These alliances were a loose form of vertical integration, enabling spinners to produce long runs of standard yarns and providing an opportunity for the synchronisation of investment in spinning and weaving. This is an interesting finding, and a study by Dore suggests that alliances between Japanese spinners and weavers may have been an important factor in slowing the decline in competitiveness of the Japanese textile industry in the 1970s.[32] Higgins concludes that even Alfred Chandler, the foremost authority on the growth of American big business, judged that few technical economies of scale could be expected from the mass production of textiles. Given the fragmentation of markets and the uncertain nature of demand in the 1950s, the high throughput strategy advocated by Lazonick may have been particularly inappropriate.[33]

Singleton argues that the causes of low investment in the post-war cotton industry are to be found in the industry's gloomy prospects. The current level and rate of change in demand, and the state of expectations about future demand, are crucial determinants of investment expenditure. In Lancashire's cotton industry, a sector blighted by contracting markets, falling profits, surplus capacity and declining confidence, few firms were prepared to take the risk of buying new equipment. Firms will not invest, unless they are confident that the new machinery will generate an adequate financial return.[34] Should Lancashire have been bolder? Singleton argues that firms' pessimism was fully justified, given the long run tendency for the balance of competitive advantage in labour intensive industries, such as textiles, to move towards developing countries with low wages.[35] Singleton also criticizes Lazonick's suggestion that more vertical integration would have revived Lancashire's fortunes. The American cotton textile industry, which Lazonick compares favourably with Lancashire, had a much higher degree of vertical integration. US textile wages were well above those in Lancashire, so that ring spindles and automatic looms, machines that economised on labour, were very well suited to American conditions. Yet, despite its vertically integrated structure, and its preference for rings and automatic looms, the American industry was reduced to campaigning for protection, claiming that it could not compete with Asian mills using cheap labour. In the early 1960s, the US textile industry was the principal architect of the new protective regime in world textile trade which resulted in the Multi Fibre Arrangement.[36] If Lazonick's strategy failed in the United States, where the conditions were ideal, why should it have worked in Britain?

Overseas investment and diversification were tried by some firms, but it is questionable whether many had the management skills required to make such initiatives succeed. The Rossendale firm of David Whitehead & Sons opened weaving mills in colonial Africa in the 1950s and 1960s, and, in the early 1960s, the Cyril Lord group closed down two of its Lancashire mills and established factories behind the South African tariff wall.[37] Large companies, such as the Scottish cotton thread manufacturer, J. & P. Coats, had a number of overseas plants, but small and medium sized cotton firms were reluctant to take the risk of setting up mills abroad. It would be difficult to argue that Lancashire's failure to invest overseas was due to the modest size of most of its firms: many small Japanese textile and apparel companies were prepared to engage in direct foreign investment in South Korea and Taiwan in the late 1960s and early 1970s.[38] Falling profits in Britain would have made it difficult for firms to raise the funds for direct investment abroad and managers were pre-occupied with achieving day-to-day survival.

As for diversification, in the finishing section, the Bleachers' Association acquired a motley collection of firms in engineering, laundering, timber merchanting and tanning, as well as carpet-making and knitting, between the 1930s and early 1960s. The Bleachers' Association's diversification strategy appears to have been deficient in purpose and in execution: the company was reluctant to stray too far from Lancashire and its directors tended to conduct takeover negotiations over drinks with golfing chums.[39] The Lancashire Cotton Corporation bought a brick works and an electrical equipment manufacturer, for reasons which remain obscure, while British Cotton and Wool Dyers purchased coffee houses and a producer of kitchen units.[40] A more promising strategy was that of specialising in niche markets. During the 1950s James Kenyon & Sons had considerable success producing wet felts for industrial uses; E. & E. Bottomley prospered in the tyre fabric business; and James Nelson concentrated on the weaving of man-made fibres.[41]

Lobbying for protection was probably the dominant strategy in Lancashire after the crisis of 1952. Dupree and Singleton show that the leaders of the cotton industry devoted a great deal of energy to seeking collusive agreements and pressing the government for protection against overseas competitors. However, Dupree and Singleton disagree in their interpretation of this behaviour. Dupree endorses the Cotton Board's view that the regulation of domestic and overseas competition was necessary to stabilize demand, and thereby to provide Lancashire with the sense of security which it regarded as a precondition for embarking on an aggressive policy of modernisation.[42] But Singleton doubts whether protection over the medium term would have led to the restoration of competitiveness in the long term. He argues that Lancashire really wanted permanent import controls because it had no other hope of survival.[43] By 1956, even the Cotton Board was beginning to doubt whether the industry would ever be able to compete on an unfettered basis with Asia.[44]

The campaign got off to a bad start for the protectionists. When the Conservatives became the governing party in 1951, they announced that the cotton industry could expect no favours. Nevertheless, an incessant campaign was mounted by the Cotton Board and the unions, with the objective of changing the government's mind. Cyril Lord, feeling that the Cotton Board was too soft, launched his own more dramatic offensive against both the 'Japs' and the unfortunate President of the Board of Trade, Peter Thorneycroft, whom he described as the 'hangman of Lancashire'. A world cotton textile conference was hosted by the Cotton Board at Buxton in 1952, in a vain attempt to whip the Japanese and Indians into restraining their exports. Delegations from Manchester were usually given a polite hearing in Whitehall – on one occasion they had an audience with the Prime Minister, Winston Churchill – but Lancashire was offered nothing of substance. The government argued that, if Britain wanted to sell machinery and munitions to developing countries such as India, it would have to accept textiles in return. There was logic in this reasoning.[45] Alongside their lobbying, the spinning masters operated a scheme, designed to fix sales margins, called the Yarn Spinners' Agreement, in a forlorn attempt to stop price competition. This too fell foul of the government; it was

FIGURE 114. Peter Thorneycroft, President of the Board of Trade. (Photograph courtesy of Times Newspapers Ltd)

referred to the Restrictive Practices Court in 1958 and judged to be illegal.[46]

Towards the end of the 1950s, the new Conservative Prime Minister, Harold Macmillan, appeared to show more sympathy for Lancashire. He feared that marginal Tory seats in cotton towns were being put in jeopardy by the government's indifference to the industry's fate. Labour's Harold Wilson and the cotton unions were demanding that Asian countries be forced to accept 'voluntary' quotas on cotton textile exports to Britain. Wilson called for vigorous state intervention in the cotton industry and contemplated the partial nationalisation of some companies.[47] Macmillan needed a vote-catching initiative of his own. He duly approached India, Pakistan and Hong Kong, and persuaded, and in the case of Hong Kong instructed, these countries to accept voluntary quotas on cotton cloth exports to Britain.[48] Macmillan also passed the 1959 Cotton Industry Act, offering spinners and weavers another round of subsidies for installing new machinery, on condition that they scrapped older plant.[49]

Assessments of Macmillan's strategy have tended to be rather jaundiced. The voluntary quotas did not actually reduce Commonwealth cloth exports to Britain; rather they put limits on their future growth. Moreover, the quotas could be evaded by exporting finished garments instead of cloth. As for the 1959 Cotton Industry Act, it certainly led to the scrapping of 48 per cent of the spindles and 27 per cent of the looms in place in April 1959, but it induced only £53.5 million of re-equipment spending, out of a target figure of £80–90 million. Miles calculates that state aid under the 1959 Act was equivalent to a mere 5 per cent tariff for two years.[50] Disillusion was rapid. After the Conservative triumph in the 1959 election, the government reverted to a policy of ignoring Lancashire and in the early 1960s the industry's future was no more secure than it had been a few years earlier.

FIGURE 115. Prime Minister Harold Macmillan. Source: *Preston By-Pass Opening by the Prime Minister* (Lancashire County Council, 1958, frontispiece)

## The 1960s mergers and the end of the cotton industry

A dramatic merger wave swept through the textile industry during the 1960s and resulted in the disappearance of many of Lancashire's most famous companies. This revolution in the cotton industry's pattern of ownership was engineered by outsiders, especially the giant man-made fibre producers, Courtaulds and ICI. By 1970, it was difficult, if not impossible, to distinguish the cotton industry from the textile industry in general, since all the major firms now had productive capacity in a variety of fibres and processes.

After the Second World War, the competitive position of Courtaulds declined because the company failed to match ICI in the development and production of synthetic fibres.[51] Courtaulds was overcommitted to rayon and this older fibre offered fewer opportunities for market growth. In the late 1950s, Courtaulds began a programme of acquisition and diversification, and moved into paints and plastics, but these typically disjointed initiatives failed to revive the company's performance. A particular problem for Courtaulds was its dependence on the threatened

FIGURE 116. Sir Frank Kearton, chairman of Courtaulds. (Photograph courtesy of Times Newspapers Ltd, by Sally Soames)

Lancashire cotton industry to spin and weave 30 per cent of its domestic viscose staple rayon sales. If the cotton industry collapsed, where would Courtaulds find new outlets for this fibre? Courtaulds' weakness was highlighted when the company almost fell to an ICI takeover bid launched in November 1961. Courtaulds was in a trap of its own making and judged that its only hope of escape was to integrate forwards into textiles, in order to safeguard the market for its core rayon business. Since it would take time to rationalise and modernise the cotton industry, Courtaulds wanted an assurance that imports would be brought

FIGURE 117. Protesters from Lancashire in London in 1962. *Left to right*: Nelson MP, Samuel Sidney Silverman; Mayor of Nelson, Harold Ingham; the Mayor of Burnley; Burnley MP, Daniel Jones; Councillor Davidson from Colne.

under firmer control in the interim period. Arthur Knight, a senior Courtaulds executive, states that in 1962, Board of Trade officials hinted that, if Courtaulds agreed to sort out Lancashire, the government might look more favourably on the industry's plight. Despite the vagueness of this offer, Courtaulds resolved to press ahead.[52]

Courtaulds bought many of the leading cotton firms in the mid-1960s, including the Lancashire Cotton Corporation and the Fine Spinners' and Doublers' Association. By 1968, Courtaulds had taken control of 30 per cent of the Lancashire spinning section and 12 per cent of the weaving section, and had extensive capacity in finishing, knitting and merchanting. Courtaulds now had the potential to become a vertically integrated fibre group, of the type discussed earlier in this chapter. ICI did not want Courtaulds to monopolize the textile industry and was forced to respond in kind. The ICI board predicted that, if Courtaulds gained control of Lancashire's mills, it would be able to smother the demand for ICI fibres. Unlike Courtaulds, ICI did not make direct purchases of cotton textile companies and instead chose to fund acquisitions made by its smaller allies, Viyella International and Carrington

& Dewhurst. Viyella was the vehicle of a London ladies' clothing manufacturer, Joe Hyman, who arrived in Lancashire by a circuitous route, having become a major player in the textile industry of the east midlands. Viyella grabbed a number of firms during the merger scramble, including the Bradford Dyers Association and Combined English Mills. Carrington & Dewhurst was an unusually forward-looking cotton weaving company in central Lancashire, which had concentrated on man-made fibre fabrics since the 1950s. After several scrapes, Hyman was deposed by his own board and in 1970 Viyella and Carrington & Dewhurst were merged to form Carrington Viyella, with ICI holding a 35 per cent stake in the new group.[53]

The mergers of the 1960s were followed by the closure of obsolete

FIGURE 118. Joe Hyman, Chairman and Chief Executive of Viyella International. (Photograph courtesy of *The Financial Times*, by Trevor Humphries)

FIGURE 119.
Courtaulds and
Dunlops Ltd,
Pimbo Industrial
Estate, Skelmers-
dale. (Photograph
courtesy of
Lancashire County
Library, Skelmers-
dale Local Studies
Collection)

mills, the appointment of new managers and the installation of modern types of equipment. New and highly capital-intensive technologies, notably break spinning and shuttleless loom weaving, were becoming available and stimulated the most innovative firms to move beyond the ring spindle and the automatic loom. A report published by the Cotton Board's successor, the Textile Council, calculated that, on the basis of 1967–8 costs and prices, firms could make substantial savings by introducing break spinning and shuttleless looms.[54] Courtaulds alone spent £57 million on textile machinery and the construction of modern textile factories, in places such as Skelmersdale, between 1962 and 1969.[55] The rate of installation of shuttleless looms in Britain rose after 1966 and 22 per cent of looms in the UK textile industry were shuttleless in 1980, a proportion exceeded in only Sweden, the Netherlands and the Soviet Union.[56] But the British textile machinery industry proved incapable of meeting the demand for the most sophisticated items and there was increasing recourse to imports from Switzerland and West Germany. A survey of 107 British textile firms showed that 89 per cent had purchased foreign machinery between 1970 and 1976,

FIGURE 120.
Modern, shuttleless looms in operation. (Photograph courtesy of Hilden Manufacturing Co. Ltd, Oswaldtwistle)

often because there was no British alternative of acceptable price and quality.[57]

Despite these technological changes, it is generally agreed that the intervention of Courtaulds and ICI failed to restore the competitiveness of the Lancashire section of the textile industry and in the 1970s many of the spinning frames and looms purchased in the 1960s were standing idle. Carrington Viyella was not a success and it was involved in further restructuring, being taken over by Vantona in 1982, at which point ICI disposed of its shares for a fraction of their original value.[58] Some large firms saw little future in textile production in Britain. Between 1980 and 1984, Tootals virtually abandoned spinning, weaving and knitting in the UK, finding it more profitable to concentrate on the design and trading aspects of the business and the importation of textiles ordered from factories in the Far East.[59]

What went wrong at Courtaulds? Knight argues, in a rather round-about way, that the government did not live up to its obligation to grant Courtaulds, and the cotton industry, adequate levels of protection.[60] The 1960s saw the imposition of further voluntary quotas on imports of Asian textiles by the UK and other western governments, under the American-inspired Short Term Arrangement and Long Term Agreement. As with the previous controls on Commonwealth textiles, these measures merely restricted the rate of growth of imports and induced a switch in the composition of imports from textiles to clothing.[61] Import restrictions could also be avoided by 'quota hopping': in the early 1960s, Hong Kong firms set up plants in Singapore, a place which was not yet subject to quotas, in order to produce textiles for the British market.[62] Given the continuing instability of textile markets, firms which had invested in shuttleless looms lacked the standardised orders that were needed to keep them running for twenty four hours a day, seven days a week. Consequently, overheads were too high, and it became even more difficult for British firms to compete.

## Today's textile industry

Serious doubts have been expressed about the viability of the high throughput strategies of Courtaulds and the alliance of Viyella International, Carrington & Dewhurst and ICI, for coping with the conditions in the textile industry in the late-twentieth century. On purely technical grounds, there was no need for huge combines. Pratten estimated that 60,000 spindles and 1,000 looms were the minimum efficient scales of modern cotton spinning and weaving units in the late 1960s.[63] On this basis, there would have been room for several dozen efficient companies in Lancashire in the 1960s, not just two or three firms, as Courtaulds and ICI seemed to think was the case. One study concludes that it was a strategic error for the large British firms to try to compete with cheap mass market Asian textiles.[64] Was there an alternative?

One of the most successful western textile industries since 1960 has been that of Italy.[65] After the collapse of the wool textile industry in the 1950s and 1960s, a new textile sector, based on collaboration among networks of small firms, developed in northern Italy. These small firms were controlled by skilled workers, technicians and designers, many of whom had previously worked in the mills. Their wage costs were low, but their mechanical and design skills were high. Italian firms concentrated on supplying textiles for fashion-conscious consumers and avoided direct competition with lower quality products from Asian countries. Businesses had to be prepared to change their product lines at very short notice, in order to keep up with the latest fashions and this required the development of more versatile types of machinery. Italian firms put more emphasis on forward integration into marketing than they did on the integration of spinning and weaving. Successful enterprises introduced computerised communications systems for linking sales tills in retail shops to head office, so that an immediate response could be made to shifts in consumer demand. The production of cloth and the making up of garments would often be subcontracted to allied firms.[66] Benetton and Stefanel are the outstanding examples of Italian firms employing this strategy. In the 1980s, Benetton's performance was unsurpassed in the European textile industry and by the end of the decade, textile and clothing firms in other countries were adopting similar methods of organising their businesses.[67]

Should – and could – Lancashire have followed a similar strategy to that of the Italians? This might have been difficult, since Lancashire has never been regarded as an international centre of fashion, not even in the heyday of the Beatles and George Best in the 1960s. Even German consumers, remarked a shocked Cotton Board pamphlet in 1958, regarded British designs as tasteless and their finish shoddy.[68] Lancashire would have found the going tough, but other European textile and clothing complexes, including the West German, made great strides towards emulating the move upmarket of the Italians in the 1970s and 1980s, so the task cannot have been hopeless.

In the early 1980s, many British firms were still trying to compete in low quality textiles and garments.[69] A comparison of the British and German clothing industries concluded that one of the main constraints faced by British firms was a shortage of skilled workers and technicians, which resulted in low labour productivity, poor maintenance of machinery and an inability to do intricate work. The lack of skills, it was argued, reflected the low priority given to industrial training by the British government and the stranglehold of British retail chains over their domestic suppliers. Marks & Spencer alone accounted for 16 per cent of British clothing sales in the mid-1980s. Large retail groups demanded long runs of standardised garments from their captive suppliers. It was argued that these satellite firms became so reliant on the large retailers they failed to learn how to act on their own initiative and neglected to develop their own design skills.[70]

It is just possible that new technological developments may give Britain another chance to make up lost ground. In the 1980s, the application of computers to the clothing industry, especially at the design and cutting – rather than sewing – stages, opened up new opportunities for garment manufacturers in western countries.[71] Since this form of computerisation economizes on skilled labour, it may be of greater advantage to British firms than to those of, say, Germany or Sweden. Kell and Richtering show that, between 1980 and 1988, the developed countries regained some of their lost competitiveness in textiles by installing open-ended rotor spinning and shuttleless weaving equipment. They argue that the machinery now available to the OECD countries is far more flexible and productive than that on offer in the

1960s, when Courtaulds launched its ill-fated assault on world cloth markets.[72] In 1985, Britain (14 per cent) was an impressive fourth in the non-communist world in terms of open-end rotors as a proportion of total cotton spinning capacity, behind Sweden (45 per cent), Hong Kong (35 per cent) and West Germany (16 per cent).[73] Recent research into the factors contributing to employment change in the British textile and clothing sector, indicates that improvements in labour productivity were responsible for approximately twice as many net job losses as rising import penetration between 1980 and 1989.[74] This suggests that many firms are fighting back against their overseas competitors, but it is too early to know whether they will be successful.

## Conclusion

The world textile industry is intensely competitive. Lancashire's cotton mills failed to match and overcome this competition. But Lancashire's contraction has not been unparalleled and for a similar chronicle of decline it is necessary to look no further than France and its textile producers.[75] One interpretation of cotton's decline states that Lancashire's problems were insurmountable, given the low wages enjoyed by developing countries. Another explanation claims that the cotton industry could have been saved by the amalgamation of family firms into modern business corporations. Yet another interpretation suggests that governments could have encouraged a revival of confidence in the industry, by providing it with greater security against imports.

A substantial decline in the Lancashire cotton industry had been on the cards for many years. The industry was bloated by 1914, having risen to dominate world markets at a time when it faced few, if any, serious competitors. Many people took Lancashire's superiority for granted, but they ought to have had the sense to know that this extraordinary state of affairs could not last forever. As other countries developed their own manufacturing sectors, their cotton industries were bound to eat into Lancashire's markets, with or without the help of protective measures in their home markets, as actually occurred from the 1920s onwards.

The strategy of creating big, vertically integrated firms did not seem to work, either in the United States or in Britain. Large textile groups, such as Courtaulds, had great difficulty fending off competition from small textile producers in Taiwan, Hong Kong and South Korea in the 1960s and 1970s. Bureaucratic firms were not at their best in the conditions that prevailed in the textile industry, where it was vital that producers should be responsive to subtle changes in demand and consumer tastes. In large capital-intensive plants, it was costly and time-consuming to alter the firm's production plans, while the need for endless committee meetings and paperwork clogged up the decision-making process.

Italy provides the most positive example of a thriving textile industry in post-war western Europe. Italy's small firms, however, were very different from those in Clitheroe or Chorley. The new Italian textile industry grew on the ruins of an older and quite hopelessly inefficient mill sector, and it put the emphasis on design and informal networks of co-operation between businesses. Lancashire's mills, by contrast, were geared up to supplying the empire with blankets and other cheap fabrics; British mills accepted whatever orders the merchants gave them and knew very little about modern trends in design. The Italians proved that a high wage economy could be successful in textiles, once it had found an appropriate niche and once the dead wood had been cleared away. In Lancashire, the dead wood was not cleared away quickly enough, hence little progress was made towards building a new textile and clothing industry.

The cotton industry could have been preserved after 1945 by import controls and generous subsidies, but these would have imposed a painful burden on consumers and taxpayers. It would have become a museum piece, comparable with many of the industries of the former Soviet bloc. British consumers are familiar with the sorry effects of the European Union's Common Agricultural Policy on food prices. Would Britain also have been willing to pay more for its clothing, simply to keep hundreds of cotton mills open in Lancashire?

# CHAPTER 12

# Cotton's legacy

CHRIS ASPIN

L ET US LOOK at Lancashire from two much-visited vantage points: the Peel Monument above Holcombe and, some twenty miles away, the north-facing summit of Jeffrey Hill.

The square stone tower at the entrance to the Rossendale Valley rewards those who climb its winding staircase with a comprehensive view of a landscape created almost totally by the cotton industry and the myriad developments the industry set in train. Extending almost as far as the eye can see is one of the world's most densely-populated districts, where town is joined to town, village to village, and where all, with hardly a break, are linked to the tall buildings of Manchester in the middle distance. There are few better spots from which to see how vast and complete was the impact of the cotton plant on an area covering more than 600 square miles of the Lancashire Plain.

Above this great conurbation, as above the other towns of industrial Lancashire, there drifted for a century and a half a pall of dust and dirt and smoke which often turned into an impenetrable smog and only rarely thinned sufficiently to allow the watcher on this hilltop to glimpse Cheshire and the Pennine peaks of Derbyshire. Sometimes, when there was a wind from the south-east, the black cloud would reach the Isle of Man and smudge the grazing sheep. The tower, the stone walls on the moor and many buildings visible from this and many other Lancashire uplands still bear the imprint of the smoke-filled years; and while much time and money has been spent on removing the dark deposits, one can occasionally admire what Nikolaus Pevsner called 'the dignity of blackened stone.' No such thoughts crossed the mind of Charles Dickens, who distilled his observations of industrial Lancashire into Coketown, a place dominated by '. . . machinery and tall chimneys, out of which interminable serpents of smoke trailed themselves for ever and ever and never got uncoiled . . . You saw nothing in Coketown but what was severely workful'. [1]

Two centuries ago, the Manchester landmarks one could have made out with certainty from Holcombe Hill were the new cotton factories, the first of which were Richard Arkwright's in Shude Hill and Joseph

Thackeray's on the River Medlock. These rose during the mid-1780s when the two spinners installed steam engines to return spent water to their water wheels. The mill chimneys were soon joined by many larger companions – usually stone and square to begin with, then octagonal or circular in brick – until the whole area became a sort of red and black forest. 'What have you done to Lancashire?' cried William Morris, horrified by a district that hid its face from the sun. But this dark world with its blackened buildings and its closely-knit communities was the quintessential Lancashire for the generations that were born and grew up there. Disraeli, who realised that the cotton trade had changed the course of history, has Coningsby in his novel of that name, ask the question, 'What would I not give to see Athens!' And the hero's companion replies, 'I have seen it. The Age of Ruins is passed. Have you seen Manchester? Manchester is as great a human exploit as Athens.' Those who read the book when it was published in 1844 would have been astonished had someone told them that factories and factory chimneys would one day be preserved and protected to remind future generations of the once-universal power of cotton and coal and steam.

On the site of Arkwright's mill rises the CIS Building, the most easily distinguished of Manchester's twentieth-century skyscrapers. Thackeray's mill has been replaced by a part of UMIST; and so we find in these landmarks appropriate and powerful reminders that the cotton era has left a rich legacy of ideas, of which the co-operative movement and the Manchester region's huge contribution to science and technology are among the most widespread and influential.

It is not too fanciful to imagine a nineteenth-century visitor to the Peel Monument looking over the busily-smoking landscape and seeing it as an immense social cauldron or melting pot out of which were emerging not only Karl Marx's 'new-fangled men', but also some of the most important developments of modern times: free trade, the co-operative movement, parliamentary reform, factory legislation, local government, trade unionism, engineering insurance (prompted by the explosion of many early cotton mill boilers), public health and town planning. The Blackburn mill owner, Thomas Boys Lewis, had similar thoughts and being also a poet, he put them into a sonnet which begins:

> Scorn not, O stranger from a clearer sky,
> This grim, grey sunless town; here men have learned
> To summon to their aid dread powers that lie
> Deep in the frame of things.[2]

Visitors to east Lancashire in the early part of the nineteenth century often mentioned the large numbers of red-headed inhabitants, 'a testimony of Nature,' as William Howitt commented in 1838, 'to the

FIGURE 121. The way in which the cotton industry dominated the larger Lancashire towns is seen to almost overwhelming effect in the Weavers' Triangle at Burnley. Fifteen Victorian mills and other industrial buildings line the Leeds and Liverpool Canal to provide urban vistas unique in Britain. (Photograph courtesy of Lancashire County Library, Burnley Local Studies Collection)

ancient prevalence of the Dane on these hills'.[3] The rarity of redheads today is a good indication of the change brought about by the arrival from all parts of the country of people who found work in the cotton mills. Most came willingly, but some had no choice. These were the pauper children shipped in large numbers from the workhouses of London and other distant places to begin a new life as apprentices to entrepreneurs like the Peels, who ran a clutch of mills within a few miles of Holcombe Hill. In this century, there have been two further waves of newcomers: displaced persons driven from central Europe in the Second World War and the Asian workers who responded to appeals from the mill owners in the 1950s and '60s and made their homes in the cotton towns.

## Water and steam mills

If we turn our backs on the Peel Monument and make our way to Jeffrey Hill, we see a landscape that has been only lightly touched by industry and looks very much as it did long before the cotton trade reached Lancashire. To the right, a Roman road heads with unerring directness towards Pen-y-Ghent. On the other side of the valley are

the banks and ditches of a medieval deer park; and down below, green meadows, hedgerows, woodland and scattered farmhouses make up picture of unchanging rural ways, for there is neither a mill chimney nor a railway nor a wide modern road. The tallest building is the square tower of Chipping church, the central point of the only settlement in the whole valley. This is Lancashire as most of it might have remained but for the explosive growth of the cotton trade.

Yet it is here, rather than among the urban sprawl of Greater Manchester, that we can see one of the first cotton factories to be built in Lancashire. Arkwright had made a fortune by supplying the trade with the warp thread needed for an ever-growing range of all-cotton cloths and when his patents were nullified, many men rushed to follow in his footsteps. Among them in 1785 were the founders of the water-powered Kirk Mill at Chipping. Though slightly enlarged, it retains much of its original character and is among only a handful of eighteenth-century mills still standing in Lancashire. Others are at Backbarrow (now an hotel) and (transformed into private dwellings) at Caton, Cleveley, Wray and Bury Fold in Darwen.

These early mills, like many that followed them over the next half century, relied on water power and that is why there are few Pennine valleys that cannot show some evidence of the cotton trade. Choose almost any stream and follow it to its source on the high moorland and you will pass weirs and watercourses, mill sites and workpeople's cottages, many in ruins, but some still lived in. The Cheesden Brook,

FIGURE 122. From the late nineteenth century, spinning mills with tall chimneys and short names became familiar landmarks in the Oldham area. Bee Mill at Royton is one of the survivors. There was a good reason for choosing names with three or four letters – skips with large letters on the side tended to be returned promptly once customers had emptied them. Source: Platt Brothers & Co. Ltd, *Particulars and Calculations Relation to Cotton Spinning* (Platt Brothers & Co. Ltd, 1904), p. 286.

which hurries beneath the Rochdale to Edenfield road, gathered no fewer than fifteen mills to its banks in a six-mile descent to the outskirts of Bury and Heywood. It served most of them for the best part of a century, creating in this now largely-deserted valley a community of several hundred people.

Though fulling came first in the 1780s, this was essentially a cotton stream with ten mills spinning waste from other factories and weaving it into cloth. Other sites were involved in bleaching and calico printing. Much ingenuity went into conserving, using and reusing the water, and the present-day mountaineer who climbs to the source of the brook on the edge of Scout Moor will discover, at a height of almost 1,500 feet, the Great Lodge, which still collects water from the surrounding moss. A little downstream, but still above the 1,000ft contour, is the site of Four Acre Mill and its 36ft wheel. Cheesden Pasture Mill, built on the edge of the moor in 1830 by George and James Ramsbottom, farmer-weavers with a strong religious bent, was probably unique in having its own pulpit and in being the setting for an annual performance of Handel's *Messiah*, for which a borrowed harmonium was carried over the fields on two mop staves. Little of this mill and its row of cottages remains, though the circular gasholder pit is easily traced.

As one accompanies the Cheesden Brook to its lower reaches, one finds few stretches without some evidence of a busy industrial past, for it was never allowed to go far before being diverted along mill races or coaxed into reservoirs. And though steam was used in some of the larger mills – coal was mined locally – the Cheesden Valley is perhaps the most concentrated memorial in Lancashire to the once all-powerful waterwheel.

Availability of water also determined the siting of steam-driven mills and, as well as the principal rivers and their tributaries, the canals became important providers. The Ancoats district of Manchester, the first industrial suburb, began its spectacular growth alongside the Rochdale Canal in the 1790s. Before the turn of the century, an eight-storey mill, built by the Scottish brothers Adam and George Murray, and probably the first anywhere to employ more than 1,000 workers, towered over the surrounding streets. Other giants followed and were added to until the early years of the twentieth century. An operative who praised the Ancoats factories in verse was reminded of 'gorgeous palaces'. Others were less flattering. 'Colossal prisons' and 'brick boxes' were among the epithets used. Karl Friedrich Schinkel, the leading German architect of his day, was astonished in 1826 to find that Manchester had factories 'as long as the Palace in Berlin'; and he observed that buildings only three years old were as blackened with smoke as if they had been in use for a century.[4] Many of the Ancoats factories remain and even in a city of tall buildings, they continue to impress the visitor by their daunting bulk and take on a strange beauty when lit up at night.

The largest concentration of Victorian mills – some fifteen stone buildings as well as three ironworks that made mill engines and looms – occupy what is known in Burnley as the Weavers' Triangle. The former spinning mills and weaving sheds line both banks of the Leeds and Liverpool Canal to provide industrial vistas unlike any other either in this country or abroad. In recent years, the Weavers' Triangle has become a place of pilgrimage for students of urban Britain and a guide book is available for the tourist who sets out on a half-hour exploration from the former Wharfmaster's House and Canal Toll Office. Cheek by jowl with the mills are two public houses and buildings that were formerly a school, a mill owner's mansion, Burnley's first public library and working- and middle-class housing. Slater Terrace, built in the late 1840s, is especially interesting, for here lived eleven families above a

canal-side warehouse. Surrounded and overshadowed by cotton mills, these houses had front doors that opened onto an iron landing projecting over the water.

A different pattern of mill building is seen when one crosses the moor from Burnley to Rossendale, where the Irwell, its tributaries and the local coal mines provided such abundant power that by the middle of the nineteenth century, people spoke of the Golden Valley, because of the great profits then being made. Among the plain stone mills strung out along the streams are several that were built and run on co-operative principles by shareholding workpeople, who hired and fired professional managers in the way football clubs do today. At Stacksteads is Farholme Mill, which wove its first pieces in 1854 and astonished the trade in 1859 and '60 by paying successive half-yearly dividends of 31, 44 and 62 per cent, an achievement no other company equalled.[5] Lower down the Irwell at Cloughfold, another group of co-operators built the five-storey Victoria Mill and opened it in 1861 with a tea party attended by more than 3,000 people. The datestone, transferred from the demolished chimney to a new building, includes the names of the company's first chairman and vice chairman. A feature of the narrow Pennine valleys are mill chimneys detached from their engine houses and placed high up the adjoining hillsides in order to produce a sufficient draught.

FIGURE 123. Houldsworth's Mill at Reddish, near Stockport, is a rare and striking example of a double spinning mill: two five-storey blocks, each of eighteen bays, separated by a warehouse and office block flanked by stair towers. The Oldham architect A. H. Stott chose an Italianate style when he produced his design for the mill, which was completed in 1865. (Photograph courtesy of Stockport Metropolitan Borough, Heritage Library)

## A land of contrasts

Though Manchester and the mill towns are cotton's most obvious legacy, their characters are remarkably diverse, reflecting the wide-ranging ingenuity and spirited independence of the Lancastrians who created them. There are also striking differences in the places of work, most obviously between the tall spinning mills in the southern half of the county and the single-storey weaving sheds with their saw-toothed and north-facing roofs that abound in the more northerly towns and villages.

In contrast to the stone buildings of the east Lancashire valleys are the later and larger brick spinning mills that dominate the skylines of Oldham, Bolton and the smaller towns in the south of the county. Climb to the high ground above Shaw and you can look down on a landscape dominated by huge red boxes that spun many fortunes and gave the district the reputation of having more millionaires to the square mile than any other place on earth. Most of the Oldham spinning mills have found other uses, but their names can be read in large letters on their chimneys. Because it cost less to paint a short name on returnable skips and cases and because the letters could be big, the mill owners chose words like Ace, Bee, Elk, Fir, Fox, Oak, Owl, Ram and Roy.

Mill architects were usually given only limited freedom to make their buildings outwardly attractive, though there were exceptions to the purely functional approach. Houldsworth's Mill at Reddish, built in 1865, has an arresting Italianate facade with a large clock and cupola on the parapet. From the same period, Gidlow Works at Wigan, with its adventurous inclusion of white and blue Staffordshire brick, is equally striking. Lord Derby observed on its completion that it was 'a pleasure to the eye to rest on,' an opinion shared by many subsequent visitors, for the building is now at the centre of a conservation area. It was here that John Rylands established the leading firm in the trade and made the fortune which, after his death, his widow used to establish the John Rylands Library in Manchester. At Summerseat, between Bury and Ramsbottom, the handsome spinning mill, built in the mid-1870s by Isaac and Edward Hoyle, pioneers of industrial partnership, has been lovingly cleaned and restored and under its new name, The Spinnings, offers private accommodation to several families.

The mill-dominated townscape of the Bolton district enables the visitor to trace building developments from the era of water power to that of electricity, though almost all of the 100 survivors relied on steam. The Atlas group of eight huge mills built between 1864 and

FIGURE 124. This former cotton spinning mill at Summerseat has been turned into luxury flats. It was built in the mid-1870s by Isaac and Edward Hoyle, pioneers of industrial partnership. (Photograph courtesy of Bury Metropolitan Borough Council)

1887, and the three at Swan Lane (1903, 1906 and 1914), radiate their founders' unbounded optimism and powerfully remind us that Bolton's consumption of Egyptian and Sudan cotton was so vast that the Nile Valley was made to bloom in order to satisfy the demand for fine mule-spun yarns.

Villages also had their big mills, two of the most impressive survivors being the tower-topped Ring and Mavis Mills, opened in 1906 and 1908, by separate companies at Coppull.

Of the surviving chimneys that of India Mill in Darwen (1864–68) is the most astonishing. Rising more than 300 feet is what appears at first sight to be an Italian bell tower built of brick. It stands on one of the largest stones ever quarried and, because of its great height, has become a nesting place for peregrine falcons.

## Manchester and Liverpool

John Jones, the Manchester operative who thought the city's first big mills were like palaces, would probably have been lost for words had

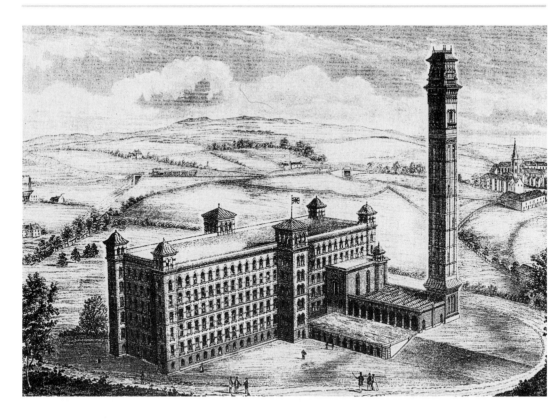

he lived to see the Royal Exchange or the great warehouses. These really were palatial and Schinkel, the German architect who was dismayed by the 'monstrous shapeless' mills, would surely have approved of a building like the Italianate S. & J. Watts warehouse built during the 1850s in Portland Street. We admire it today as the Britannia Hotel and it reminds us that Manchester was much more a city of warehouses than of mills. Many of these buildings survive as offices, shops and stores.

In the centre of Manchester is the Royal Exchange, now the home of a modern theatre company, but once the meeting place of 10,000 cotton men, most of whom in the heyday of the trade wore silk top hats. The more prosperous tended to live by the sea and those who made St Annes their home travelled to Manchester in a luxuriously-appointed train that no one else could board. The building was completed in 1921 – there had been earlier cotton exchanges – and it has now found other uses. Mount the steps from Cross Street or St Ann's Square and you enter a vast hall with three glass domes and massive pillars. Here merchants, manufacturers and spinners met to do business alongside representatives of textile machinery companies and the suppliers of mill furnishings. Close to the roof is the large long board which displayed the world's cotton prices. Those quoted on the last day of business in 1968 can still be read. Manchester Town Hall,

FIGURE 126. Darwen gained an impressive, if incongrous, landmark when the India Mill chimney rose to a height of more than 300 feet in the 1860s. It has the elaborate shape of an Italian bell tower and stands on a foundation of one of the largest stones ever quarried. Source: E. Leigh, *Science of Modern Cotton Spinning* (Manchester, Palmer & Howe, 1873), facing p. 25.

completed in 1877, is a splendid monument to a city that grew to greatness as the world's great cotton centre. Among its many ornamentations you will find a handloom weaver carved in stone and an heraldic ceiling with the arms of cities with which Manchester did business. Close by, the Free Trade Hall reminds the visitor of a campaign that gave Britain a public policy for two generations. The hall is to become an hotel, but it will be remembered as the home of the Hallé Orchestra and remain a symbol of the city's many contributions to the arts. The subject can be only lightly touched on here, but the range of cotton-influenced achievements is considerable: from novels like Mrs Gaskell's *Mary Barton*, the 'Tale of Manchester Life' first published in 1848, to the quirky mill town scenes painted by L.S.Lowry in our own century.

Like Manchester, Liverpool grew prosperous as the cotton trade expanded. The two cities were linked in 1830 by the world's first professionally-run railway and, in 1894, by the Manchester Ship Canal. The Leeds and Liverpool Canal, begun in 1775, was another of the industry's main arteries and shaped the growth of a string of manufacturing communities. The original Liverpool basin and its warehouses can still be seen along with the preserved entrance locks from the Stanley Dock.

If the Ancoats mills and the converted city centre warehouses are Manchester's most notable reminders of cotton production and the sales of cloth, then Liverpool's huge dockland is a memorable pointer to both the huge inflow of cotton bales and to the exporting of finished goods. Princes and Bramley-Moore were the two raw cotton docks; and they await redevelopment. Liverpool lost its Cotton Exchange in the early 1970s, though its name lives on in the building which took its place. Exchange Flags, the open area behind the Town Hall where cotton was also traded, remains much as it was. Vulcan Street has warehouses that once held cotton in vast quantities and among the Victorian mansions built by cotton merchants, Greenbank House (now part of the university) and Liscard Hall are outstanding examples.

## Cotton colonies and villages

In the centre of the bus turn-round at Barrow Bridge, just to the north of Bolton, is the carved keystone from the engine house facade of Dean Mills. It marks the centre of an industrial settlement widely regarded during the middle years of the nineteenth century as a model of enlightened paternalism. By good fortune, much of it survives and is a living memorial to Robert Gardner and Thomas Bazely, its two farsighted founders.

To this narrow wooded valley in 1851 came Prince Albert who was anxious examine at first hand what the *Illustrated London News* called

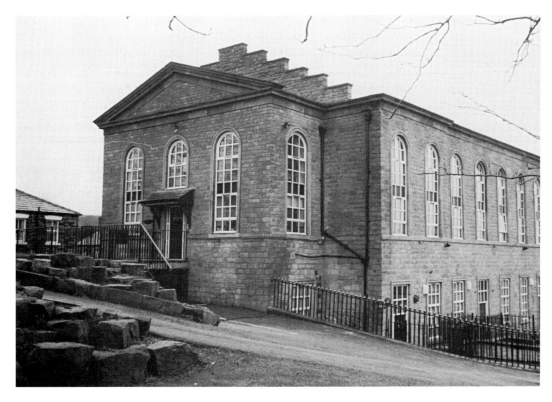

'a well organised community never equalled in the Utopias of philosophy'.[6] He went away much impressed, never having seen anything to compare with it and certainly never having toured a place of toil to the sounds of 'sweet music' played by a workmen's band.

Though the two six-storey mills, which stood beside the stream, were taken down in 1913, the rest of the settlement has survived. Here are the workers' houses, each with its own garden; and close by is the splendidly-restored educational institute building. Climb the footpath to the top of the slope and you reach Bazely Street, off which run solid stone terraces called simply First, Second, Third, Fourth and Fifth Streets. On the end house and on another in the valley bottom, where the managers lived, clusters of plaques record Barrow Bridge's many successes in the Beautiful Britain in Bloom Competition, something which would surely have pleased the hamlet's founders, who by treating their employees humanely did so much to repair the tattered reputation of the early factory system.

Gardner built the mills in the early 1830s and was joined by Bazely in 1843. Both were men of vision, for as well as providing 300 of their 1,000 workers with gas-lit homes, they set up a sick and burial club and built a reading room, a dining room, a co-operative store, a bathhouse (opened in 1844 with a performance of Handel's *Messiah*)

FIGURE 127. Barrow Bridge on the outskirts of Bolton was one of a number of model villages established by Victorian industrialists who took a close interest in the welfare of their workpeople. The former school and lecture hall, which could accommodate 2,000 people, has been turned into flats. (Photograph courtesy of Lancashire County Library, Headquarters Local Studies Collection)

and, most astonishing of all, the large school above which was a lecture hall with room for more than 2,000 people. After years of neglect, the building was tastefully restored, and in 1992 it began a new life as a group of up-market flats. Now its stone shines again on sunny days with a honey-coloured radiance that the soot deposits of a century and a half had totally obscured. It is a remarkable building for a hamlet and is far bigger and better-looking than many similar meeting places in large towns. Today it is the centrepiece of a settlement that reminds us of one of the cotton trade's most admirable social achievements. On the outskirts of the hamlet is an octagonal brick chimney, said to be the biggest in Bolton, and now a listed building. It served the bleach works of Richard Ainsworth Son & Company.

Barrow Bridge was one of several factory colonies in the district to benefit from the attentions of enlightened employers. Henry and Edmund Ashworth created mill villages at Egerton and New Eagley, where the houses, in the opinion of Lord Ashley, were 'the best I ever saw for working-men'.[7] Every time a cottage became vacant, there were at least twenty applicants who were well aware that the Ashworth brothers made 'frequent and irregular' inspections. As we admire these well-built and now much sought-after homes, we can picture the two masters 'minutely examining' the state of cleanliness of the rooms, the bedding, the furniture, the condition of the children and the income and habits of the tenants. 'Remarks on the visit are entered in books kept for the purpose,' Henry Ashworth told the Factory Commissioners in 1833. These two Quakers acted as they did for sound economic reasons. They received a much better return on their investments by employing workpeople who were well-housed and more contented than those who lived in the damp cellars of Bolton.

Ashworth houses, which were regularly whitewashed and painted at the firm's expense, were high on the list of places visited by eminent Victorians like Disraeli who made industrial Grand Tours of the north. Bright Street and Cobden Street at Egerton are reminders of Henry Ashworth's association with the two leading free-traders in the Anti-Corn Law League of the 1840s.

Another factory village on the moorland edge of Bolton is straggling Belmont. Like the others it came into being because it had a good supply of water and a good road. It grew up alongside the Sharples to Hoghton turnpike, opened in 1801 and because of its remoteness it has retained much of its original character. The cotton trade was represented by the 'Top Works' (first spinning, then bleaching) and the 'Bottom Works' (bleaching and dyeing) and by the time of the Cotton Famine (1863–64), Belmont had more than 1,000 inhabitants. Lack of work then resulted in a great exodus and for many years travellers passed through an almost deserted village. Today the people who buy the characterful old stone houses for their retirement have many reminders of the textile years. The northern part of the village with its terraces, its pub and its chapel, is much as it was. And the newcomer with a taste for local history finds many links with the distant past. Maria Square is named after the daughter of the Ryecroft family, who ran the 'Bottom Works,' and Deakin Terrace is another link with a mill-owning family.

On the other side of the moor, the road passes through Abbey Village, the creation of John Parke, a Preston cotton manufacturer, who built a spinning and weaving mill on a greenfield site in the early 1840s. The cotton era ended in 1971, but ninety-two workers' houses still line the main street in what must be the longest rows of the period.

Some factory settlements have been absorbed into towns. Freetown at Bury and the southern part of Preston developed by John and Samuel Horrocks and their successors spring to mind. John Horrocks built his first factory in 1792 and the firm was still growing one hundred years later. The huge Centenary Mill with its square tower continues to dominate the skyline, though the Horrockses link with the town ended in 1988.

Summerseat is another creation of the cotton trade and as well as the Hoyle brothers' handsome mill, the village, through its older buildings, has many other links with an active industrial past. Among the well-preserved workpeople's cottages and terraced houses are Robin Road (late eighteenth-century), Hamer Terrace (early nineteenth-century)

FIGURE 128. The breadwinners in this long row of cottages at Abbey Village worked in the local cotton mill; and one can picture them setting out together, their clogs ringing on the stone pavements, in time for the 6 o'clock start. (Photograph courtesy of Lancashire County Library, Headquarters Local Studies Collection)

named after Richard Hamer, a millowner who learned his trade in the village under Robert Peel and his partners, East View (1837), Miller Street (1855) and the 'Brick Houses' of the mid-1880s. The Wesleyan school, built by Hamer in 1840, and co-operative store of 1861, are now private dwellings. Sunk into the ground at the junction of Queen's Place and Rowlands Road is a domed cast iron retort, which was doubtless used in a gas-making plant attached to one of the village mills. These sturdy seven-foot cylinders are used as gateposts in several parts of east Lancashire and a mid-nineteenth-century engraving of Summerseat, shows the gas holders and retort house at the now-vanished Twist Mill, only a few hundred yards from the solitary survivor.

The River Darwen drew to its banks several eighteenth-century entrepreneurs who created industrial settlements around spinning mills and calico printing works. These communities continue to flourish, though the remaining mill buildings have found new uses. Lower Darwen has one hundred houses built before 1850, there are cottages and converted mills at Hoghton Bottoms and lower downstream Samlesbury Bottoms and Roach Bridge are other former cotton hamlets where one can see mill buildings and the homes of the workpeople.

The hamlet of Irwell Vale, near Haslingden, is probably unique among the surviving factory settlements of Lancashire in having been built as a speculation. In January, 1832, the *Manchester Guardian* carried the following advertisement

> WATER POWER MILL – TO BE LET, with immediate possession, a New Substantial STONE BUILDING four stories high, 41 yards long by 16 yards wide, with water wheels, &c., a supply of water equal to 30 horses' power in the dryest seasons. Situated in the Vale of the Irwell, near Edenfield, fifteen miles from Manchester. For further particulars, apply Mr Bowker, Prestwich.

John Bowker, a merchant, had acquired the site in 1798 and he later bought the adjoining Ravenshore Farm, which gave him a source of water from the River Ogden. This must have involved considerable expense, for as well as constructing a substantial weir at Ravenshore Bowker had to tunnel through solid rock for more than one hundred yards to take his water to a channel which ran for a third of a mile to the mill. The weir, tunnel and channel survive, but the mill was demolished in 1957.

In 1833, Bowker built thirty stone houses near the mill. The two rows with a few additions account for most of the present settlement and their names, Bowker Street and Aitkin Street, remind the visitor of both the speculative builder and Thomas Aikten, a cotton spinner who leased the mill and whose family ran it for more than a century Irwell Vale provided an income for Bowker and his descendants unt

1905. Neither Bowker nor Aitkin, both of whom lived some distance from the hamlet, appears to have taken much interest in the social life of the workpeople, almost all of whom were self-motivated Primitive Methodists. Over the years, there evolved in Irwell Vale a tightly-knit community which by the end of the nineteenth century had its own chapel, co-operative store, newsroom, temperance society, mutual improvement class and burial club.

Another village with quite different links with its industrial past is Tottington. A good starting point is the imposing house known as Stormer Hill, a rare example of a wealthy manufacturer's home of the domestic period. It was built in 1762 by Edward Smalley and continued as a 'cotton mansion' for two centuries. Its most notable tenant was Joshua Knowles, a calico printer at Tottington Mill. He leased the house in the mid-1830s and in what is known as the long room on the top floor, built two fireplaces using large wooden printing blocks from the works. He is also remembered for providing the west gallery of Tottington church 'for the benefit of poor children' and for Tower Court, which overlooked his mill. This, the most notable building in the district, has what Nikolaus Pevsner called 'a dramatically medievalising façade, all embattled.' Knowles is said to have lavished money on his tower in order to rival a now-vanished one built in the same style by his old employers, the Grants, of Ramsbottom, and also as a means of dispelling rumours that he was becoming financially insecure. The tower, with its large 1840 datestone, forms part of a courtyard incorporating a former farm, stables for the factory horses and an earlier fustian workshop. The whole has been converted into luxury apartments.

In the valley below the tower are striking reminders of the time when the Kirklees Brook quenched the thirst of a string of bleaching and calico printing works. Here among isolated walls and the tumbled stones of old engine beds and buildings is a miniature Lake District: a dozen or so reservoirs that stored the water for an industry that has now almost gone. Across the largest reservoir stride the nine arches of Island Lodge Viaduct, which carried the Bury and Tottington Railway to the foot of Holcombe Hill and to the doors of the works it was built to serve. Though it had five stations and two halts on its three and three-quarter miles, it was principally a cotton line promoted by local men with an interest in the trade. The first train ran in November, 1882 and six years later the line became a limb of the Lancashire and Yorkshire Railway system, the chief means of the county's cotton transport for more than a century.

A little downstream from the viaduct are some of the strangest of all the many relics the cotton trade has left us. Among the trees of a young wood are huge and curiously-shaped masses of clinker, fused solid from the smouldering loads brought from the engine house of Tottington Mill.

In January, 1819, James Watkins, a Bolton magistrate, visited the factories in and around Tottington as required by Peel's neglected Health and Morals of Apprentices Act of 1802, and found much to alarm him. One mill at Elton was

> most filthy; no Ventilation; the Apprentices and other Children ragged, puny, not half clothed, and seemingly not half fed; no Instruction of any sort; no human Beings can be more wretched.[8]

The parliamentary reports that record the findings of Watkins and others, together with the evidence of many people who were sent as young children to work in factories like that described above, present us with the most disquieting of all our surviving links with the cotton trade. That children under ten spent as long as fifteen hours a day in such places and that it took a long and bitterly-fought campaign to remedy the evil have prompted many later commentators to seize on William Blake's phrase 'dark satanic mills.' There were, however, owners with a sense of responsibility and while factory life until well into the twentieth century entailed long hours, much tedium and, for those confined to weaving sheds, the day-long deafening din of clattering looms, it offered, when conditions were improved, a better means of earning a decent living than was available in most other industries.

## Remains of the Cotton Famine

When the American Civil War cut the supply of cotton to Lancashire, it caused widespread distress not only to the 420,000 people directly employed in the mills, but also to thousands more who supplied both the trade and the workpeople. The response of the operatives, who had enjoyed a period of rising prosperity and were beginning to run their own mills on the co-operative principle, was of heroic proportions. There was much sympathy for the north in its struggle to abolish slavery and the visitor to Manchester can see in Brazennose Street the statue of Abraham Lincoln and read on the plinth his letter of thanks to the Lancashire working men who supported him.

Out of the Cotton Famine of 1861 to 1865 came much good. As the mills closed or went on short time, local authorities, relief committees and a number of generous individuals began schemes to provide road-making and other work for the unemployed. The laying out of the Ribbleton Estate in Preston was among the many tasks found for the mill workers but as the crisis deepened, Lancashire looked to the Government for extra help. And here we must record the achievements of an unsung benefactor who did much to transform the cotton towns and villages during the years of distress. Despite much opposition from politicians who lamented the large sums wasted in Ireland during the Potato Famine, the Government decided to offer 'work for wages' schemes to the distressed districts. The Public Works (Manufacturing Districts) Act received Royal Assent on July 21, 1863; and to put the policy into operation, the Home Secretary chose Robert Rawlinson, a Chorley builder's son who had risen from being a stonemason to the Local Government Board's Chief Engineering Inspector. He arrived in Lancashire in 1863 with instructions

> . . . to inspect towns and their suburbs, and ascertain the character of their drainage; the quantity and quality of the water supplies; the condition of the streets; and the provision made for parks and other grounds for the recreation of the inhabitants; and the general sanitary arrangements of each locality.

The Government offered loans at 3 per cent and almost £2m was usefully spent during the next four years. In some places Rawlinson met strong prejudice against works designed to improve public health. In others he had to contend with indifference 'based on want of knowledge and appreciation of the results of main sewers, house drains, and other similar works.' His weapons were 'discussion and explanation'; and so successful was he in this that some ninety-four towns and districts undertook improvement schemes, the results of which we can see in many areas today. As the sanitary state of Lancashire came to match that of London, Rawlinson estimated that more than 10,000 lives were being saved every year. And when the Cotton Famine ended, he was able to report

> the public works in the Lancashire towns have benefited trade by giving 400 miles of road for tracts of mud; and they have further added to local means of health and pleasure by providing public parks and recreation grounds, which otherwise might not have been formed . . . There are well-paved and clean river courses where all was previously swamp, mud and garbage.[9]

Waterworks were completed at Burnley, Manchester, Oswaldtwistle, Ashton, Bolton and Wigan; public parks were laid out or extended at Oldham, Preston, Bolton and Blackburn; cemeteries at Bury, Manchester and Chorley, built away from the towns and looking more like parks than traditional graveyards, set a standard that was to be copied throughout the county. There were also less tangible, but equally important benefits. The use of government loans for town improvements soon became widespread and speeded the development of urban Britain in the years after the Cotton Famine. The Second Reform Act of 1867, which gave the vote to ordinary householders, would hardly have been possible but for the responsible behaviour of the cotton workers during the years of acute deprivation.

In Miller Park, Preston, is a statue to Lord Derby, who laboured hard during the Cotton Famine to bring relief to the needy, and who was also responsible for introducing the Second Reform Bill into Parliament. Among those who contributed to its cost, were some 20,787 working folk from the cotton towns.

## Handloom weaving

Why some houses in the older parts of most Lancashire towns and villages have their ground floors above street level puzzles many people. It does seem odd that they were built in such a way that those who went to live there had to climb four, five and sometimes as many as eight stone steps to reach their front doors. There is, of course, a good reason. At pavement level there were (and sometimes still are) narrow windows that let light into cellars. And cellars for thousands of handloom weavers, especially those working at the finer end of the trade, were once the favoured places of work. The weavers needed light, but more importantly they needed to throw their shuttles in an atmosphere sufficiently moist to prevent the threads from breaking. In April, 1821, when Blackburn experienced 'the most dreadful storm ever remembered,' the *Blackburn Standard* reported that 'the workshops of the weavers (principally in cellars) were inundated, burying the looms, materials &c in the water.'

Weavers' cottages are of several types, but probably all the survivors were built between 1790 and 1840, by which time the powerloom was rapidly gaining ground, especially at the coarser end of the trade. Better methods of sizing – stiffening the warps with paste – were also coming into use, eventually freeing the weavers from the necessity of working in their damp cellars. Loomshops built at ground-level, originally with earth floors, were widely used, but it seems that only in the wettest parts of Lancashire, in towns like Haslingden and Colne, which specialised in the coarser kinds of cloth, did the cotton weavers work, as did their colleagues in the wool, silk and linen trades, on the top floors of their homes. Occasionally, a manufacturer would build a small factory and fill it with handlooms, but most weavers worked alone, though rarely in complete isolation. Good examples have survived both of rows of domestic weavers' cottages and of colonies extending over several streets.

Club Houses is a name common to several such developments, one of the largest of which has survived intact at Horwich. It grew during the early years of the nineteenth century into a settlement of fifty houses and a stroll along Church Street, Duncan Street and Nelson Street gives the visitor an excellent feel of the original character. That many subterranean weavers worked here is obvious from the steps and pavement-level windows, but there are indications that groundfloor loomshops were used as well.

Blackburn has retained many of its weavers' cottages, the group of sixty above the town at West View and Revidge Road being well worth a visit. Their construction by the Mile End Subscription Building Society occupied the years 1817 to 1830 and while not all the houses are identical, their semicircular, arched doors give the rows a striking unity. The 1851 census returns show that the colony had 279 people, with most of them employed working at the loom.

The traveller entering Longridge by the Preston road can hardly fail to notice a large red plaque on the side of a bus shelter. It was put there in 1981 to mark the completion of the town's first 'improvement area' covering thirty terraced houses in two rectangular blocks. Disappointingly, the inscription is silent about the history of the property, for what we see today is one of the best-preserved handloom weaving colonies in the county. Newtown, as it was originally known, took shape between 1825 and 1840 at the behest of Dr Edmund Eccles, who lived in the largest house (much elaborated in 1911) fronting the main road. Doctor's Row reminds us of his unusual achievement, but Pancake Row has become Lodge View, and Pump Street, which divides the two blocks and is a reminder of the original water supply, has been transformed into Southern Court. More than 200 people worked in Newtown and though most were weavers, there were two nailers who repaired the looms and also a household that prepared warps. One building was used as a warehouse. The Newtown weavers had ground-floor loomshops next to their living quarters. These could be entered either from the front or rear, but not from the living room.

Some of the streets near the centre of Longridge have weavers' houses from an earlier period and Club Row (6 to 44 Higher Lane) is famous for being the oldest to have been erected by a building society. The twenty dwellings, which took shape between 1793 to 1804, are unusual in alternating their fronts and backs to the road and being separated by passages. Each house had a cellar loomshop. Club Houses in King Street have steps to the front doors and blocked-up loomshop windows at pavement level.

Another row of twenty-six well-preserved cottages can be admired in Union Street, Leyland; and as the name suggests, this was the work of a local building society. Construction began in the 1790s, with blocks of dwellings being added over the next fifteen years or so as the money came in. Leyland people refer to the row as the 'step houses', for here one climbs up to the front doors and down to the cellars. The cottages are of hand-made brick, but the much-worn steps are of gritstone. Two of the houses – No. 22 and No. 48 – have fire marks that were fixed above their doors in 1803 by the Royal Exchange Insurance Company. They are probably unique in being found on a building of this kind and they provide evidence of the trade's prosperity at that time.

An irregular frontage is often the sign of a former handloom weaver's cottage which had a loomshop at ground level. There are several patterns. Triplet windows to one side of the door provide a common variation throughout the old cotton districts. A good example can be seen at New Row in Knowle Green. Coal Hey, close to the centre of Haslingden, had a loomshop on the top floor which was reached by an outside staircase.

A rare example of a handloom weaving factory can be seen at Horncliffe between Rawtenstall and Edenfield. It had thirty six looms when it was offered for sale in 1799 along with a small spinning factory at Topwood, above Ramsbottom.

## The great and famous

Everyone learns something at school of four Lancastrians – John Kay, James Hargreaves, Richard Arkwright and Samuel Crompton – whose revolutionary inventions brought about the great changes in the eighteenth-century cotton trade. How well have they been remembered?

FIGURE 129. Club Row, Longridge, is made up of twenty handloom weavers' cottages built between 1793 and 1804 by a group of local people. Each house had a cellar loomshop at the rear.
(Photograph courtesy of Lancashire County Library, Headquarters Local Studies Collection)

John Kay, who was born on a farm at Park, near Ramsbottom, in 1704, and died at the age of 76 in France, invented the fly shuttle in 1733, thus enabling a handloom weaver to produce far more cloth than had previously been thought possible. Bury early claimed him as its own and in 1908, with money provided by Harry Whitehead, one of Kay's descendants, laid out a memorial garden in the town centre. Four bronze panels on the sides of a large domed monument depict Kay, hand- and powerlooms, and also give details of his career and of his other inventions. From 1877 until 1974, a life-size statue of Kay looked over the town from the top of Robert Hall's loom-making works, but when the business was wound up, it was taken to Barnsley by another of the inventor's family and displayed in the entrance to a textile engineering company. Kay in Pre-Raphaelite guise can be seen escaping from anti-patent opponents in Ford Maddox Brown's series of wall paintings in Manchester Town Hall. Attempts in the 1950s to turn Kay's birthplace into a museum failed through lack of funds and the building's historic link was in danger of being forgotten until 1991, when Bury Metropolitan Council placed a plaque over the front door.

James Hargreaves (1720–1778) was born in Oswaldtwistle, worked there for Robert ('Parsley') Peel and in about 1764 completed an eight-spindle jenny in the stone cottage that is now Stanhill Post Office. A plaque on the wall records the achievement, though the

FIGURE 130. Arkwright House, Preston, now renovated. (Photograph courtesy of Lancashire County Library, Preston Local Studies Collection)

jenny depicted is of an improved version of the machine. Hargreaves later moved to Lower Ramsclough (close to the present Blackburn–Haslingden road) and began to build jennies in a barn. Fears that the invention would put hand spinners out of work prompted a mob to destroy the frames of about twenty machines and all the inventor's tools. Later that year (1768) Hargreaves moved to Nottingham. Lancashire's first textile machinery workshop has long been in ruins. When the borough of Hyndburn was formed by the merger of Oswaldtwistle and other towns, the new authority included a spinning jenny in its coat of arms.

Richard Arkwright was born in Preston in 1732, and having worked as a barber in Bolton, he returned to the town with the Warrington clockmaker, John Kay, in 1768 to carry out secret experiments in roller

FIGURE 131. In 1862, some thirty-five years after his death, Bolton remembered Samuel Crompton, inventor of the spinning mule, and placed a statue in Nelson Square. By then the number of mule spindles at work throughout the world ran in to many millions. (Photograph courtesy of Lancashire County Library Headquarters, Local Studies Collection)

spinning and to complete the first successful frame. Arkwright rented a first-floor room in the school master's house at the bottom of Stoneygate, a fact remembered when the building became the Arkwright Arms public house in the 1850s. In later years the building was a lodging house and was then turned into workshops. The house was saved from demolition in the late 1970s.

The passing years have been kinder to Samuel Crompton (1753–1827), whose statue, unveiled in September 1862, looks down on Nelson Square in Bolton, where he spent most of his life. On the outskirts of the town, a little beyond Crompton Way, one can also see the inventor's birthplace in Firwood Fold and visit Hall i' th' Wood, now a folk museum, in which he secretly built his first spinning mule. Darwen, where Crompton spent the years 1812–17 as an unsuccessful bleacher, has marked its link with the inventor by affixing a plaque on Low Hill House, near Bury Fold.

The most handsomely remembered of the cotton trade's other great innovators has been John Mercer (1791–1866), the self-made industrial chemist, who gave the English language the verb to mercerise: the process, developed in 1850, by which fabrics are treated with caustic alkali under tension to give them greater strength and lustre. Great Harwood, his native town, has the Mercer Hall and a memorial clock tower topped by a mortar and pestle. The family mansion and grounds at Clayton-le-Moors, have become Mercer Park.

Several cotton men have been cast in bronze or carved in marble. 'Honest John' Fielden (1784–1849), the Radical reformer who, though a large employer, fought to cut the long hours worked by factory children, now broods in a leafy park bower at Todmorden, the town he did so much to create. Close to Blackburn Town Hall, William Henry Hornby, who took more interest in the welfare of his workers than many of his nineteenth-century contemporaries, owes his reincarnation to one of his employees. John Margarison so enjoyed the fifty years he spent as a roller coverer at Brookhouse Mill that he left instructions in his will for a 10ft 9in statue of his former boss. It cost

FIGURE 132. The
clock tower in
Town Hall Square
is Great Harwood's
memorial to John
Mercer (1791–
1866), the self-
taught industrial
chemist who, as the
inscription says, in-
vented 'the world-
wide process of
mercerisation as ap-
plied to cotton and
other fabrics'. The
tower, completed
in 1903, is topped
by a weather-vane
incorporating a
mortar and pestle.
(Photograph court-
esy of Lancashire
County Library,
Accrington Local
Studies Collection)

£3,000 and was unveiled in 1912 (see figure 46). The working classes of Bolton were quick to remember J. F. Fielding (1850–1894), for many years secretary of both the spinners' union and the town's trades council. Thousands subscribed when a fund was set up pay for a statue of a much-loved townsman. It stands in Queen's Park. And in Victoria Park, Haslingden, a clock tower stands to the memory of Alderman W. H. Wilkinson (1850–1906), a weavers' leader who, as a plaque tells us, served his members 'with zeal and ability.'

## Saved for posterity

Lancashire was slow to preserve relics of its great industry and, by the time the significance of cotton's contribution to the nation's greatness was recognised, much had been lost for ever.

The county's first museum curators were anxious to show people who were unlikely to travel very far a range of artifacts from distant countries. Many of these exhibits were donated by wealthy cotton men with a taste for foreign travel, but who were blind to the historic value of machinery in their own mills. The industry was already old before anyone thought seriously of saving items from it and it is only because of a strange quirk of fortune that some of Arkwright's own machines, including carding engines and spinning frames, have come down to us. So rapid were technical advances in the late eighteenth and early nineteenth centuries that equipment was regularly scrapped and re-placed. But at Cromford, the Arkwright mills continued to use original wooden-framed machines long after other firms had thrown them out. In 1883, when Oldham decided to stage an industrial exhibition, the Arkwright company loaned the town a collection of its eighteenth-century machines and these later formed the nucleus of a private museum at the works of Platt Brothers, a leading maker of textile machinery. In the 1970s, the Platt collection was transferred to the company's research plant in Helmshore.

At Bolton, the other great spinning town, a local philanthropist, Dr S. T. Chadwick paid for the building in 1885 of a museum in Queen's Park. Because of the corporation's support of archaeological expeditions to Egypt, Bolton received many excavated items for the Chadwick Museum, but it also acquired a number of textile machines, including some from Cromford and part of a mule that had belonged to Samuel Crompton. When a new museum opened in the town centre in 1939, Egyptology had pride of place, and the textile display went to the Tong Moor branch library, where it was on view until 1993. It is now in store along with a large collection of early twentieth-century Bolton-made machinery, including an unused self-actor mule and a steam engine.

One millowner who was conscious of cotton's legacy and who was determined to give the public some permanent record of it was Thomas Boys Lewis (1869–1942) of Blackburn. Unusually, he combined cotton spinning with a very wide range of interests, and having sold his business during the boom that followed the First World War, he stayed in his native town doing good works. In 1938, he set up and endowed the Lewis Textile Museum in the centre of Blackburn. His aim, he said, was to provide an adequate memorial to the great inventors who revolutionised the textile industries and in doing so affected the trade and social structure of the whole world. Lewis looked back to the introduction of the famous machines, but since no originals had survived, he commissioned working copies, which he set in rooms furnished in period style. The novel approach proved popular and thousands of visitors flocked to the museum to see cotton spun and woven as it had been before the coming of factories. In recent years, later machines, including Blackburn-built power looms, have been added to the reconstructed spinning jennies (Hargreaves's original and the improved version), a cut-down mule and the models showing the principles of Arkwright's water frame. There is also an original handloom, though it was brought from Scotland, no survivor from the thousands once at work in Lancashire having been found. The Lewis Museum has a large collection of costumes and textile samples, which can be seen by appointment.

The idea of a working textile mill had to wait until the cotton industry was in terminal decline. The water-powered Higher Mill at Helmshore, where woollen cloth had been fulled and finished since 1789, closed in 1967 and following efforts by the Helmshore Local History Society, it was scheduled an ancient monument and taken over by a charitable trust. Room was then found for the Platt collection, from which a water frame and a carding engine were put into working order. Higher Mill passed into the control of Lancashire County Council, which acquired the adjoining hard waste spinning mill and much of its twentieth-century equipment, including carding engines and mules.

The development of the Helmshore mill museums has been complemented by preservation at Burnley of Queen Street Mill, a complete weaving shed of Lancashire looms powered by a steam engine.

Helmshore was followed by Quarry Bank at Styal, near Manchester Airport, where the well-preserved industrial settlement that developed around a water-powered spinning mill of 1784, has been turned into both a working museum (spinning mules, power and handlooms) and a study centre with a growing archive. The National Trust owns Quarry Bank Mill, Styal village and the surrounding country park and the Quarry Bank Mill Trust, which runs the museum, continues a commendable restoration programme, which has included the installation of a huge waterwheel very similar to one that drove the mill.

The Museum of Science & Industry in Manchester has a large collection of working cotton machines, ranging from an original Arkwright spinning frame, believed to have been built as a prototype in the 1770s, to high-speed equipment developed in the second half of the twentieth century. Staff take raw cotton and pass it through all the stages needed to produce cloth. The museum's aim is to tell the story of the city's wide range of industrial and commercial activities, not least its busy years as the cotton trade's greatest *entrepôt*. With this in mind, the collection of samples of the many types of cloth sold in the numerous warehouses has a high priority. A merchant's office is another feature reflecting Manchester's importance as a trading centre. An extensive archive is constantly being enlarged.

Manchester is also the home of the National Museum of Labour History, where the visitor can see a wide spread of exhibits from the cotton industry: trade union banners, emblems and notices, mill and trade tokens, workers' tools, merchants' samples; photographs and cartoons and a medal struck to mark the passing of the Ten-Hours Bill. The extensive archive includes pamphlets on the industry and early Labour Party correspondence with thirty-three textile trade unions in Lancashire.

The Liverpool Life Museum has a small section devoted to the now-vanished Cotton Exchange, the centrepiece being the Brokers' Ring. This is a circular barrier of wood and brass, about ten feet in diameter, behind which the brokers stood while a clerk inside relayed their deals to a colleague on a gallery above them. The second clerk wrote the prices on a blackboard for the benefit of newcomers. In the Whitaker Park Museum at Rawtenstall, the visitor can gain some idea of Victorian factory life by studying a typical set of rules and punishments from the 1840s.

> Any Weaver or other Person neglecting work during the time the Steam Engine is going, or Reading, or Sewing, shall for every such offence forfeit Twopence.

> Any Person smoking Tobacco or any other ingredients, or having Gunpowder or other combustibles upon the Premises or buying or having Ale or Spirituous Liqueurs in the Mill or Premises shall be subject to be instantly discharged.[10]

A Burnley-made powerloom and tacklers' tools are among items in the local industries annex at Towneley Hall, which has one of the few oil paintings inspired by the cotton trade. It depicts the now-vanished spinning mill and calico printing works at Lowerhouse in the 1830s.

The Bacup Natural History Society's museum has a working power-loom and a bell from a local mill.

The cotton trade has been well served by the North West Sound Archive, established in 1979 and now based at Clitheroe Castle. Among the thousands of recordings are not only the once-familiar sounds of looms and mules and carding engines, but also the voices of men and women who tended them. In the many dialects of the cotton towns, the workers tell of the strict discipline of factory life – the six o'clock hooter and the loss of pay for late arrival – but often stress the companionship most of them found. Several reminiscences take us back to the weaving sheds and spinning rooms of the Victorian era; others include stories passed down from previous generations and provide links with even earlier periods. Edith Smith recalls being struck by a shuttle that flew from a loom at Hoyle's mill in Summerseat. When she was taken into the office, she thought she was going to be given a glass of brandy, but had to make do with a whiff of *sal volatile*. From Mary Donaldson come stories not only of her own experiences in a Manchester factory, but also descriptions passed down by her ancestors of the Peterloo Massacre in 1819. The Sound Archive has also collected trade and technical terms and expressions and these, along with the recordings, are available on loan or may be heard at both Clitheroe and the outstation in the Manchester Record Office.

To record the loss of hundreds of superbly-built steam engines is perhaps the saddest task of anyone who undertakes a survey of the cotton industry's demise. But by good fortune, what is said to be the largest working mill engine in the world was saved by enthusiasts when the Ellenroad Ring Mill, near Milnrow, was demolished. Volunteers now give guided tours of the 3,000 horsepower engine and its coal-fired boiler house. Other preserved engines are at Queen's Street Mill, Burnley, Bancroft Mill, Barnoldswick and at Wigan Pier.

## Reminders of a great industry

As well the things already listed, the cotton industry left behind many lesser, or less obvious, reminders of its vigorous years. Every industrial town and village has streets named after cotton magnates and their families, though research is needed to discover who they were. Accrington has a group of stone terraces with a surprisingly romantic history. They were built on land belonging to Frederick Steiner (1787–1869), a Frenchman who settled in the district and made his fortune after discovering a cheap method of printing cotton cloth in a once popular colour called Turkey red. Frederick Street and Steiner Street provide a double reminder of the industrial chemist, whose daughters, Lina and Emma, became society beauties and close friends of Edward VII. They,

FIGURE 133.
Though Ellenroad
Mill near Milnrow
has gone, its huge
steam engine has
been preserved and
is run for visitors.
The 3,000-horse-
power engine was
installed in 1892. (Il-
lustration courtesy
of the Ellenroad
Trust)

too, have streets named after them. Bolton, appropriately, has its Mule
Street and there is a street named after the spinning jenny in Leigh,
which claims Thomas Highs, a native of the town, as the true inventor.

Flying Shuttle public houses provide hospitality in Bury and Farnworth
and one can also drink at the Spinning Jenny in either Accrington or
Leigh. Numerous Cotton Trees have blossomed, Spinners and Weavers
Arms are often met with, and crofters, carders and spindlemakers live
on in pub signs. Arkwright's Ale House in Bolton reminds us of the
inventor's early years in the town. The Sun Mill Inn at Chadderton
takes its name from a mill built in 1860 and run by working men. The
Clog and Shawl, at Rochdale, commemorates the mill girls' traditional
dress and The Engine Inn at Cark owes it name to the Boulton and
Watt 'fire engine' installed in 1786 at the village spinning mill.

The weather vane of St John's Church in Blackburn takes the form
of a shuttle, an apt symbol to top a building closely linked to many
of the town's first merchants and manufacturers. Todmorden Town
Hall, built in the style of the Parthenon, boasts an imposing pediment
incorporating a group of pseudo-classical figures holding an engine
crankshaft, a box of spindles and a bale of cotton. At a similar height
on the former Technical School in Blackburn are other figures busy
at the loom and spinning wheel. Rossendale is the only local authority
with a Town Hall that was built as a stock exchange. It opened as the
Exchange Club in 1876 and was 'fitted up regardless of cost' by brokers
who traded principally in the shares of Lancashire's joint-stock cotton
companies. Climb the wide stone staircase in Accrington Public Library
and you will come face to face with the town's coat-of-arms in coloured

glass and including a roll of cloth printed with the parsley leaf pattern that set the Peels on the road to fame and fortune. Another stained-glass window in the Wagon and Horses public house at Westhoughton depicts the burning down by rioters in 1812 of a local powerloom factory.

Darwen has placed a number of industrial relics in the open air. Painted in cheerful colours, a 450-hp steam engine and its 16-ft flywheel, catch the eye in Bolton Road. The machine, built in 1905, drove Bowling Green Mill. At the opposite approach to Darwen, a powerloom is one of the items in an industrial garden.

Near the television mast on Winter Hill above Horwich stands a lone pillar from a cotton spinning room. This is the second Scotsman's Stump, a memorial to a pedlar murdered nearby in 1838. The first 'stump' was of wood, but when this disintegrated, local people, who were fighting to keep open moorland footpaths, set up the present memorial in 1912.

If you pass Textile Hall in Bury, note on the front wall the excellent carvings of a powerloom and a ring frame. The hall, opened in 1894, had unusual origins. Union leaders decided to build a place of their own after finding it almost impossible to rent offices in the town because of the noise made by the clogs of visiting mill workers. Spinners' Hall opened in Bolton in 1911 is another elegant building which reflects the strength of the unions.

Of the cotton mansions, Woodfold Park at Mellor, near Blackburn, is the most spectacular despite its having been allowed to become a largely roofless shell. It was built in a large landscaped park between 1796 and 1800 for the town's leading merchant, Henry Sudell. For his architect, Sudell engaged James Wyatt, who designed a house with a nine-bay front and a central portico supported on four pillars. At Sunderland Point is the grave of 'Poor Samboo, A Faithful Negro, who Attending his Master from the West Indies,' died on his arrival in 1736. The epitaph was composed in 1796 by the Rev. James Watson, whose younger brothers invested heavily in Lancaster slave ships. Some of the money made from slaving found its way into cotton mills; and in Brookhouse Church, near Caton, one can read the memorial to Thomas Hodgson, 'for many years an eminent merchant in Liverpool and founder of the cotton and silk works in this, his native place.'

Graveyards have many reminders of the cotton trade, though space must restrict us to three neglected inventors. A stone at Altham informs the visitor that John and Ellen Hacking 'invented and made the first carding engine and turned it by hand. They carded cotton-wool for their neighbours in Huncoat in the year 1772.' At Tockholes is the tomb of John Osbaldeston, inventor of the weft fork, a simple but vital device, which stopped a powerloom when a thread broke in the weaving. Osbaldeston died in a workhouse in 1862, but not before composing his own epitaph in which he described himself as 'the dupe of false friends and the victim of misplaced confidence.' Osbaldeston had in mind James Bullough, co-founder of the Accrington textile machinery firm of Howard and Bullough. Bullough made a fortune, as did his son, Sir George Bullough, who bought the Scottish island of Rhum. There he built Kinloch Castle and, on the seashore facing the Atlantic, a mausoleum in the style of a Grecian temple.

Let us end where we began. If we look to the west from Jeffrey Hill, we see Blackpool and the other holiday resorts which were as much the creation of the cotton trade as the mill towns themselves. And though east Lancashire no longer sends its entire population to the coast each summer, it still observes the cotton town holidays, a tradition that will probably puzzle future generations when all the mills are gone.

# Glossary of technical terms

| | |
|---|---|
| *Automatic loom* | A loom where the supply of weft is replenished automatically. |
| *Barragon* | A light corded cotton for summer wear. |
| *Blowing* | Process where cotton fibres are cleaned and smoothed in preparation for carding. |
| *Broadcloth* | Best plain-woven and dressed woollen cloth woven on a double width. |
| *Camblet* | Originally camel or goat hair textile. Later of wool and hair, silk and hair, plain or twilled. |
| *Calico* | Cotton cloth with patterns printed in one or more colours; the name comes from Calicut, a port on the west coast of Malabar, south of Madras. |
| *Card* | Machine for disentangling and ranging cotton fibres |
| *Chintz* | Printed or painted calico. |
| *Cop* | The conical ball of cotton or any yarn wound on the spinning frame; a tube for carrying yarn. |
| *Corduroy* | An English word, although supposedly of French origin, for fustian with a corded pile. |
| *Count* | The measure of yarn by length and weight, stating how many hanks of a given length will weigh a pound. The higher the count the finer the yarn. |
| *Coutil* | A French species of jean but lighter in weight; a twilled cloth. |
| *Denim* | Originally a wool serge, later a twilled cotton used for work clothes. |
| *Diaper* | A linen, cotton or mixed fabric woven with a small raised diamond pattern. |
| *Dimity* | A stout white cotton fabric, plain or twilled with a raised pattern on one side, sometimes printed. |
| *Dowlas* | A coarse, strong calico. |
| *Drabbet* | A drab, whitey-brown twilled linen or fustian, particularly used for smocks. |

| | |
|---|---|
| *Drugget* | A coarse woollen fabric, often with a linen or cotton warp, much used for floor and table coverings. |
| *Duck* | A strong, untwilled linen or cotton, lighter or finer than canvas, used for small sails and men's outerwear. |
| *Dyeing* | Impregnating cloth with colouring substances. |
| *Fustian* | A coarse, stout cotton, originally linen and by the eighteenth century a cotton/linen mixture. |
| *Finishing* | A series of operations (including bleaching, dyeing and printing). |
| *Gingham* | A stout cloth with a woven chequered pattern, originally linen but later cotton. |
| *Grey cloth* | Unbleached cotton or linen cloth. |
| *Grinding* | Giving new points to the teeth of the carding wires by grinding with an emery band or wheel. |
| *Herringbone* | A fustian with a woven pattern like the bone of a herring, that is in crossed parallel lines. |
| *Jacquard loom* | Loom fitted with harness consisting of cards, card cylinder, needles, hooks and cords, which control the warp in weaving. |
| *Jean* | A twilled cotton fustian, thick and strong, later a twilled sateen. |
| *Jenny* | Name given to Hargreaves' spinning machine − a corruption of the word 'engine'. |
| *Linsey-woolsey* | A coarse mixture of wool and linen. |
| *Moleskin* | A strong, soft, fine-piled cotton fustian, the surface of which is 'shaved' before dyeing. |
| *Mule* | Cotton spinning machine invented by Samuel Crompton, so named becaue it combines the roller-drawing principle of Arkwright's water frame with the carriage-drawing of Hargreaves' jenny. |
| *Muslin* | A fine, thin, semi-transparent cotton. Originally any cloth made from superfine cotton yarns. |
| *Nankeen* | A plain, closely woven cotton, yellowish or buff colour. |
| *Outwork* | (or putting out system). System of organising production where merchant manufacturers employ people to produce work at home. |
| *Piece Goods* | Fabrics sold by the piece (definite length). |
| *Piecer* | The operative who mends the broken ends of thread in the spinning process. |
| *Piece work* | Payment by output rather than by the hour. |
| *Pillow* | A plain fustian with a four-leaved twill. |

| | |
|---|---|
| *Printing* | Applying patterns to cloth using a block, roller or screen. |
| *Rayon* | This name was chosen in 1924 by the National Retail Dry Goods Association of America for the new man-made fabric from regenerated cellulose, also known as artificial silk. |
| *Ring frame* | Spinning machine on which the spindle revolves within a ring. |
| *Roving* | The sliver after it has been brought to fineness prior to spinning. |
| *Sateen* | A cotton textile with a satin face. |
| *Scutching* | *See* blowing. |
| *Self-acting mule* | The mule frame which automatically performs drawing, twisting, winding on and copping motions. |
| *Serge* | A hard-wearing twilled material of worsted, or with the warp of worsted, the weft of linen. |
| *Shirting* | Common grey-cloth, woven 36–45 inches long and cut into piece lengths 36 yards long. |
| *Shuttle* | Spool carrier in the loom. |
| *Size* | Substance used for stiffening and binding fabrics. |
| *Spinning* | Drawing and twisting fibres to make yarns or threads. |
| *Stripping* | Clearing cards of matted fibres. |
| *Thickset* | A stout, twilled cotton fustian with a short, very close nap. |
| *Ticking* | A strong, hard, linen or cotton canvas from which bed ticks were made. |
| *Throstle* | A bobbin and fly spinning machine. |
| *Velveteen* | An imitation silk velvet, with a cotton fustian twill-weave backing and a cotton or silk pile. |
| *Union* | A stout material, being a mixture of linen and cotton, much dressed and stiffened. |
| *Warp* | Threads which lie lengthways in the cloth. |
| *Warping* | Winding warp onto the beam. |
| *Water frame* | Arkwright's spinning invention. |
| *Weft* | Threads which lie widthwise in the cloth. |
| *Winding* | Making bobbins of yarn. |
| *Yarn* | A spun thread. |

# Notes

## Notes to Chapter 1

1. I am grateful to the contributors to this volume for comments they made on an earlier draft of this chapter.

2. John K. Walton, *Lancashire: A Social History, 1558–1939* (Manchester University Press, 1987), p. 25.

3. A. P. Wadsworth and J. de L. Mann, *The Cotton Trade and Industrial Lancashire, 1600–1780* (Manchester University Press, 1931), p. 3.

4. E. Baines, *History of the Cotton Manufacture in Great Britain* (Manchester, 1935).

5. G. W. Daniels, *The Early English Cotton Industry* (Manchester University Press, 1920), pp. 26–8; Wadsworth and Mann, *The Cotton Trade*, p. 171; M. M. Edwards, *The Growth of the British Cotton Trade* (Manchester University Press, 1967), p. 5; J. K. Walton, 'Proto-industrialisation and the First Industrial Revolution: The Case of Lancashire', in P. Hudson, *Regions and Industries* (Cambridge University Press, 1989), pp. 41–67.

6. G. H. Tupling, *The Economic History of Rossendale* (Manchester University Press, 1927), p. 203.

7. J. K. Walton, 'Proto-industrialisation and the First Industrial Revoluion: The Case of Lancashire', in P. Hudson (ed.), *Regions and Industries* (Cambridge University Press).

8. Daniels, *The Early English*, pp. 61–4; Wadsworth and Mann, *The Cotton Trade*, pp. 232–43.

9. Wadsworth and Mann, *The Cotton Trade*, pp. 73, 78.

10. Walton, *Social History*, p. 63.

11. Edwards, *The Growth*, p. 107.

12. Wadsworth and Mann, *The Cotton Trade*, pp. 233–6.

13. Wadsworth and Mann, *The Cotton Trade*.

14. S. D. Chapman, *The Cotton Industry and The Industrial Revolution* (Macmillan, 1987, 2nd ed.), p. 12.

15. Wadsworth and Mann, *The Cotton Trade*, p. 91.

16. Wadsworth and Mann, *The Cotton Trade*, pp. 71–91.

17. J. Hoppit, 'The Use and Abuse of Credit in the Eighteenth Century', in N. McKendrick and R. B. Outhwaite (eds), *Business Life and Public Policy* (Cambridge University Press, 1984), pp. 91–2.

18. Wadsworth and Mann, *The Cotton Trade*, pp. 248–9; B. L. Anderson, 'The Attorney and the Early Capital Market in Lancashire during the Eighteenth Century', in F. Crouzet (ed.), *Capital Formation in the Industrial Revolution* (Methuen, 1972), pp. 252–5.

19. Anderson, 'The Attorney'; B. L. Anderson, 'Aspects of Capital and Credit in Lancashire During the Eighteenth Century' (unpublished MA thesis, University of Liverpool, 1966); P. Hudson, *The Genesis of Industrial Capital: A Study of the West Riding Wool Textile Industry, c. 1750–1850* (Cambridge University Press, 1986), pp. 211–34.

20. Arthur Young, *A Six Months Tour Through the North of England*, vol. 3 (London, W. Strahan, 1771), p. 163.

21. Walton, *Social History*, p. 67.

22. Daniels, *The Early English*, pp. xxviii–ix, 3–6.

23. Daniels, *The Early English*, pp. 20–3; Wadsworth and Mann, *The Cotton Trade*, p. 150; P. O'Brien, T. Griffiths and P. Hunt, 'Political Components of the Industrial Revolution: Parliament and the English Cotton Textile Industry, 1660–1774', *Economic History Review*, second series, 44 (1991), pp. 395–423.

24. Walton, *Social History*, p. 67.

25. D. A. Farnie, *The English Cotton Industry and the World Market, 1815–1896* (Clarendon Press, 1979).

26. B. Lemire, *Fashion's Favourite: The Cotton Trade and Consumer in Britain* (Oxford University Press, 1991), pp. 3–42.

27. B. R. Mitchell, *British Historical Statistics* (Cambridge University Press, 1988), pp. 330–1.

28. P. Deane and H. J. Habakkuk, 'The Take-Off in Britain', in W. Rostow (ed.), *The Economics of the Take-Off into Self Sustained Growth* (Cambridge University Press, 1963), pp. 77–80.

29. R. Davis, *The Industrial Revolution and British Overseas Trade* (Leicester University Press, 1979), p. 65.

30. Edwards, *The Growth*, pp. 243, 247.

31. The Calicoe Acts of 1721 . . . forbad the wearing of printed calicoes, though Lancashire was not subject to them.

32. B. Lemire, *Fashion's Favourite: The Cotton Trade*

and the Consumer in Britain, 1660–1800 (Oxford University Press, 1979), pp. 3–42.

33. Lemire, Fashion's Favourite, pp. 51–2.

34. R. L. Hills, 'Hargreaves, Arkwright and Crompton, why three inventions?', Textile History, 10 (1979); S. Chapman, The Cotton Industry in the Industrial Revolution (Macmillan, 1987).

35. Victor C. Clark, History of Manufactures, vol. 1, 1607–1860 (Carnegie Institute of Washington, 1929), p. 272.

36. Chapman, The Cotton Industry.

37. Davis, The Industrial Revolution, p. 14.

38. Edwards, The Growth, p. 63.

39. D. C. Coleman, The Domestic System in Industry (Historical Association, 1967), pp. 4–7.

40. Marglin, 'What do Bosses Do?', Review of Radical Political Economy, 6 (1974), pp. 60–112; Oliver E. Williamson, 'The Organisation of Work: A Comparative Institutional Assessment', Journal of Economic Behaviour and Organisation, 1 (1980), pp. 5–38; H. Medick, 'The Proto-industrial Family Economy: The Structural Function of Household and Family During the Transition from Peasant Society to Industrial Capitalism', Social History, 1 (1976), pp. 291–316.

41. E. P. Thompson, 'Time Work Discipline and Industrial Capitalism', Past and Present, 38 (1967).

42. Wadsworth and Mann, The Cotton Trade, pp. 395–401.

43. John Styles, 'Embezzlement, Industry and the Law in England, 1500–1800', in M. Berg, P. Hudson and M. Sonenscher (eds), Manufacture in Town and Country (Cambridge University Press, 1983).

44. Williamson, 'The Organisation of Work', pp. 5–38.

45. K. L. Wallwork, 'The Calico Printing Industry of Lancastria in the 1840s', Transactions of the Institute of British Geographers, 45 (1968), p. 144.

46. Walton, Social History, p. 105.

47. Walton, Social History, pp. 109–10. G. Timmins, The Last Shift (Manchester University Press, 1993).

48. D. Bythell, The Handloom Weavers (Cambridge University Press, 1968), p. 254.

49. J. S. Lyons, 'Vertical Integration of the British Cotton Industry, 1825–1850', Journal of Economic History, 45 (1985), pp. 419–26. See also Timmins, Last Shift.

50. S. D. Chapman, 'The Arkwright Mills', Industrial Archaeology Review, 6 (1981), pp. 5–27.

51. Katrina Honeyman, Origins of Enterprise: Business Leadership in the Industrial Revolution (Manchester University Press, 1982), p. 61.

52. G. W. Daniels, 'Samuel Crompton's Census of the Cotton Industry in 1811', Economic Journal, Economic History Supplement II (1933), pp. 107–11.

53. H. D. Fong, Triumph of the Factory System (Tientsin, China, Chihli Press, 1932), p. 25; V. A. C. Gatrell, 'Labour Power and the Size of Firms in Lancashire Cotton in the Second Quarter of the Nineteenth Century', Economic History Review, 30 (1977), p. 98.

54. Wallwork, 'Calico Printing', p. 144.

55. Farnie, The English Cotton Industry, p. 24.

56. Walton, Social History, p. 103.

57. F. F. Mendells, 'Proto-industrialisation: The First Phase of the Industrialisation Process', Journal of Economic History, 32 (1972), pp. 241–61.

58. Walton, 'Proto-industrialisation'.

59. Wadsworth and Mann, The Cotton Trade, p. 113.

60. C. Sabel and J. Zeitlin, 'Historical Alternatives to Mass Production: Politics, Markets and Technology in Nineteenth-Century Industrialisation', Past and Present, 108 (1985), pp. 133–76.

61. R. L. Hills, Power in the Industrial Revolution (Manchester University Press, 1970), p. 91; Owen Ashmore, The Industrial Archaeology of Lancashire (Plymouth: Latimer Trend & Co., 1969), p. 44.

62. Ashmore, Industrial Archaeology, p. 40; Mary B. Rose, The Gregs of Quarry Bank Mill: The Rise and Decline of a Family Firm, 1750–1914 (Cambridge University Press, 1986), p. 17.

63. J. D. Marshall and Michael Davies-Shiel, Industrial Archaeology of the Lake Counties (David and Charles, 1969), pp. 223–4.

64. Ashmore, Industrial Archaeology, p. 52.

65. A. E. Musson, 'Industrial Motive Power in the United Kingdom, 1800–1870', Economic History Review, second series, 29 (1976), pp. 415–39.

66. G. N. Von Tunzelmann, Steam Power and British Industrialisation to 1860 (Oxford University Press, 1978), pp. 116–60, 287; Ashmore, Industrial Archaeology, p. 52 .

67. H. B. Rodgers, 'The Lancashire Cotton Industry in 1840', Transactions of the Institute of British Geographers, 28 (1960), p. 138.

68. Farnie, The English Cotton Industry, pp. 45–77.

69. D. A. Farnie, 'The Textile Machine Making Industry and the World Market, 1870–1960', Business History, 32 (1990), pp. 150–65.

70. S. Chapman and J. Butt, 'The Cotton Industry, 1775–1856', in C. H. Feinstein and S. Pollard (eds), Studies in Capital Formation in the United Kingdom, 1750–1820 (Clarendon Press, 1988), pp. 124–5.

71. S. D. Chapman, 'Fixed Capital Formation in the British Cotton Industry, 1770–1815', Economic History Review, second series, 23 (1970).

72. K. Honeyman, The Origins of Enterprise: Business Leadership in the Industrial Revolution (Manchester University Press, 1982), pp. 62–3.

73. A. C. Howe, *The Cotton Masters, 1830–1860* (Clarendon Press, 1984).

74. Edwards, *The Growth*, pp. 182–215.

75. S. D. Chapman, 'Financial Constraints on the Growth of Firms in the Cotton Industry, 1790–1850', *Economic History Review*, second series, 32 (1979), pp. 50–69.

76. Julian Hoppit, *Risk and Failure in English Business, 1700–1800* (Cambridge University Press, 1987), pp. 76, 135; S. D. Chapman, *European Textile Printers in the Eighteenth Century: A Study of Peel and Overkampf* (Heinemann Educational Books, 1981), pp. 29–33.

77. Mary B. Rose, 'The Family Firm in British Business, 1780–1914', in M. W. Kirby and Mary B. Rose, *Business Enterprise in Modern Britain* (Routledge, 1994), pp. 66–7.

78. Midland Bank Archive, Preston Bank Records.

79. Rose, *The Gregs*, p. 344.

80. Wadsworth and Mann, *The Cotton Trade*.

81. Mary B. Rose, 'Social Policy and Business: Parish Apprenticeship and the Early Factory System, 1750–1834', *Business History*, 31 (1990), pp. 5–32.

82. 42 Geo 3 73, *An Act for the Preservation of the Health and Morals of Apprentices and Others Employed in Cotton Mills and Other Factories*.

83. Lancashire Record Office, QSO 2/153, Quarter Sessions Orders, 1784.

84. *Select Committee on the State of Children employed in the Manufactories of the United Kingdom*, p. 312, evidence of William David Evans, Manchester magistrate.

85. Westminster City Record Office, Vestry Minutes, St Clement Danes, 1797 and 1801.

86. R. Boyson, *The Ashworth Cotton Enterprise: The Rise and Fall of a Family Firm, 1818–80* (Oxford University Press, 1970), pp. 184–99.

87. S. J. Chapman, 'Some Policies of the Cotton Spinners' Trade Unions', *Economic Journal*, 10 (1900), pp. 468–9.

88. W. Lazonick, *Competitive Advantage on the Shopfloor* (Cambridge, MA.: Harvard University Press), p. 95.

89. Honeyman, *Origins of Enterprise*, pp. 87–114.

90. Timmins, *Last Shift*; John T. Swain, *Industry Before the Industrial Revolution: North East Lancashire, 1500–1640*, Chetham Society, 3rd series, 32 (1986), p. 147.

91. Daniels, 'Samuel Crompton's Census', p. 107; S. D. Chapman, *The Early Factory Masters* (David and Charles, 1967), p. 51; Edwards, *The Growth*, p. 5; C. Aspin, *James Hargreaves and the Spinning Jenny* (Helmshore Local History Society, 1964), p. 46.

92. Daniels, 'Samuel Crompton's Census', p. 108.

93. Manchester Central Library f. 677 c38, typescript of the Crompton Census.

94. Aspin, *James Hargreaves*, pp. 52–7; Chapman, *The Early Factory*, p. 60.

95. R. Lloyd-Jones and A. A. le Roux, 'The Size of Firms in the Cotton Industry, 1815–1841', *Economic History Review*, 33 (1980), pp. 72–82.

96. N. F. R Crafts and C. K. Harley, 'Output Growth and the British Industrial Revolution: A Restatement of the Crafts-Harley View', *Economic History Review*, second series, 45 (1992).

97. W. W. Rostow, *The Stages of Economic Growth* (Cambridge University Press, 1968), p. 25.

98. E. Hobsbawm, *Industry and Empire* (Penguin, 1968).

99. D. Landes, *Unbound Prometheus* (Cambridge University Press, 1969), p. 42.

100. P. Deane and W. A. Cole, *British Economic Growth, 1688–1959* (Cambridge University Press, 1962), pp. 191–2.

101. S. Pollard, *Peaceful Conquest* (Oxford University Press, 1981), p. 17.

102. Pollard, *Peaceful Conquest*, p. 25

## Further reading

S. D. Chapman, *The Cotton Industry and The Industrial Revolution* (Macmillan, 1987, 2nd ed.).

M. M. Edwards, *The Growth of the British Cotton Trade* (Manchester University Press, 1967).

D. A. Farnie, *The English Cotton Industry and the World Market, 1815–1896* (Clarendon Press, 1979).

R. L. Hills, *Power in the Industrial Revolution* (Manchester University Press, 1970).

S. Horrocks, *Lancashire Bibliography* (1991).

A. C. Howe, *The Cotton Masters, 1830–1860* (Oxford, Clarendon Press, 1984).

Mary B. Rose, *The Gregs of Quarry Bank Mill: The Rise and Decline of a Family Firm, 1750–1914* (Cambridge University Press, 1986).

G. Timmins, *The Last Shift* (Manchester University Press, 1993).

A. P. Wadsworth and J. de L. Mann, *The Cotton Trade and Industrial Lancashire, 1600–1780* (Manchester University Press, 1931).

John K. Walton, *Lancashire: A Social History, 1558–1939* (Manchester University Press, 1987).

# Notes to Chapter 2

1. S. D. Chapman, *The Cotton Industry in the Industrial Revolution* (Macmillan, 1972), p. 17.

2. A. P. Wadsworth and J. de L. Mann, *The Cotton Trade and Industrial Lancashire, 1600–1780* (Manchester University Press, 1931), pp. 29–48, 72–91.

3. A. Ure, *The Cotton Manufacture of Great Britain*, vol. 1 (London, Bohn's Scientific Library, 1861), pp. 226–8, 233–5; W. English, *The Textile Industry* (Longmans, 1969), pp. 1–9; R. Marsden, *Cotton Spinning: Its Development, Principles, and Practice* (London, 1886), pp. 195–9, 206–7; R. L. Hills, *Power in the Industrial Revolution* (Manchester University Press, 1970), pp. 17–19; H. Lemon, 'The Development of Hand Spinning Wheels', *Textile History*, 1 (1965), pp. 83–91; A. Rees, *The Cyclopaedia or, Universal Dictionary of Arts, Sciences, and Literature* (London, 1819), article on 'Cotton'.

4. R. Marsden, *Cotton Weaving: Its Development, Principles, and Practice* (London, 1895), pp. 250–3.

5. E. Baines, *History of the Cotton Manufacture in Great Britain* (1835, reprinted Cass, 1966), pp. 245–7.

6. Wadsworth and Mann, *Cotton Trade*, pp. 413–15.

7. Detailed consideration of Paul and Wyatt's invention is given in Baines, *Cotton Manufacture*, pp. 119–41; Wadsworth and Mann, *Cotton Trade*, pp. 419–48; Hills, *Power*, pp. 32–52.

8. C. Singer, *et al.* (eds), *A History of Technology*, vol. III (Clarendon Press, 1958), pp. 153–5; Baines, *Cotton Manufacture*, pp. 171–7.

9. See Rose, above, pp. 6–10

10. Wadsworth and Mann, *Cotton Trade*, pp. 415, 425–6.

11. Wadsworth and Mann, *Cotton Trade*, pp. 417–18. For more general discussion on this issue, see C. MacLeod, *Inventing the Industrial Revolution* (Cambridge University Press, 1988), pp. 159–73.

12. Wadsworth and Mann, *Cotton Trade*, pp. 14, 103–4, 326; A. Barlow, *The History and Principles of Weaving by Hand and by Power* (1884), pp. 217–28; English, *Textile Industry*, pp. 35–40.

13. Wadsworth and Mann, *Cotton Trade*, pp. 450, 452, 467, 470–1; English, *Textile Industry*, pp. 27–34.

14. Wadsworth and Mann, *Cotton Trade*, p. 462.

15. The annual average rose from 1.72 million lbs in the 1830s to reach 3.68 million lbs in the 1760s (Wadsworth and Mann, *Cotton Trade*, p. 170).

16. Wadsworth and Mann, *Cotton Trade*, p. 472; A. E. Musson, *The Growth of British Industry* (Batsford, 1978), p. 80; C. Aspin and S. D. Chapman, *James Hargreaves and the Spinning Jenny* (Helmshore Local History Society, 1964), p. 14; G. N. von Tunzelmann, 'Technical Progress During the Industrial Revolution', in R. Floud and D. McCloskey, *The Economic History of Britain*, 1 (Cambridge University Press, 1981), p. 146.

17. Wadsworth and Mann, *Cotton Trade*, pp. 415, 432; T. Griffiths, P. A. Hunt and P. K. O'Brien, 'Inventive Activity in the British Textile Industry, 1700–1800', *Journal of Economic History*, 52 (1992), p. 886.

18. For further discussion, see Baines, *Cotton Manufacture*, pp. 155–63; Ure, *Cotton Manufacture*, I, pp. 228–33; Wadsworth and Mann, *Cotton Trade*, pp. 476–82; English, *Textile Industry*, pp. 45–51; Aspin and Chapman, *Spinning Jenny*, pp. 42–6; H. Catling, *The Spinning Mule* (David and Charles, 1970), pp. 25–30; and Rees, *Cyclopaedia*, 'Cotton'.

19. Useful accounts of Arkwright's water-frame are to be found in Baines, *Cotton Manufacture*, pp. 147–55; Wadsworth and Mann, *Cotton Trade*, pp. 482–5; Catling, *Spinning Mule*, pp. 21–4; Ure, *Cotton Manufacture*, I, pp. 249–56, 275–7; English, *Textile Industry*, pp. 55–61; Rees, *Cyclopaedia*, 'Cotton'; Hills, *Power*, pp. 61–71; R. S. Fitton, *The Arkwrights, Spinners of Fortune* (Manchester University Press, 1989), ch. 2.

20. Baines, *Cotton Manufacture*, pp. 167–70; Wadsworth and Mann, *Cotton Trade*, p. 485; Fitton, *The Arkwrights*, pp. 33–5.

21. Baines, *Cotton Manufacture*, pp. 171–83; Singer, *Technology*, IV, pp. 280–1; Fitton, *The Arkwrights*, chs 2 and 3; J. Tann, 'Richard Arkwright and Technology', *History*, 58 (1973), pp. 29–44; D. Jeremy, 'British and American Entrepreneurial Values in the Early Nineteenth Century', in R. A. Burchell (ed.), *The End of Anglo-America* (Manchester University Press, 1991), pp. 34–9.

22. Aspin and Chapman, *Spinning Jenny*, pp. 31–2; Wadsworth and Mann, *Cotton Trade*, pp. 479–82; S. D. Chapman and S. Chassange, *European Textile Printers in the Eighteenth Century* (Heinemann, 1981), p. 37.

23. Aspin and Chapman, *Spinning Jenny*, pp. 48–9. For comment on opposition to the jenny because of its threat to women's work, see M. Berg, 'Workers and Machinery in Eighteenth-Century England', in J. Rule, *British Trade Unionism, 1750–1850* (Longmans, 1988), pp. 67–8.

24. MacLeod, *Industrial Revolution*, pp. 102–3.

25. S. D. Chapman, *The Factory Masters* (David and Charles, 1967), pp. 73–6; H. I. Dutton, *The Patent System and Innovative Activity During the Industrial Revolution, 1750–1852* (Manchester University Press, 1984), pp. 134, 203–4.

26. Baines, *Cotton Manufacture*, pp. 197–211; Singer, *Technology*, IV, pp. 279–80, 287–90; Catling,

*Spinning Mule*, chs 2–6; Ure, *Cotton Manufacture*, I, pp. 277–80 and II, pp. 117–36; English, *Textile Industry*, pp. 71–7; Marsden, *Cotton Spinning*, pp. 217–30; G. N. von Tunzelmann, *Steam Power and Industrialisation* (Clarendon Press, 1978), p. 194.

27. Singer, *Technology*, IV, pp. 283–4 and 291; J. R. Barford, *The Progress of Cotton* (*c.* 1840), pp. 2 and 3; Marsden, *Cotton Spinning*, pp. 291–6; Baines, *Cotton Manufacture*, pp. 241–2.

28. This figure is based on details given in a letter written to John Wyatt in 1743. They suggest that a spinner could produce about 15 skeins in a 7.5 hour shift and that 12 skeins were obtained from 1lb of cotton (Wadsworth and Mann, *Cotton Trade*, p. 437).

29. Catling, *Spinning Mule*, p. 54. Other figures for mule spinning productivity are given in von Tunzelmann, *Steam Power*, p. 203.

30. D. Bythell, *The Handloom Weavers* (Cambridge University Press, 1969), pp. 67–8 and 73–4; Baines, *Cotton Manufacture*, pp. 229–31; English, *Textile Industry*, p. 90.

31. Bythell, *Handloom Weavers*, p. 79; Singer, *Technology*, IV, pp. 300–3.

32. Bythell, *Handloom Weavers*, pp. 199–203; W. Turner, *Riot* (Lancashire County Books, 1993).

33. R. Guest, *A Compendious History of the Cotton Manufacture* (1823, reprinted Frank Cass), p. 46.

34. Baines, *Cotton Manufacture*, p. 240.

35. For a discussion of this point, see von Tunzelmann, *Steam Power*, pp. 195–202.

36. R. Marsden, *Cotton Weaving: Its Development, Principles and Practice* (London, 1895), p. 95.

37. G. Timmins, *The Last Shift* (Manchester University Press, 1993), p. 158.

38. Marsden, *Cotton Weaving*, p. 94–5.

39. The sizing process was quickened when slasher sizing was introduced in 1853. This fed the warp directly from the beam into the sizing trough without passing it through a reed, healds and ravel (which formed the parallel strips of warp). See English, *Textile Industry*, p. 193 and Marsden, *Cotton Weaving*, p. 334.

40. W. Radcliffe, *Origin of the New System of Manufacture* (Stockport, 1828), pp. 18–31; Marsden, *Cotton Weaving*, 328–33; von Tunzelmann, *Steam Power*, pp. 201–2; Barlow, *History of Weaving*, p. 245; Jeremy, 'Entrepreneurial Values', pp. 24–6.

41. Bythell, *Handloom Weavers*, p. 84.

42. Baines, *Cotton Manufacture*, pp. 247–53.

43. *An Illustrated Itinerary of the County of Lancaster* (London, 1842), pp. 50–1.

44. O. Ashmore, *The Industrial Archaeology of Lancashire* (David and Charles, 1969), p. 69.

45. Baines, *Cotton Manufacture*, pp. 264–8; W. Farrer,

J. Brownbill (eds), *A History of the County of Lancaster* (London, 1908), pp. 395–7; Wadsworth and Mann, *Cotton Trade*, p. 142. For evidence of plate-printing at the Bury works of Haworth, Peel & Co. in 1768, see F. Montgomery, *Printed Textiles: English and American Cotton and Linens, 1700–1800* (Thames and Hudson, 1970), p. 31. An early improvement was made to roller printing by an employee of Livesey & Company's competitors, the Peels. It comprised an endless, woollen blanket which fed colour evenly onto the roller. See Chapman and Chassagne, *Textile Printers*, pp. 43–4.

46. S. R. H. Jones, 'Technology, Transaction Costs, and the Transition to Factory Production in the British Silk Industry, 1700–1870', *Journal of Economic History* (1987), pp. 71–96. See also J. S. Cohen, 'Managers and Machinery: An Analysis of the Rise of Factory Production', *Australian Economic Papers* (June, 1981), pp. 24–39.

47. Wadsworth and Mann, *Cotton Trade*, p. 105. They also note instances of Dutch looms being driven by mechanical power, a patent to achieve this having been taken out by John Kay and Joseph Stell in 1745 (pp. 301–2).

48. Wadsworth and Mann, *Cotton Trade*, pp. 302–3.

49. Bythell, *Handloom Weavers*, pp. 33–4.

50. D. Hunt, *A History of Preston* (Carnegie Publishing, 1992), p. 151.

51. A. Barlow, *History of Weaving*, pp. 69–73; Marsden, *Cotton Weaving*, pp. 253–5; S. J. Chapman, *The Lancashire Cotton Industry* (Manchester University Press, 1904), p. 15.

52. Jones, 'Technology', p. 94.

53. R. Samuel, 'Workshop of the World: Steam Power and Hand Technology in mid-Victorian Britain', *History Workshop Journal* (1977), p. 19.

54. G. W. Daniels, 'Samuel Crompton's Census of the Cotton Industry in 1811', *Economic History*, II (1930), pp. 107–8; S. D. Chapman, 'Fixed Capital Formation in the British Cotton Industry, 1770–1815', *Economic History Review*, 23 (1970), p. 248.

55. Griffiths, 'Inventive Activity', p. 889; von Tunzelmann, *Steam Power*, p. 183.

56. M. M. Edwards, *The Growth of the British Cotton Trade, 1780–1815* (Manchester University Press, 1967), p. 8.

57. Aspin and Chapman, *Spinning Jenny*, p. 46.

58. PP, 1833 (690) VI, *Report from the Select Committee on the Present State of Manufactures, Commerce and Shipping*, Q. 10,555.

59. Baines, *Cotton Manufacture*, p. 198. For further discussion on the persistence of the jenny, see Rose, above, pp. 25–6.

60. Baines, *Cotton Manufacture*, pp. 207–8; M. Freifeld, 'Technological Change and the "Self-acting"

Mule: a Study of Skill and the Sexual Division of Labour', *Social History*, 11 (1986), pp. 319, 336.

61. R. Boyson, *The Ashworth Enterprise* (Clarendon Press, 1970), pp. 15, 54, 75; von Tunzelmann, *Steam Power*, p. 188; Chapman, *Lancashire Cotton Industry*, p. 70. Employers pressured Roberts to develop the self-actor mule as a means of curbing mule spinners' bargaining power. For a time, however, trade recession helped employers to achieve this objective, so that sales of self-actors were limited and Roberts did not make a profit from his invention for ten years. See C. MacLeod, 'Strategies for Innovation: the Diffusion of New Technology in Nineteenth-century Britain', *Economic History Review*, 45 (1992), p. 291,

62. Catling, *Spinning Mule*, pp. 67, 83.

63. Baines, *Cotton Manufacture*, p. 235.

64. Timmins, *Last Shift*, pp. 20-1.

65. Bythell, *Handloom Weavers*, p. 90; Timmins, *Last Shift*, p. 21.

66. Timmins, *Last Shift*, pp. 110–11.

67. Timmins, *Last Shift*, p. 110.

68. PP, 1842 (380) XV, *Children's Employment Commission: Second Report*, Part I, p. B3.

69. J. Graham, *The Chemistry of Calico Printing from 1799–1835 and History of Printworks in the Manchester District from 1760 to 1846* (Manchester Central Reference Library manuscript copy, 1846), pp. 401, 410.

70. Baines, *Cotton Manufacture*, p. 266.

71. D. Hogg, *A History of Church and Oswaldtwistle, 1860–1914* (Accrington and District Local History Society, 1973), pp. 16, 24; Ashmore, *Industrial Archaeology*, p. 66.

72. Marsden, *Cotton Spinning*, pp. 289–90.

73. *Illustrated Itinerary*, p. 21.

74. Freifeld, 'Technological Change', pp. 326–8.

75. Timmins, *Last Shift*, p. 158.

76. D. A. Farnie, *The English Cotton Industry and the World Market, 1815–1896* (Clarendon Press, 1979), p. 282.

77. Baines, *Cotton Manufacture*, p. 270.

78. C. O'Neill, *A Dictionary of Calico Printing and Dyeing* (London, 1862), p. 29. For some time after it was introduced, cylinder printing was chiefly used to produce single-colour wares, because of the difficulty of adjusting several cylinders to work effectively with one another. See Chapman and Chassange, *Textile Printers*, pp. 43–4.

79. W. S. Murphy, *The Textile Industries*, VIII (London, 1911), p. 4.

80. Timmins, *Last Shift*, pp. 161–70.

81. H. J. Habakkuk, *British and American Technology in the Nineteenth Century* (Cambridge University Press, 1962), pp. 147–9. For comment see Timmins, *Last Shift*, pp. 151–2.

82. Timmins, *Last Shift*, p. 131.

83. Bythell, *Handloom Weavers*, pp. 120–1.

84. Freifeld, 'Technological Change', pp. 319–39.

85. *Preston Chronicle*, 23 July 1836.

86. G. Turnbull, *A History of the Calico Printing Industry of Great Britain* (Altrincham, 1951), p. 89; J. G. Hurst, *The Principles and Practice of Textile Printing* (London, 1912), p. 18.

87. PP, 1840 (639) XXIV, p. 13.

## Further reading

C. Aspin and S. D. Chapman, *James Hargreaves and the Spinning Jenny* (Helmshore Local History Society, 1964).

E. Baines, *History of the Cotton Manufacture in Great Britain* (1835, reprinted Cass, 1966).

H. Catling, *The Spinning Mule* (David and Charles, 1970).

H. Dutton, *The Patent System and Innovative Activity during the Industrial Revolution* (Manchester University Press, 1984).

W. English, *The Textile Industry* (Longmans, 1969).

R. L. Hills, *Power in the Industrial Revolution* (Manchester University Press, 1970).

P. A. Hunt and P. K. O'Brien, 'Inventive Activity in the British Textile Industry, 1700–1800', *Journal of Economic History*, 52 (1992).

C. MacLeod, *Inventing the Industrial Revolution* (Cambridge University Press, 1988).

R. Marsden, *Cotton Spinning: Its Development, Principles, and Practice* (London, 1886).

R. Marsden, *Cotton Weaving: Its Development, Principles, and Practice* (London, 1895).

C. Singer, *et al.*, *A History of Technology*, vols III and IV (Clarendon, 1958).

G. Timmins, *The Last Shift* (Manchester University Press, 1993).

A. Ure, *The Cotton Manufacture of Great Britain*, 2 vols (London, 1861).

A. P. Wadsworth and J. de L. Mann, *The Cotton Trade and Industrial Lancashire, 1600–1780* (Manchester University Press, 1931).

# Notes to Chapter 3

1. B. Lemire, *Fashion's Favourite. The Cotton Trade and the Consumer in Britain 1660–1800* (Oxford University Press, 1991), p. 153.

2. Analysis of *Universal British Directory*, III (1794), Manchester section.

3. A. P. Wadsworth and J. de L. Mann, *The Cotton Trade and Industrial Lancashire 1600–1780* (Manchester University Press, 1931), pp. 238–9; Lemire, *Fashion's Favourite*, pp. 80 ff.

4. Wadsworth and Mann, *Cotton Trade*, pp. 243–4.

5. S. D. Chapman, *Merchant Enterprise in Britain* (Cambridge University Press, 1992), pp. 94–5.

6. E. Baines, *History of the Cotton Manufacture in Great Britain* (1835, reprinted Cass, 1966), pp. 318–19; reprinted Frank T. Ellison, *The Cotton Trade of GB* (1886), pp. 195–6. PRO E112/1758/5286, Harrison *v*. Harrison (1794).

7. House of Lords Record Office, Evidence on Irish Commercial Propositions, 10–30 June 1785.

8. Quoted in T. M. Doerflinger, *A Vigorous Spirit of Enterprise: Merchants and Economic Development in Revolutionary Philadelphia* (University of North Carolina Press, 1986), pp. 53, 88.

9. S. D. Chapman, 'James Longsdon (1745–1821), Farmer and Fustian Manufacturer', *Textile History*, 1 (1970).

10. G. Meinertzhagen, *From Ploughshare to Parliament: the Potters of Tadcaster* (John Murray, 1908), esp. pp. 2, 140–2.

11. R. Gatty, *Portrait of a Merchant Prince: James Morrison 1789–1857* (privately published, 1981), esp. pp. 1–23. *Select Committee on Trade Marks Bill*, 1862, PP. XII, pp. 542–4.

12. Journals of Joshua Gilpin (1765–1840), LII (Sept. 1799), Pennsylvania Historical Commission, Harrisburg, USA.

13. S. D. Chapman, 'British Marketing Enterprise . . . 1700–1860', *Business History Review*, 53 (1979).

14. *Ibid.*

15. R. Lloyd-Jones and M. J. Lewis, *Manchester and the Age of the Factory* (Croom Helm, 1988), pp. 30–1, 90, 108.

16. John Mortimer, *Mercantile Manchester Past and Present* (Bannerman, 1896), p. 69. West Sussex Record Office, Cobden Papers.

17. R. Davis, *The Industrial Revolution and British Overseas Trade* (Leicester University Press, 1979), esp. ch. 1.

18. S. D. Chapman, 'Financial Restraints on the Growth of Firms in the Cotton Industry 1790–1850', *Economic History Review*, 32 (1979).

19. Davis, *Industrial Revolution and Trade*, p. 15.

20. S. D. Chapman, *Merchant Enterprise in Britain from the Industrial Revolution to World War I* (Cambridge University Press, 1993), ch. 4.

21. Chapman, 'British Marketing Enterprise', citing Hodgson Robinson Mss, Rylands Library, Manchester.

22. Chapman, *Merchant Enterprise*, ch. 5.

23. S. D. Chapman, 'Merchants and Bankers', in W. E. Mosse (ed.), *Second Chance: Two Centuries of German Jews in the UK* (Tubingen, J. C. B. Mohr, 1991), pp. 341–3.

24. *Royal Commission on Depression in Trade*, Third Report, PP, 1886, p. 21.

25. Chapman, *Merchant Enterprise*, ch. 5, The 1877 estimate is cited in D. A. Farnie, *John Rylands* (Manchester, 1993), p. 38.

26. Edgar Jaffe, 'Die englishe Baumwollindustrie und die Organisation des Exporthandels', *Schmollers Jahrbuch für Gesetzgebung*, 24 (1900), esp. p. 200.

27. R. Spencer, *The Home Trade of Manchester* (Simpkin, Marshall & Co., 1988), p. 51; W. S. Murphy (ed.), *Modern Drapery* (Gresham, 1914), I, p. 22. Rylands' leadership appears in the City of London rate books, Guildhall Library, EC.

28. D. A. Farnie, *John Rylands of Manchester* (1993). For the size of firms see J. S. Toms, 'Profits, Capital Accumulation and the Development of the Lancashire Cotton Spinning Industry 1885–1914', *Accounting, Business and Financial History*, 4 (1994), esp. p. 372.

29. The best summary of the system is Henry Clay, *Report on the Position of the English Cotton Industry* (1931), pp. 2, 37–40.

30. H. B. Heylin, *Buyers and Sellers in the Cotton Trade* (Griffin, 1913), p. 123; W. T. Caves, *Wholesale Textile Distribution* (Mirror Printing Co., Eastbourne, 1951), p. 64; Chapman, *Merchant Enterprise*, ch. 8.

31. *Dictionary of Business Biography*, III, Sir Frank Hollins; *The Times*, 17 January 1906; J. S. Toms, 'The Profitability of the First Lancashire Merger: Horrocks, 1887–1905', *Textile History*, 24 (1993).

32. Tootal, Broadhurst, Lee Mss, Manchester Public Library, M461, esp. Board Minutes 1888–93.

33. Henry Clay, *Report*, p. 40.

34. S. J. Chapman, *Lancashire Cotton Industry* (Manchester University Press, 1904), pp. 135–40; H. B. Heylin, *Buyers and Sellers*, p. 122.

35. Chapman, *Merchant Enterprise*, ch. 7.

36. Samuel Smith MP, *My Life-Work* (Hodder and Stoughton, 1902), p. 36.

37. S. D. Chapman, 'The Decline and Rise of Textile Merchanting 1880–1990', *Business History*, 32 (1990).

38. D. A. Farnie, 'An Index of Commercial Activity: The Membership of the Manchester Royal Exchange, 1809–1948', *Business History*, 21 (1979).

39. United Turkey Red Co. (Glasgow), credit registers, 1920s and 1930s. Glasgow University Archives.

40. United Turkey Red Co. register. W. T. Caves, *Wholesale Textile Distribution*, p. 53.

41. Clay, *Report*, pp. 22–6.

42. Simon Pitt, *Strategic and Structural Change in the CPA 1899–1973*, Ph.D. thesis, London Business School, 1990; *Dictionary of Business Biography* III, article on Lennox Lee. Ralli Mss, Guildhall Library, London.

43. Clay, *Report*, p. 69.

44. R. Robson, *The Cotton Industry in Britain* (Macmillan, 1957), p. 125.

## Further reading

The extensive literature on the Lancashire cotton industry is very largely focused on manufacturers, workers and the factory system; there is surprisingly little on commercial enterprise and organisation. Very broadly, this list proceeds from the general to particular and specialised studies.

A. P. Wadsworth and J. de L. Mann, *The Cotton Trade and Industrial Lancashire, 1600–1780* (Manchester University Press, 1931), chs 1–15.

S. D. Chapman, *Merchant Enterprise in Britain from the Industrial Revolution to World War I* (Cambridge University Press, 1993).

N. S. Buck, *The Development of the Organisation of Anglo-American Trade, 1800–1850* (Yale University Press, 1925). Some of the perspectives of this early book have now been redrawn by Chapman (1993).

T. Ellison, *The Cotton Trade of Great Britain* (1886), Part II, 'History of the Liverpool Cotton Market' (reprinted Cass, 1968).

M. M. Edwards, *The Growth of the British Cotton Trade, 1780–1815* (Manchester University Press, 1969).

D. A. Farnie, *John Rylands of Manchester* (Rylands Library, Manchester, 1993).

B. W. Clapp, *John Owens, Manchester Merchant* (Manchester University Press, 1965).

E. F. Rathbone, *William Rathbone* [of Liverpool] (Macmillan, 1905).

*Dictionary of Business Biography* (5 vols, Butterworth, 1984–6), articles on Sir E. T. Broadhurst, Sir F. Hollins, H. E. Hollins, Henry and J. C. Lee, L. B. Lee, J. Rylands and others.

Henry Clay, *Report on the Position of the English Cotton Industry* (privately printed, 1931).

## Notes to Chapter 4

1. A. Howe, *The Cotton Masters, 1830–1860* (Oxford Historical Monographs, 1984); D. A. Farnie, *The English Cotton Industry and the World Market, 1815–1896* (Clarendon Press, 1979), p. 38.

2. F. M. L. Thompson, *English Landed Society in the Nineteenth Century* (Routledge, 1963); A. C. Howe, 'From "Old Corruption" to "New Probity": the Bank of England and its Directors in the Age of Reform', *Financial History Review*, 1 (1994), pp. 23–41; Y. Cassis, *City Bankers, 1870–1914* (Cambridge, 1994).

3. Quoted in D. A. Farnie, 'The English Cotton Industry, 1850–1896' (Manchester MA thesis, 1953), pp. 473–4.

4. Howe, *Cotton Masters*, pp. 1–6.

5. R. Lloyd-Jones and M. J. Lewis, *Manchester and the Age of the Factory* (Croom Helm, 1988).

6. R. Boyson, *The Ashworth Cotton Enterprise* (Oxford University Press, 1970); C. H. Lee, *A Cotton Enterprise, 1795–1840, a History of M'Connel and Kennedy, Fine Cotton Spinners* (Manchester University Press, 1972); M. B. Rose, *The Gregs of Quarry Bank Mill* (Cambridge University

Press, 1986); *Fortunes Made in Business* (3 vols, 1884–87).

7. V. A. C. Gatrell, 'Labour, Power and the Size of Firms in Lancashire Cotton in the Second Quarter of the Nineteenth Century', *Economic History Review*, second series, 30 (1977), pp. 95–139; cf. Lloyd-Jones and A. A. Le Roux, 'The Size of Firms in the Cotton Industry in Manchester, 1815–1841', *Economic History Review*, second series, 33 (1980), pp. 72–82.

8. Farnie, *Cotton Industry*, ch. 7; 'John Bunting', *Dictionary of Business Biography* [hereafter *DBB*]; D. J. Jeremy (ed.) (5 vols, Butterworth, 1984–86), I, pp. 506–10; Marrison, ch. 9 below.

9. Farnie, *Cotton Industry*, ch. 8; Marrison, ch. 9 below.

10. Ch. 3.

11. For one example, see W. F. M. Weston-Webb, *The Autobiography of a British Yarn Merchant* (Cayme Press, 1929).

12. *The Diary of Beatrice Webb: vol. 1 1873–1892* N. and J. MacKenzie (eds) (Virago with L.S.E., 1982), p. 306 [26 Nov. 1889]; H. R. Fox-Bourne, *English*

*Merchants* (Chatto 1886), ch. 19; G. Meinertzhagen [née Potter], *From Ploughshare to Parliament* (Murray, 1908).

13. See Chapman, ch. 3 above and Dupree, ch. 10 below.

14. In general, Farnie, *Cotton Industry*, pp. 31–5; Lloyd-Jones and Lewis, *Age of the Factory*, pp. 155–91; in particular, L. H. Grindon, *Manchester Banks and Bankers: Historical, Biographical and Anecdotal* (Manchester, Palmer & Howe 1878); R. N. Holden, 'The Architect in the Lancashire Cotton Industry, 1850–1914', *Textile History*, 23 (1992), pp. 243–57; V. Parrott, 'Manchester Solicitors', *Manchester Region History Review* [hereafter *MRHR*] 8 (1994), 74–82. Among accountants, Henry Whitworth played a leading organisational role in business life, for example, as secretary of the National Association of Factory Occupiers and of the National Federation of Associated Employers of Labour.

15. D. A. Farnie, 'John Worrall of Oldham, Directory-Publisher to Lancashire, and to the World, 1868–1970', *MRHR*, 4 (1990), pp. 30–35.

16. S. H. Jones, 'The Cotton Magnates Move Into Banking', *Textile History* (1977), pp. 90–111; R. Pearson, 'Collective Diversification: Manchester Cotton Merchants and the Insurance Business in the Early Nineteenth Century', *Business History Review* 65 (1991), pp. 379–414; Howe, *Cotton Masters*, pp. 32–43.

17. Howe, *Cotton Masters*, p. 51. The former included Engels, whose profits from the cotton spinners Ermen and Engels helped finance the career and writings of Marx. For a brief study, see R. Whitfield, 'The Double Life of Friedrich Engels', *MRHR*, 2 (1988), 13–19.

18. Chapman, ch. 3 above; Manchester Central Library, J. Scholes, 'A List of Foreign Merchants residing in Manchester 1784–1870' (Ms); N. Frangopulo, 'Foreign Communities in Victorian Manchester', *Manchester Review*, 10 (1965); B. Williams, *The Making of Manchester Jewry, 1740–1875* (Manchester University Press, 1976); S. Coates, 'Manchester's German Gentlemen', *MRHR*, 5 (1991–92), pp. 21–30.

19. S. Smiles, *Self-Help* (1859); F. Crouzet, *The First Industrialists: the Problem of Origins* (Cambridge, 1985).

20. *The Dictionary of National Biography: Missing Persons*, C. S. Nicholls (ed.) (Oxford University Press, 1993), pp. 230–1. Later generations more typically sought *rentier* and professional status. For one such, Lees Mayall, *Fireflies in Aspic* (1991).

21. Crouzet, *First Industrialists*, *passim*; see also J. H. Fox, 'The Victorian Entrepreneur in Lancashire',

in S. P. Bell (ed.), *Victorian Lancashire* (David & Charles, 1974); K. Honeyman, *Origins of Enterprise: Business Leadership in the Industrial Revolution* (Manchester University Press, 1982).

22. Howe, *Cotton Masters*, pp. 41–6, 49–54.

23. H. Berghoff and R. Moller, 'Tired Pioneers and Dynamic Newcomers? A Comparative Essay on English and German Entrepreneurs, 1870–1914', *Economic History Review*, 47 (1994), pp. 266–7; H. Berghoff, 'Regional Variations in Provincial Business Biography: the case of Birmingham, Bristol and Manchester, 1870–1914', *Business History*, 37 (1995), pp. 64–85. For fuller details, see H. Berghoff, *Englische Unternehmer 1870–1914: Eine Kollektivbiographie führender Wirtschaftsbürger in Birmingham, Bristol und Manchester* (Göttingen, 1991).

24. Classically, S. J. Chapman and F. J. Marquis, 'The Recruiting of the Employing Class from the Ranks of the Wage-earners in the Cotton Industry', *Journal of the Royal Statistical Society*, 75 (1912); cf. E. Thorpe, 'The Taken-for Granted Reference', *Sociology*, 7 (1973), pp. 361–76.

25. Farnie, 'The English Cotton Industry', pp. 222–30.

26. *Preston Pilot*, 28 Feb. 1846; D. A. Farnie, *John Rylands of Manchester* (John Rylands University Library, 1993).

27. R. Burn, *Statistics of the Cotton Trade* (1847); Farnie, *Cotton Industry*, *passim*.

28. W. D. Rubinstein, *Men of Property* (Croom Helm, 1981) and 'The Victorian Middle Classes: Wealth, Occupation, Geography', *Economic History Review*, 30 (1977), pp. 602–23; Howe, *Cotton Masters*, pp. 44–5; Langworthy (1796–1874) was alderman and mayor of Salford, briefly its MP in 1857, benefactor of several educational charities, *Salford Weekly News*, 11 April 1874. His wealth at death (£1.2m.) was dispersed among his large family.

29. For this thesis, M. Wiener, *English Culture and the Decline of the Industrial Spirit* (Cambridge University Press, 1981); cf. B. Collins and K. Robbins (eds), *British Culture and Economic Decline* (Weidenfeld, 1990) and W. D. Rubinstein, *Capitalism, Culture and Decline in Britain, 1750–1990* (Routledge, 1994).

30. Howe, *Cotton Masters*, pp. 54–7; H. Berghoff, 'Public Schools and the Decline of the British Economy', *Past and Present*, 129 (1990), p. 164.

31. *DBB*, v, pp. 418–25.

32. See Marrison, ch. 9 below.

33. E. L. Jones, 'Industrial Capital and Landed Investment: the Arkwrights in Herefordshire, 1809–1843', in E. L. Jones and G. E. Mingay (eds), *Land, Labour and Population in the Industrial Revolution* (1967); D. Brown, 'From "Cotton

Lord" to Landed Aristocrat: the Rise of Sir George Philips, Bart, 1766–1847', *Historical Research* (forthcoming).

34. Howe, *Cotton Masters*, pp. 29–32; for the wider debate, see F. M. L. Thompson, 'Business and Landed Elites in the Nineteenth Century' in F. M. L. Thompson (ed.), *Landowners, Capitalists, and Entrepreneurs* (Oxford University Press, 1994), pp. 139–70.

35. F. Baker, *The Moral Tone of the Factory System Defended* (1850), p. 30.

36. M. Lane, *The Tale of Beatrix Potter* (rev. ed., Warne 1985); D'Urberville was the scion of Simon Stokes, 'an honest merchant (some said money-lender) in the North' (*Tess of the D'Urbervilles* (1891, ch. 5).

37. A. Thackray, 'Natural Knowledge in Cultural Context: the Manchester Model', *American Historical Review*, 79 (1974), pp. 672–709; T. S. Ashton, *Economic and Social Investigations in Manchester, 1833–1933: A Centenary History of the Manchester Statistical Society* (P. S. King & Son, 1934); S. MacDonald, 'The Royal Manchester Institution', in J. G. Archer (ed.), *Art and Architecture in Victorian Manchester* (Manchester University Press, 1985), pp. 28–45.

38. T. N. L. Brown, *The History of the Manchester Geographical Society 1884–1950* (Manchester University Press, 1971).

39. See, *inter alia*, F. S. Stanniclffe, *John Shaw's, 1738–1938* (Sherratt & Hughes, 1938); A. Brooks and B. Haworth, *Boomtown Manchester, 1800–1850: the Portico Connection* (Manchester, The Portico Library: 1993); H. Whittaker, *The Union Club, Blackburn, 1849–1949* (Blackburn, 1950).

40. Howe, *Cotton Masters*, pp. 72–80. This picture is broadly confirmed by Berghoff, *Englische Unternehme*, p. 132.

41. For a valuable study of French business wives, see B. Smith, *Ladies of the Leisure Class* (Princeton, 1981). See also L. Davidoff and C. Hall, *Family Fortunes: Men and Women of the English Middle Class, 1750–1850* (Hutchinson, 1987).

42. For example, Hugh Mason of Ashton, on whom W. Haslam Mills, *Grey Pastures* (Chatto, 1924). See, too, P. Joyce. *Work, Society and Politics: the Culture of the Factory in Later Victorian England* (Harvester Press, 1980).

43. T. Baker, *Memorials of a Dissenting Chapel* (Simpkin, Marshall, 1884); J. Seed, 'Unitarianism, Political Economy, and the Antinomies of Liberal Culture in Manchester', *Social History*, 7 (1982), pp. 1–25; *idem.*, 'Theologies of Power: Unitarianism and Social Relations of Religious Discourse', in R. J. Morris (ed.), *Class, Power, and Social*

*Structure in British Nineteenth-Century Towns* (Leicester University Press, 1986). Possibly, Manchester's merchants were more inclined to Nonconformity than Lancashire industrialists; Manchester bankers, on the other hand, may have inclined to high churchmanship.

44. Jane Garnett and A. C. Howe, 'Churchmen and Cotton Masters in Victorian England', in D. J. Jeremy (ed.), *Business and Religion in Britain* (1988), pp. 72–94; M. Smith, *Religion in Industrial Society: Oldham and Saddleworth, 1740–1865* (Oxford Historical Monographs, 1994).

45. In a Manchester Unitarian context, see H. W. Wach, 'Religion and Social Morality', *Journal of Modern History*, 63 (1991), pp. 425–56.

46. Howe, *Cotton Masters*, *passim*, esp. pp. 92–3.

47. Farnie, *John Rylands of Manchester*.

48. *Culture and Anarchy* (1869).

49. *DNB*; Howe, *Cotton Masters*, *passim*.

50. *DBB*, III, pp. 359–69.

51. E. F. Simpson, *A Sketch of the History of the Manchester Royal Exchange* (Manchester, 1875); J. G. C. Parsons, *The Centenary of the Manchester Royal Exchange, 1804–1904: A Historical Sketch* (Manchester Royal Exchange, 1904). See too ch. 3 above, and ch. 12 below.

52. D. A. Farnie, 'An Index of Commercial Activity: the Membership of the Manchester Royal Exchange, 1809–1948', *Business History*, 21 (1979), pp. 96–106; N. Taylor, *Monuments of Commerce* (RIBA, 1968), pp. 46–7, for plans for a new Exchange building *c*. 1866.

53. W. Cooke Taylor, *Notes of a Tour of the Manufacturing Districts of Lancashire* (Duncan & Malcolm), p. 10.

54. R. A. J. Walling (ed.), *The Diaries of John Bright* (Cassell & Co., 1930), p. 67; A. Redford, *Manchester Merchants and Foreign Trade* (Manchester University Press, 2 vols, 1934, 1956), ii, pp. 277–8.

55. Redford, *Manchester Merchants*, ii, pp. 298–300.

56. Lloyd-Jones and Lewis, *Age of the Factory*, pp. 145–50.

57. M. J. Turner, 'Before the Manchester School: Economic Theory in Early Nineteenth-Century Manchester', *History*, 79 (1994), pp. 216–41.

58. Quoted in Howe, *Cotton Masters*, p. 202.

59. For the Chamber, see besides Redford, A. Briggs, *Victorian Cities* (Penguin, 1968), p. 130; V. A. C. Gatrell, 'The Commercial Class in Manchester *c*. 1820–1857', unpublished Cambridge Ph.D. thesis, 1971; Howe, *Cotton Masters*, pp. 202–5; M. W. Dupree (ed.), *Lancashire and Whitehall: The Diary of Sir Raymond Streat* (2 vols, Manchester University Press, 1987).

60. Howe, *Cotton Masters*, pp. 163–78; A. Bullen,

'Pragmatism *vs* Principle: Cotton Employers and the Origins of an Industrial Relations System', in J. A. Jowitt and A. J. McIvor (eds), *Employers and Labour in the English Textile Industries, 1850–1939* (Routledge 1988), pp. 27–43.

61. Howe, *Cotton Masters*, pp. 197–8.

62. A. W. Silver, *Manchester Men and Indian Cotton, 1847–1872* (Manchester, 1966); W. O. Henderson, *The Lancashire Cotton Famine, 1861–65* (Manchester University Press, 1969). See below chapter five for the important social implications of the Famine.

63. R. J. Moore, *Sir Charles Wood's Indian Policy, 1853–66* (Manchester University Press, 1966).

64. Redford, *Manchester Merchants*, ii, chs 3, 4; P. Harnetty, 'The Indian Cotton Duties Controversy, 1892–96', *English Historical Review*, 77 (1962), pp. 684–702. See, too, Marrison, ch. 9 below.

65. The main issues are dealt with in E. H. H. Green, 'Rentiers versus Producers? The Political Economy of the Bimetallic Controversy *c*.1880–1898', *English Historical Review*, 103 (1988), pp. 588–612 and in A. C. Howe, 'Bimetallism, *c*. 1880–1898: a controversy re-opened?', *English Historical Rreview*, 105 (1990), pp. 377–91. For the local context, T. Wilson, 'The Battle for the Standard: the Bimetallic Movement in Manchester', *MRHR*, 6 (1992), pp. 49–58.

66. Farnie, *John Rylands of Manchester*, p. 50.

67. I. Harford, 'The Ship Canal: Raising the Standard for Popular Capitalism', *MRHR*, 8 (1994), pp. 2–13; idem, *Manchester and its Ship Canal Movement: Class, Work, and Politics in late-Victorian England* (Keele, Ryburn Publishing, 1994).

68. A. Prentice, *History of the Anti-Corn Law League* (2 vols, Cash, 1853) cf. N. McCord, *The Anti-Corn Law League* (George Allen & Unwin, 1958). See too N. Longmate, *The Breadstealers* (Temple Smith, 1984).

69. For a general study along these lines, see G. R. Searle, *Entrepreneurial Politics in Mid-Victorian Britain* (Oxford, 1993).

70. Howe, *Cotton Masters*, p. 213.

71. *Ibid.*, p. 215.

72. For the involvement of one millowning family, see Rose, *The Gregs*; for the issue as a whole, Howe, *Cotton Masters*, 178–93.

73. *Factory Legislation: Report of the Central Committee of the Association of Millowners and Manufacturers* (1845), p. 4.

74. T. Bazley, quoted in *A Sketch of the Foundation and Past Fifty Years of the Manchester Steam Users' Association* (Manchester, Taylor, Garnett & Evans, 1905), p. 16; P. W. J. Bartrip, 'The State and the Steam Boiler in 19th-century Britain', *International Review of Social History*, 25 (1980), pp. 77–105.

75. N. McCord, 'Cobden and Bright in Politics, 1846–57', in R. Robson (ed.), *Ideas and Institutions of Victorian Britain* (Bell, 1967); J. Vincent, *The Formation of the British Liberal Party, 1857–68* (Constable, 1966); Howe, *Cotton Masters*, pp. 215–49; Searle, *Entrepreneurial Politics*.

76. M. Taylor, *The Decline of British Radicalism* (Oxford, 1995), pp. 280–4.

77. Stanley to Disraeli, 13 October 1860, quoted in W. F. Monypenny and G. E. Buckle, *The Life of Benjamin Disraeli* (John Murray, 1916), iv, 274n.

78. Joyce, *Work, passim*. See too chapter 5 below.

79. P. F. Clarke, *Lancashire and the New Liberalism* (Cambridge University Press, 1971), pp. 114, 429.

80. D. Foster, 'Class and County Government in early 19th-century Lancashire', *Northern History*, 9 (1974), pp. 48–61; J. M. Lee, *Social Leaders and Public Persons* (Oxford University Press, 1963).

81. J. Garrard, *Leadership and Power in Victorian Industrial Towns 1830–80* (Manchester University Press, 1983); Howe, *Cotton Masters*, ch. 4.

82. Lloyd-Jones and Lewis, *Age of the Factory*, pp. 135–8; Howe, *Cotton Masters*, p. 135.

83. M. Harrison, 'Art and Philanthropy: T. C. Horsfall and the Manchester Art Museum', in A. J. Kidd and K. W. Roberts (eds), *City, Class and Culture: Studies in Cultural Production and Social Policy in Victorian Manchester* (Manchester University Press, 1985), pp. 120–47. See too in this volume, M. E. Rose, 'Culture, Philanthropy and the Manchester Middle Classes', pp. 103–17; 'Ancoats: the first industrial suburb', *MRHR* (special number, 7, 1993); F. W. Hawcroft, 'The Whitworth Art Gallery', in Archer, *Art and Architecture*, pp. 208–29.

84. Howe, *Cotton Masters*, pp. 301–10.

85. M. Tylecote, *The Mechanics' Institutes of Lancashire and Yorkshire* (Manchester University Press, 1957); D. S. L. Cardwell, *Artisan to Graduate: Essays to Commemorate the Foundation in 1824 of the Manchester Mechanics' Institution* (Manchester University Press, 1974).

86. B. W. Clapp, *John Owens, Manchester Merchant* (Manchester University Press, 1965); A. Guagnini, 'The Fashioning of Higher Technical Education in Britain: the Case of Manchester, 1851–1914', in H. Gospel (ed.), *Industrial Training and Technological Innovation: a Comparative and Historical Study* (1991), 69–92; K. Tribe and A. Kadish (eds), *The Market for Political Economy: the Advent of Economics in British University Culture, 1850–1905* (1993).

87. 'Shall Manchester have a University?', *Nineteenth Century*, 2 (1877), pp. 113–23.

88. Farnie, *Cotton Industry*, ch. 6.

89. Nevertheless, as Marrison rightly notes below, this did not substantially undermine the numerical dominance of small and medium-sized firms.

90. L. E. Davis and R. A. Huttenback, *Mammon and the Pursuit of Empire: the Political Economy of British Imperialism, 1860–1912* (Cambridge, 1987), esp. p. 210.

91. See above, n. 67.

92. *DBB*, III, pp. 703–14.

93. W. H. Mills, *Sir Charles Macara, Bart: A Study of Modern Lancashire* (Manchester, 1917); *DBB*, IV, pp. 7–14.

94. K. M. Wilson, *Channel Tunnel Visions, 1850–1945* (1995); *DBB*, IV, pp. 609–14; V, pp. 682–5.

95. W. B. Tracy and W. T. Pike, *Manchester and Salford at the Close of the Nineteenth Century* (Brighton, Pike, 1899), p. 111.

96. A. McIvor, 'Cotton Employers' Organisations and Labour Relations, 1890–1939', in Jowitt and McIvor, *Employers and Labour*, pp. 1–26.

97. B. Webb, *Diary*, i, p. 296 [18 September 1889].

98. O. Westall (ed.), *Windermere in the Nineteenth Century* (rev. ed., Lancaster University, Centre for North-West Regional Studies, 1991).

99. Clarke, *Lancashire and the New Liberalism, passim*.

100. H. D. Henderson, *The Cotton Control Board* (Oxford University Press, 1922); 'Sir Alfred Herbert Dixon', *DBB*, II, pp. 107–12; J. Singleton, 'The cotton industry and the British war effort, 1914–1918', *Economic History Review*, 47 (1994), pp. 601–

18; F. Trentmann, 'The Transformation of Fiscal Reform: Reciprocity, Modernisation, and the Fiscal Debate within the British Business Community, c. 1900–1918', *Historical Journal* (forthcoming).

101. See chs 10 and 11 below.

*Further reading*

R. Boyson, *The Ashworth Cotton Enterprise* (Oxford University Press, 1970).

B. W. Clapp, *John Owens, Manchester Merchant* (Manchester University Press, 1965).

D. A. Farnie, *The English Cotton Industry and the World Market, 1815–1896* (Clarendon Press, 1979).

D. A. Farnie, *John Rylands of Manchester* (John Rylands University Library, 1993).

W. Hinde *Richard Cobden: A Victorian Outsider* (1987).

A. Howe, *The Cotton Masters, 1830–1860* (Oxford, 1984).

P. Joyce, *Work, Politics and Society: the Culture of the Factory in Later Victorian Britain* (Hassocks, 1980).

B. R. Law, *The Fieldens of Todmorden: a Nineteenth-Century Business Dynasty* (Kelsall, 1995).

N. McCord, *The Anti-Corn Law League* (1958).

A. Redford, *Manchester Merchants and Foreign Trade* (2 vols, Manchester, 1934 and 1956).

K. G. Robbins, *John Bright* (1979).

M. B. Rose, *The Gregs of Quarry Bank Mill* (Cambridge University Press, 1986).

# Notes to Chapter 5

1. E. Baines jnr, 'The History of Cotton Manufacture', in Edward Baines, *History of the County Palatine and Duchy of Lancaster*, vol. 2 (Fisher & Son, 1836), pp. 507, 521.

2. Andrew Ure, *The Philosophy of Manufactures* (Cass, 1835), pp. 17–19, quoted in J. T. Ward, *The Factory System*, vol. 1 (David and Charles, 1970), p. 143.

3. PRO, MH32/57. Letter from Assistant Poor Law Commissioner Charles Mott to Poor Law Commission, 28 January 1839.

4. A. Bullen and A. Fowler, *The Cardroom Workers Union: a Centenary History of the Amalgamated Association of Card and Blowing Room Opertives* (Amalgamated Textile Workers Union, Rochdale, 1986), p. 68.

5. A. McIvor, 'Work, Wages and Industrial Relations in Cotton Finishing, 1880–1914', in J. A. Jowitt and A. J. McIvor (eds), *Employers and Labour in the English Textile Industries, 1850–1939* (Routledge, 1988), p. 135.

6. Butterworth Manuscripts, March 1842; Oldham Local Studies Library.

7. K. Burgess, *The Origins of British Industrial Relations: the Nineteenth-Century Experience* (Croom Helm, 1975), p. 234.

8. For example, J. Foster, *Class Struggle and the Industrial Revolution* (Weidenfeld and Nicolson, 1974), pp. 231–4; M. Holbrook-Jones, 'Spinners: the Modern Plebeians', in *Supremacy and Subordination of Labour* (Heinemann, 1982), pp. 155–85; W. Lazonick, 'Industrial Relations and Technical Change: the Case of the Self-Acting Mule', *Cambridge Journal of Economics*, 3 (1979), pp. 231–62; R. Penn, 'Trade Union Organisation and Skill in the Cotton and Engineering Industries in Britain, 1850–1960', *Social History*, 8 (1983); I. Cohen, 'Workers' Control in the Cotton Industry: A Comparative Study of British and American Mule Spinning', *Labor History*, 26 (1985).

9. M. Freifeld, 'Technological Change and the "Self-

Acting" Mule: a Study of Skill and the Sexual Division of Labour', *Social History*, 11 (1986), p. 323.

10. H. Catling, *The Spinning Mule* (David and Charles, 1970; reprinted Lancashire County Council, 1986), p. 149.

11. M. Savage, 'Women and Work in the Lancashire Cotton Industry, 1890–1939', in Jowitt and McIvor, *Employers and Labour*, p. 214.

12. S. J. Chapman, *The Lancashire Cotton Industry: a Study in Economic Development* (Manchester University Press, 1904), p. 112.

13. *Children's Employment Commission*, PP, 1843, xiv, B62; Evidence of Samuel Robinson of Dukinfield interviewed by Assistant Commissioner Joseph Kennedy, March 1841.

14. A. H. Robson, *The Education of Children Engaged in Industry in England, 1833–1876* (Kegan Paul, 1931); M. W. Thomas, *The Early Factory Legislation* (Thames Bank, 1948).

15. There is, however, no consensus on this issue. For the debates see U. R. Q. Henriques, *The Early Factory Acts and their Enforcement* (Historical Association, 1971); C. Nardinelli, 'Child Labor and the Factory Act', *Journal of Economic History*, 4 (1980); A. E. Peacock, 'The Successful Prosecution of the Factory Acts, 1833–1855', *Economic History Review*, 37 (1984) pp. 197–210; P. W. J. Bartripp, 'Success or Failure? The Prosecution of the Early Factory Acts', *Economic History Review*, 38 (1985).

16. H. Silver, 'Ideology and the Factory Child: Attitudes to Half-time Education', in P. McCann (ed.), *Popular Education and Socialization in the Nineteenth Century* (Methuen, 1977), pp. 141–66.

17. C. Nardinelli, *Child Labor and the Industrial Revolution* (Indiana University Press, 1990), ch. 5.

18. D. A. Farnie, *The English Cotton Industry and the World Market, 1815–1896* (Clarendon Press, 1979), p. 301.

19. P. Bolin-Hort, *Work, Family and the State: Child Labour and the Organisation of Production in the British Cotton Industry, 1780–1920* (Lund University Press, Sweden, 1989), is a meticulous exploration of all these issues. See also, H. Challand and M. Walker, '"No School, No Mill; No Mill, No Money": the Half-time Textile Worker', in M. Winstanley, *Working Children in Nineteenth-Century Lancashire* (Lancashire County Books, 1995).

20. B. Simon, *Education and the Labour Movement, 1870–1920* (Lawrence and Wishart, 1974), pp. 137–41; E. and R. Frow, *A Survey of the Half-Time System in Education* (E. J. Morten, 1970).

21. For full details of these and other Factory Acts see B. L. Hutchins and A. Harrison, *A History of Factory Legislation* (P. S. King, 1911).

22. J. T. Ward, *The Factory Movement, 1830–1855* (David & Charles 1962); J. T. Ward, 'The Factory Movement in Lancashire, 1830–1855', *Transactions of the Lancashire and Cheshire Antiquarian Society*, 75–6 (1966), pp. 186–210.

23. R. Sykes, 'General Unionism, Class and Politics: the Cotton Districts, 1829–1834', *Bulletin of Society for the Study of Labour History*, 49 (1984). pp. 20–1.

24. R. Sykes, 'Popular Politics and Trade Unionism in South-East Lancashire, 1829–42' (unpublished Ph.D. thesis, University of Manchester, 1982), ch. 3; J. Mason, 'Spinners and Minders', in A. Fowler and T. Wyke, *The Barefoot Aristocrats: a History of the Amalgamated Association of Operative Cotton Spinners* (George Kelsall, 1987), ch. 2.

25. Memorial of Preston spinners in 1856 quoted by Mason, 'Spinners and Minders', p. 53.

26. Chapman, *Cotton Industry*, pp. 266–8; for a full explanation of these lists see J. Jewkes and E. M. Gray, *Wages and Labour in the Lancashire Cotton Industry* (Manchester University Press, 1935), chs 5 and 6.

27. H. A. Turner, *Trade Union Growth, Structure and Policy: a Comparative Study of the Cotton Unions in England* (Toronto University Press, 1962), pp. 132–4; E. Hopwood, *The Lancashire Weavers' Story* (Amalgamated Weavers Association, 1969), chs 7 and 8; A. Fowler and L. Fowler, *The History of the Nelson Weavers' Association* (Burnley, Nelson, Rossendale and District Textile Workers Union, 1984).

28. Bullen and Fowler, *Cardroom Workers*, p. 11.

29. N. Kirk, *The Growth of Working-Class Reformism in Mid-Victorian England* (Croom Helm, 1985), p. 265.

30. Burgess, *British Industrial Relations*, p. 235; Hopwood, *Weavers' Story*, p. 53. For the Preston strike see H. Dutton and J. King, *'Ten Per Cent and No Surrender': the Preston Strike, 1853–54* (Cambridge University Press, 1981).

31. Quoted in Kirk, *Working-Class Reformism*, p. 267.

32. A. Bullen, 'A Modern Spinners Union', in Fowler and Wyke, *Barefoot Aristocrats*, pp. 90–1.

33. Bullen and Fowler, *Cardroom Workers*, p. 41; Turner, *Trade Union Growth*, p. 154.

34. E. H. Hunt, *British Labour History, 1815–1914* (Weidenfeld and Nicolson, 1981), p. 299.

35. J. L. White, 'Lancashire Cotton Textiles', in C. J. Wrigley (ed.), *A History of British Industrial Relations, 1875–1914* (Harvester, 1982), p. 216; McIvor, 'Cotton Finishing', p. 132.

36. Bullen and Fowler, *Cardroom Workers*, p. 114.

37. White, 'Lancashire Cotton Textiles', provides a

succinct overview; for more detail, see his *The Limits of Trade Union Militancy: the Lancashire Textile Workers, 1910–1914* (Westport, CT, 1978).

38. A. Bullen, 'The Making of Brooklands', in Fowler and Wyke, *Barefoot Aristocrats*, ch. 6.

39. Hopwood, *Weavers' Story*, pp. 68–72;

40. Foster, *Class Struggle*, p. 117; see also M. Jenkins, *The General Strike of 1842* (Lawrence and Wishart, 1980).

41. A. E. Musson, 'Class Struggle and the Labour Aristocracy', *Social History*, 1 (1976) pp. 335–56; G. Stedman Jones, 'Class Struggle and the Industrial Revolution', *New Left Review*, 90 (1976); D. Gadian, 'Class Consciousness in Oldham and other North-West Industrial Towns, 1830–1850', *Historical Journal*, 21 (1978), pp. 161–72; R. Sykes, 'Some Aspects of Working-Class Consciousness in Oldham, 1830–1842', *Historical Journal*, 23 (1980), pp. 167–79; M. Winstanley, 'Oldham Radicalism and the Origins of Popular Liberalism, 1830–52', *Historical Journal*, 36 (1993), pp. 619–43.

42. T. D. W. Reid and C. A. N. Reid, 'The 1842 "Plug Plot" in Stockport', *International Review of Social History*, 24 (1979), pp. 55–79.

43. Winstanley, 'Oldham Radicalism', pp. 636–8; P. Taylor, *Popular Politics in Early Industrial Britain: Bolton, 1825–1850* (Ryburn/Keele University Press, 1995), ch. 4.

44. H. J. Hanham, *Elections and Party Management: Politics in the Time of Gladstone and Disraeli* (Longmans, 1959), p. 286.

45. J. Vincent, *The Formation of the Liberal Party, 1857–68* (Constable, 1966, Penguin, 1972), p. 138.

46. J. K. Walton, *Lancashire: A Social History, 1558–1939* (Manchester University Press, 1987), pp. 255–64, offers a succinct overview of these.

47. Walton, *Lancashire*, p. 263 gives an excellent review of these debates.

48. P. F. Clarke, *Lancashire and the New Liberalism* (Cambridge University Press, 1971), pp. 64–9.

49. R. Greenall, 'Popular Conservatism in Salford, 1868–86', *Northern History*, 9 (1974), pp. 123–38; Kirk, *Working-Class Reformism*, ch. 7.

50. P. Joyce, *Work, Society and Politics: the Culture of the Factory in Late-Victorian England* (Harvester, 1980), pp. 292–5.

51. M. Pugh, *The Tories and the People, 1880–1935* (Blackwell, 1985), pp. 240–2.

52. Bullen and Fowler, *Cardroom Workers*, p. 48; Fowler and Wyke, *Barefoot Aristocrats* pp. 120–1, 127.

53. Joyce, *Work, Society and Politics*, passim.

54. A. Russell, 'Local Elites and the Working-Class Response in the North-West, 1870–1985: Paternalism and Deference Reconsidered', *Northern History*, 23 (1987).

55. M. E. Rose, 'Rochdale Man and the Stalybridge Riot: the Relief and Control of the Unemployed during the Lancashire Cotton Famine', in A. P. Donajgrodzki (ed.), *Social Control in Nineteenth-Century Britain* (Croom Helm, 1977); Kirk, *Working-Class Reformism*, pp. 258–61.

56. J. McHugh and B. Ripley, 'The Spinners and the Rise of Labour', in Fowler and Wyke, *Barefoot Aristocrats*, ch. 7.

57. Walton, *Lancashire*, pp. 274–5.

58. Savage, 'Women and Work', in Jowitt and McIvor, *Employers and Labour*, pp. 210–12.

59. J. Liddington and J. Norris, *'One Hand Tied Behind Us': the Rise of the Women's Suffrage Movement* (Virago, 1978), p. 262.

60. Fowler and Wyke, *Barefoot Aristocrats*, p. 141.

61. Walton, *Lancashire*, p. 280.

62. M. Savage, *The Dynamics of Working-Class Politics: the Labour Movement in Preston, 1880–1940* (Cambridge University Press, 1987), pp. 70–80

63. W. J. Lowe etc 'The Irish in Lancashire' (unpublished Ph.D. thesis, University College, Dublin, 1974), copy in LRO.

64. M. Anderson, *Family Structure in Nineteenth-Century Lancashire* (Cambridge University Press, 1971), pp. 37–8.

65. Foster, *Class Struggle*, p. 77.

66. Anderson, *Family Structure*, pp. 66, 101.

67. E. Roberts, *A Woman's Place: an Oral History of Working-Class Women, 1890–1940* (Blackwell, 1984), pp. 168ff.

68. For discussions of this see N. J. Smelser, *Social Change in the Industrial Revolution* (Routledge, 1959); M. M. Edwards and R. Lloyd-Jones, 'N. J. Smelser and the Cotton Factory Family: a Reassessment', in N. B. Harte and K. G. Ponting (eds), *Textile History and Economic History* (Manchester University Press, 1973), pp. 304–19; M. Anderson 'Sociological History and the Working-Class Family: Smelser Revisited', *Social History*, 1 (1976), pp. 317–54.

69. S. J. Chapman and W. Abbott, 'The Tendency of Children to Enter their Fathers' Trades', *Journal of the Royal Statistical Society*, 74 (1912–13), pp. 599–604.

70. Dr John Watts, 1866, quoted in Walton, *Lancashire*, p. 242.

71. M. Purvis, 'The Development of Co-operative Retailing in England and Wales, 1851–1901: a Geographical Study', *Journal of Historical Geography*, 16 (1990), pp. 314–31; G. D. H. Cole, *A Century of Co-operation* (George Allen and Unwin, 1944), pp. 176–7.

72. P. Joyce, *Visions of the People: Industrial England and the Question of Class, 1848–1914* (Cambridge Univeristy Press, 1991), esp. chs 11–13.

73. R. Poole, *Popular Leisure and Music Hall in 19th-Century Bolton* (Centre for North-West Regional Studies, University of Lancaster, 1982); J. Richards, *Stars in Our Eyes: Lancashire Stars of Stage, Screen and Radio* (Lancashire County Books/Lancaster Historical Association branch, 1994).

74. T. Mason, *Association Football and English Society, 1863–1915* (Harvester, 1980), ch. 2; Walton, *Lancashire*, pp. 297–8.

75. R. Poole, *The Lancashire Wakes Holidays* (Lancashire County Books/Lancaster Historical Association branch, 1994); R. Poole, 'Oldham Wakes', in J. K. Walton and J. Walvin (eds), *Leisure in Britain, 1750–1939* (Manchester University Press, 1983).

76. J. K. Walton, 'The Demand for Working-Class Seaside Holidays in Victorian England', *Economic History Review*, 34 (1981), pp. 249–65.

77. J. K. Walton, *The Blackpool Landlady: a Social History* (Manchester University Press, 1978).

78. Joyce, *Visions of the People*, has explored these themes in detail.

79. Walton, *Lancashire*, is the best introduction to the experience of other regions in the county.

80. Farnie, *Cotton Industry*, p. 327.

## Further reading

M. Anderson, *Family Structure in Nineteenth-Century Lancashire* (Cambridge University Press, 1971).

I. Cohen, *American Management and British Labor: A Comparative Study of the Cotton Spinning Industry* (New York, Greenwood Press, 1990).

H. I. Dutton and J. King, *'Ten Per Cent and No Surrender': The Preston Strike, 1853–4* (Cambridge University Press, 1981).

A. Fowler and T. Wyke, *The Barefoot Aristocrats: A History of the Amalgamated Association of Operative Cotton Spinners* (George Kelsall, 1987).

P. Joyce, *Work, Society and Politics: the Culture of the Factory in Late Victorian England* (Harvester, 1980).

A. Jowitt and A. J. McIvor (eds), *Employers and Labour in the English Textile Industries* (Routledge, 1988).

P. Bollin-Hort, *Work, Family and the State: Child Labour and the Organisation of Production in the British Cotton Industry, 1780–1920* (Lund University Press, Sweden, 1989).

P. Taylor, *Popular Politics in Early Industrial Britain: Bolton 1825–50* (Ryburn/Keele University Press, 1995).

N. Kirk, *The Growth of Working-Class Reformism in Mid-Victorian England* (Croom Helm, 1985).

H. A. Turner, *Trade Union Growth, Structure and Policy: a Comparative Study of the Cotton Unions in England* (Toronto University Press, 1962).

J. K. Walton, *Lancashire: A Social History, 1558–1939* (Manchester University Press, 1987).

## Notes to Chapter 6

1. M. Spufford, *The Great Reclothing of Rural England. Petty Chapmen and their Wares in the Seventeenth Century* (Hambledon Press, 1984), p. 92.

2. R. Latham and W. Matthews (eds), *The Diary of Samuel Pepys* (G. Bell, 1971), vol. 4, p. 391.

3. Quoted in B. Lemire, *Fashion's Favourite, The Cotton Trade and the Consumer in Britain 1660–1800* (Pasold Research Fund and Oxford University Press, 1991), p. 35, from *Old Bailey Records*, July 1719, 7.

4. Lemire, *Fashion's Favourite*, p. 113; Barbara Johnson's sample book, Textile Department, Victoria and Albert Museum, London, T219-1973.

5. A. Ribeiro, *Dress in Eighteenth-Century Europe, 1715–1789* (Batsford, 1984), p. 155.

6. J. Farrell, *Socks and Stockings* (The costume accessory series, Batsford, 1992), pp. 34–7.

7. 'Sylvia', *How to Dress Well on a Shilling a Day* (Ward, Lock & Co., 1875).

8. E. E. Perkins, *Treatise on Haberdashery and Hosiery*, 8th ed. (W. Tegg & Co., 1853), p. 123.

9. Place Collections, vol. 39, Add. MS 27827, pp. 50–2, quoted in Ribeiro, p. 64.

10. Ribeiro, *Dress in Eighteenth-Century Europe*, p. 62.

11. G. Clark, 'Infant Clothing in the Eighteenth Century: a New Insight', *Costume*, 28 (1994), pp. 47–59.

12. Lemire, *Fashion's Favourite*, pp. 96–7.

13. Mrs Gaskell, *Mary Barton, a Tale of Manchester Life* (Chapman & Hall, 1848), ch. 25. Hoyle's prints are discussed in more detail by Mary Schoeser in chapter 7.

14. Quoted in J. Tozer and S. Levitt, *Fabric of Society, a Century of People and Their Clothes, 1770–1870* (Laura Ashley Ltd, 1983), p. 135.

15. S. W., *Directions for Cutting Out and Making Articles of Clothing, with Practical Rules and Suggestions on Needlework, Chiefly Applicable to Villages* (Society for Promoting Christian Knowledge, 1854), pp. 9–12.

16. Anon., *Instructions for Cutting out Apparel for the Poor; Principally Intended for the Assistance of the*

*Patronesses of Sunday Schools* (published for the benefit of the Sunday School Children of Hertingfordbury, 1789, undated facsimile, Costume and Textile Association for Norfolk Museums).

17. F. Litchfield, *Three Years' Results of the Farthinghoe Clothing Society with a Few Remarks Upon the Policy of Encouraging Provident Habits Among the Working Classes* (J. Freeman, Northampton, 1832), pp. 4–19.

18. *Old Bailey Records*, January 1714/15, 5. Quoted in Lemire, *Fashion's Favourite*, p. 90.

19. Press cuttings in 'law and order' file, Hounslow Libraries Local Studies Section.

20. Quoted in Lemire, *Fashion's Favourite*, p. 102.

21. F. Engels, *The Condition of the Working Class in England in 1845* (reprinted Granada, 1982), p. 99.

22. S. W., *Directions for Cutting Out . . .*, p. 7.

23. J. Schmeichen, *Sweated Industries and Sweated Labor, the London Clothing Trades, 1860–1914* (Croom Helm, 1984), p. 14.

24. S. P. Dobbs, *The Clothing Workers of Great Britain* (Routledge, 1928), p. 3.

25. R. Roberts, *The Classic Slum: Salford Life in the First Quarter of the Century* (Pelican Books, 1971), p. 38.

26. S. Levitt, 'Bristol Clothing Trades and Exports in the Georgian Period', *Per una Storia della Moda Pronta, problemi e ricerche* (CISST and Edifir Edizione, Firenze, 1991), pp. 29ff.

27. Dobbs, *The Clothing Workers of Great Britain*, p. 51.

28. T. S. Ashton, 'A Century of Commerce and Industry', *Manchester Guardian*, 16 May 1938, p. 22.

29. B. Williams, *The Making of Manchester Jewry* (Manchester University Press, 1976), p. 69.

30. Williams, *The Making of Manchester Jewry*, p. 115.

31. S. Levitt, 'Manchester Mackintoshes, a History of the Rubberised Garment Trade in Manchester', *Textile History*, 17 (1986), pp. 51–70.

32. For further details see S. Levitt, *Victorians Unbuttoned, Registered Designs for Clothing, Their Makers and Wearers, 1839–1900* (George Allen and Unwin, 1986).

33. Levy, BT45 1774; Hyam, BT45 1015; BT45 2852; Thacker and Radford, BT45 952; Flusheim and Hesse, BT45 413; BT45 695; BT45 1580.

34. *Children's and Young Persons' Employment Commission, Evidence upon the Manufacture of Wearing Apparel*, PP. 1864, XXII, p. 99ff.

35. *Children's and Young Persons' Employment Commission*, para. 24.

36. *Children's and Young Persons' Employment Commission*, para. 9.

37. BT43/13 397083, 397226.

38. *Children's and Young Persons' Employment Commission*, para. 55.

39. *Children's and Young Persons' Employment Commission*, para. 257.

40. F. Godfrey, *An International History of the Sewing Machine* (Robert Hale, 1982), p. 236.

41. BT43/13 79986.

42. M. Wray, *The Women's Outerwear Industry* (Duckworth & Co. Ltd, 1957), p. 23.

43. L. A. Stocks, *The History of John Maden & Son Ltd* (John Maden, 1977), p. 45.

44. Anon., *Manchester Makes: a Review of Industries, Other Than Cotton, Carried On in the Great Industrial Area of South East Lancashire and North East Cheshire* (Manchester Chamber of Commerce, 1937), p. 117.

45. Anon., *An Industrial Survey of the Lancashire Area* (University of Manchester for the Board of Trade, 1932), p. 179.

46. Anon., *An Industrial Survey . . .*, p. 183.

47. *Crook's Clothing Magazine*, vol. 1, 1923, Central Reference Library Manchester, Local Studies Section.

48. R. Redmayne, *Ideals in Industry, Being the Story of Montague Burton Ltd, 1900–1950* (Montague Burton, 1950), pp. 139ff.

49. Anon., *An Industrial Survey . . .*, p. 190.

50. Anon., *An Industrial Survey . . .*, p. 184.

51. Wray, *Women's Outerwear Industry*, p. 25.

52. Anon., *An Industrial Survey . . .*, p. 193.

53. Anon., *An Industrial Survey . . .*, p. 194.

54. Anon., *An Industrial Survey . . .*, p. 197.

55. Anon., 'Raw cotton to finished garment, activities of the house of Bannerman', *Empire Mail*, June 1925, p. 333.

56. Anon., *An Industrial Survey . . .*, p. 184.

57. H. Clay and K. Russell Brady (eds), *Manchester at Work, a Survey* (Manchester Civic Week Committee, 1929), p. 118.

58. Wray, *Women's Outerwear Industry*, p. 281.

59. Anon., *The Lancashire Clothing Industry* (Lancashire County Planning Department, 1985), pp. 2, 32.

60. D. C. Gibbs, *Employment Change, the Labour Process and Manchester's Clothing Industry* (University of Newcastle upon Tyne Centre for Urban and Regional Development Studies, 1983), p. 2.

61. Anon., *The Lancashire Clothing Industry*, p. 11.

62. Anon., *The Lancashire Clothing Industry*, p. 43.

## Further reading

A. Briggs, *Friends of the People, a Centenary History of Lewis's* (Batsford, 1956).

P. Byrde, *Nineteenth-Century Fashion* (Batsford, 1992).

F. Chenoune, *A History of Nen's Fashion* (Thames and Hudson, 1993).

A. Carter, *Underwear, the Fashion History* (Batsford, 1992).

A. Jarvis, *Liverpool Fashion, its Makers and Wearers: The Dressmaking Trade in Liverpool 1830–1940* (Merseyside County Museums, 1981).

S. Levitt, 'Clothing Production and the Sewing Machine', *Textile Society Magazine*, 9 (1988), pp. 2–13.

N. Rothstein (ed.), *Barbara Johnson's Album of Fashion and Fabrics* (Thames and Hudson, 1987).

J. Tozer, *British Cotton Couture, 1941–61* (The Gallery of English Costume picture book number 11, Manchester City Art Galleries, 1985).

## Notes to Chapter 7

1. Peel sample book, Human History Department, Bolton Museum and Art Gallery, August 28, *c.* 1806: 'Enclosed you have a pattern of one of the Bury Houses . . . Plate furnitures; Joseph Peel desires you will draw up and engrave two or three patterns similar. They must be shewey and full of work.'

2. The number of surviving sample books and designs relating to Lancashire production is difficult to estimate accurately; of the print, weave and dye sample books, there are certainly about 1,000 held in public collections in Britain and at least 200, and quite probably many more, in private collections. Given that at least one-third of these contain woven fabrics (that is, un-printed), for the printing and dyeing industry as a whole there are perhaps some 800 volumes. This is a very small number when compared to other regional collections, such as the volumes, numbering about 750, which document the production of only fourteen Macclesfield firms. Fortunately, to the Lancashire sample books can be aded the Patent Office Design Registers of 1842–1910 held by the Public Record Office (PRO), Kew, which has among its samples and designs many that were made in Lancashire; for the eighteenth century there are also some small but significant holdings overseas.

3. Edmund Potter, *Calico Printing as an Art Manufacture. A Lecture on Calico Printing read before the Society of Arts*, 22 April 1852, p. 3.

4. John Graham, 'The Chemistry of Calico Printing from 1790 to 1835 and History of Printworks in the Manchester District from 1760–1846', manuscript in MCRL (1847). A typed transcription of the section on printworks has been made by David Greysmith, who gives an excellent summary of bibliographic material in his unpublished M.Phil. dissertation, 'The Printed Textiles Industry in England 1830–1870', Middlesex Polytechnic, 1985, and to which this paragraph is indebted.

5. *English Printed Textiles* (HMSO, 1960), p. 8. In Floud and Barbara Morris's *Catalogue of an Exhibition of English Chintz: Two Centuries of Changing Taste* (HMSO, 1955), the coverage extends to 1951; the section on 1837–73, however, includes a comment on 'the general level of mediocrity' (p. 36).

6. S. D. Chapman and S. Chassagne, *European Textile Printers in the Eighteenth Century: A Study of Peel and Oberkampf* (Heinemann Educational Books/ The Pasold Fund, 1981), p. 34; hereafter referred to as *Peel and Oberkampf*.

7. See Godfrey Smith, *The Laboratory; or, School of Arts*, vol. 2, 6th ed. (C. Wittingham, London, 1799), p. 51.

8. Eric Kerridge, *Textile Manufactures in Early Modern England* (Manchester University Press, 1985), pp. 124–5. Even in the early nineteenth century the term fustian still included cotton corduroy, thickset, velveret and velveteen; see Florence Montgomery, *Textiles in America, 1650–1870* (W. W. Norton & Co., New York, 1984), p. 244

9. *Livre d'Echantillons*, presented by Marc Morel to M. De Montigny *c.* 1750; see Florence M. Montgomery, 'John Holker's Mid-Eighteenth-Century *Livre d'Echantillons*', in Veronic Gevers (ed.), *Studies in Textile History* (Royal Ontario Museum, 1977), p. 220

10. *Peel and Oberkampf*, p. 26

11. *Studies in Textile History*, p. 219

12. *Textiles in America*, p. 399. Prepared by Thomas Smith, 1783; by Nathaniel and Joshua Gould, 1775–85; and for Benjamin and John Bower, Manchester, 1771.

13. The early cotton velvets were probably printed in spirit colours, which combined the colouring matter and mordant, but were not as fast as colours obtained by printing only the mordant and then dyeing.

14. *Peel and Oberkampf*, p. 28.

15. James Ogden, *A Description of Manchester* (Manchester, N. Falkner, 1783), p. 53

16. It was, according to Turnbull, introduced into Lancashire in 1788 by Dr Thomas Henry of Thomas Ridgeway & Son, of Wallsuches, Horwich, a firm founded in 1777 and 'one of the largest and most enterprising bleaching firms of the time [and] the first firm to erect a glazing

calendar . . .' (one of the processes that had previously distinguished London chintzes); the use of chlorine was difficult until Tennant's 1799 patent for bleaching powder, which between 1805 and 1812 reduced in cost from £112 to £60 per ton, with production increasing during the same time by more than double. Geoffrey Turnbull, *A History of the Calico Printing Industry of Great Britain* (John Sherratt & Son, 1951), pp. 33–4, hereafter referred to as *History*.

17. Peel pattern book, The Human History Department, Bolton Museum and Art Gallery. The cheapest process listed was 'Black and purple honeycomb' at 12s, and was quite probably a semi-discharge, using a weak bleach solution to turn the black to purple.

18. See Wendy Hefford, *The Victoria and Albert Museum's Textile Collection: Design for Printed Textiles in England from 1750 to 1850* (Victoria and Albert Museum, 1992), plate 134 for an example which demonstrates this style on a black ground.

19. See the sample page in Ackermann's *Repository*, March 1811, which includes 'A bright permanent morone printed cambric for intermediate order of dress. It admits of repeated washing without any detriment to its colours'. The pattern is a three-quarter-inch 'hop' in red, black, blue and yellow, placed so that a generous amount of Turkey red ground is displayed.

20. *Repository*, July 1809; and The Human History Department, Bolton Museum and Art Gallery, John Heywood & Son correspondence.

21. See *Victoria and Albert Museum: English Printed Textiles* (HMSO, 1960), illustrations 42–9. It was not until about 1815 that rollers of sufficient size – allowing a downward pattern repeat of about 22 inches – were available (although in 1862 reference was made to 43 inch rollers for furnishings; see F. C. Calvert, 'On Improvements and Progress in Dyeing and Calico Printing since 1851', *Journal of the Society of Arts* (February 1862), p. 176.

22. Joseph Lockett introduced the die-and-mill process to copper roller engraving in 1808; this repeated a small design (up to six inches) over the roller.

23. Turnbull, *History*, p. 27. Graham noted that their peak production was in 1834–5, when they produced nearly three million yards; by the time they closed in 1841, they had five printing machines.

24. *Peel and Oberkampf*, citing the *Manchester Mercury*, 14 November 1786. For a full discussion of the 1787 Act, see Ada Leask, 'William Kilburn and the earliest Copyright Acts for Cotton Printing Design', *Burlington Magazine*, vol. 95 (July 1953), pp. 230–3.

25. Hefford, *V. and A.*, p. 10, citing Charles O'Brien, *The Calico Printers' Assistant*, vol. 2 (1792, from internal evidence written in 1790), unpaginated. The major saving was probably in the price of the cloth, although some reduction in cost occurred because the copiest did not have to pay for designs or designers, which cost London printers up to £1,000 a year. O'Brien nevertheless stretched the point, since a half-price version of a London pattern would look very different by virtue of the necessarily limited colouring of the copy.

26. Journal of Samuel Rowland Fisher, of the Philadelphia dry-goods importing firm, Joshua Fisher & Sons, 1783, cited in Florence Montgomery, *Printed Textiles: English and American Cottons and Linens, 1700–1850* (Thames and Hudson, 1970), p. 31. A year later the Peel and Livesey works alone were producing nearly 30 per cent of all British printed textiles, see *Peel and Oberkampf*, p. 58.

27. Evidence of this dates from as early as 1808, see M. Schoeser and C. Rufey, *English and American Textiles: 1790 to the Present* (Thames and Hudson, 1989), p. 44.

28. Turnbull, *History*, p. 136, citing a speech by George Wallis to the Society of Arts, 23 May 1849.

29. Greysmith, dissertation, pp. 103–5, and citing Edmund Potter, 'Calico Printing as an Art Manufacture' in *Monthly Literary and Scientific Lecturer*, vol. 3 (1852), note 8, p. 23.

30. Greysmith, *ibid*.

31. Hefford, *V and A*, pl. 217 (the gothic stripe) and 195–6 for other examples; a large number of such designs survive in American collections.

32. Richard Redgrave, *Report on the Present State of Design Applied to Manufactures, as shown in the Paris Universal Exhibition*, vol. 3 (1955), p. 398.

33. Turnbull, *History*, p. 137, citing George Wallis, 'A Fifty Year Retrospect of British Art', paper read before the Arts Society on 31 October 1882.

34. *Peterson's Magazine*, vol. 36, no. 6 (December 1859), p. 44.

35. George S. Cole, *A Complete Dictionary of Dry Goods* . . . (J. B. Herring Publishing Co., Chicago, 1894), p. 53.

36. see David J. Jeremy, *Transatlantic Industrial Revolution: The Diffusion of Textile Technologies Between Britain and America, 1790–1830s* (Basil Blackwell, 1981), pp. 109–12; and see Diane L. Fagan Affleck, *Just New From the Mills: Printed Cottons in America* (Museum of American Textile History, 1987), for numerous examples of fourth-quarter nineteenth-century American printers patterns – especially p. 54, showing an example almost identical to an early Hoyle's print (Allen 1428).

37. J. Emerson Tennent, *A Treatise on the Copyright of Designs* (1841), p. 3, note 16. At this time there were said to be ten times more designers in Paris than in London and Manchester combined. Freelance designing appears to have been prevalent; in 1833 James Thomson stated that his printworks at Primrose, Clitheroe, was one of only about six employing in-house designers.

38. See Mary Schoeser and Kathleen Dejardin, *French Textiles from 1760 to the Present* (Lawrence King, London, 1991), pp. 100–2.

39. For a complete discussion, see David Greysmith, 'Patterns, Piracy and Protection in the Textile Printing Industry 1787–1850', *Textile History*, 14, no. 2, 1983), pp. 165–94. The author wishes to point out that the figure given for registered furnishing designs on page 186 should read 3,000.

40. See Stuart Robinson, *A History of Dyed Textiles* (Studio Vista Ltd, 1969), plates 33 and 35–7.

41. See *Fine Costume, Haute Couture, Needlework, Textiles and an Archive of Printed Cottons* (Christie's, South Kensington, 5 March 1991), pp. 18–25. Three volumes, two of 1872 and one covering 1897–1905, were purchased by the Department of Textiles and Dress, Victoria and Albert Museum.

42. 'Owen Jones and his Contemporaries: Chapter II', *The Journal of Decorative Art* (February 1881), p. 15.

43. Charles Eastlake, *Hints on Household Taste in Furniture, Upholstery and Other Details*, 4th rev. ed. (Longman, Green & Co., London, 1878), p. 103; first edition 1868.

44. Turnbull, *History*, pp. 349, 370.

45. See Linda Parry, *The Victoria and Albert Museum's Textile Collection: British Textiles from 1850 to 1900* (Victoria and Albert Museum, 1993), pp. 16–20.

46. Christie's, p. 20, lot 162 (illustrated), noting that one of the dolls was printed by Samuel Finburgh & Company, Manchester.

47. See, for example, *Ideas for New Designs*, samples books of Gregson and Monk Ltd, Preston, 1884–1908, Harris Museum, Preston.

48. See Mary Schoeser, *Fabrics and Wallpapers: Twentieth-Century Design* (Bell and Hyman, 1986), pp. 29–31. Cited hereafter as *Fabrics*.

49. Five years later Walter Crane published his Manchester lectures in *The Bases of Design*, dedicated to Charles Rowley, the school's chairman.

50. The 1932 (St Anne's) Conference Committee of the National Association of Head Teachers, *Education in Lancashire* (Ginn & Co. Ltd, London, 1932), p. 80.

51. Schoeser, *Fabrics*, pp. 41–3 and 55; their second exhibition, held in Manchester in 1916, was of textiles.

52. Basil Ionides, 'Textiles', *Architectural Review*, vol. 59 (1926), p. 184.

53. See *Ideal Home*, vol. 17 (28 March and 28 June 1928), unpaginated advertisements, naming the designers as G. Day, H. R. Thomson, Elsie McNaught, John Revel, Helen McKenzie, Herbert Budd, A. M. Talmage, J. S. Tunnard, T. C. Dugdale, Jacqueline Cundall and Lucy Revel.

54. Cyril Connolly, 'Genuine Arts and Crafts', *Architectural Review* (January–June 1932), p. 23; this information courtesy of Dr Christine Boydell.

55. 'Textiles and Furnishing', *Catalogue of the Exhibition of Contemporary Industrial Design in the Home* (Dorland Hall, 1934), p. 107.

56. H. G. Hayes Marshall, *British Textile Designers Today* (F. Lewis Ltd, Leigh-on-Sea, 1939), p. 326.

57. N. Pevsner, *Industrial Art in England* (Cambridge University Press, 1937), p. 48; he does not name the firm, but describes it as 'a house famous for dress materials, employing a staff of over 4,000'. It may well have been Horrockses.

58. *Exhibition of British Art in Industry* (Royal Academy, 1935), p. 162.

59. Hayes Marshall, *British Textile Designers*, pp. 315–21; and catalogue of *Britain Can Make It* (1945) for information regarding clients.

60. Michael Farr, *Design in British Industry*, 2nd ed. (Cambridge University Press, 1955), p. 223.

61. Alan Peat, *David Whitehead Ltd: Artist Designed Textiles, 1952–1969* (Oldham Leisure Services, 1993), p. 24.

62. Grace Lovat Fraser, *Textiles by Britain* (George Allen and Unwin, 1948), pp. 103–4.

63. Hayes Marshall, *British Textile Designers*, p. 222.

64. Turnbull, *History*, p. 405 (citing a report written by himself in 1935).

## Further reading

Veronic Gevers (ed.), *Studies in Textile History* (Royal Ontario Museum, 1977).

David Greysmith, 'Patterns, Piracy and Protection in the Textile Printing Industry, 1787–1850', *Textile History*, 14 (1983).

Wendy Hefford, *The Victoria and Albert's Textile Collection: Design for Printed Textile in England from 1750 to 1850* (Victoria and Albert Museum).

Florence Montgomery, *Textiles in America, 1650–1870* (W. W. Norton & Co., 1984).

Linda Parry, *The Victoria and Albert Museum's Textile Collection: British Textiles from 1850–1900* (Victoria and Albert Museum, 1993).

N. Pevsner, *Industrial Art in England* (Cambridge University Press, 1937).

M. Schoeser, *Fabrics and Wallpapers: Twentieth-Century Design* (Bell and Hyman, 1986).

M. Schoeser and C. Rufey, *English and American Textiles: 1790 to the Present* (Thames and Hudson, 1989).

# Notes to Chapter 8

1. I am most grateful to Dr D. A. Farnie for his critical and magisterial comments on the first draft of this chapter; and I am obliged to Dr Mary Rose for her editorial appraisal. I remain responsible for the final draft.

2. David J. Jeremy, *Technology and Power in the Early American Cotton Industry: James Montgomery, the Second Edition of His 'Cotton Manufacture' (1840), and the 'Justitia' Controversy about Relative Power Costs* (American Philosophical Society, 1990), p. 32.

3. V. A. C. Gatrell, 'Labour, Power, and the Size of Firms in Lancashire Cotton in the Second Quarter of the Nineteenth Century', *Economic History Review*, 2nd series, 30 (1977), p. 127.

4. George Henry Wood, *The History of Wages in the Cotton Trade During the Past Hundred Years* (Sherratt and Hughes, 1910), p. 125.

5. J. H. Clapham, *The Economic Development of France and Germany, 1815–1914* (Cambridge University Press, 1928), p. 63.

6. USA, *Eighth Census of the United States*, 1860, 3 (Government Printing Office, 1865), p. xix; D. T. Jenkins, 'The Validity of the Factory Returns, 1833–50', *Textile History*, 4 (1973), pp. 40, 43.

7. Jeremy, *Technology and Power*, p. 29.

8. *Statistics of Lowell Manufactures*, 1 January 1837.

9. Gatrell, 'Labour, Power', pp. 100, 135; Mary B. Rose, *The Gregs of Quarry Bank Mill: The Rise and Decline of a Family Firm, 1750–1914* (Cambridge University Press, 1986), p. 55.

10. In this essay I am using the terms 'sharing technology', 'technology transfer' and 'technology diffusion' interchangeably to denote the complex process under discussion. While transfer can occur between countries, regions, firms or individuals, I am almost always considering transfer between countries.

11. James Foreman-Peck, *A History of the World Economy: International Economic Relations Since 1850* (Wheatsheaf, 1983), pp. 37–45.

12. Michael E. Porter, *The Competitive Advantage of Nations* (Macmillan, 1990).

13. Raymond Vernon, 'International Investment and International Trade in the Product Cycle', *Quarterly Journal of Economics*, 80, no. 2 (May 1966).

14. Nathan Rosenberg, *Technology and American Economic Growth* (Harper and Row, 1972); idem, *Inside the Black Box* (Cambridge University Press, 1982).

15. Everett M. Rogers and F. Floyd Shoemaker, *Communication of Innovations: A Cross-Cultural Approach* (Free Press, 1971).

16. Kenneth J. Arrow, 'Classificatory Notes on the Production and Transmission of Technological Knowledge', *American Economic Review*, 59, no. 2 (1969), p. 33.

17. David J. Jeremy (ed.), *Technology Transfer and Business Enterprise*, vol. 9 in *The International Library of Critical Writings in Business History*, Geoffrey Jones (ed.) (Edward Elgar, 1994), pp. xxii–xxiii.

18. W. W. Rostow, *The Stages of Economic Growth* (Cambridge University Press, 1960).

19. David J. Jeremy (ed.), *Henry Wansey and His American Journal, 1794* (American Philosophical Society, 1970), p. 146; Howard Robinson, *Carrying British Mails Overseas* (Allen and Unwin, 1964), p. 115; Robert G. Albion, *The Rise of New York Port (1815–1860)* (David and Charles, 1970), pp. 38–43.

20. David J. Jeremy, *Transatlantic Industrial Revolution: The Diffusion of Textile Technologies between Britain and America, 1790s–1830s* (Cambridge, MA: MIT Press, 1981), p. 149.

21. Robert Owen, *The Life of Robert Owen, Written by Himself* (2 vols, Wilson, 1857), I, p. 31; Jeremy, *Transatlantic Industrial Revolution*, pp. 36–9.

22. Jeremy, *Technology and Power*, p. 18.

23. Jeremy, *Transatlantic Industrial Revolution*, pp. 68–9; Negley B. Harte, 'On Rees's Cyclopaedia as a Source for the History of the Textile Industries in the Early Nineteenth Century', *Textile History*, 5 (1974); Jeremy, *Technology and Power*, pp. 6–12.

24. Jeremy, *Transatlantic Industrial Revolution*, pp. 36–9. For some discussion of skills see David J. Jeremy, 'British Textile Technology Transmission to the United States: The Philadelphia Region Experience, 1770–1820', *Business History Review*, 47 (1973).

25. John A. Cantrell, *James Nasmyth and the Bridgewater Foundry. A Study in Entrepreneurship in the Early Engineering Industry*, Chetham Society, 3rd series, 31 (1984), pp. 44, 136–9.

26. Christine MacLeod, 'Strategies for Innovation: The Diffusion of New Technology in Nineteenth-Century British Industry', *Economic History Review*, 45 (1992).

27. David J. Jeremy, 'Damming the Flood: British Government Efforts to Check the Outflow of Technicians and Machinery, 1780–1843', *Business History Review*, 51 (1977).

28. Public Record Office, BT 5/21, p. 70, minutes of 4 December 1811.

29. Bruce Sinclair, 'At the Turn of a Screw: William Sellers, the Franklin Institute, and a Standard American Thread', *Technology and Culture*, 10 (1969).

30. Jeremy, *Transatlantic Industrial Revolution*, pp. 50–1.

31. GB, PP *(House of Commons)* 1820 (314), VII, 'Second Report of the Commissioners . . . [on] Weights and Measures', Appendix A.

32. H. I. Dutton, *The Patent System and Inventive Activity during the Industrial Revolution, 1750–1852* (Manchester University Press, 1984), p. 2. See also Trevor Griffiths, Philip A. Hunt and Patrick K. O'Brien, 'Inventive Activity in the British Textile Industry, 1700–1800', *Journal of Economic History*, 52 (1992).

33. Jeremy, *Transatlantic Industrial Revolution*, p. 55.

34. W. W. Rostow, *British Economy of the Nineteenth Century* (Clarendon Press, 1948), p. 8.

35. PP *(Commons)* 1829 (332) 3, 'Report from the Select Committee on the Law Relative to Patents for Inventions'.

36. Jeremy, *Transatlantic Industrial Revolution*, pp. 45–9.

37. PP *(Commons)* 1824 (51) v, 'Six Reports from the Select Committee on Artizans and Machinery', p. 545.

38. Jeremy, *Transatlantic Industrial Revolution*, p. 43.

39. Charlotte Erickson, *Invisible Immigrants: The Adaptation of English and Scottish Immigrants in Nineteenth-Century America* (University of Miami Press, 1972), p. 269.

40. Public Record Office, BT 1/76, f. 36, James Kipping, Liverpool Customs Surveyor on Special Service, to the Collector of Liverpool, 8, 9, 12 March 1811.

41. Jeremy, *Transatlantic Industrial Revolution*, p. 138.

42. Henry Ainley took drawings with him to Japan in 1866 (Dr Farnie tells me).

43. A. E. Musson, 'Continental Influences on the Industrial Revolution in Great Britain', in B. M. Ratcliffe, *Great Britain and Her World, 1750–1914* (Manchester University Press, 1975).

44. A. P. Wadsworth and J. de Lacy Mann, *The Cotton Trade and Industrial Lancashire, 1600–1780* (Manchester University Press, 1931), pp. 449–64.

45. Arthur L. Dunham, *The Industrial Revolution in France, 1815–1848* (Exposition Press, 1955), p. 257. Wadsworth and Mann, *Cotton Trade*, pp. 503–4. Henderson noted that an Englishman, Morgan, who owned a factory at Amiens, made improvements in the jenny in 1755: presumably a misprint for 1775 or 1795. See W. O. Henderson, *Britain and Industrial Europe, 1750–1870* (Leicester University Press, 1972), p. 21. The fullest and definitive account of the Holkers' activities is given by Professor John R. Harris in his forthcoming volume on technology transfer.

46. Wadsworth and Mann, *Cotton Trade*, p. 504; Henderson, *Britain and Industrial Europe*, p. 21.

47. Henderson, *Britain and Industrial Europe*, p. 22; Wadsworth and Mann, *Cotton Trade*, pp. 504–5.

48. Henderson, *Britain and Industrial Europe*, p. 24.

49. Henderson, *Britain and Industrial Europe*, p. 27.

50. J-M. Schmitt, 'Relations between England and the Mulhouse Textile Industry in the Nineteenth Century', *Textile History* 17, no. 1 (Spring 1986); Henderson, *Britain and Industrial Europe*, p. 25.

51. Dunham, *Industrial Revolution in France*, p. 263.

52. Henderson, *Britain and Industrial Europe*, p. 21.

53. David S. Landes, *The Unbound Prometheus: Technological Change and Industrial Development in Western Europe from 1750 to the Present* (Cambridge University Press, 1969), p. 140.

54. Kristine Bruland, *British Technology and European Industrialisation: The Norwegian Textile Industry in the Mid-Nineteenth Century* (Cambridge University Press, 1989).

55. PP *(Commons)* 1824 (51) v, 'Six Reports from the Select Committee on Artizans and Machinery', pp. 108, 299; W. W. Rostow, *British Economy*, p. 33.

56. PP *(Commons)* 1824 (51) v, 'Six Reports from the Select Committee on Artizans and Machinery', p. 545.

57. For descriptions of these districts see the accounts of travellers seeking industrial information, e.g. W. O. Henderson (ed.), *Industrial Britain under the Regency: The Diaries of Escher, Bodmer, May and de Gallois, 1814–1818* (Cass, 1968) and Zachariah Allen, *Practical Tourist*, 2 vols, (A. S. Beckwith, 1832).

58. Henderson, *Industrial Britain under the Regency*, pp. 7–16, 75–111.

59. PP *(Commons)* 1824 (51) v, 'Six Reports from the Select Committee on Artizans and Machinery', pp. 546, 548.

60. PP *(Commons)* 1824 (51) v, 'Six Reports from the Select Committee on Artizans and Machinery', p. 17.

61. J-P. Chaline, 'The Cotton Manufacturer in Normandy and England during the Nineteenth Century', *Textile History*, 17, no. 1 (Spring 1986), p. 22.

62. PP *(Commons)* 1824 (51) v, 'Six Reports from the Select Committee on Artizans and Machinery', p. 579.

63. Henderson, *Britain and Industrial Europe*, pp. 22, 28–9, 52–8.

64. Stuart Thompstone, 'Ludwig Knoop, "The Arkwright of Russia"', *Textile History*, 15, no. 1 (Spring 1984)

65. Eric Robinson, 'The Transference of British Technology to Russia, 1760–1820: A Preliminary Enquiry', in Ratcliffe (ed.), *Great Britain and Her World*.

66. Thompstone, 'Ludwig Knoop'.

67. R. S. Fitton, *The Arkwrights: Spinners of Fortune* (Manchester University Press, 1989); Jeremy, *Transatlantic Industrial Revolution* pp. 14–19, 76–91; Anthony F. C. Wallace and David J. Jeremy, 'William Pollard and the Arkwright Patents', *William and Mary Quarterly*, 3rd series, 34 (1977); Barbara M. Tucker, *Samuel Slater and the Origins of the American Textile Industry, 1790–1860* (Cornell University Press, 1984).

68. See Robert F. Dalzell, Jnr, *Enterprising Elite: The Boston Associates and the World They Made* (Cambridge, MA: Harvard University Press, 1987), pp. 5–25.

69. Jeremy, *Transatlantic Industrial Revolution*, pp. 109–10.

70. Jeremy, *Technology and Power*.

71. Jeremy, *Transatlantic Industrial Revolution*, pp. 161–3.

72. Jeremy, *Transatlantic Industrial Revolution*, pp. 104–15.

73. New Hampshire Historical Society, Concord, NH, Dover Manufacturing Company, Agent's Letterbooks (three spanning January 1825 to September 1828), John Williams (company agent at Dover, NH) to William Shimmin (company treasurer in Boston), 26 January 1827. I am grateful to the NHHS for permission to read and quote from these letterbooks.

74. For further data and discussion of industrial espionage see David J. Jeremy, 'Transatlantic Industrial Espionage in the Early Nineteenth Century: Barriers and Penetrations', *Textile History*, 26 (1995).

75. Robert Kirk and Colin Simmons, 'Lancashire and the Equipping of the Indian Cotton Mills: A Study of Textile Machinery Supply, 1854–1939', *Salford (University) Papers in Economics*, 81–6 (1981), pp. 2–4, 17.

76. By 1913 73.5 per cent of India's spindles were rings whilst in Japan at that date the proportion was 97.74 per cent (information from Dr D. A. Farnie).

77. S. D. Mehta, *The Cotton Mills of India, 1854 to 1954* (Bombay: The Textile Association (India), 1954), pp. 13–20. Mehta diverges at points from Rutnagur (next note). I have followed Mehta's account which seems more thoroughly researched.

78. S. M. Rutnagur, *Bombay Industries: The Cotton Mills* (Bombay: Indian Textile Journal, 1927), pp. 9–10.

79. Daniel R. Headrick, *The Tentacles of Progress: Technology Transfer in the Age of Imperialism, 1850–1940* (Oxford University Press, 1988), pp. 361–6.

80. Mehta, *Cotton Mills of India*, pp. 43–44.

81. Rutnagur, *Bombay Industries*, p. 19.

82. Rutnagur, *Bombay Industries*, pp. 297–311.

83. Yukihiko Kiyokawa, 'Technical Adaptations and Managerial Resources in India: A Study of the Experience of the Cotton Textile Industry from a Comparative Viewpoint', *The Developing Economies*, 21, no. 2 (June 1983).

84. Stanley Chapman, *Merchant Enterprise in Britain from the Industrial Revolution to World War I* (Cambridge University Press, 1992), p. 268.

85. For this fact I am grateful to Dr D. A. Farnie.

86. Tetsuro Nakaoka, 'The Transfer of Cotton Manufacturing Technology from Britain to Japan' in David J. Jeremy (ed.), *International Technology Transfer: Europe, Japan and the USA, 1700–1914* (Edward Elgar, 1991).

87. Nakaoka, 'Transfer of Cotton Manufacturing Technology'.

88. G. C. Allen, *A Short Economic History of Japan* (Macmillan, 1981), pp. 73–5, 123, 261.

89. Information from Dr D. A. Farnie.

90. Julia de L. Mann, 'The Textile Industry: Machinery for Cotton, Flax, Wool, 1760–1850', in Charles Singer *et al.* (eds), *A History of Technology*, 7 vols (Clarendon Press, 1954–78), vol. 4; D. A. Farnie, 'The Textile Industry: Woven Fabrics', in *ibid.* vol. 5.

91. Jeremy, *Transatlantic Industrial Revolution*, pp. 196, 206–8; David J. Jeremy, 'Technological Diffusion: The Case of the Differential Gear', *Industrial Archaeology Review*, 5 (1981).

92. David J. Jeremy, 'Invention in American Textile Technology during the Early Nineteenth-century, 1790–1830' in *Working Papers from the Regional Economic History Research Centre* vol. 5, no. 4 (1982); Jeremy, *Technology and Power*, pp. 99–103; John W. Lozier, 'Taunton and Mason: Cotton Machinery and Locomotive Manufacture in Taunton, Massachusetts, 1811–1861' (Ohio State University Ph.D,. 1978), pp. 203–44; Thomas R. Navin, *The Whitin Machine Works since 1831: A Textile Machinery Company in an Industrial Village* (Cambridge MA: Harvard University Press, 1950), pp. 180–203.

93. William Mass, 'Mechanical and Organisational Innovation: The Drapers and the Automatic Loom', *Business History Review* 63 (1989).

94. Jeremy, *Transatlantic Industrial Revolution*, pp. 240–51.

95. D. A. Farnie, 'The Textile Machine-Making Industry and the World Market, 1870–1960', *Business History*, 32, no. 4 (October 1990), p. 154; Idem., 'The Marketing Strategies of Platt Bros & Co. Ltd of Oldham, 1906–1940', *Textile History*, 24, no. 2 (Autumn 1993).

## Further reading

Kristine Bruland, *British Technology and European Industrialization: The Norwegian Textile Industry in the Mid-Nineteenth Century* (Cambridge University Press, 1989).

D. A. Farnie, 'The Textile Machine Making Industry and the World Market, 1870–1960', *Business History*, 32 (1990).

Daniel R. Headrick, *The Tentacles of Progress: Technology Transfer in the Age of Imperialism, 1850–1940* (Oxford University Press, 1988).

W. O. Henderson, *Britain and Industrial Europe, 1750–1850* (Leicester University Press, 1972).

David J. Jeremy (ed.), *Transatlantic Industrial Revolution: The Diffusion of Textile Technologies between Britain and America* (MIT Press, 1981).

David J. Jeremy (ed.), *Technology Transfer and Business Enterprise* (Edward Elgar, 1994).

David J. Jeremy, 'British Technology Transmission to the United States: The Philadelphia Region Experience, 1770–1820', *Business History Review*, 47 (1973).

David J. Jeremy, 'Damming the Flood: British Government Efforts to Check the Outflow of Technicians and Machinery, 1780–1843', *Business History Review*, 51 (1977).

David S. Landes, *The Unbound Prometheus: Technological Change and Industrial Development in Western Europe From 1750 to the Present* (Cambridge University Press, 1969).

Tetsuro Nakaoka, 'The Transfer of Cotton Manufacturing Technology from Britain to Japan', in David J. Jeremy (ed.), *International Technology Transfer: Europe, Japan and the USA, 1700–1914* (Edward Elgar, 1991).

# Notes to Chapter 9

1. B. Bowker, *Lancashire Under the Hammer* (Hogarth Press, 1928), pp. 9–21.

2. R. Robson, *The Cotton Industry in Britain* (Macmillan, 1957), pp. 2–3; D. A. Farnie, 'The Structure of the British Cotton Industry, 1846–1914', in Akio Okochi and Shin-Ichi Yonekawa (eds), *The Textile Industry and Its Business Climate: Proceedings of the Fuji Conference*, International Conference on Business History, 8 (University of Tokyo Press, 1982), p. 46; S. J. Stein, *The Brazilian Cotton Manufacture* (Harvard University Press, 1957); S. D. Mehta, *The Cotton Mills of India, 1854 to 1954* (Bombay, The Textile Association, 1954).

3. See, for example, J. R. Campbell to editor, *Manchester Guardian*, 10 June 1905, p. 7; cf. H. Smalley to editor, *Manchester Guardian*, 13 June 1905, p. 3.

4. A. E. Musson, *The Growth of British Industry* (Batsford, 1978), pp. 202–3.

5. S. J. Chapman, *A Reply to the Report of the Tariff Commission on the Cotton Industry* (Sherratt and Hughes, 1905), p. 53.

6. P. Deane and W. A. Cole, *British Economic Growth, 1688–1959* (Cambridge University Press, 1962), table 43, p. 187.

7. A. J. Robertson, 'The Decline of the Scottish Cotton Industry, 1860–1914', *Business History*, 12 (1970); R. Lloyd-Jones and M. J. Lewis, *Manchester and the Age of the Factory* (Croom Helm, 1988), pp. 205–7; Farnie, 'Structure', pp. 68–9.

8. H. W. Macrosty, *The Trust Movement in British Industry* (Longman, Green & Co., 1907); L. Hannah, *The Rise of the Corporate Economy* (Methuen, 1976), ch. 2; A. D. Chandler, *Scale and Scope: The Dynamics of Industrial Capitalism* (Harvard University Press, 1990), part III.

9. D. A. Farnie, *The English Cotton Industry and the World Market 1815–1896* (Clarendon Press, 1979), p. 215; Farnie, 'Structure', table 3, p. 61.

10. Macrosty, *Trust Movement*, ch. 5; Christine Shaw, 'The Large Manufacturing Employers of 1907', in R. P. T. Davenport-Hines (ed.), *Business in the Age of Depression and War* (Frank Cass, 1990), pp. 1–19; J. S. Toms, 'The Profitability of the First Lancashire Merger: The Case of Horrocks, Crewdson & Co. Ltd, 1887–1905', *Textile History*, 24 (1993), pp. 129–46.

11. D. A. Farnie and Shin'ichi Yonekawa, 'The Emergence of the Large Firm in the Cotton Spinning Industries of the World, 1883–1938', *Textile History*, 19 (1988), pp. 171–210.

12. For the merchant's public activities in the Manchester Chamber of Commerce, see Arthur Redford's classic *Manchester Merchants and Foreign Trade, II, 1850–1939* (Manchester University Press, 1956), chs 3–14. Also Stanley Chapman, 'The Decline and Rise of Textile Merchanting, 1880–1990', *Business History*, 23 (1990), pp. 171–8.

13. L. G. Sandberg, *Lancashire in Decline: a Study in*

*Entrepreneurship, Technology, and International Trade* (Ohio State University Press, 1974), pp. 6, 108.

14. No detailed aggregate analysis has ever been attempted, but cotton production in the late nineteenth century is generally considered to have yielded only modest returns, whilst, especially in weaving, entry and exit levels were high, business of short duration. Compiling figures from Tattersall's *Cotton Trade Review*, Robson found that during the years 1884–1914 limited companies in spinning declared dividends of 8 per cent or more only in three years, 1906, 1907, and 1908. Losses were declared in 1885–6, 1892–3, 1902–3 and 1909–10. See Robson, *Cotton Industry*, A4, p. 338.

15. R. E. Tyson (ed.), 'The Cotton Industry', in D. H. Aldcroft, *The Development of British Industry and Foreign Competition, 1875–1914* (George Allen and Unwin, 1968), pp. 101–2.

16. A convenient map is found in J. L. White, *The Limits of Trade Union Militancy: The Lancashire Textile Workers, 1910–1914* (Greenwood Press, 1978), p. 2. For 1936, see W. Smith, *An Economic Geography of Great Britain* (Methuen, 2nd ed. 1953), map facing p. 466.

17. Farnie, 'Structure', pp. 61–9

18. Farnie, *English Cotton Industry*, pp. 252, 220–43.

19. F. W. Taussig, *Tariff History of the United States* (G. P. Putnam's Sons, 1888), pp. 34–6, 135–42. Cf. M. Bils, 'Tariff Protection and Production in the Early U.S. Cotton Textile Industry', *Journal of Economic History*, 44 (1984), pp. 1033–46.

20. R. B. Zevin, 'The Growth of Cotton Textile Production after 1815', in R. W. Fogel and S. Engerman, *The Reinterpretation of American Economic History* (Harper and Row, 1971), pp. 122–47; P. A. David, 'Learning by Doing and Tariff Protection: A Reconsideration of the Case of the Ante-Bellum United States Cotton Textile Industry', *Journal of Economic History*, 30 (1970), pp. 521–601.

21. Sandberg, *Lancashire in Decline*, pp. 152–6.

22. See, for example, T. M. Young, *The American Cotton Industry* (Methuen, 1902), pp. 11–13.

23. A. J. Marrison, 'Great Britain and Her Rivals in the Latin-American Cotton Piece-Goods Market, 1880–1914', in B. M. Ratcliffe (ed.), *Great Britain and Her World: Essays in Honour of W. O. Henderson* (Manchester University Press, 1975), pp. 329–33.

24. Robson, *Cotton Industry*, p. 4.

25. An arrogance lampooned with effect in Bowker, *Lancashire Under the Hammer*, ch. 4.

26. Australia and New Zealand are probably the only examples, whilst the Argentine industry was of negligible proportions. I am indebted to D. A. Farnie for this information.

27. Farnie, *English Cotton Industry*, p. 179; Robson, *Cotton Industry*, p. 2.

28. *Annual Statement of Trade of the United Kingdom, House of Commons, Sessional Papers*, various years.

29. On finer counts, see, for example, *Textile Mercury*, August 1890, p. 104, September 1892, p. 105; *Textile Recorder*, January 1893, p. 239, July 1896, p. 188, September 1911, p. 143; S. L. Besso, *The Cotton Industry of Switzerland, Vorarlberg and Italy* (Manchester University Press, 1910), pp. 10–11, 19. On finishing, see *Report of the Tariff Commission*, vol. 2, part 1, *The Cotton Industry* (P. S. King & Son, 1905), paras 69, 73; S. J. Chapman, 'The Report of the Tariff Commission', *Economic Journal*, 15 (1905), pp. 420–1.

30. H. B. Heylin, *Buyers and Sellers in the Cotton Trade* (Griffin, 1913), p. 104; *Report of the Tariff Commission*, paras 20–8.

31. In 1908, dyed goods were further split into two: goods dyed 'in the piece', and goods 'manufactured wholly or in part of dyed yarn, commonly known as coloured cottons'.

32. As calculated by dividing total export values by quantity, giving, in effect, average f.o.b. export prices.

33. *The Economist*'s index was composed only of grey cloths. Though the relative prices of grey and more highly finished clothes in Britain's exports were fairly stable in the period 1871–1900, this was not so after 1900. For this period, Sandberg performed two calculations, one assuming that the grey : coloured export price ratio reflected changes in their relative quality, the other assuming it did not. The differences are relatively small.

34. L. G. Sandberg, 'Movements in the Quality of British Cotton Textile Exports, 1815–1913', *Journal of Economic History*, 28 (1968), pp. 1–27.

35. Marrison, 'Great Britain and Her Rivals'. One revealing facet of the US print trade, which may have been more widely applicable of more highly finished goods generally, is that US producers used state-of-the-art printing machinery to produce long runs of high-quality prints in several colours, only to find that Latin American consumers preferred individuality.

36. Figures for 1904 would show a much larger penetration of the Chinese market by printed and dyed goods. China (along with Western Europe) was unusual in that these categories declined as a proportion of imports from Britain in 1904–13.

37. A. Silver, *Manchester Men and Indian Cotton, 1847–1872* (Manchester University Press, 1966); P. Harnetty, *Imperialism and Free Trade: Lancashire and India in the Mid-Nineteenth Century* (Manchester University Press, 1972), chs 6–7.

38. Redford, *Manchester Merchants*, II, chs 3–4; R. Smith, 'The Manchester Chamber of Commerce and the Increasing Foreign Competition to Lancashire Cotton Textiles', *Bulletin of the John Rylands Library*, 38 (1956), pp. 518–19.

39. C. Dewey, 'The End of the Imperialism of Free Trade: The Eclipse of the Lancashire Lobby and the Concession of Fiscal Autonomy to India', in C. Dewey and A. G. Hopkins (eds), *The Imperial Impact: Studies in the Economic History of Africa and India* (Athlone Press, 1978), p. 35.

40. Dewey, 'End of Imperialism', pp. 35–67.

41. For the events in the war and the concession of fiscal autonomy, see also B. Chatterji, *Trade, Tariffs, and Empire: Lancashire and British Policy in India, 1919–1939* (Delhi, Oxford University Press, 1992).

42. For basic descriptions of the mule- and ring-spinning processes, see J. Jewkes and E. M. Gray, *Wages and Labour in the Lancashire Cotton Spinning Industry* (Manchester University Press, 1935), pp. 3–14; Sandberg, *Lancashire in Decline*, pp. 18–20.

43. M. T. Copeland, *The Cotton Manufacturing Industry of the United States* (Harvard University Press, 1912), p. 70; Robson, *Cotton Industry*, p. 355; W. Lazonick, 'Industrial Organization and Technological Change: The Decline of the British Cotton Industry', *Business History Review*, 57 (1983), p. 196. Allowing for higher yarn output from the ring spindle would show ring spinning to be even more dominant in the USA than the figures presented above.

44. D. A. Farnie, 'The Marketing Strategies of Platt Bros & Co. Ltd of Oldham, 1906–1940', *Textile History*, 24 (1993), pp. 147–50; Shaw, 'Large Manufacturing Employers'.

45. G. T. Jones, *Increasing Return* (Cambridge University Press, 1933), parts I and III.

46. Tyson, 'Cotton Industry', p. 121.

47. Jones, *Increasing Return*, p. 53; W. Mass and W. Lazonick, 'The British Cotton Industry and International Competitive Advantage: The State of the Debates', *Business History*, 23 (1990), p. 28.

48. Jones used the same index of grey cloths, the *Economist*'s index, that Sandberg later used in his study of cloth quality. But in 1903 the index was changed to reflect products more typical of the new century. It was necessary, therefore, to splice the two indexes, a task which *The Economist* had made possible by projecting the new index back to 1898, so that it overlapped with the old. But, at the turn of the century, the old index was behaving so erratically that the choice of year in which the splice was made is critical, and Sandberg argued that Jones' choice of the year 1899

introduced serious distortions which disappeared if 1898 were used instead. See Sandberg, *Lancashire in Decline*, pp. 96–7, 101–2.

49. Copeland, *Cotton Manufacturing Industry*, pp. 70–2.

50. Jewkes and Gray, *Wages and Labour*, p. 121.

51. This condition did not apply above counts of 100, for which qualities the US practice was still to use mules.

52. Sandberg, 'American Rings and English Mules: The Role of Economic Rationality', *Quarterly Journal of Economics*, 83 (1969).

53. Sandberg, *Lancashire in Decline*, p. 221.

54. See W. Lazonick and W. Mass, 'The Performance of the British Cotton Industry, 1870–1913', *Research in Economic History*, 9 (1984), pp. 20–2, where the output series was smoothed with a (rather short) three-year moving average, but the employment series was left unadjusted. Compare S. N. Broadberry, *Made in Britain: Productivity in British Manufacturing: an International Perspective, 1850–1990* (forthcoming).

55. These factors were also recognized by Copeland, *Cotton Manufacturing Industry*, pp. 79–80.

56. W. Lazonick, 'Industrial Relations and Technical Change: The Case of the Self-Acting Mule', *Cambridge Journal of Economics*, 3 (1979), pp. 257–8; W. Lazonick and W. Mass, 'Performance of the British Cotton Industry', pp. 5–13.

57. Implicit in the stagnation of labour productivity after 1900 and the escalation of labour disputes is the inference that 'hard driving' of the labour force was nearing its limit.

58. W. Lazonick, 'Factor Costs and the Diffusion of Ring Spinning in Britain Prior to World War I', *Quarterly Journal of Economics*, 96 (1981); Lazonick, 'Competition, Specialization, and Industrial Decline', *Journal of Economic History*, 41 (1981), pp. 31–8.

59. W. Lazonick, 'Competition, Specialization and Industrial Decline', p. 37.

60. Lazonick, 'Factor Costs'; cf. Sandberg, *Lancashire in Decline*, p. 29. Subsequently, Sandberg essentially conceded the validity of Lazonick's revisions to his figures on output-mix and replacement rate: L. G. Sandberg, 'The Remembrance of Things Past: Rings and Mules Revisited', *Quarterly Journal of Economics*, 99 (1984), pp. 387–9.

61. Japanese exports surpassed imports in 1898, and grew rapidly, but were still composed predominantly of yarn.

62. G. R. Saxonhouse and G. Wright, 'New Evidence on the Stubborn English Mule and the Cotton Industry, 1878–1920', *Economic History Review*, second series, 37 (1984), pp. 507–19.

63. W. Lazonick, 'Stubborn Mules: Some Comments',

*Economic History Review*, second series, 40 (1987), p. 85.

64. Saxonhouse and Wright, 'New Evidence', p. 519; G. R. Saxonhouse and G. Wright, 'Stubborn Mules and Vertical Integration: The Disappearing Constraint', *Economic History Review*, second series, 40 (1987), pp. 87–94. It is also salutary to remember that Massachusetts could also be guilty of technological inertia. In 1926 65 per cent of automatic looms in the US were in the Southern states. See W. Mass, 'Technological Change and Industrial Relations: the Diffusion of the Automatic Loom in the United States and Britain', unpublished Ph.D. Dissertation, Boston College (1984), p. 98. I am indebted to Mary Rose for this reference.

65. G. Clark, 'Why Isn't the Whole World Developed? Lessons from the Cotton Mills', *Journal of Economic History*, 47 (1987), p. 144.

66. W. Lazonick, 'Industrial Organization and Technological Change: The Decline of the British Cotton Industry', *Business History Review*, 57 (1983), pp. 208–10; Mass and Lazonick, 'British Cotton Industry and International Competitive Advantage', pp. 53–7.

67. Mass and Lazonick, 'British Cotton Industry and International Competitive Advantage', p. 23; Lazonick, 'Industrial Organization and Technological Change', pp. 211–12.

68. Lazonick, 'Competition, Specialization, and Industrial Decline', p. 32.

69. J. S. Toms, 'Financial Constraints on Economic Growth; Profits, Capital Accumulation and the Development of the Lancashire Cotton-spinning Industry, 1885–1914', *Accounting, Business and Financial History*, 4 (1994), pp. 363–83.

70. Mass and Lazonick, 'British Cotton Industry and International Competitive Advantage', pp. 40–1.

71. I am indebted to D. A. Farnie for allowing me to use these preliminary findings.

## Further reading

D. A. Farnie, *The English Cotton Industry and the World Market, 1815–1896* (Clarendon Press, 1979).

D. A. Farnie, 'The Structure of the British Cotton Industry, 1846–1914', in Akio Okochi and Shin-Ichi Yonekawa (eds), *The Textile Industry and its Business Climate: Proceedings of the Fuji Conference*, International Conference on Business History, 8 (University of Tokyo Press, 1982).

W. Lazonick, 'Factor Costs and the Diffusion of Ring Spinning in Britain Prior to World War I', *Quarterly Journal of Economics*, 96 (1981).

W. Lazonick, 'Competition, Specialization, and Industrial Decline', *Journal of Economic History*, 41 (1981).

W. Lazonick and W. Mass, 'The Performance of the British Cotton Industry, 1870–1913', *Research in Economic History*, 9 (1984).

A. J. Marrison, 'Great Britain and her Rivals in the Latin-American Cotton Piece-Goods Market, 1880–1914', in B. M. Ratcliffe (ed.), *Great Britain and Her World: Essays in Honour of W. O. Henderson* (Manchester University Press, 1975).

W. Mass and W. Lazonick, 'The British Cotton Industry and International Competitive Advantage: The State of the Debates', *Business History*, 23 (1990).

Arthur Redford, *Manchester Merchants and Foreign Trade, II, 1850–1939* (Manchester University Press, 1956).

L. G. Sandberg, *Lancashire in Decline: a Study in Entrepreneurship, Technology, and International Trade* (Ohio State University Press, 1974).

G. R. Saxonhouse and G. Wright, 'New Evidence on the Stubborn English Mule and the Cotton Industry, 1878–1920', *Economic History Review*, second series, 37 (1984).

G. R. Saxonhouse and G. Wright, 'Stubborn Mules and Vertical Integration: The Disappearing Constraint', *Economic History Review*, second series, 40 (1987).

R. E. Tyson, 'The Cotton Industry', in D. H. Aldcroft (ed.), *The Development of British Industry and Foreign Competition, 1875–1914* (George Allen and Unwin, 1968).

## Notes to Chapter 10

1. Benjamin Bowker, *Lancashire Under the Hammer* (Hogarth Press, 1928), p. 43.

2. Robert Robson, *The Cotton Industry in Britain* (Macmillan & Co. Ltd, 1957), pp. 333; G. W. Furness, 'The Cotton and Rayon Textile Industry', in D. L. Burn (ed.), *The Structure of British Industry*, vol. 2 (Cambridge University Press, 1958), pp. 185–7; Board of Trade, *Working Party Report – Cotton* (HMSO, 1946), pp. 5–7.

3. Bowker, *Lancashire Under the Hammer*, p. 31.

4. J. D. Tomlinson, 'The First World War and British Cotton Piece Exports to India', *Economic History Review*, second series, 32 (1979), pp. 494–5.

5. John Singleton, 'The Cotton Industry and the

British War Effort, 1914–1918', *Economic History Review*, second series, 47 (1994), pp. 610–11.

6. A. C. Howe, 'Sir Alfred Herbert Dixon', in D. J. Jeremy and C. Shaw (eds), *Dictionary of Business Biography*, vol. 2 (Butterworths, 1984), pp. 110–11; M. W. Dupree, 'Sir Edward Tootal Broadhurst', in D. J. Jeremy (ed.), *Dictionary of Business Biography*, vol. 1 (Butterworths, 1984), p. 455.

7. Singleton, 'The Cotton Industry and the British War Effort', p. 611.

8. *Ibid.*, p. 612.

9. Maurice Kirby and Mary B. Rose, 'Productivity and Competitive Failure: British Government Policy and Industry, 1914–19' in G. Jones and M. W. Kirby (eds), *Competitiveness and the State* (Manchester University Press, 1991), pp. 20, 23, 33.

10. Mike Savage, 'Women and Work in the Lancashire Cotton Industry, 1890–1939', in J. A. Jowitt and A. J. McIvor (eds), *Employers and Labour in the English Textile Industries, 1850–1939* (Routledge, 1988), p. 215; Alan Fowler, 'War and Labour Unrest', in Alan Fowler and Terry Wyke (eds), *The Barefoot Aristocrats: A History of the Amalgamated Association of Operative Cotton Spinners* (George Kelsall, 1987), pp. 146–7.

11. Singleton, 'The Cotton Industry and the British War Effort', p. 613.

12. Savage, 'Women and Work', pp. 215–16. This had implications for undermining the overlooker and, as a result, female labour was directed into employment through the state rather than male working-class contact.

13. H. D. Henderson, *The Cotton Control Board* (Oxford, 1922); Singleton, 'The Cotton Industry and the British War Effort', pp. 612, 614–16; Fowler, 'War and Labour Unrest', p. 148.

14. Singleton, 'The Cotton Industry and the British War Effort', pp. 604–6.

15. M. Dupree (ed.), *Lancashire and Whitehall: the Diary of Sir Raymond Streat, 1931–1957*, vol. 2 (Manchester University Press, 1987), pp. 47–8.

16. Committee on Industry and Trade, *Minutes of Evidence Taken Before the Committee on Industry and Trade, 1924–1927* (for departmental use), vol. 1, p. 466.

17. Bowker, *Lancashire Under the Hammer*, p. 32.

18. *Ibid.*, p. 34.

19. Robson, *Cotton Industry*, p. 338.

20. *Ibid.*, pp. 5, 338. Over 70 per cent of the 17 million spindles installed in the industry between 1900 and 1914 were installed during the 1905–7 boom.

21. Bowker, *Lancashire Under the Hammer*, p. 38; Jim Bamburg, 'Rationalization of the British Cotton Industry in the Interwar Years', *Textile History*, 19 (1988), p. 84.

22. Bowker, *Lancashire Under the Hammer*, pp. 63–4. For the emergence of the system, see D. A. Farnie, *The English Cotton Industry and the World Market, 1815–1896* (Clarendon Press, 1979), esp. pp. 251–64.

23. Bowker, *Lancashire Under the Hammer*, p. 65. Bamberg, 'Rationalization', pp. 84–5.

24. G. W. Daniels and J. Jewkes, 'The Post-War Depression in the Lancashire Cotton Industry', *Journal of the Royal Statistical Society*, 41 (1928), pp. 170–82.

25. Bowker, *Lancashire Under the Hammer*, pp. 40–1.

26. Tomlinson, 'The First World War and British Cotton Piece Exports to India', pp. 494–504, gives a full account of effects of the war on Lancashire's piece goods exports to India.

27. *Ibid.*, p. 497.

28. Tomlinson, 'The First World War and British Cotton Piece Exports to India', p. 499; J. Tomlinson, *Government and the Enterprise Since 1900: the Changing Problem of Efficiency* (Clarendon Press, 1994), p. 347; Committee on Industry and Trade, *Survey of Textile Industries: Cotton, Wool, Artificial Silk* (HMSO, 1928), pp. 100, 102. Milward's comment that, of the 53 per cent decline in Britain's cotton cloth exports between 1913 and 1923, only one-quarter of that decline was attributed to the development of the Indian cotton goods industry during the war is misleading (A. S. Milward, *The Economic Effects of the World Wars on Britain* (Macmillan, 1970), p. 50). It is true that only about one-quarter of the decline in Lancashire's exports between 1913 and 1923 was due to the increase in output of the Indian mill industry *during the war*, but the war covered only part of the period between 1913 and 1923. The total volume of piece goods consumed in the Indian market was essentially the same in 1913 and 1923. The increase in output of the Indian mills over the whole period between 1913 and 1923 was equivalent to nearly 80 per cent of the decline in piece goods imports from Lancashire during the period, while imports from Japan accounted for about 15 per cent of Lancashire's decline, and handloom production in India encouraged by Gandhi accounted for the rest.

29. B. Chatterji, *Trade, Tariffs, and Empire: Lancashire and British Policy in India, 1919–1939* (Oxford University Press, 1992), p. 199; Tomlinson, 'The First World War and British Cotton Piece Exports to India', pp. 502–3.

30. Robson, *Cotton Industry*, pp. 10, 265; see also Tomlinson, 'The First World War and British Cotton Piece Exports to India', pp. 501–3, and Ian M. Drummond, *British Economic Policy and*

*Empire, 1919–1939* (George Allen and Unwin, 1972), p. 123 for discussion of the wartime position.

31. G. R. Saxonhouse and G. Wright, 'New Evidence on the Stubborn English Mule and the Cotton Industry 1878–1920', *Economic History Review*, second series, 37 (1984), p. 519.

32. W. Mass and W. Lazonick, 'The British Cotton Industry and International Competitive Advantage: the State of the Debates', *Business History*, 32 (1990), p. 50; L. Sandberg, *Lancashire in Decline* (Ohio State University Press, 1974), pp. 182–97.

33. Board of Trade, *Working Party Report – Cotton* (HMSO, 1946), p. 5.

34. M. W. Kirby, 'The Lancashire Cotton Industry in the Inter-War Years: a Study of Organisational Change', *Business History*, 16 (1974), pp. 148–9, 156.

35. The Federation of Master Cotton Spinners' Associations.

36. The Cotton Spinners' and Manufacturers' Association.

37. Allied Association of Bleachers, Dyers, Printers and Finishers.

38. The Shipping Merchants' Committee of the Manchester Chamber of Commerce.

39. Dupree (ed.), *Lancashire and Whitehall*, vol. 1, p. 253.

40. Dupree (ed.), *Lancashire and Whitehall*, vol. 2, pp. 768–9.

41. Kirby, 'The Lancashire Cotton Industry', pp. 146–7.

42. Clemens Wurm, *Business, Politics and International Relations: Steel, Cotton and International Cartels in British Politics, 1924–1939*, trans. by P. Salmon (Cambridge University Press, 1993), p. 288.

43. *Ibid.*

44. J. H. Bamberg, 'The Rationalization of the British Cotton Industry in the Interwar Years', *Textile History*, 19 (1988), pp. 86–7; Kirby, 'The Lancashire Cotton Industry', pp. 148–51.

45. Bamberg, 'The Rationalization of the British Cotton Industry', p. 87.

46. *Ibid.*, pp. 87–94.

47. Tomlinson, *Government and the Enterprise Since 1900*, pp. 353–4.

48. W. Lazonick 'The Cotton Industry', in B. Elbaum and W. Lazonick (eds), *The Decline of the British Economy* (Oxford University Press, 1986), p. 45.

49. *Ibid.*, pp. 20–1.

50. Board of Trade, *Working Party*, p. 9.

51. A. McIvor, 'Cotton Employers' Organisations and Labour Relations 1890–1939', in A. McIvor and J. A. Jowett (eds), *Employers and Labour in the English Textile Industries, 1850–1939* (Routledge,

1988), p. 14; A. Fowler, 'Lancashire Cotton Trade Unionism in the Interwar Years', *idem.*, pp. 112, 114.

52. Fowler, 'War and Labour Unrest', pp. 149–64.

53. Fowler, 'Lancashire Cotton Trade Unionism', pp. 115, 116.

54. *Ibid.*, p. 115.

55. McIvor, 'Cotton Employers' Organisations', p. 14.

56. *Ibid.*, pp. 15, 21.

57. Fowler, 'Lancashire Cotton Trade Unionism', p. 116.

58. *Ibid.*, pp. 122–3.

59. *Ibid.*, pp. 117–18.

60. McIvor, 'Cotton Employers' Organisations', pp. 16–17.

61. Board of Trade, *Working Party*, p. 9.

62. Bowker, *Lancashire Under the Hammer*, pp. 80–7; Kirby, 'Lancashire Cotton Industry', pp. 154–5.

63. Kirby, 'Lancashire Cotton Industry', pp. 155–6.

64. Tomlinson, 'The First World War and British Cotton Piece Exports to India', pp. 494–506; Robson, *Cotton Industry*, p. 10.

65. Robson, *Cotton Industry*, p. 265. Chatterji, *Trade, Tariffs and Empire*, pp. 211–65.

66. Robson, *Cotton Industry*, p. 265. In 1933 the Indian and Japanese industries negotiated a reduction to 50 per cent and an import quota for Japanese goods related to purchases of Indian raw cotton.

67. Dupree (ed.), *Lancashire and Whitehall*, vol. 1, pp. 95–9.

68. The Board of Trade official who suggested an industry-to-industry approach comments on its seeming novelty and describes its adoption by the Board of Trade in relation to Anglo-Japanese negotaitions in 1933. See A. Meynell, *Public Servant, Private Woman: An Autobiography* (Victor Gollancz, 1988), pp. 142–3.

69. For Churchill's views on India see M. Gilbert, *Winston S. Churchill*, vol. 5 (Heinemann, 1976), esp. pp. 367–405, 464–84, 496–548, 581–619.

70. B. Chatterji, 'Business and Politics in the 1930s: Lancashire and the Making of the Indo-British Trade Agreement, 1939', *Modern Asian Studies*, 15 (1981), p. 556. See also, Chatterji, *Trade, Tariffs, and Empire*.

71. *Monthly Record*, 48 (1937), x.

72. Chatterji, 'Business and Politics in the 1930s', p. 573.

73. Tomlinson, *Government and the Enterprise Since 1900*, p. 348; Committee on Industry and Trade, *Survey of Textile Industries*, pp. 100, 102.

74. For the development of the Japanese cotton industry see Alex J. Robertson, 'Lancashire and the

Rise of Japan, 1910–1937', in Mary Rose (ed.), *International Competition and Strategic Response in the Textile Industries Since 1870* (Frank Cass, 1991), pp. 88–96.

75. *Ibid.*, p. 96; Mass and Lazonick, 'The British Cotton Industry and International Competitive Advantage', pp. 39, 42–3.

76. Robertson, 'Lancashire and the Rise of Japan', p. 96.

77. E. R. Streat, 'Cotton Between the Wars', *Manchester Guardian*, 5 Dec 1957, cited in Dupree, *Lancashire and Whitehall*, vol. 1, p. xxiv.

78. Wurm, *Business, Politics and International Relations*, pp. 203–98.

79. Tim Rooth, *British Protectionism and the International Economy: Overseas Commercial Policy in the 1930s* (Cambridge University Press, 1993), p. 24.

80. Dupree (ed.), *Lancashire and Whitehall*, vol. 1, p. 12.

81. P. J. Cain and A. G. Hopkins, 'Gentlemanly Capitalism and British Expansion Overseas II: New Imperialism, 1850–1945' *Economic History Review*, second series, 40 (1987), p. 1.

82. Meynell, *Public Servant, Private Woman*, pp. 132, 136.

83. Rooth, *British Protectionism and the International Economy*.

84. Dupree (ed.), *Lancashire and Whitehall*, vol. 1, pp. 194–5.

85. Dupree (ed.), *Lancashire and Whitehall*, vol. 1, p. 313.

86. Mass and Lazonick, 'The British Cotton Industry and International Competitive Advantage', pp. 46–7. The Indian factory industry, however, was handicapped by its dependence on overseas supplies and unable to take full advantage of the reduction of competition from imports during the war, see Tomlinson, 'The First World War and British Cotton Piece Exports to India', pp. 497–501, 504.

## Further reading

J. Bamburgh, 'The Rationalisation of the British Cotton Industry in the Interwar Years', *Textile History*, 19 (1988), pp. 83–102.

Benjamin Bowker, *Lancashire Under the Hammer* (Hogarth Press, 1928).

B. Chatterji, *Trade, Tariffs and Empire: Lancashire and British Policy in India, 1919–1939* (Delhi: Oxford University Press, 1992).

Marguerite Dupree (ed.), *Lancashire and Whitehall: The Diary of Sir Raymond Streat 1931–1957*, vol. 1 (Manchester University Press, 1987).

Marguerite Dupree, 'Fighting Against Fate: the Cotton Industry and the Government During the 1930s', *Textile History*, 21 (1990), pp. 101–17.

Alan Fowler and Terry Wyke (eds), *The Barefoot Aristocrats: A History of the Amalgamated Association of Operative Cotton Spinners* (Littleborough, George Kelsall, 1987).

M. Gilbert, *Winston S. Churchill*, vol. v (Heinemann, 1976).

M. W. Kirby, 'The Lancashire Cotton Industry in the Inter-war Years: a Study of Organisational Change', *Business History*, 16 (1974), pp. 145–59.

W. Lazonick, 'The Cotton Industry', in B. Elbaum and W. Lazonick (eds), *The Decline of the British Economy* (Oxford University Press, 1986).

A. McIvor and J. A. Jowett (eds), *Employers and Labour in the English Textile Industries, 1850–1939* (Routledge, 1988), especially articles by Alan Fowler, Arthur McIvor, Steve Jones, Michael Savage.

Mary Rose (ed.), *International Competition and Strategic Response in the Textile Industries Since 1870* (Cass, 1990), especially: W. Mass and W. Lazonick, 'The British Cotton Industry and International Competitive Advantage: the State of the Debates', pp. 8–65; and A. J. Robertson, 'Lancashire and the Rise of Japan, 1910–1937', pp. 87–105.

Clemens Wurm, *Business, Politics and International Relations: Steel, Cotton and International Cartels in British Politics, 1924–1939*, transl. by P. Salmon (Cambridge University Press, 1993).

# Notes to Chapter 11

I would like to thank Gordon Boyce, Andy Marrison, Paul Robertson and Mary Rose for comments on the previous drafts. All remaining mistakes are my own.

1. William Lazonick, 'Industrial Organization and Technological Change: The Decline of the British Cotton Industry', *Business History Review*, 57 (1983), pp. 195–236.

2. Marguerite Dupree, 'Struggling with Destiny: The Cotton Industry, Overseas Trade Policy and the Cotton Board, 1940–1959', *Business History*, 32 (1990), pp. 106–28, reprinted in Mary B. Rose (ed.), *International Competition and Strategic Response*

in the Textile Industries Since 1870 (Cass, 1991); Marguerite Dupree, 'The Cotton Industry: A Middle Way Between Nationalisation and Self-Government', in Helen Mercer, Neil Rollings, and Jim Tomlinson (eds), Labour Governments and Private Industry: The Experience of 1945–1951 (Edinburgh University Press, 1992), pp. 137–61. Dupree is the editor of an invaluable commentary on events in the cotton industry up to 1957: Sir Raymond Streat (edited by Marguerite Dupree), Lancashire and Whitehall: The Diary of Sir Raymond Streat, vol. 2 (Manchester University Press, 1987).

3. John Singleton, 'Showing the White Flag: The Lancashire Cotton Industry, 1945–65', Business History, 32 (1990), pp. 129–49, reprinted in Mary B. Rose (ed.), International Competition and Strategic Response in the Textile Industries Since 1870 (Cass, 1991); John Singleton, Lancashire on the Scrapheap: The Cotton Industry, 1945–1970 (Oxford University Press for Pasold Research Fund, 1991).

4. R. W. Lacey, 'Cotton's War Effort', Manchester School of Economic and Social Studies, 15 (1947), pp. 26–74; E. L. Hargreaves and M. M. Gowing, Civil Industry and Trade (HMSO, 1952), pp. 343–76; H. E. Wadsworth, 'Utility Cloth and Clothing Scheme', Review of Economic Studies, 16 (1949–50), pp. 82–101; W. Hubball, 'The Cotton Trade's War Time Commodity Supplies', Transactions of the Manchester Statistical Society (1946–7). The war-time economy is described in Sidney Pollard, The Development of the British Economy, 1914–1990 (Edward Arnold, 4th ed., 1992), ch. 5.

5. Singleton, Lancashire on the Scrapheap, chs 2–5. For general background on the British economy in the early post-war period, see Alec Cairncross, The British Economy Since 1945 (Blackwell, 1992), ch. 2, and Pollard, Development of the British Economy, ch. 6.

6. Singleton, Lancashire on the Scrapheap, pp. 36–45.

7. Singleton, Lancashire on the Scrapheap, ch. 4; L. H. C. Tippett, 'The Study of Industrial Efficiency, with Special Reference to the Cotton Industry', Journal of the Royal Statistical Society, 110 (1947), pp. 108–22; L. H. C. Tippett and P. D. Vincent, 'Statistical Investigations of Labour Productivity in Cotton Spinning', Journal of the Royal Statistical Society, 116 (1953), pp. 256–71.

8. G. Evans, 'Wage Rates and Earnings in the Cotton Industry from 1946 to 1951', Manchester School of Economic and Social Studies, 21 (1953), pp. 224–57.

9. D. C. Shaw, 'Productivity in the Cotton Spinning Industry', Manchester School of Economic and Social Studies, 18 (1950), pp. 14–30; K. S. Lomax, 'Recent Productivity Changes in the British Cotton

Industry', Bulletin of the Oxford University Institute of Statistics, 15 (1953), pp. 147–50.

10. Singleton, Lancashire on the Scrapheap, ch. 3; W. Crofts, 'The Attlee Government's Pursuit of Women', History Today, 36 (August 1986), pp. 29–35.

11. Ministry of Production, Report of the Cotton Textile Mission to the United States of America (HMSO, 1944); Singleton, Lancashire on the Scrapheap, pp. 25, 28–9, 91–2.

12. Cotton Board, Report of the Cotton Board Committee to Enquire into Post-War Problems (Cotton Board, 1944).

13. United Textile Factory Workers' Association, Report of the Legislative Council on Ways and Means of Improving the Economic Stability of the Cotton Textile Industry (Rochdale: UTFWA, 1943); John Singleton, 'Debating the Nationalisation of the Cotton Industry', in Robert M. Millward and John Singleton (eds), The Political Economy of Nationalisation in Britain, 1920–50 (Cambridge University Press, 1995), pp. 212–33.

14. Jack Wiseman and B. S. Yamey, 'The Raw Cotton Commission, 1948–52', Oxford Economic Papers, 8 (1956), pp. 1–34; W. Robertson, 'The Raw Cotton Commission: An Experiment in State Trading', Journal of Industrial Economics, 4 (1956), pp. 224–39; Charlotte Leubuscher, Bulk Buying from the Colonies: A Study of the Bulk Purchase of Colonial Commodities by the United Kingdom Government (Oxford University Press, 1956), pp. 53–66.

15. Board of Trade: Working Party Reports: Cotton (HMSO, 1946); G. C. Allen, 'The Report of the Working Party on the Cotton Industry', Manchester School of Economic and Social Studies, 14 (1946), pp. 60–73; Singleton, Lancashire on the Scrapheap, pp. 219–34; Dupree, 'The Cotton Industry: A Middle Way', pp. 143–51.

16. Dupree, 'The Cotton Industry: A Middle Way', p. 159.

17. Singleton, Lancashire on the Scrapheap, ch. 5.

18. Dupree (ed.), Lancashire and Whitehall, vol. 2, pp. 540–5; Singleton, Lancashire on the Scrapheap, pp. 45–6. For a contemporary discussion of the Japanese cotton industry in the late 1940s see Keizo Seki, The Cotton Industry of Japan (Japan Society for the Promotion of Science, 1956), esp. pp. 217–63.

19. H. A. Turner and R. Smith, 'The Slump in the Cotton Industry, 1952', Bulletin of the Oxford University Institute of Statistics, 15 (1953), pp. 105–32; Singleton, Lancashire on the Scrapheap, pp. 126–9.

20. For contemporary analyses of the cotton industry

in the 1950s and early 1960s, and the challenges it faced, see Robert Robson, *The Cotton Industry in Britain* (Macmillan, 1957); B. Vitkovitch, 'The UK Cotton Industry, 1937–54' *Journal of Industrial Economics*, 3 (1955), pp. 241–65. G. W. Furness, 'The Cotton and Rayon Textile Industry', in Duncan Burn (ed.), *The Structure of British Industry: A Symposium*, vol. 2 (Cambridge University Press, 1958), pp. 184–221; F. Vibert, 'Economic Problems of the Cotton Industry', *Oxford Economic Papers*, 18 (1966), pp. 313–43; L. H. C. Tippett, *A Portrait of the Lancashire Textile Industry* (Oxford University Press, 1969). For informative, comparative studies of cotton industries around the world see OECD, *Modern Cotton Industry: A Capital Intensive Industry* (OECD, 1965) and GATT, *A Study on Cotton Textiles* (GATT, 1966). Wider developments in the British economy in the 1950s and 1960s are discussed in Cairncross, *The British Economy Since 1945*, chs 3–4, and Pollard, *Development of the British Economy*, chs 7–9.

21. S. J. Wells, *British Export Performance: A Comparative Study* (Cambridge University Press, 1964), pp. 23, 211. This book has detailed statistics on British cotton textile exports to all significant markets, 1953–9.

22. Siu Lun Wong, *Emigrant Entrepreneurs: Shanghai Industrialists in Hong Kong* (Oxford University Press, 1988).

23. F. A. Wells, *The British Hosiery and Knitwear Industry: Its History and Organisation* (David and Charles, 1972), pp. 181–2.

24. Calculated from data in Clive H. Lee, *British Regional Employment Statistics, 1841–1971* (Cambridge University Press, 1979).

25. Singleton, *Lancashire on the Scrapheap*, ch. 8.

26. Singleton, *Lancashire on the Scrapheap*, pp. 141–6.

27. Lazonick, 'Industrial Organization and Technological Change', p. 213.

28. John Jewkes and Sylvia Jewkes, 'A Hundred Years of Change in the Structure of the Cotton Industry', *Journal of Law and Economics*, 9 (1966), p. 122.

29. Lazonick, 'Industrial Organization and Technological Change', pp. 228–9.

30. David M. Higgins, 'Rings, Mules, and Structural Constraints in the Lancashire Textile Industry, *c.* 1945–*c.* 1965', *Economic History Review*, second series, 46 (1993), pp. 342–62.

31. David M. Higgins, 'Structural Constraints and Financial Performance in the Lancashire Textile Industry, *c.* 1945–*c.* 1960' (Sheffield University Management School, Discussion Paper no. 51, 1992).

32. David M. Higgins, 'Re-equipment as a Strategy for Survival in the Lancashire Spinning Industry, *c.* 1945–*c.* 1960', *Textile History*, 24 (1993), pp. 211–34; Ronald Dore, *Flexible Rigidities: Industrial Policy and Structural Adjustment in the Japanese Economy 1970–80* (Stanford University Press, 1986), chs 7–10.

33. Higgins, 'Re-equipment as a Strategy', p. 227; Alfred D. Chandler, *Scale and Scope: The Dynamics of Industrial Capitalism* (Harvard University Press, 1990), p. 22.

34. Singleton, *Lancashire on the Scrapheap*, ch. 7.

35. Kym Anderson, 'The Changing Role of Fibres, Textiles and Clothing as Economies Grow', in Kym Anderson (ed.), *New Silk Roads: East Asia and World Textile Markets* (Cambridge University Press, 1992), pp. 2–14; UNIDO, *International Comparative Advantage: Changing Profiles of Resources and Trade* (UNIDO, 1986).

36. Vinod K. Aggarwal and Stephan Haggard, 'The Politics of Protection in the U.S. Textile and Apparel Industries', in John Zysman and Laura Tyson (eds), *American Industry in International Competition: Government Policies and Corporate Strategies* (Cornell University Press, 1983), pp. 249–312.

37. George Kay, *Rhodesia: A Human Geography* (University of London Press, 1970), p. 154; Singleton, *Lancashire on the Scrapheap*, p. 119; R. David, 'Lord, Cyril', in D. J. Jeremy (ed.), *Dictionary of Business Biography*, vol. 3 (Butterworths, 1985), pp. 852–5.

38. K. Yoshihara, *Japanese Investment in Southeast Asia* (University of Hawaii Press, 1978), pp. 111–16.

39. David J. Jeremy, 'Survival Strategies in Lancashire Textiles: The Bleachers' Association Ltd to Whitecroft plc, 1900–1980s', *Textile History*, 24 (1993), pp. 195–8.

40. John A. Blackburn, 'The British Cotton Textile Industry Since World War II: The Search for a Strategy', *Textile History*, 24 (1993), p. 238.

41. A. Muir, *The Kenyon Tradition: The History of James Kenyon & Sons Ltd* (Cambridge: Heffer & Sons, 1964), pp. 93–110; Alan Hess, *Some British Industries: Their Expansion and Achievements, 1936–1956* (London: Information in Industry, 1957), pp. 35–7, 180–3.

42. Dupree, 'Struggling with Destiny', p. 107.

43. Singleton, *Lancashire on the Scrapheap*, chs 6, 9.

44. Cotton Board, *The Cotton Industry and the Consequences of Unlimited Imports* (Cotton Board, 1956).

45. Singleton, *Lancashire on the Scrapheap*, pp. 130–2; Dupree, 'Struggling with Destiny', pp. 116–23.

46. Alister Sutherland, 'The Restrictive Practices Court and Cotton Spinning', *Journal of Industrial Economics*, 8 (1959), pp. 58–79; Singleton, *Lancashire on the Scrapheap*, pp. 193–202.

47. United Textile Factory Workers' Association, *Plan

*for Cotton* (Ashton-under-Lyne: UTFWA, 1957). This report was written by the prominent Labour politician and economist, Harold Wilson.

48. Harold Macmillan, *Riding the Storm, 1956–1959* (Macmillan, 1971), pp. 739–46.

49. Caroline Miles, *Lancashire Textiles, A Case Study of Industrial Change* (Cambridge University Press, 1968).

50. Caroline Miles, 'Protection of the British Textile Industry', in W. M. Corden and G. Fels (eds), *Public Assistance to Industry: Protection and Subsidies in Britain and Germany* (Macmillan, 1976), p. 206.

51. Donald C. Coleman, *Courtaulds: An Economic and Social History*, vol. 3 (Oxford University Press, 1980); Arthur Knight, *Private Enterprise and Public Intervention: The Courtaulds Experience* (George Allen and Unwin, 1974).

52. Knight, *Private Enterprise and Public Intervention*, p. 52.

53. Singleton, *Lancashire on the Scrapheap*, ch. 10; Coleman, *Courtaulds*, vol. 3, pp. 270–88; Knight, *Private Enterprise and Public Intervention*, ch. 3; Blackburn, 'British Cotton Textile Industry'.

54. Textile Council, *Cotton and Allied Textiles: A Report on Present Performance and Future Prospects* (Textile Council, 1969).

55. Blackburn, 'British Cotton Textile Industry', p. 247.

56. G. F. Ray, *The Diffusion of Mature Technologies* (Cambridge University Press, 1984), pp. 44–5.

57. Roy Rothwell, 'Innovation in Textile Machinery', in Keith Pavitt (ed.), *Technical Innovation and British Economic Performance* (Macmillan, 1980), pp. 125–41.

58. Singleton, *Lancashire on the Scrapheap*, pp. 227–30; Blackburn, 'British Cotton Textile Industry', pp. 253–8.

59. Stanley Chapman, 'The Decline and Rise of Textile Merchanting, 1880–1990', *Business History*, 32 (1990), p. 185.

60. Knight, *Private Enterprise and Public Intervention*, pp. 183–5.

61. There is a voluminous literature on the western countries' attempts to control textile and clothing imports since the 1960s. See D. B. Keesing and M. Wolf, *Textile Quotas Against Developing Countries* (Trade Policy Research Centre, 1980); Z. A. Silberston, *The Multi-Fibre Arrangement and the UK Economy* (HMSO, 1984); William R. Cline, *The Future of World Trade in Textiles and Apparel*, rev. ed. (Institute of International Economics, 1990); Carl B. Hamilton (ed.), *Textiles Trade and the Developing Countries: Eliminating the Multi-Fibre Arrangement in the 1990s* (World Bank, 1990).

62. Helen Hughes and Poh Seng You, *Foreign Investment and Industrialisation in Singapore* (Australian National University Press, 1969), pp. 121–4.

63. C. F. Pratten, *Economics of Scale in Manufacturing Industry* (Cambridge University Press, 1971), p. 238.

64. B. Toyne, J. Arpan, D. A. Ricks, T. A. Shimp, and A. Barnett, *The Global Textile Industry* (George Allen and Unwin, 1984), p. 163. This book surveys the textile industries in developed countries in the late 1970s.

65. M. J. Piore and C. F. Sabel, *The Second Industrial Divide: Possibilities for Prosperity* (Basic Books, 1984), pp. 213–16; Geoffrey Shepherd, 'Textiles: New Ways of Surviving in an Old Industry', in G. Shepherd, F. Duchene and C. Saunders (eds), *Europe's Industries: Public and Private Strategies for Change* (Frances Pinter, 1983), pp. 26–51.

66. D. Bigarelli and P. Crestanello, 'An Analysis of Changes in the Knitwear/Clothing District of Carpi during the 1980s', *Entrepreneurship and Regional Development*, 6 (1994), pp. 127–44; R. Camagni and R. Rabellotti, 'Technology and Organisation in the Italian Textile-Clothing Industry', *Entrepreneurship and Regional Development*, 4 (1992), pp. 271–85; Enzo Rullani and Antonello Zanfei, 'Networks Between Manufacturing and Demand – Cases from Textile and Clothing Industries', in Christiano Antonelli (ed.), *New Information Technology and Industrial Change: The Italian Case* (Kluwer Academic Press, 1988), pp. 57–95.

67. Benetton's strategy and performance are discussed in John Kay, *Foundations of Corporate Success* (Oxford University Press, 1993).

68. Cotton Board, *Western Germany: The Market for Britain's Cottons* (Cotton Board, 1958), pp. 56–7.

69. Toyne *et al.*, *Global Textile Industry*, p. 164.

70. Hilary Steedman and Karin Wagner, 'Productivity, Machinery and Skills: Clothing Manufacture in Britain and Germany', *National Institute Economic Review*, 128 (1989), pp. 40–57. A more positive view of Marks and Spencer's role in the textile industry is to be found in Goronwy Rees, *St Michael: A History of Marks and Spencer* (Weidenfeld and Nicolson, 1969), pp. 191–6. For an overall analysis of the modern UK clothing industry, see Jonathan Zeitlin, 'The Clothing Industry in Transition: International Trends and British Response', *Textile History*, 19 (1988), pp. 211–38.

71. Kurt Hoffman and Howard Rush, *Micro-electronics and Clothing: The Impact of Technical Change on a Global Industry* (Praeger, 1988); A. Mody and D. Wheeler, *Automation and World Competition: New Technologies, Industrial Location and Trade* (Macmillan, 1990).

72. George Kell and Jurgen Richtering, 'Technology

and Competitiveness in the Textile Industry' (UNCTAD, Discussion Paper no. 42, 1991).

73. Cristiano Antonelli, 'The Role of Technological Expectations in a Mixed Model of International Diffusion of Process Innovations: The Case of Open-End Spinning Rotors', *Research Policy*, 18 (1989), p. 281.

74. V. N. Balasubramanyam and M. A. Salisu, 'International Trade and Employment in the UK Textiles and Clothing Sector', *Applied Economics*, 25 (1993), pp. 1477–82.

75. Lynn Krieger Mytelka, 'The French Textile Industry: Crisis and Adjustment', in Harold K. Jacobson and Dusan Sidjanski (eds), *The Emerging International Order: Dynamic Processes, Constraints, and Opportunities* (Sage, 1982), pp. 129–66.

### Further reading

J. Singleton, *Lancashire on the Scrapheap: The Cotton Industry 1945–70* (Oxford University Press, 1991).

John A. Blackburn, 'The British Cotton Textile Industry Since World War II: The Search for a Strategy', *Textile History*, 24 (1993), pp. 235–58.

E. L. Hargreaves and M. M. Gowing, *Civil Industry and Trade* (HMSO, 1952), pp. 343–76.

Board of Trade: *Working Party Reports: Cotton* (HMSO, 1946).

Marguerite Dupree, 'Struggling with Destiny: The Cotton Industry, Overseas Trade Policy and the Cotton Board, 1940–1959', *Business History*, 32 (1990), pp. 106–28.

Robert Robson, *The Cotton Industry in Britain* (Macmillan, 1957).

Caroline Miles, *Lancashire Textiles: A Case Study of Industrial Change* (Cambridge University Press, 1968).

Arthur Knight, *Private Enterprise and Public Intervention: The Courtaulds Experience* (George Allen and Unwin, 1974).

William R. Cline, *The Future of World Trade in Textiles and Apparel*, rev. ed. (Institute of International Economics, 1990).

Kym Anderson (ed.), *New Silk Roads: East Asia and World Textile Markets* (Cambridge University Press, 1992).

## Notes to Chapter 12

1. Charles Dickens, *Hard Times* (1854). The description of Coketown is at the start of Chapter 5.

2. T. B. Lewis, 'In a Northern Town', in *Meditations of a Cotton Spinner* (London, 1929), p. 17.

3. C. Aspin, *Lancashire: The First Industrial Society* (Helmshore Local History Society, 1969), p. 53.

4. D Bindman and G. Reimann (eds), *Karl Freidrich Schinkel: 'The English Journey'* (New Haven and London: Yale University Press, 1993), pp. 175–9.

5. C. Aspin, *Mr Pilling's Short-Cut to China* (Helmshore Local History Society, 1983), p. 6.

6. C. Aspin, *Lancashire: The First Industrial Society*, p. 137

7. R. Boyson, *The Ashworth Cotton Enterprise* (Oxford University Press, 1970), p. 119.

8. *House of Lords Committee on the State and Condition of the Children employed in the Cotton Manufactories of the United Kingdom*, PP, 1919, cx, pp. 279–81.

9. Robert Rawlinson, *Public Works in Lancashire for the Relief of Distress Among the Unemployed Factory Hands During the Cotton Famine, 1863–66* (London, 1898), p. 53. The book includes all the reports made by Rawlinson between 1863 and 1869.

10. That identical rules were enforced throughout the cotton districts is clear from the fact that the printer left a space for each mill owner to enter the name of his premises. The set preserved in the museum came from Broadclough Mill, Bacup.

### Further reading

O. Ashmore, *Industrial Archaeology of Lancashire* (David & Charles, 1969).

C. Aspin, *The Water Spinners* (forthcoming).

C. Aspin, *Lancashire: The First Industrial Society* (Helmshore Local History Society, 1969 and Preston, Carnegie, 1995).

J. H. Longworth, *The Cotton Mills of Bolton 1780–1985* (Bolton, 1987).

N. Morgan, *Vanished Dwellings: Early Industrial Housing in a Lancashire Cotton Town.* (Preston, Mullion Books, 1990).

G. Timmins, *The Last Shift. The Decline of Handloom Weaving in Nineteenth-Century Lancashire* (Manchester University Press, 1993).

M. Rothwell, *Industrial Heritage.* An ongoing series covering the industrial archaeology of east Lancashire. Titles include Accrington, Clayton-le-Moors, Church, Great Harwood, Oswaldtwistle, Rishton, Blackburn, Ribble Valley and Padiham.

M. Williams and D. A. Farnie, *Cotton Mills in Greater Manchester* (Preston, Carnegie, 1992).

L. S. Wood and A. Wilmore, *The Romance of the Cotton Industry in England* (Oxford University Press, 1927).

# Index